DYSLEXIA IN SECONDARY SCHOOL

A practical handbook for teachers, parents and students

DYSLEXIA IN SECONDARY SCHOOL

A practical handbook for teachers, parents and students

Jenny Cogan BA

Westminster School, London

and

Mary Flecker MA

City of London School

Consultant in Dyslexia
Professor Margaret Snowling
University of York

x

x
W

x

x
WHURR PUBLISHERS
LONDON AND PHILADELPHIA

© 2004 Whurr Publishers Ltd
First published 2004
by Whurr Publishers Ltd
19b Compton Terrace, London N1 2UN England and
325 Chestnut Street, Philadelphia PA 19106 USA

British Library Cataloguing in Publication Data

A catalogue record for this book
is available from the British Library.

ISBN 1 86156 272 1

Printed and bound in the UK by Athenaeum Press Ltd,
Gateshead, Tyne & Wear.

Contents

Chapter 4   Note-taking   **117**

Chapter 5 Essay writing 153

xii Contents

Preface

The aim of this book is to focus the attention of classroom teachers on the help they can give to dyslexic children in secondary school. It makes a further point that, as few students have perfect learning skills, the methods put forward as essential to students with dyslexia will also help to raise academic standards for every other pupil in secondary school classrooms. Finally, what is crucial to success for dyslexic pupils in secondary school will continue to be so in any form of further or higher education that they undertake; this book will therefore be of interest beyond the framework of school.

Generally speaking, educational practice is currently preoccupied with raising standards of attainment, whereas educational research is increasingly centred on the idea of learning how to learn. Meanwhile, however, in secondary school classrooms across the country, many unsuccessful and poorly motivated children struggle day by day to master – or avoid – their curriculum. If students spend five years or more trying unsuccessfully to learn, giving up, feeling a failure, behaving badly, they are likely to move out of school ill-equipped, both in skills and in attitude, to contribute usefully to the adult world. These are children who are particularly in need of teaching methods that raise their standards and self-confidence, and of learning styles that suit their individual cognitive strengths.

Many of our struggling children have dyslexia, i.e. they function poorly in one or two specific cognitive areas. In the classroom, students are constantly required to do several things at the same time, e.g. listening, understanding, remembering, writing and spelling. All this happens at speed, and when one or two weaker skills break down, they cause the whole learning system to fail. It is during such activities involving several skills that teachers can often identify the specific underlying difficulties that frustrate the efforts of their dyslexic students.

Dyslexic difficulties are specific to certain skills and, more often than not, they mask competence or excellence in other cognitive areas. Children with dyslexia are likely to be as interested as anyone else in the content of their courses and just as able to appreciate the concepts – witness their lively oral contribution in class. Their strengths, unfortunately, may be hidden by the fact that they are unable to read or write about the subject as well as others.

Dyslexic children are also just as keen to please, but their underlying difficulties may cause them to appear stupid, incompetent or disaffected. Those same difficulties may frustrate them to the point where they respond with lazy or annoying behaviour. Teachers must take responsibility for distinguishing cause and effect and for keeping dyslexic children at the centre, not the periphery, of their classroom.

For some teachers this could mean a shift of emphasis. At secondary school level it is reasonable for teachers to see themselves primarily as subject teachers: 'I teach chemistry', not 'I teach David', and most teachers instinctively teach in the way that they learned so successfully themselves – using the written word as their medium. This seems all the more reasonable given that GCSE and A level are written assessments. It might also seem reasonable for teachers to assume that basic skills were learned at primary school and could now be counted on for tackling new content and new expertise. However, those skills that teachers hope to assume – in reading, writing, spelling, remembering, organizing – are the very ones in which dyslexic students will continue to be deficient as they work through their secondary school.

Conventional instruction leans heavily on such skills, yet, all too often, teachers and those of their students with dyslexia do not understand either the low-level difficulties that make high-level classroom skills so hard to perform, or what alternative strategies there might be for teaching and learning.

We have found that teenagers who are dyslexic will flourish in school, given that their individual learning styles are understood and nurtured by appropriate teaching methods. We aim to explain to teachers, and also to pupils and their parents, how underlying difficulties affect the specific skills needed for the range of curriculum subjects. In doing so, we allude to current research and highlight typical difficulties and solutions from the experience of students at this moment in secondary school.

These chapters describe practical ways of teaching and learning, illustrated through current curriculum material for 11–18-year-olds. The book provides a collection of sheets for immediate use in class or for homework, as a way of introducing new and perhaps initially uncomfortable methods. It proposes small but significant adjustments to teaching style that could make all the difference to individuals in the classroom.

Noting a lead in current Government policy, the book stresses the value of computers for all schoolchildren, but in particular it points to the potential of good touch-typing, word-processing and the use of a laptop instead of a pen to transform the learning experience for many children with dyslexia. The Government also recently allocated funds for schools to purchase teacher laptops. As growing numbers of teachers acquire laptops this should help to address teacher confidence where it is lacking.

In parallel with Government research initiatives into 'learning how to learn' (see Joint Project of the Economic and Social Research Council's Teaching and Learning Research Programme), the book recommends that the best learning/teaching strategies are based on appreciating the particular needs of an individual child. Such an appreciation – the responsibility equally of teacher and of child – is at the heart of this book.

There is no attempt at political correctness in this book. We happen to teach in predominantly boys' schools therefore most of the students and teachers referred to are male, but not all.

Nearly all of the figures and quotations in the book are original work, often written in class or in haste, some of them photocopied. The spelling errors and lack of polish are deliberately not corrected or 'improved', so that the reader has a true picture of dyslexic children coping in school.

Jenny Cogan
Mary Flecker

Acknowledgements

The authors and publishers thank the following for permission to use copyright material:

The National Gallery Picture Library for 'The Ambassadors' by Hans Holbein;
Routledge for 'Photosynthesis' from *The Biochemist's Songbook* by Professor Harold Baum;
Faber and Faber for 'The Jaguar' from *The Hawk in the Rain* by Ted Hughes.
The terms 'mind-map' and 'mind-mapping' are the copyright of Tony Buzan.

Our thanks to all our students, not just those whose work enlivens this book, to colleagues for their contributions and help, and to our families for their shrewd and kindly criticism.

Chapter 1
Reading

Introduction

In school, the symptoms of reading difficulty are sometimes hard to identify. There are children with dyslexia whose fluent reading of words hides a serious lack of comprehension. There are those who read fast, evidently understand what they read and yet retain very little. At the other end of the scale are those who love books and take refuge between their covers, but who read to themselves slowly and avoid reading aloud at all costs. Such readers are nearly always behind with a class set book. They can appear lazy or reluctant, when in fact their response to the content, when they do manage to read, may be fitting and original. Frequently, there are those who read too slowly to build up any interest whatsoever in a concept, argument, character or story. These convince themselves that they hate books, when in fact what they hate is reading.

This dislike of reading is often strengthened, in a school context, by the dread of being asked to read aloud in class. Although children with dyslexia may really enjoy listening to others read, they should not themselves be asked to read aloud in public, nor should they be left wondering if they will be asked. They should, however, practise in private, because oral and aural channels will act to support their weak reading skills.

Their dislike of reading is also influenced by the size of a book, by how easy it is to hold open and by the appearance of its text – the background colour, the size and clarity of print, the length of line and layout on the . Where one student tolerates magazine articles, another detests columns of newsprint. One will pore over technical manuals whereas another, despite labouring at every , may still lose himself happily in the world of a long novel. Dyslexia is never more confusing than when it relates to reading.

Teachers' checklist

Teachers who wish to help poor readers in the subject they teach could start by identifying their students' specific difficulties. A checklist of warning signs is given in Figure 1.1 and ticks scattered or clustered on this list should prompt a discussion about the skills needed to read in that subject – the first step towards dealing with a reading difficulty.

Where dyslexia is the problem, pupils are likely to have difficulty (sometimes an acute difficulty) relating letter sounds to letter shapes: s = (s, z), qu = (kw), ph = (f), ch = (ch, k, sh). This skill is known as 'phonological processing'. It is the foundation step to synthesising letters into syllables, then words, and attaching meaning to them. It underpins all aspects of literacy, and most children develop a high-speed fluency in it. Definitions of dyslexia usually, however, emphasise a lack of fluency in this skill. Although poor phonological processing affects speaking and writing, it is most damaging to reading, hence dyslexia's early history as a 'reading difficulty'.

The fact that readers with dyslexia may have to work out even the simplest one-syllable words, letter by letter, often goes undetected in ordinary school life. Meanwhile their peers

Difficulties in reading – a checklist of warning signs for teachers
Do you teach students who...

In general:

- rarely read any book not required for school? ☐
- read comics and technical magazines but avoid books? ☐
- dread reading books with small print and tight binding? ☐

Speed:

- often fail to complete reading homework? ☐
- like to discuss characters and scenes but are too far behind in required reading to be able to join in class discussions? ☐

Comprehension and memory:

- have done the reading but understand very little of the content? ☐
- read fast, enjoy the book as they read, but remember little? ☐
- read unusually slowly but digest information and inference? ☐

Reading aloud:

- read aloud hesitantly or in a monotone or with odd emphasis? ☐
- read aloud fluently but cannot answer questions about content? ☐
- lose their place easily and omit or repeat words/lines? ☐
- cannot pronounce or remember names or unfamiliar words? ☐
- mispronounce familiar words (perfect/prefect)? ☐
- change tenses (add or omit 'ed')? ☐
- ignore or add 'not' and reverse the meaning? ☐
- substitute synonyms (house/home)? ☐
- disregard punctuation? ☐

Reading silently:

- yawn, fidget, rub eyes, cover one eye, lay head on arm? ☐
- mouth words? ☐
- use finger as guide? ☐
- daydream or give up? ☐

Extracting information:

- can't scan a book or magazine to find specific material in it? ☐
- can't extract information from notices or posters, or even find their own name on a posted list? ☐
- misread examination questions or overlook part of a question? ☐

Figure 1.1 Use this checklist to raise pupils' interest in their own reading skills.

are taking in the meaning of whole groups of words at a glance. The consequence of poor phonological processing is that sufferers devote their prime attention to working out or 'decoding' individual words, so they can pay only residual attention to syntax and to integrating the meaning of the text as a whole. This can be equally true when reading numbers and equations, the symbolic language of mathematics and chemistry or physics. In addition, the short-term memory and sequencing problems so typical of dyslexia make symbolic language an even more difficult medium to work in.

Good readers retain a lot of what they read and absorb it into their own experience of life without conscious effort. People with dyslexia will be preoccupied, consciously or unconsciously, with decoding and cannot guarantee to retain much of what they read. To achieve the same quality of assimilation as good readers, they may need to take a different, more conscious route. They will need to personalise text in some way in order to realise and retain its meaning – they need a method that is both creative and less dependent on words. The most effective method for this is to imagine, or visualise, the content as they read.

Visualising

What is visualising?

Visualising is the technique of representing ideas as mental images rather than words. It is a spontaneous speciality of the brain's right hemisphere. Once a reader has turned text into image, he probably won't be able to forget it. Sharma (1992), a respected writer and speaker on dyslexic difficulties in mathematics, maintains that 'Anything visualised goes straight into long-term memory'.

How is visualising relevant to secondary school reading?

Visualising – usually as a step towards drawing cartoons or posters – is popular with teachers. It is often set in school as an exercise to consolidate learning, but it is not used as a primary technique for reading. It would not be practicable to draw every time one read, and many teachers may not have discovered how useful making mental pictures can be. Although they do not ask pupils to imagine the content of their reading, they are quite likely, instead, to ask pupils to 'take notes' on it. Language, not imagery, is a secondary schoolteacher's tool.

Three points may account for this. First, teachers have learned successfully themselves, using words as their medium, and they would naturally wish to employ that successful medium to teach their pupils. Second, assessment at all levels is couched in words. As a result, secondary schoolteachers have rarely formed image-making habits when they become teachers and feel impatient (if not downright hostile) with such an apparently irrelevant medium. This is all the more understandable when they are focusing intently on the content of their course rather than on their teaching method, and when most of the class learns perfectly well using words anyway. Third, teachers might argue that, as reading is all about language, transposing words into images may involve the reader in misleading interpretation and enhancement. They might feel that this is particularly true in text where the words are carrying either precise technical meaning, as in a science textbook, or resonance from the writer's personal use of language, as in poetry.

However, some readers find words a serious barrier to realisation and memory (leaving aside any expectation of interest and pleasure). For them, visualising can be a powerful alternative. Weak readers who think in images can create for themselves a sharp and, if Sharma is correct, lasting realisation of text. This realisation may be in the form of a single holistic image or of a visual sequence, like a film. It may have colour, movement, sound or smell associated with it, and the image maker may learn more thoroughly from this way of reading than do efficient readers who simply read. Visualising is valuable in any school subject and usually gives the image maker feelings of pleasure and success. These are two highly motivating emotions that readers with dyslexia rarely associate with their experience of conventional reading, but which teachers depend on for their best teaching.

How does visualising work?

Speaking at a conference on mathematics and dyslexia, Professor Sharma gave a light-hearted demonstration of how visualising works. He asked members of his lecture audience to write '69' on a scrap of paper that they were holding on their foreheads, and then he described the steps that they would be taking. Here is the gist of his description:

- Raise a mental picture, from long-term memory store, of how '69' normally looks to you.
- Relate this familiar image to the new problem of orientation and direction.
- Try to 'see in your mind' this new '69' as it should appear on the paper.
- Then attempt to realise a new image from the old; your mental screen will help to guide your hand and peg the new image in memory as you write it on your forehead.

Visualising is creative, personal and fast

When visualising, readers draw on their own unique store of experience to make visual links to the text. The process is creative and entirely personal; other people's connections and images do not work half so well. Raising familiar images prompted by new reading material helps the process of understanding and draws the new ideas, attached to these familiar images, into long-term memory. Thence the new ideas are easily retrieved, still hooked up to the familiar images with which they have been integrated.

It is well known that the funnier, the more vulgar or the more out of scale the integration between idea and image, the more likely it is to work as a mnemonic peg. This creative process in the imagination of the reader can take place at such speed that it seems instantaneous. Speed is important to dyslexic students, who will not want to add delaying business to their already slow reading.

Drawing as a way to explain visualising

The easiest way to explain visualising is to give examples, and the most direct way to do that is to draw what is visualised. Allowance has to be made for the fact that drawing is never as detailed and expressive as imagining. This first very simple example shows a 10-year-old boy visualising the making of shadows while quoting from his science textbook (Figure 1.2).

The next example (Figure 1.3) was drawn to represent information in a textbook's account of the battle in which the Romans defeated the Iceni under Boudicca in AD 61. A different reader would imagine the scene quite differently (how do you visualise a 'dense wood'?) and find his own images more memorable than these. In either case, colour (blue woad-covered faces, for instance) will enhance the initial realisation and the resultant memory.

To strengthen recall – re-visualise and talk

It is usually easier to recall images than words but, if words and images have been integrated, recalling images may evoke original phrases too, particularly if the images are recalled more than once. However, if words are a problem and examination success is the aim, students should re-visualise their reading in a way that reinforces the original link between words and images. First, they should recall the images and then take the further step of describing them

<u>*Alexander*</u>

<u>*stopping light*</u>

We know that light travels in staight lines. If we place an object in front of a light ray, the ray can't travel forward.

The ray will either be absorbed or reflected back. this is how shadows are formed.

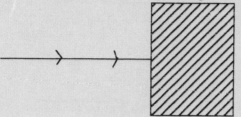

projector   light rays

silly boy

No light rays can pass through the hand nor can it bend aroud the hand. So the area behind the hand is in darkness : it forms a shadow.

<u>*Implication for the Earth*</u>
<u>*1. day and night*</u>

The main luminous source for the Earth is the Sun. The sun's rays work in the same way as any other light ray.

Figure 1.2 The computer gives time and scope for satisfying presentation – and jokes.

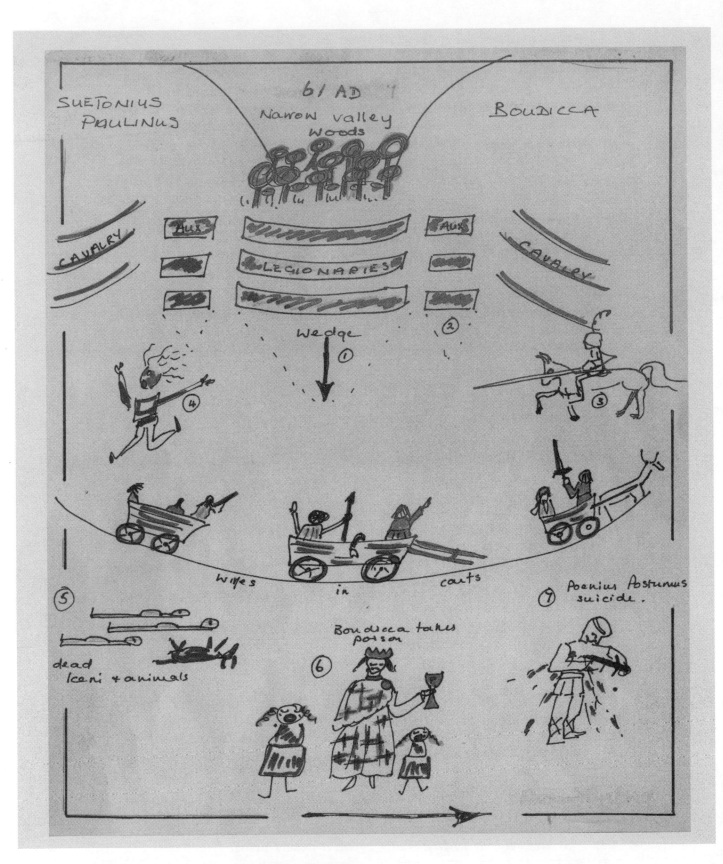

Figure 1.3 Boudicca's battle with the Romans – visualisations are more memorable than words. Numbering the images adds a checking device – 'I need to remember seven pictures to tell this story'.

in their own words, preferably out loud – not silently, in the mind, where it is possible to gloss over precise terms and syntax.

Following this method, the student who drew Figure 1.3 would put the picture aside and re-visualise it on his mental screen. He would talk through the image he 'sees' – telling the story his own way, but making a point of saying important names and terms as he speaks. Because there is a memory in the ear and the muscles of the lips and tongue, out loud is best. Such a version might sound like this:

> **Suetonius plans a swift and certain end to Boudicca's rebellion. He chooses his battlefield carefully with steep hills and a dense wood at his back. With his crack troops, the legionaries, in wedge formation in the centre, he reserves his precious cavalry on each wing. His auxiliaries, who are mostly impressed native tribesmen for whom the Romans cared little, are positioned in between. Boudicca's tribesmen, the Iceni, made reckless by previous success, bring their wives and families in carts and, mysteriously, their animals too and range them in a circle enclosing the battlefield to watch, as they imagine, their menfolk destroy the Roman army.**
>
> **The Romans advance, hurling javelins with ferocious accuracy. The Iceni, vivid in blue woad, cannot escape; they are trapped between the advancing Romans and their own families. There is tremendous slaughter. Boudicca and her daughters take poison. Poenius Postumus, disgraced as a coward, falls on his sword.**

Any student who has turned his textbook into images and words of his own and integrated the two together will remember far more in an examination, however many weeks later, than if he had simply read and reread the original description or taken notes.

Research shows that visualising improves comprehension and memory

In 1991 a research project investigated the proposal that 'poor comprehenders' could improve their reading comprehension and memory by thinking in images as they read (Oakhill and Yuill, 1991). In previous research, Oakhill and Yuill had shown that:

> **When poor comprehenders are not specifically instructed about what they should get out of a text, they are not usually aware of their comprehension problems.**

This is a useful warning to teachers that there may be members of their classes who, despite being quite self-aware in other areas of learning, still need specific instruction about what they are looking for when they read.

Oakhill and Yuill described a second characteristic of poor comprehension as an inability to draw inferences while reading. This, in part, led them to their research proposal. They thought that 'image training' would make the meaning of the text explicit in a picture. It might therefore both improve comprehension and, at the same time, train poor comprehenders to make inferences when reading. They found from the ensuing research that:

> **Poor comprehenders, given imagery training, showed a marked improvement in memory for the passages; they performed significantly better on the test questions than did the control group of poor comprehenders.**

Image training for research

The training consisted of imagining and discussing a sequence of cartoon pictures to represent events in a number of stories. In particular, the children were asked to make a single image in their heads to represent the main point of each text. The researchers found that deriving this final image did most to improve the children's understanding and recall. Their explanation was that, in creating an image for the main point of the story, the children had to relate parts to the whole in a way they would not normally do. The reason for this was, in the researchers' opinion, that dyslexic readers lack the skill of integrating meaning in a text while simultaneously decoding its words.

Oakhill and Yuill had also found, in previous research, that good comprehension was associated with strong short-term working memory. As a result, in this later research, they concluded that 'seeing' images, rather than 'hearing' a sequence of words, probably gave poor comprehenders, with their inefficient working memories, a 'different and more economical way of representing the information'.

Research method as teaching method

Teachers, seeing the relevance of this research to the pupils they teach, may wish them to learn the habit of visualising. The following way of teaching it mirrors the research format of Oakhill and Yuill's image training. The one major difference is that here, in Step 2, pupils draw their images. This is to make certain that they do actually visualise – that is transform the words they are reading into images – instead of trying to internalise the information in its original verbal form.

The role and limitations of drawing

There may well be two objections raised against drawing as part of the method: it takes too long, and very few people can draw to their own satisfaction. There are two counterbalancing arguments. The first is that it is pointless to spend any time at all on reading that fails to achieve its aim, and the second is that drawing is merely a provisional step on the way to visualising – that is making images in the head rather than on paper.

The role of drawing is like the part scaffolding plays in building. Just as builders remove scaffolding when it has served its purpose, so students can dispense with drawing once they trust themselves to transform text into images rather than clinging onto the words. Anyone unused to visualising could find relinquishing words in favour of images a big leap. For that reason, drawing (however poor) is a useful step on the way (Figure 1.4).

Use an image training format to practise visualising

The following give a format for learning to visualise. To that end, they involve readers in drawing their images, not just imagining them. The format mirrors Oakhill and Yuill's research – successful research procedures often make successful teaching methods too.

The text in Figure 1.5 comes from Chapter 14 of *Great Expectations*, a novel currently set for the MEG GCSE English literature paper. It shows Pip looking back to his time as Joe's apprentice and the selfish misery he felt as he looked from that point towards what seemed to him a mean and dreary future. It is a critical moment in the development of Pip's character, and a detailed memory of it would matter to anyone studying the book.

Three steps to teach visualising in the classroom
(use current curriculum texts of convenient length)

Step 1 Students are given a text and told they will be learning to think in pictures as they read

- Students read text to themselves.

- Teacher shows three or four pictures, in cartoon form, representing sequence of events in text.

- Teacher shows one picture illustrating main event or idea in text.

- Teacher and class discuss how pictures relate to text.

- After removing pictures, teacher asks students to imagine that the pictures are in their minds and that they are to use them to help them answer some questions about the text.

- Teacher presents a series of questions (factual, descriptive and inferential) to which students write answers: this is to encourage them to 'use' the images in their minds.

Step 2   Students are given a new text

- Students read text to themselves.

- They draw cartoon sequence with 3 or 4 frames to represent sequence of events in text.

- They draw one picture for main event.

- Teacher and students discuss drawings, in particular one of main event.

- Teacher removes drawings and presents questions for students to answer.

- Students re-visualise their drawings to help them answer questions.

Step 3 Students are given a new text

Students repeat the procedure, but this time they form mental pictures without drawing. Discussion and feedback about their images and how they might be improved are important. Finally, students re-visualise their own improved images to help them to answer questions on the text.

The research did not include drawing as in Step 2. However, secondary school students, dispirited by years of failure in conventional reading, may be unwilling to take risks. They may resist image-making and continue to try to remember words instead, if not obliged to draw (and therefore think up) some images. So Step 2 is a temporary, but helpful, stage in learning to visualise.

Figure 1.4 Follow this method to teach visualising to a class.

Visual imagery for comprehension and memory

- Draw three to four representational pictures in sequence like a cartoon.

- Draw one picture to represent the main idea of the passage.

Great Expectations Chapter Fourteen

Once, it had seemed to me that when I should at last roll up my shirt-sleeves and go into the forge, Joe's 'prentice, I should be distinguished and happy. Now the reality was in my hold, I only felt that I was dusty with the dust of the small coal, and that I had a weight upon my daily remembrance to which the anvil was a feather. There have been occasions in my later life (I suppose as in most lives) when I have felt for a time as if a thick curtain had fallen on all its interest and romance, to shut me out from anything save dull endurance any more. Never has that curtain dropped so heavy and blank, as when my way in life lay stretched out straight before me through the newly entered road of apprenticeship to Joe.

I remember that at a later period of my 'time', I used to stand about the churchyard on Sunday evenings, when night was falling, comparing my own perspective with the windy marsh view, and making out some likeness between them by thinking how flat and low both were, and how on both there came an unknown way and dark mist and then the sea. I was quite as dejected on the first working-day of my apprenticeship as in that after-time; but I am glad to know that I never breathed a murmur to Joe while my indentures lasted. It is about the only thing I am glad to know of myself in that connection.

1.
 Pip, sleeves rolled, at anvil.
'Dusty with the dust of the small coal.'
Heavy weight 'to which the anvil was a feather'.
Looks wretched.

2.
Thick curtain 'dropped so heavy and blank'.
Shuts out romance.
'Life lay stretched out straight.'
Nothing but blacksmithing and 'dull endurance'.

3.
Sundays in churchyard, 'when night was falling'.
'Windy marsh view', flat, low, dark mist, the sea.
Compared to Pip's life.

4.
Pip pleased he managed never to betray his feelings to Joe –
'never breathed a murmur'.

Summary Picture:

Only dreary misery ahead for Pip.
Loss of dreams and hope.
Contempt for self.

Figure 1.5 Read the text and imagine the scene. Decide what ideas to draw.

Dickens describes Pip's feelings in a series of multisensory images – rolled shirtsleeves, coal dust, the anvil as a feather, the heavy curtain falling on romance, the featureless road stretching ahead, the darkening churchyard, wind and flat marsh, mist and sea. Each image thickens the emotional gloom, and the reader needs to weigh each one if he is to feel the full impact of Pip's bleak depression.

To follow the visualising format, think which ideas to draw – regardless of how difficult that might prove to be. Selecting phrases and thinking how to draw their meaning is the creative process that personalises Dickens' images and fixes them in long-term memory – however badly they may then be drawn. It is the inner not the outer eye that matters (see Figure 1.5).

While the reader either visualises or draws, he will process certain phrases from the text, perhaps these: 'roll up my shirt-sleeves', 'Never has that curtain dropped so heavy and blank', 'an unknown way and dark mist and then the sea'. As a result, he is likely to learn the actual words. Quoting these will strengthen his essays and he should practise doing so, whenever he recalls the images he made to represent them (Figures 1.6–1.8).

Figure 1.6

Figure 1.7

Figure 1.6 and 1.7 Pupil and teacher drawings: students need to see their teachers practise the visualising they recommend. The quality of drawing is irrelevant. Discussion about the content of each drawing will improve the readers' visualisation

Visual imagery for comprehension and memory

- Draw three to four representational pictures in sequence like a cartoon.

- Draw one picture to represent the main idea of the passage.

Great Expectations Chapter Fourteen

Once, it had seemed to me that when I should at last roll up my shirt-sleeves and go into the forge, Joe's 'prentice, I should be distinguished and happy. Now the reality was in my hold, I only felt that I was dusty with the dust of the small coal, and that I had a weight upon my daily remembrance to which the anvil was a feather. There have been occasions in my later life (I suppose as in most lives) when I have felt for a time as if a thick curtain had fallen on all its interest and romance, to shut me out from anything save dull endurance any more. Never has that curtain dropped so heavy and blank, as when my way in life lay stretched out straight before me through the newly entered road of apprenticeship to Joe.

I remember that at a later period of my 'time', I used to stand about the churchyard on Sunday evenings, when night was falling, comparing my own perspective with the windy marsh view, and making out some likeness between them by thinking how flat and low both were, and how on both there came an unknown way and dark mist and then the sea. I was quite as dejected on the first working-day of my apprenticeship as in that after-time; but I am glad to know that I never breathed a murmur to Joe while my indentures lasted. It is about the only thing I am glad to know of myself in that connection.

Figure 1.8 A GCSE candidate draws.

Poetry lends itself especially well to visualisation, because so much of it is conceived as imagery. A poem visualised is a poem learned, so visualisation can be the best way for some readers to familiarise themselves with their curriculum set texts. Short poems with strong visual impact also make good material for visualising exercises (Figure 1.9).

Sheets A, B and C in the Worksheet Section at the end of this book are formats that can be used for visualising practice.

Visualising helps understanding and remembering

- Read the poem at least three times.

- Translate the words into pictures in your mind.

Now draw four representational pictures in sequence like a cartoon.

'Child on Top of a Greenhouse' Theodore Roethke

The wind billowing out the seat of my britches,
My feet crackling splinters of glass and dried putty,
The half-grown chrysanthemums staring up like accusers,
Up through the streaked glass, flashing with sunlight,
A few white clouds all rushing eastward,
A line of elms plunging and tossing like horses
And everyone, everyone pointing up and shouting!

Formulate one picture to represent the idea of the poem

Figure 1.9 Roethke's poem 'Child on top of a Greenhouse' with drawings that represent one reader's mental images. The final picture is a matter of personal interpretation; in this set it conveys exhilaration. Another reader might draw images of terror.

Visualising in maths and science

Bearing in mind Sharmah's assertion, when speaking about learning maths, that 'anything visualised goes straight into long-term memory', a current secondary head of physics was asked to comment on an extract about visualising for maths in Adams' book *Straight A's in GCSE* (Adams, 1995) (Figure 1.10).

'Wherever possible, problems should be worked out from basic principles and processes linked to real life. Even at A-level I try to get students to abandon rules, to work from first principles, to make diagrams and mental images. Creating *understanding* is superior to learning *rules*. You will develop confidence and become far better at maths.

'VISUALISING
For good learning it is essential to be able to visualise an operation or principle in your mind. Transformations, in particular, need this treatment when trying to reflect or rotate a pattern; but you also learn better if you visualise algebraic operations. The clearer the mental picture, the easier it is to work out a problem or memorise a process.

'Close your eyes or stare at a blank space on a wall and try to create the picture in front of you. The best students are those who are the most capable at doing this. They are also the best at recognising patterns in problems and are efficient in dissecting convergent problems. Practice, therefore, in these elements is most effective if a conscious effort is made to visualise your mathematics; and setting down the elements of problems and sums very clearly in diagrammatic and picture form *reinforces* visualisation. Practice of this *conscious* type creates deep understanding, creating a memory to which it is easy to link further knowledge. Simply practising examples, without conscious (mental picturing) application, does not build a foundation on which more advanced work can be based.'

Mary,
Yes, absolutely – this is the way
I do maths, and explain scientific
models to myself. Further, I think that
" if you can draw it, you can understand
it."
MLAK.

Figure 1.10 A head of physics endorses the value of visualising in maths.

The maths teacher writing in Figure 1.11 gives an instance where imagery would help to establish a basic principle and, in Figure 1.12, a student takes up the idea, drawing her own pictures for each step in solving an equation.

One of the most useful pictorial ideas applicable to any situation involving equations, formulae and, later, inequalities is that of simple kitchen scales or chemical balance:

Any mathematical statement involving the sign '=' inevitably must have a balance. The balance is maintained provided any change in weight (or number) on one side is also effected on the other.

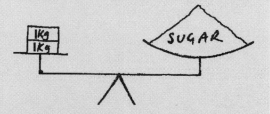

Thus in an equation any number added to (+), subtracted from (−), divided into (÷) or multiplied by (×) one side will maintain a balance (still =) provided the same operation is done to both sides.

Figure 1.11 Weighing scales – a starter for Figure 1.12 below.

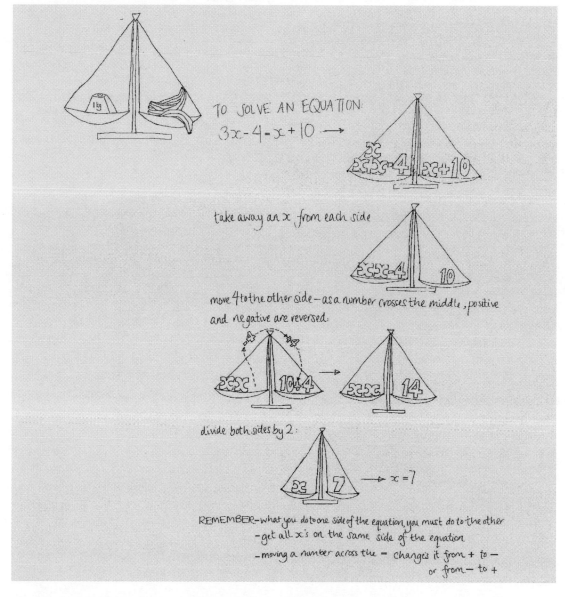

Figure 1.12 Thinking of images in the first place and then drawing them helps to separate and crystallise each step in the procedure. Eleanor drew this sequence, first to help with the original learning and, later, as a pictorial guide to solving other equations and as images in her mind to be re-visualised when necessary – in exams, for instance.

In Figures 1.13 (a) and 1.13 (b) Liam is visualising the three states of matter in his GCSE syllabus. He is interested in chemistry, but dyslexia prevents him from learning it well enough in lessons: 'We are doing this in chemistry and I can't remember about it.' Nor can he revise it by simply reading his textbook. He needs to make the text his own in some way. His favourite method is to hear the description read aloud while he visualises and draws. He prefers a mind-map format to a linear sequence of pictures, because the finished mind-map is itself an image; it plays to his visualising strength while reducing the problem of short-term sequential memory.

Structures and Bonding

Solids, liquids and gases

All of these are made up of very small particles.

Solids have a definite shape and a definite volume (that is, they take up a set amount of space). The particles are very close together. They cannot move much but only vibrate (in a very small area). This is why solids have definite shape.

Liquids have a definite volume but no definite shape. The particles are quite close together but can move around (slide past each other). This means they can be poured. It also means they take the shape of any container they are poured into.

Gases have no definite shape or volume. They can spread out into a big space and they can be squeezed (compressed) into a small space. The particles are not very close together and can move around a lot. This is why gases are very light.

Melting points and boiling points

Solids can become liquids. Liquids can become gases. You have to supply energy to do this. If you take energy away then gases can become liquids and then solids.

If energy (heat) is supplied to a solid, the particles move about more. The solid may melt (that is, become a liquid). The temperature it melts at is called its **melting point**.

If even more energy is supplied, this liquid may boil. The temperature it boils at is its **boiling point**.

If you give the particles in a liquid enough energy to overcome the forces of attraction to the other particles, then they escape and form a gas. This is called **evaporation**. The higher the temperature, the faster the evaporation. This happens at boiling point and beyond.

Diffusion

The particles of a gas move in all directions. Gases spread out in the space they are in. After a time they are evenly spread out in the space. This is called **diffusion**.

Dissolving

As the particles in a liquid move they can sometimes bump into particles of a solid and knock them apart. This happens if you add salt to water or sugar to a cup of tea. The particles of the solid then move through the liquid particles by diffusion. This is called **dissolving**.

Atoms

The particles in solids, liquids and gases are made of atoms. There are over 90 sorts. Some of the atoms you will come across include sodium, oxygen and chlorine.

Atoms have a small nucleus. The nucleus contains protons and neutrons. Whizzing around the nucleus are electrons.

	Mass	Charge
proton	1	+1 (positive)
neutron	1	0 (neutral)
electron	almost 0	−1 (negative)

Atoms have no overall charge (they are neutral). They have the same number of protons and electrons.

Figure 1.13 (a) If the text is read aloud or has been read on to tape, poor readers can visualise as they listen. If the material is taped, students can work independently, using their own best learning method, at their own pace.

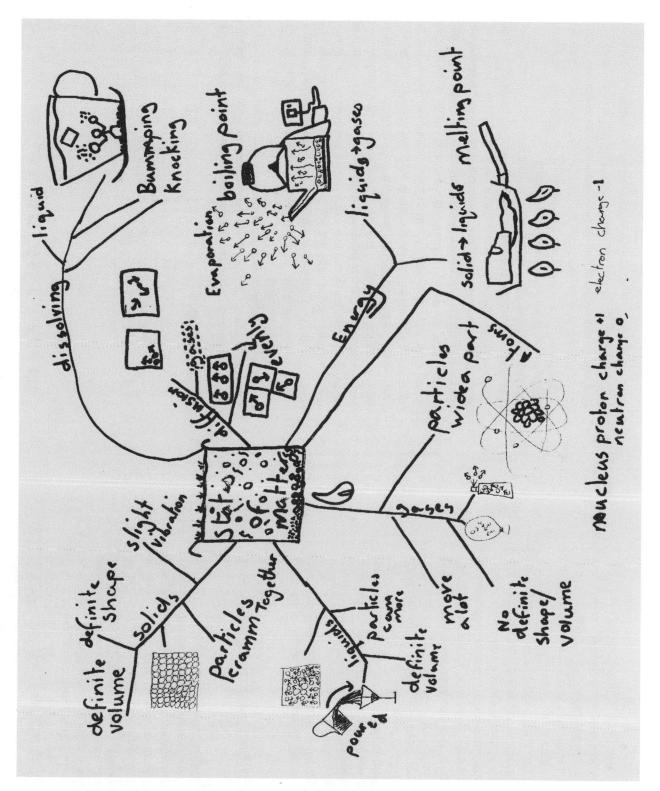

Figure 1.13 (b) Solids, liquids and gases: Liam compensates for his poor reading skills by processing text into images in the visual format of a mind-map. He keeps words on the map to a minimum, but, to revise for a test, he talks round the mind-map, putting his images back into words.

3 Electric Current

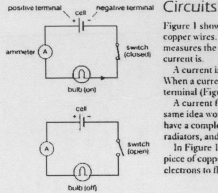

Figure 1
An electrical circuit

Circuits

Figure 1 shows an electrical circuit. The bulb is connected to an electric cell by copper wires. When the lamp lights we say there is a current. The ammeter measures the current. The needle on the meter moves to show how big the current is.

A current is a flow of charge. In copper some of the electrons are free to move. When a current goes through the wire, electrons are repelled from the negative terminal (Figure 2).

A current flows only when there is a complete circuit without any gaps. The same idea works when water flows around your central heating system. You must have a complete pathway (or circuit), so the water goes from the boiler out to the radiators, and back to the boiler to be warmed up again.

In Figure 1 there is a switch. The simplest switch can be made out of a springy piece of copper. When the switch is open there is no conducting path for the electrons to flow round. Then the bulb is off.

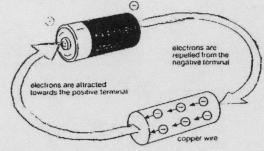

electrons are repelled from the negative terminal

electrons are attracted towards the positive terminal

copper wire

Figure 2
A current is a flow of charge

Which materials conduct?

The table (left) shows good and bad conductors, and insulators. The best conductors are metals; they contain electrons that are free to move. A current can also be carried by ions. The word ion is used to describe an atom (or molecule) that has lost or gained an electron. When an atom loses an electron it is a positive ion. When it gains an electron it is a negative ion.

Conductors	Insulators
Good	rubber
metals e.g.	plastics e.g.
copper	polythene
silver	PVC
mercury	perspex
aluminium	china
steel	air
Moderate	
carbon	
silicon	
germanium	
Poor	
water	
humans	

Your body is full of ions, so you conduct electricity. Electrical signals from your brain travel along nerves to give instructions to your muscles. Because you are a conductor, you can get a shock from the electricity mains supply.

Which way does current flow?

Figure 4 shows three examples of charge flowing. In all three cases the current is flowing to the right. The current is either carried by positive particles moving to the right, or negative particles moving to the left (or by both). It is easiest to say that current flows in the direction that positive charge moves in. So we say that current flows from the positive terminal of a cell to the negative terminal.

Measuring charge and current

We measure the current in a circuit using an ammeter. The unit of current is the ampere (A), though most of us call it an amp.

When the current is big (10 A), the charge moves round the circuit quickly. When the current is small (0.001 A) the charge moves round the circuit slowly. Current is the rate at which charge flows round a circuit.

$$\text{Current } (I) = \frac{\text{charge flowing } (Q)}{\text{time } (t)}$$

$$I = \frac{Q}{t}$$

We could measure charge by counting the number of electrons flowing. However, electrons have only a very small charge. Our unit of charge is the coulomb (C). 1 coulomb is equivalent to the charge on six million million million (6×10^{18}) electrons.

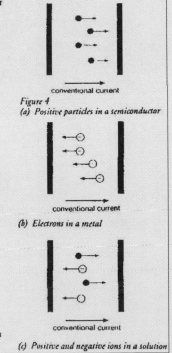

conventional current

Figure 4
(a) Positive particles in a semiconductor

conventional current

(b) Electrons in a metal

conventional current

(c) Positive and negative ions in a solution

Figure 1.14 (a) Despite the diagrams provided, poor readers may need to process the content of their textbook in a more personal manner, in order to understand and remember.

Figures 1.14 (a) and (b) show a student trying to make sense of a textbook account of electric current. The drawing illustrates the use of personal imagery to peg unfamiliar and abstract information from the text. Images here include puns – a policeman's helmet to represent 'copper', a musical conductor, two words 'am meter' with the sketch of an ammeter, and amps as 'umps' on a camel's back. They include symbols associated with the reader's home in the country – horse riding, currents and bridges in a stream, cows/'cou' and lambs/'lomb' frisking in a nearby field.

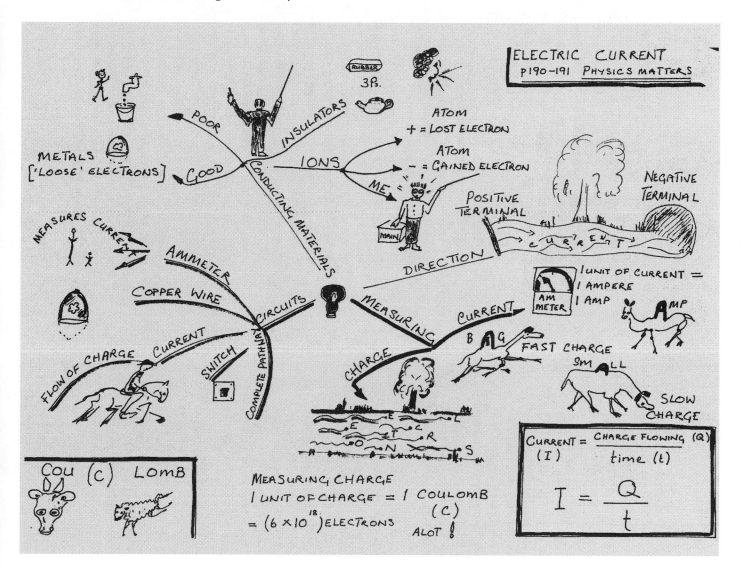

Figure 1.14 (b) The maker of this mind-map has processed the language of the text in (a) into personal imagery to help him understand and remember.

Arising out of the experience of one person, the images are uniquely meaningful to that person, though they may be barely comprehensible to a friend studying the same topic. It follows that each reader must draw or imagine his own pictures if they are to have maximum value for him as pegs on which to hang new ideas.

In Figure 1.15 the expressive faces on the water drops bring 'cohesiveness', 'high heat', 'evaporation' and 'ice floats' humorously alive.

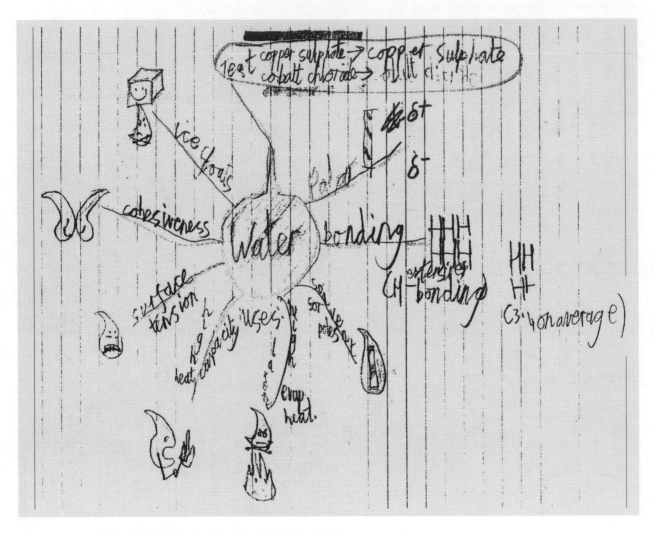

Figure 1.15 Greg is visualising the properties of water.

Teaching words

Teachers normally set reading as a way of enlarging pupils' understanding of their current topic. Visualising will achieve this goal, but dyslexic reader's will probably need help with language and individual words first – before they can pay much attention to meaning.

Why is this necessary?

Research has established that a lack of fluency in relating letter sounds to letter shapes underlies dyslexia. This 'coding' weakness makes it hard for dyslexic readers to focus on the meaning of a sentence or paragraph when their attention is chiefly taken up with decoding each of its component words.

Single words are problematic to dyslexic readers for other reasons, in addition to this phonological devil in dyslexia (see 'Subject-specific vocabulary' in Chapter 5). Words may cause trouble because they are technical (circuit, hypotenuse, mediaeval) or because they are used figuratively ('Love-devouring Death,' 'Mind-forged manacles'). They may be archaic or in dialect. They could have several meanings ('plot' a murder, 'plot' a graph, buy a 'plot' of land). They could be homophones ('key', 'quay'), tongue-twisters ('quantitative', 'preliminary'), foreign or abstract ('plagioclimax ecosystem', 'terminal velocity'). These examples show a complex mixture of problems to do with decoding words and understanding their meaning in context. Dyslexic readers have more than usual difficulty with both these aspects of written language and need strategies and practice in order to reach the point where they read new words automatically.

Other difficulties typical of dyslexia, such as poor visual perception and an inefficient memory for names, details and the order of events, make it still harder for dyslexic students to take in meaning when they read. As a first step to comprehension, they must be able to say, read, write and understand keywords that they will meet on the . They need to focus on individual important words that link the meaning of the text as a whole. They will probably need help to identify and learn these, even in the later years of secondary school.

Who should be responsible for teaching words?

Subject teachers may believe that this kind of language training is the province of the English or special needs department, but when children with dyslexia reach secondary school they usually feel they have neither the time nor the tolerance for literacy training as such. However, they will respond gratefully to being taught subject-specific language in the normal classroom, especially if this training is part of a subject teacher's programme for the class in general.

How might this work?

Two principles are useful here: the first is a school policy that expects every teacher to take responsibility for teaching his or her own subject-specific vocabulary, and the second is an understanding of the particular language difficulties that an individual student with dyslexia may have. The following classroom examples illustrate teaching approaches to various typically dyslexic difficulties with words:

1.   An oral approach to remembering names

> **Dominic in Year 7 said he could not remember events in the Old Testament stories the class was reading because he could not 'get hold of the names'. Dominic's underlying difficulties were in visual perception and working memory. His teacher allowed for these difficulties by practising Old Testament names orally with the whole class and leaving a list of them on the classroom board to serve as pegs to hang the events on. The whole class benefited.**

2.   Visualising to peg technical language

> Liam, doing GCSE physics, which he really enjoyed, found he couldn't guarantee to recall a technical word like 'evaporation', though he understood the process it stood for. Aware that 'naming' was a common problem for dyslexic individuals, his physics teacher suggested he should visualise the process and think of a mnemonic to peg the word. Liam imagined heated and fast-moving molecules breaking away from other slower molecules and 'evaping', instead of 'escaping' at the surface of a panful of water he was boiling to cook pasta. An interested cook, this image (set in his own kitchen at home) was clear in his mind's eye and, together with the silly new word, was enough to peg 'evaporation' so that he could consistently recall it. Sometimes classmates will suggest mnemonics and strengthen their own grasp of technical language at the same time.

3.   A semantic, analytical approach

> Kate, so frightened by the look of the word 'prescriptivism', in her A-level English language textbook, was convinced it stood for an abstruse idea she would never be able to understand. Her English teacher, realising that the word probably appeared to her as a tongue-twisting line-up of too many similar letters, suggested the class should write and say its separate syllables – 'pre – scrip – tiv – ism' – before they worried about its meaning. Once Kate could say it, she saw that it stood for exaggeratedly formal English. The idea was straightforward and so, she found, was reading the rest of the chapter on it. Kate's confidence to admit her problem and her teacher's recognition meant that the solution took only a few seconds and usefully involved the whole class. It probably helped some of them too.

Give time to read

Figure 1.16 (a) is taken from a Year 8 science exam. It illustrates the range of language hazards facing a dyslexic reader while, against the clock, he is trying to answer some questions on physics:

- technical words – 'bourdon gauge', 'ammeter'
- difficult spellings – 'beaker', 'measuring', 'heart', 'area'
- tongue-twister – 'irregularly'
- familiar, but probably not fully understood words – 'pressure', 'atmosphere'.

Although competent readers focus on the question in an exam, dyslexic readers struggle with the *language* of the question. Decoding will divert their attention from understanding, and they may do themselves justice only if they have enough time to process the words first, then the questions and, finally, the answers. Each step may need to be separate, each requiring conscious application and extra time. The additional stress caused by needing time to process words while others process questions can often be enough – under the added pressure of an

—— **SCIENCE** ——
Total time allowed: 75 minutes

The paper is divided into three sections, Biology, Chemistry and Physics.

The answers should be written on the question papers.

*Answer **all** the questions.*

Calculators may be used.

PHYSICS

1.

ammeter	*barometer*	*beaker*
bourdon gauge	*measuring cylinder*	*metre rule*
spring balance	*stop watch*	*tape measure*
thermometer	*top-loading balance*	*voltmeter*

Choose from the above list the apparatus you would use to make the following measurements.
You may select a particular piece once, more than once or not at all.

(a)   The mass of a book..

(b)   The temperature of a liquid..

(c)   The volume of some liquid...

(d)   The electric current in a circuit..

(e)   The pressure of the atmosphere..

(f)   The extension of a spring...

(g)   The force needed to extend a spring...

(h)   The volume of an irregularly shaped stone.......................................

(i)   The area of the base of a pencil box..

(j)   The rate at which your heart beats..

(10 marks)

Figure 1.16 (a) This page, taken at random from a Year 8 science exam, illustrates some of the technical difficulties that dyslexic students encounter when they read. The decoding problems have to be solved before the reader can absorb the content, much less answer questions on it.

exam – to wipe out the ability of a dyslexic reader to deal with content, even though, in practicals and discussion, he may be a confident scientist. Often the best thing a teacher can do for a dyslexic reader is the simplest – give him more time.

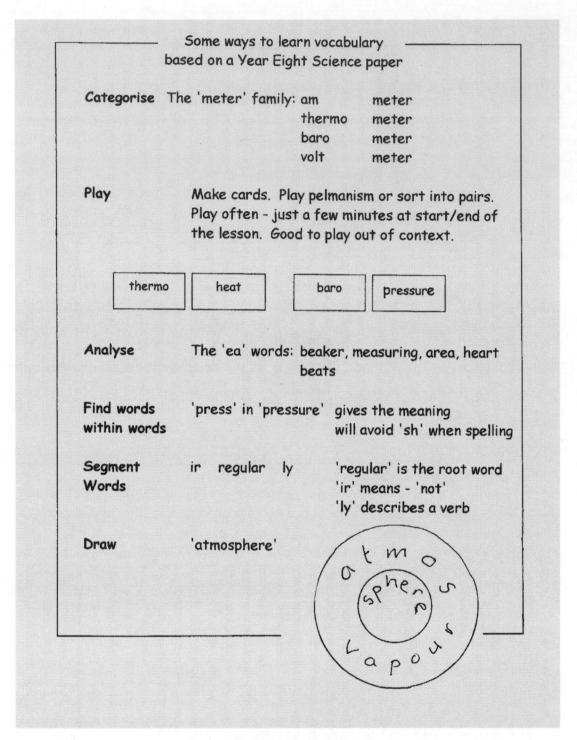

Figure 1.16 (b) Useful strategies for teaching subject-specific vocabulary.

There is, however, an additional complexity here. Research shows that readers, including those with dyslexia, may improve their reading comprehension if they are made to read faster than at their own self-paced rate of reading (Breznitz, 1991):

Dyslexic subjects gained from the experimental manipulation [that is the control and acceleration of reading rate]. Thus, they not only read about 20%

faster but, at the same time, significantly increased their comprehension score (by about 0.5 of a question). This gain took place even though the number of mistakes made (in reading aloud) did not alter.

One explanation given is that faster reading rate increases focus on the task and so there is less danger from distraction. Another explanation is that faster reading reduces the load on verbal working memory and makes it possible for people with dyslexia to build the meaning of sentences as well as process individual words, some of which, if read more slowly, will already have been forgotten before a whole sentence has been decoded.

To make sense in the classroom of the conflict between the need for extra processing time and the value of reading faster, teachers should bear in mind that reading speeds are relative. Teachers can encourage poor readers to quicken their natural pace without assuming that they will therefore read as fast or as efficiently as their classmates. It also makes sense for teachers to explain to a poor reader the value of increased reading speed as carefully as the reasons for extra reading time. Both may have a place in solving reading problems.

Use multisensory methods to teach words

Using the physics questions in Figure 1.16 (a) as illustration, Figure 1.16 (b) shows activities using eye, voice, ear and hand (simultaneously where possible) to pick out patterns of meaning, spelling and word structure in individual words. This multisensory way of categorising important words can become habitual and take very few minutes. Without the habit, many students may never manage to read, say, remember or write the keywords that carry the topic they are studying. Ultimately, dyslexic readers should act for themselves, but teachers can be very helpful if they see that the difficulty is with the language not with the topic – although that may also be difficult for other reasons.

Reading with a pencil

Familiarity with common patterns in the construction of English words is important to all dyslexic readers. It enables them to break strings of letters into meaningful units and then to synthesise them with greater accuracy and understanding. Figure 1.17 shows how to code word patterns with a pencil.

By no means all readers who are dyslexic need this basic approach, but some may. Teachers may not realise who is in this group unless they hear them read aloud. Practice using a pencil to code will train a child with dyslexia in the habit of mentally coding difficult words as he reads.

Readability

Teachers are often years adrift in estimating the reading age of a particular text or book. (Try gauging the reading age of the different sections of a Sunday paper, then check your accuracy using an established index.) Yet a mismatch between text level and an individual's level of reading skill may seriously interfere with his understanding and pleasure.

In the case of a reader with dyslexia, getting the reading age right may mean aiming off to allow for a legacy of past reading failure, with the selection of a text at a level lower than

Reading with a pencil
Example words are taken from a Geography textbook

Two ways of segmenting words:
1.   Box affixes, underline roots:
    [dis]solve   move[ment]   [oc]clud[ed]   [pre]vail[ing]

2.   Divide into syllables:
        Cor/ ro/ sion   gla/ci/ a/ ted   in/ ac/ cess/ ib/ il/ it/ y

Some coding symbols:

⌣	breve	put above a vowel to indicate short sound	excess (ĕxcĕss)
—	macron	put above a vowel to indicate long sound	relocate,
/	cross out	silent letters	fertile, quarried
			Ox-bow
___	underline	digraphs – two letters, one sound	leisure, groyne
		Trigraphs – three letters, one sound	catchment
ʂ		c before e/i/y is soft – make it look like an 's'	concentric
k		c before other letters is hard – make it look like a 'k'	arcuate
		g before e/i/y is soft – a dot links it to 'j'	plagioclimax
		y often acts as a vowel – a dot links it to 'i'	pyramidal
		ti before a vowel sound 'sh' – circle and write 'sh'	partial, conservationist

Figure 1.17 Using a pencil to code new or difficult words when reading introduces an element of play, cultivates the habit of phonological analysis and gives a weak reader increased confidence in his ability to crack the code of unfamiliar words.

his actual reading capability. Size and clarity of font, the placing of text in space on the , the quality and position of illustrations and the use of colour, subheadings, summaries, questions and contents list may all contribute to or detract from a text's readability for these disadvantaged readers.

What is a dyslexic student's reading level?

It is helpful for teachers to know of any large discrepancy between the reading ages of their students. However, knowing what sort of reading age and therefore what sort of reading assessment to look for is not straightforward. Exam boards require evidence from tests of single, unrelated words, read aloud, to grant the concession of extra time in public exams. Teachers, on the other hand, will be looking at how well their students can take in and remember information when they are reading continuous text silently to themselves.

There are few satisfactory formal tests for this at secondary school level, but teachers wishing to discover if their students can cope as might be expected with reading in their subject could do their own informal assessment, using current curriculum material. The model for this assessment might be:

- A passage of roughly 1000 words. This will give a reading task lasting about 4/5 minutes; one source suggests that the average reading speed for the general reading public is 230–250 words per minute (De Leeuw and De Leeuw, 1965).
- Ten multiple-choice questions to be answered immediately after reading the passage, but without looking back at it.
- Ten differently worded questions, covering the same points, to be asked a few days later and without warning.

Students who are already familiar with the topic in the test material will have an obvious advantage over others in the class who are not. Often dyslexic readers will have avoided previous reading assignments and will have learned less than their peers from taking notes in class. They are therefore likely to have less knowledge than others with which to associate any new reading; this makes a secondary reason for poor reading results in general, as well as in a reading assessment exercise.

Where reading assessment reveals a qualitative discrepancy between the reading of a dyslexic student and that of the rest of the class, teachers will need to gauge how disabling it is likely to be. A dyslexic student who has reading skills below the level of his class might cope, for instance, with the reading required to study A-level chemistry, biology or geography, whereas he might quail at reading *Middlemarch* for an English literature paper. He could probably build up the necessary vocabulary for science or geography through multisensory methods and repetition but would find the length of the novel, the working memory load and the subtleties of George Eliot's language and syntax overwhelming, without additional tactics and aids. Following the text while listening to an audiotape might answer this particular problem. If dyslexic readers can use tapes as a multisensory way of accessing text, then there may be no further barrier to their appreciation and pleasure in a great novel, however long and complex.

What is the reading level of a text?

The readability level of a given text is usually calculated on the number of complete sentences and words of three or more syllables in a sample of 100 words. The readability level will sometimes vary through the text of a book – from UK reading age (RA) 8 to 17 years in the case of Dickens' *Little Dorrit* – so a fair impression calls for several samples. The scale in mind for this chapter is the Flesch Kincaid Grade Level found at the end of the Spelling and Grammar Check in Microsoft Word 98, with 5 added to the American Grade Level to give a UK RA.

There is nothing very precise about readability levels. They are useful to predict rather than to measure a text's difficulty, and there are several factors to take into account when thinking about them. A higher readability level is acceptable if there is a teacher available to explain the more advanced words where necessary. If a student is determined to read a text with too high a readability level, he should be helped to do so. Scientific texts may be given an exaggerated level of difficulty because certain multisyllable words, such as chloroplast, holophytic, chlorophyll in a section on photosynthesis, recur often in the selection. Conversely, a passage of physics may be easy to read but hard to understand because the content is too concentrated and abstract to take in without study or interpretation.

Two approximate guides to estimating the suitability of a text

Readability tolerance levels:

A reader working independently may tolerate 1% error.
A reader with instruction available may tolerate 5%.
Anything beyond 10% error will cause frustration.

The 'Five-finger Test', despite its age, still helps to predict the unsuitability of a text for independent reading.

Five-finger test:

1. Select a of text from the middle of a book.
2. Start reading from the top of the .
3. When you come to a word you don't know, put a finger on it.
4. Put your next finger on the second word you don't recognise.
5. Use one hand only.

If you run out of fingers before the end of the , the text is probably too difficult for you to read with confidence or pleasure.

Sometimes there can be no alternative text with higher or lower readability level than the one given. Set texts and original sources are such cases, as is this extract, for instance, which, with a UK RA of 17 years, appeared on a Year 8 history paper.

'Witchcraft' – An extract from a law passed in 1563

If any person practises or uses any invocations of evil or wicked spirits, or uses any witchcraft, enchantment, charm or sorcery whereby any person shall be killed, being of these offences lawfully convicted shall suffer pains of death. And if any person shall practise witchcraft, enchantment, charm or sorcery whereby any person shall be damaged in his or her body, or whereby any good shall be damaged or destroyed, being of these offences lawfully convicted shall for the first offence suffer imprisonment for one year; and for the second offence suffer the pains of death.

Faced with unfamiliar language, latinate sentence structure and no modernised version to hand, it is not only the dyslexic student who might need to use some conscious strategy in following the sense of this passage.

Make questions to help with understanding and remembering

To meet such a reading challenge, students, dyslexic or otherwise, need to find a way of interacting with the text. One way, in the case of the above text, would be to reread each sentence out loud, forming questions to which parts of the sentence are answers. For the first sentence the reader might ask himself:

- What types of people are to die?

  Answer: those calling up evil spirits or using witchcraft, spells or magic.

- What two conditions would lead to their execution?

  Answer: they would have to cause their victim's death. They would have to be found guilty of this in a law court.

Questioning helps to identify the separate points apparently moulded into one by syntax.

Textbooks

Difficulties

Students are often set reading tasks for homework – to give further explanation for topics that have been covered in class, to give background to the subject that they are studying or in preparation for a class discussion or test. This is the most demanding sort of reading for a dyslexic person because:

- interest level in the subject matter may not be very great
- the material may be at too high a reading level
- the subject may be unfamiliar and therefore hard to visualise
- if the chapter is photocopied, it may be poorly reproduced and the print too small
- textbooks are unlikely to be on tape

As a result of these difficulties, the student with dyslexia often has to read the material twice to get at the meaning, so it takes him longer to read it than his peers. And at the back of his mind he knows that, unless it is followed up by some supporting activity, he is very likely to forget what he has read. It is not surprising that many students who are dyslexic hope that they can get by without doing their reading homework.

Getting to know the textbook

However, some time spent on exploring the class textbook, and showing the pupils how to use it, is particularly helpful to the dyslexic people in the class. Showing how the textbook works, which bits are the most valuable and which the least, will give the pupils confidence. To develop their critical faculties and become familiar with what may (or may not) be a valuable resource, the children could answer the following questions for homework:

- Do you like the look of the book? Why?
- Is it too difficult for you to read?
- Is there a useful table of contents?
- Are there paragraph, or chapter headings?
- Is there a glossary?
- Do the pictures or diagrams help your understanding?
- Are there questions at the end of the chapters or sections?
- Is there a summary at the end of the chapter?
- Why could it be a good idea to read the questions or summary before you start reading the chapter?

If the book is too difficult for some pupils, they may need a different one or some help with how to use the one they have.

Reading to understand and remember

A class lesson in reading techniques, on a relevant chapter, would give poor readers very useful guidance on how to get beyond simply decoding the words. One of the most effective approaches to reading for understanding and memory involves a sequence of activities: previewing, questioning, reading, summarising, testing (PQRST).

Previewing

Previewing involves the student's looking over the text before he reads it, noting the titles and subtitles, the first and last sentences of each section, the pictures and diagrams, and any summary or questions there might be at the end of the chapter.

In this way he establishes a framework for his reading – he finds out what the chapter is about and how the subject is handled, the pictures should give relevance to the theory, and the summary should provide an overview so that the detail can be read in context.

Questioning

This second activity is the one that can make the difference between active and passive reading: while previewing a passage, the reader writes down a brief list of the questions that he hopes or expects the passage to answer.

Reading

The reading should now have more relevance and the reader should feel more actively engaged with the text. The topic is familiar, he knows where it's going and he is looking for answers to his own questions and any questions that the author may have posed at the end of the passage.

If the reading material is difficult, the dyslexic student might find it helpful to read the text aloud onto tape or enlist a parent or friend to do this for him. Some students find it easier to understand when they listen rather than read the words from the . Committing the chapter to tape also provides a resource for future study and revision.

Summarising

Pausing at the end of each paragraph and asking 'What was that about?' and then summarising it in his own words, either aloud or on paper, is a very thorough way of reading for meaning. The processing involved in this will make it much more likely that he will remember the piece, as well as provide a useful summary when he comes to revise the subject.

Testing

Answering the questions he generated on previewing, answering any questions there might be at the end of the chapter, creating his own questions (see 135), summarising the whole piece, being tested by his teacher, creating a mind-map of the topic – all these activities will benefit the pupil who tends to forget what he has read. The forgetting curve (see 238) needs to be taken into account, particularly with students who are dyslexic, if the reading assignment is to be a valuable element in study.

An example

Figure 1.18 is an extract from a GCSE history textbook – *Modern World History* by McAleavy. Below are examples of how a student might preview, question, read, summarise and test a part of the chapter entitled 'Hitler's War'.

Previewing

Previewing involves some internal talking about the text while the student scans it for the first time:

> **It's a factual summary of the events of the Second World War. The main headings are 'Blitzkrieg in Poland', 'The phoney war', 'The fall of France', 'Hitler turns east', 'America joins the war', 'The attack on Pearl Harbour', 'The tide turns', 'The holocaust', 'The end game'.**
>
> **There are pictures of Hitler under the Eiffel Tower in 1940 after the defeat of France, Hitler's forces in the Ukraine in 1941, the Japanese attack on Pearl Harbour, a terrible picture of Jewish victims of the Holocaust.**

Questions

The reader then writes down some questions he expects to be answered in the chapter:

The Second World War

Blitzkrieg in Poland

The Second World War began when Germany invaded Poland on 1 September 1939. Britain and France had pledged to defend Poland. On 3 September the French and the British governments declared war on Germany. The French and the British could do very little to stop a German victory in Poland. By the end of the month, Polish resistance had collapsed. On 17 September Soviet forces crossed the Polish frontier and took control of part of eastern Poland. This was part of the deal Hitler had struck with Stalin before the war in the Nazi–Soviet Pact. Stalin also moved his troops into the Baltic states of Latvia, Lithuania and Estonia.

In Poland and each of the following campaigns Hitler's methods became known as a 'Blitzkrieg' or lightning war. Blitzkrieg involved the use of overwhelming force, in as short a time as possible, in order to crush the enemy. Extensive use was made of tanks and other armoured vehicles. The Germans had much success with this technique.

The phoney war

Having succeeded in the east, Hitler's thoughts turned west. He began to make plans for an attack on France. Meanwhile the British and the French tried to weaken Germany by stopping German trade by sea. In particular they tried to cut off the supply of iron ore from Scandinavia. From October 1939 to April 1940 there was little fighting between Britain, France and Germany. This period became known as the 'phoney war'. Fighting did take place in the winter of 1939–40 between the USSR and the small Baltic state of Finland. The Finnish army fought with great skill and ferocity and it took from October 1939 to March 1940 for the USSR to defeat her small neighbour. Eventually Finland was defeated and forced to give territory and a naval base to the USSR. The Soviet struggle to defeat Finland convinced Hitler that the Red Army could easily be beaten by Germany. His secret long-term plan was to turn against the Soviet Union and set up a new German empire in the east.

In April 1940 the French and the British started mining Norwegian waters to stop the trade in iron ore. Germany responded by invading Norway and Denmark. The fall of Finland, Norway and Denmark led to a political crisis in Britain and France. Both prime ministers were forced to resign. In Britain Winston Churchill came to power in May 1940.

The fall of France

After months of waiting Hitler struck west in May 1940. The Netherlands, Belgium and France were invaded and rapidly defeated by German forces. A British army was forced to flee from the Continent back to Britain from the port of Dunkirk. Germany took direct control of much of France, leaving part of the south and south-east of the country under a puppet French government, with its capital in the town of Vichy. At this point it seemed that Hitler had virtually won the war. France was beaten and much of Europe was occupied. Only Britain remained to fight Germany. Sensing that the war was nearly over, Mussolini joined forces with Germany in 1940. He wanted Italy to get some of the rewards of victory.

Having defeated France, Hitler prepared for a German invasion of Britain. The German air force, the Luftwaffe, set out to win control of the air over Britain. This was the first stage of the invasion plan. German planes bombed military sites, factories and the capital city, London, in August and September 1940. The British air force, the RAF, fought back and the clash of the two air forces became known as the 'Battle of Britain'. Although there were heavy losses on both sides, the RAF got the upper hand in the Battle of Britain and, as a result, Hitler was forced to put off his plans for an invasion of Britain.

An Italian attempt to share in Hitler's victory went disastrously wrong. An Italian army was defeated by Britain in North Africa, and Greece successfully stopped an Italian attempt to invade. Hitler was obliged to send German forces to North Africa and to Greece in order to help his ally.

Figure 1.18 Extract from *Modern World History,* *Tony McAleavy, C.U.P 1996.*

In what ways was Germany successful between 1939 and 1941?

Why was the attack on Pearl Harbour important?

What happened in the Holocaust?

How did the Second World War end?

I would also like to know:

What is 'blitzkrieg'?

What is a phoney war?

Why did Britain get involved?

What went wrong with the Nazi Soviet pact?

Which countries did Hitler defeat?

Where are the Baltic states?

What happened at Pearl Harbour?

What part did the Americans take in the war?

How was the Holocaust allowed to happen?

Three ways of summarising

a) Summarising with words

The student reads each paragraph and summarises it. Here is the first:

France and Britain declared war on Germany when she invaded Poland on 1 September 1939. By 17 September Soviet troops had occupied Eastern Poland, and Stalin, who had signed the Nazi–Soviet Pact with Hitler, moved his troops into Latvia, Lithuania and Estonia. Germany achieved her successes by a series of lightning strikes using overwhelming force with armoured vehicles.

b) Mind-map summary

Some students might prefer to build up a mind-map summary of the chapter they are reading. It is the visualising and the thought processing behind drawing a mind-map summary, as well as the advantage of a spatial representation of the information, that helps the person with dyslexia give substance to words and remember better what he has read (Figure 1.19).

Again, an internal dialogue:

Blitzkrieg – How shall I remember that Germany invaded Poland in September? – Mum's birthday – a birthday cake.

I'll do a flash of lightning for blitzkrieg and a tank to represent how the Germans won their victories. A swastika and the hammer and sickle will symbolise the Nazi–Soviet Pact.

Phoney War – I'll draw an iron on a boat to help me remember iron ore. And a mine to show Britain and France intercepting the German trade with Scandinavia.

And so on.

This is quite hard work, but more interesting than just reading or writing notes. It involves a great deal of processing and makes the leap from words to visualising and on to involvement in what was really going on at the time.

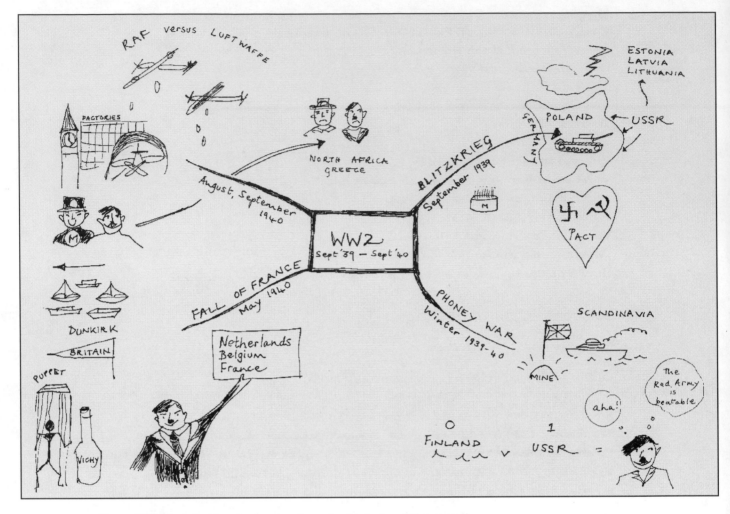

Figure 1.19 This student has clearly *enjoyed* mapping the topic, which is a good start to study. The map itself is most useful as a stimulus for him to talk through, explaining the symbols, giving more details and enlarging on the issues.

For some dyslexic people this is a far more effective way of making notes or summarising. There is little detail, so, because the symbols are just pegs for memory, it is important for the student to look at the map again and talk it through, supplying the detail. Travelling round the map in a clockwise direction, from one o'clock, the position of the symbols on the map will show and reinforce the sequence of events as they occurred.

c) Summarising by drawing a map

I don't know exactly where Poland or the Balkan states are, so I'll copy a map. I don't remember maps unless I've drawn or illustrated them myself.

The geography of Europe helps to explain a great deal of what happened in the Second World War (or any war) – working with a map is ideal for people with a strong spatial sense. Their own input into the map with pictures, arrows, colours and dates will help with both understanding and memory (Figure 1.20).

Figure 1.20 Map of Europe: enlarged onto A3, coloured, and with personal pictures and symbols added, this map will become memorable for the individual who worked on it.

Testing

a) Testing on the questions

At the end of his reading session, the pupil should answer the questions he formulated during his preview. In this way, he will consolidate his memory and practise expressing historical information in his own words. The questions will be available for further testing later.

b) Testing on the mind-map

When he has finished reading the chapter and making the mind-map, the student should cover it, re-visualise it and talk his way round it from memory, explaining the symbols and expanding on main points. Repeating this operation later will further strengthen his memory.

c) Testing on the map

The dyslexic student needs to redraw the map from memory more than once to make sure that it is fixed in his long-term memory. Ideally, he should talk about the events described in the chapter all the time he is drawing.

Books on tape

Some teachers, and even students, feel that it is cheating to listen to a book rather than read it. This is probably a hangover from the days when it was only the elite who had access to book learning – they could afford education and books, and so cultural norms became established that have been reinforced by the education and exam system – if you can't read, you can't be very intelligent. If you can't learn in the way we teach, you can't be worth educating. This was a policy of exclusion.

We now know that, because of dyslexia, about 10% of the population have mild or severe difficulties with accessing education and literature through the written word. The individuals with dyslexia in a classroom may be among the least literate – but they could be the most literary. Fortunately, our fuller understanding of the difficulties and potential of people with dyslexia has come at a time when technology offers many solutions for those who were previously disadvantaged.

Books on tape create a level playing field on the reading front. There is nothing inferior about receiving information or a story aurally rather than reading the words on the . Some would argue that, because the author thinks in the spoken word with tone of voice, timing and expression being part of his message, the written word must be a secondary medium, a translation of his original conception – capital letters, paragraphing and punctuation marks being substitutes for what the human voice can supply naturally.

Anything that gets in the way of 'hearing' the voice of the author – and there are many purely technical problems with print for the dyslexic reader that do just that – can be eliminated by actually *hearing* the written word read aloud. For someone with dyslexia, listening to books on tape has many advantages.

Visualising for comprehension and memory

Research shows that readers who visualise (see page 7) – whether it is fact or fiction that they are reading – will be able to comprehend and remember more effectively than those who do not visualise. A dyslexic individual who is struggling to decode the words and punctuation is much less likely to be able to visualise – so comprehension, memory and, of course, enjoyment all suffer. As a listener, he not only has the advantage of being free to visualise, but is also helped by tone of voice, accent, emphasis, timing and speed.

Remembering the sequence

Anyone who has listened to the tape of a play or novel on a journey will know that external landmarks of their journey can, rather incongruously, map the sequence of the story.

> 'The balcony scene in *Romeo and Juliet* was when we were on the M4/M5 interchange.'

It is also striking to remember how clearly the visual images of the story remain in the memory when one was relaxed and listening. Listening to a tape on a familiar walk can provide even clearer pegs to mark the sequence and help a student to remember the order of events in the book he is studying.

Slow readers need not lag behind the class

In classes at school, college or university, the slow reader will lag behind other students and, while they are discussing, say, Chapter 8 of the textbook or novel, he will still be on Chapter 5. Not only does he not benefit from the teaching around Chapter 8, he also loses the chance to join in the discussion – which is often the best way of learning for the person with dyslexia. Listening to the tape before the lessons will put him in a much stronger position.

Listening to books helps with writing style

Children with dyslexia are often reluctant writers as well as reluctant readers. Much of this can be put down to spelling, handwriting and short-term memory difficulties. However, if these children have not read much either, they will have missed out on the conventions of story-telling, familiarity with formal written structures and perhaps a more extensive use of vocabulary than they are used to in their everyday conversations. Their own ability to express themselves on paper will be affected. Listening to books on tape can fill this gap.

Following the text while listening

Listening to tapes can actually improve the reading skills of a dyslexic reader. If he follows the text while listening, he will both increase his reading speed and, by seeing the letters and words while he hears the sounds, improve his spelling and his word recognition. Using text and tape together, the pupil will experience the pleasure and satisfaction, perhaps for the first time, of being able to read the printed word fluently.

Full, unabridged texts are essential for students, particularly if they want to follow the text while listening. Another reason for avoiding abridged versions is that often they leave out the descriptive passages – and for the visualiser these may be essential for him to be able to imagine how the characters look and where and when the action is taking place.

Some readers may find the pace of a reading too slow to follow the text while listening. For them, just listening or just reading is the obvious solution.

You've heard the tape – now read the book

Booksellers will confirm that once a novel or play has been filmed, or serialised on the radio or television, sales of the book will rocket. Not all the buyers will have dyslexia, but many of them will be reluctant or new readers who are usually diffident about investing time and effort in a book unless they know in advance that they are going to enjoy it. For people with dyslexia there is also enormous advantage in being familiar with the setting, the characters and the plot before they start the novel. Having the framework in place, they can really enjoy everything the book has to offer.

Dialect and conversation

Much fiction contains large portions of conversation written in dialect – for example the novels of Walter Scott, Mark Twain, Harper Lee and Irvine Welsh. The author's attempts to

Huckleberry
Finn (an extract)

Well, when it come dark I tuck out up de river road, en went 'bout
two mile er more to whah dey warn't no houses. I'd made up my mine
'bout what I's a-gwyne to do. You see ef I kep' on tryin' to git away
afoot, de dogs 'ud track me; ef I stole a skift to cross over, dey'd miss
dat skift, you see, en dey'd know 'bout whah I'd lan' on de yuther side
en whah to pick up my track. So I says, a raff is what I's arter; it doan'
make no track.

I see a light a-comin' roun' de p'int, bymeby, so I wade' in en shove'
a log ahead o'me, en swum more'n half-way acrost de river, en got in
'mongst de drift-wood, en kep' my head down low, en kinder swum
agin de current tell the raff come along. Den I swum to de stern uv
it, en tuck aholt. It clouded up en 'uz pooty dark for a little while. So
I clumb up en laid down on de planks. De men 'uz all 'way yonder in
de middle, whah de lantern wuz. De river wuz a-risin' en dey wuz a
good current; so I reck'n'd 'at by fo' in de mawnin' I'd be twenty-five
mile down de river, en den I'd slip in, jis' b'fo' daylight, en swim
asho' en take to de woods on de Illinoi side.

Figure 1.21 *Huckleberry Finn* is a wonderful book – but the passages in dialect are
quite hard going if you haven't got automatic phonological skills. If you have dyslexia
and this is your set text, you will enjoy the book much more if you listen to the tape.

make the language come alive by spelling the words in the way they sound (a novel concept in English!) are a great barrier to people with dyslexia, whose phonological skills are not automatic (Figure 1.21).

Textbooks on tape

Dyslexic pupils are entitled to the same access to the syllabus as the rest of the class, but providing this is not easy. Sometimes a textbook or handout that is appropriate for the class as a whole is unsuitable for those in the class with dyslexia: the content level may be right, but the reading age too high or the layout confusing ('I have to read it two or three times to get at the meaning').

Unfortunately, children with dyslexia are the very ones who really need the back-up of a textbook – their note-taking or copying may be poor and they need reinforcement of what they have learnt in class. If the rest of the class needs an appropriate textbook, then they do too. And more so.

There are alternatives: the teacher could try to find a comparable textbook or handout at the right content and reading level, or he could have the textbook read aloud onto tape for those children who need that help. The latter option is the best – the tape can be used with the book that everyone else is using, and the tape can be copied for several members of the class. The teacher could even edit the text or interpolate his own comments and guidance while recording.

A main objection to this idea is that it is time-consuming and needs extra planning and organisation. Once done, however, it is a resource that can be used again and again and is a real help to that underachieving group of every class whose literacy skills hold them back in every subject. The hard-pressed subject teachers need not do the reading themselves – a parent, a pupil in the school, another teacher who enjoys reading, any of these could supply the need.

Sources for tapes

Books on tape or CD are available from public libraries – a note from a dyslexia therapist or educational psychologist would enable anyone with dyslexia to borrow tapes free. Lists of audio books are available from the library. There are now many sources for obtaining unabridged recorded books – surf the web to find who publishes and stocks the title you want.

Listening Books provides a postal audio-book library service to anyone who has difficulty reading in the ordinary way. For an annual fee you can borrow as many titles as you can listen to during a year. You will be sent catalogues that contain a wide range of (abridged and unabridged) fiction and non-fiction titles, as well as audio books which support the National Curriculum (see Reading and Resources, page 329).

Shakespeare's plays on tape

For most schoolchildren the unfamiliarity of Shakespeare's language can prevent understanding of the plot and appreciation of the poetry. Many have difficulties with the subtleties of the verse forms. For dyslexic students the problems are compounded because of their poor short-term memory and sequencing, and their slow and inaccurate reading.

One of the earliest indicators of dyslexia in young children may be their inability to recognise rhyme and rhythm. It is a skill that can be learnt (W. B. Yeats taught himself) and one of the best ways of appreciating stress and metre is to hear it *while looking at* the verse on the – seeing where the line ends, seeing where the stress falls, recognising sound patterns visually while listening.

Reading aloud round the class is a less satisfactory introduction to a play than reading the text while listening to good actors reading on tape. The cast of a BBC recording of *Hamlet*, for example, is as follows:

Hamlet	Kenneth Branagh
Claudius	Derek Jacobi
Gertrude	Judi Dench
Polonius	Richard Briars
Horatio	Michael Williams
Ophelia	Sophie Thompson
Laertes	James Wilby
First Gravedigger	Michael Elphick
Player King	Michael Hordern
Player Queen	Emma Thompson
The Ghost	John Gielgud

Few classrooms can boast such talent!

Until the children are already familiar with the language, with the characters whose words they are reading and with what the play is about, too much is lost to make reading round the class a good use of time. For those with dyslexia too, the fear of being asked to read is enough to put them off Shakespeare for life ('I can't hear what I'm saying when I'm reading aloud' is a common complaint). Reading the play at a very slow rate, lesson by lesson with weekends in between can mean that details are forgotten and the momentum is lost. When they know the play, pupils will enjoy taking the parts themselves, and it will be a much more enriching experience. Shakespeare is operating on so many levels that, as with other complex tasks where there is overload, it is a good idea for students with dyslexia to break the study down into small steps.

An ideal classroom approach for them might be to make pupils familiar with the characters and the plot (the teacher telling the story, *Lamb's Tales*, etc.), drawing them, describing them, mind-mapping acts or characters, and then watching a performance on video and retelling in their own words. When this framework is established, they will be ready to listen to the tape as they study the text – either at home or in the classroom – and will appreciate the play much more, perhaps 'hearing' the poetry for the first time. This is not a way of avoiding serious study – but of encouraging and enhancing it.

Tapes make literature accessible to all

There are some problems of prejudice with suggesting multisensory learning – drawing pictures, listening rather than reading and mind-mapping are sometimes perceived as childish, rather a cop-out, methods to be used only in emergencies with the less bright pupils. There is no evidence to suggest that people who are dyslexic are less intelligent, responsive or creative than others – only that, for them, the written rather than the spoken word often makes literature inaccessible.

There may well be other children in the class whose weak reading skills are the main obstacle to academic success. They will find listening to a book easier and more enjoyable than reading it off the . Introducing them to books on tape might give them their best access to the world of ideas and the imagination, and could make the crucial difference for those who avoid subjects where there is a big reading component.

Conclusion

Teachers who understand the skills required to read for their particular subject are in a good position to help those in the class whose reading ability does not match the task. This is all the more true when teachers also have a clear picture of the specific skills, or lack of them, that individual pupils bring to their reading.

Chapter 2
Mind-mapping

Why mind-mapping works for people with dyslexia

Hearing is sequencing in time

The problems experienced by many people with dyslexia stem from their weak memory for an auditory sequence. This has implications not only for reading – as you read the words, you hear them in your mind, and then they are gone – but also for most other aspects of formal learning.

If this is where the dyslexic student's weakness lies, it is understandable that he will have problems with planning, organising and remembering words. He cannot rely solely on his auditory sequential memory but must be helped to support and supplement it with other strategies.

Seeing is sequencing in space

An auditory sequence can be turned into a spatial sequence. Just as a conventional map uses colours, symbols, numbers, print and scale to convey information – and some people can work from a map much more easily than from a verbal account – so some dyslexic students will find a visual presentation of ideas, a mind-map, easier to work from. If they learn to lay out their ideas spatially, with phrases or symbols, they will have more control over them – be able to re-sequence them if necessary, see links between them and, having a clear visual picture of the , will be able to remember not only the content but also the order and relationships.

Mind-mapping is one of the most useful writing and learning tools for the student with dyslexia – but it is one that is seldom taught because most teachers and learners can think and write sequentially without difficulty and so manage quite well without it. In fact, some teachers may feel quite hostile to this way of working because it lacks the formal, logical approach that they regard as the hallmark of academic competence.

Objections to mind-mapping

> 'Other people's mind-maps look very confusing.'

> 'You can't get enough detail on them.'

> 'What if you can't draw?'

> 'I think in a linear way.'

Teaching mind-mapping

It is difficult to teach something that you are not committed to and don't do yourself. It is therefore most important for sympathetic teachers to learn about mind-mapping, to recognise its value and to encourage their pupils to use it. A significant number of each class would benefit from and enjoy using this technique – so we owe it to them to offer it as an option. If the whole class learns it, then those with dyslexia will feel more confident in using a method that, for them, could make the difference between success and failure – and even the most linear thinkers in the class may also find advantages and produce more interesting work.

The technique needs to be taught and practised before the full benefits are felt. Students who initially met the idea of mind-maps with suspicion have gone on to use them as a routine part of their working: first with brainstorming, then with essay planning, summarising, revision and, finally, as a crucial part of exam technique.

Mind-maps are a practical demonstration of all we know about multisensory learning. In making a mind-map, we use many different areas of the brain, processing and integrating the material with which we are working.

How to start

Watching Tony Buzan's video on mind-mapping (*Get Ahead: A Short Cut to Straight 'A's*) would be a good introduction. It is a good idea to watch the video with the class or the pupil so that you can keep stopping it in order to discuss the merits of the techniques – and why they might be particularly helpful for people with dyslexia. There are some good ideas and some good examples on the video. Obviously, the most effective way of encouraging your pupils to use the technique is to get them to mind-map something that they actually need to learn or revise at that moment – a school topic in preparation for a test, perhaps. They should not only make the mind-map themselves but also talk about it, and re-visualise it afterwards so that it will stay in the memory. If the technique is used properly and works well, students will want to use it again and again.

These points are worth remembering:

- Plain white paper, turned round to the horizontal, landscape view seems to be most satisfactory for mind-mapping.
- A3 paper gives more space than A4.
- Single words or phrases are more effective than a lot of writing.
- A well-spaced mind-map is easier to visualise.
- Symbols should be used wherever possible – because they will make the map more memorable.
- Humour, colour and striking images should be used wherever possible.
- Other people's mind-maps don't work for you in the same way. You need to do your own.

Types of mind-map

There is no one generic mind-map to suit all tasks: symbols and pictures would be inappropriate for mind-mapping an essay; brainstorming would not be suitable for structuring or summarising.

The student should ask himself, therefore, 'What is this map for?' – and then it will become clear which type of mind-map he should use.

"Is it to get me started on an essay?"
(A brainstorm with single words or phrases)

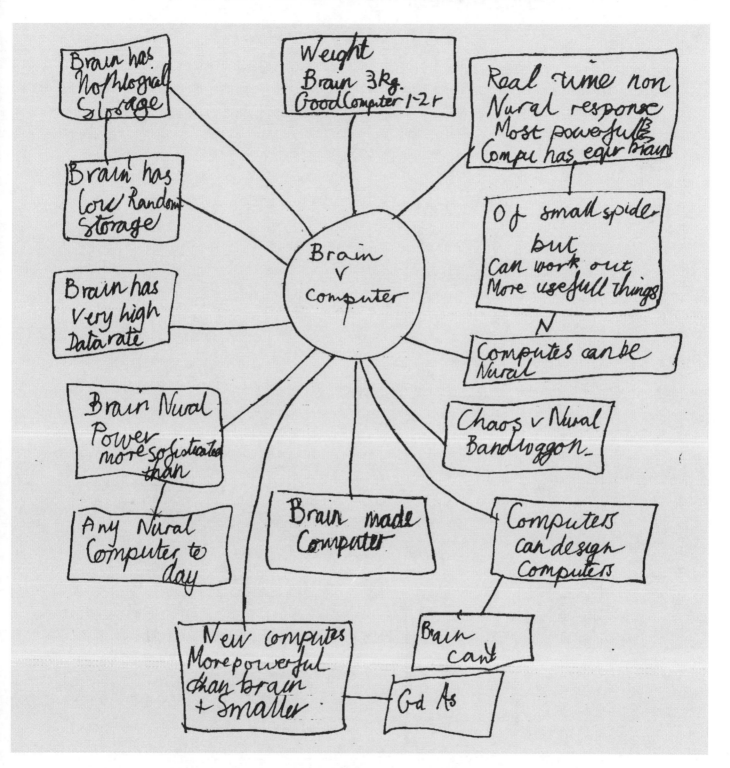

Figure 2.1 This pupil was brainstorming the relative merits of the brain and a computer. He put down ideas as they occurred to him and sorted them later.

"Is it to help sort ideas?"
(Exploring topics and looking for themes to link them)

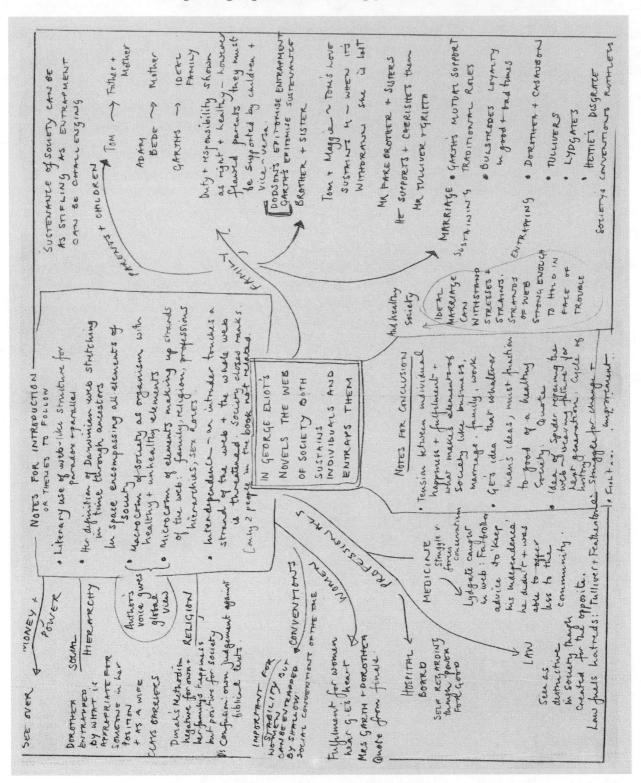

Figure 2.2 This essay question needed to have some time spent on brainstorming before the student could commit herself to a plan.

"Is it to help sort ideas?"
(Main branches with subtopics coming off)

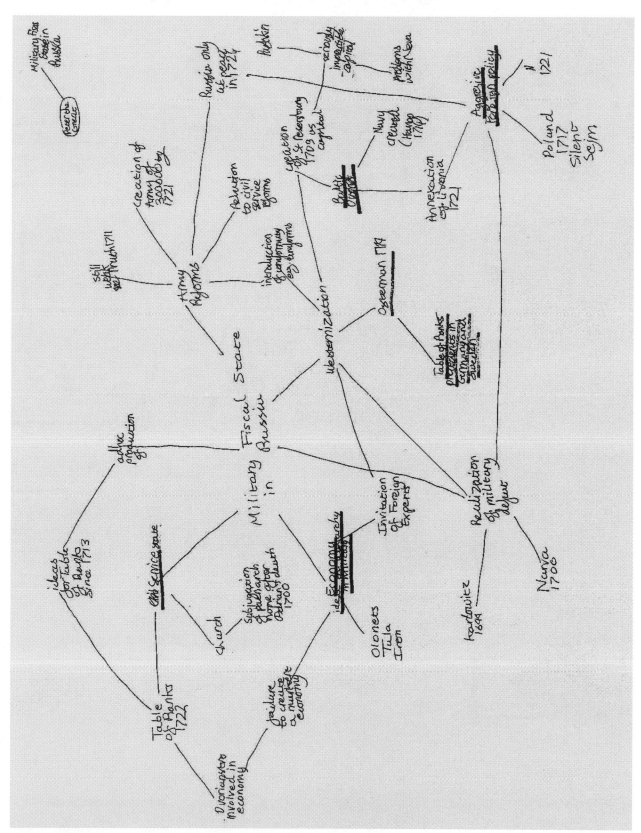

Figure 2.3 A mind-map encourages flexibility of thinking. This pupil is deciding on main topics, giving examples, seeing links. The spatial arrangement gives a good overall picture of the links.

"Is it to help me put my ideas into a relevant order?"
(Numbering or linking topics in a plan)

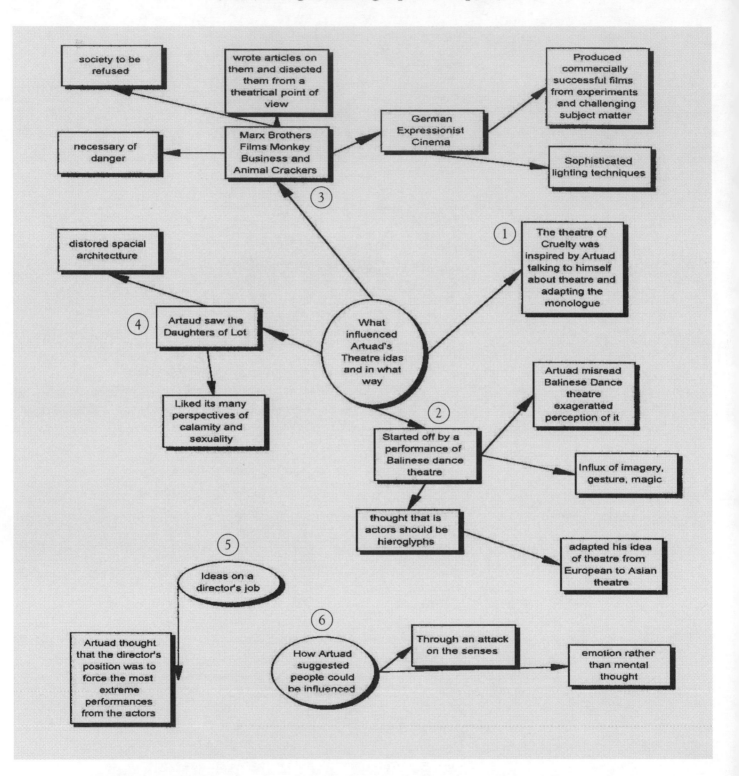

Figure 2.4 Robert has put down his responses to an essay question using mind-mapping software called *Inspiration*. He subsequently printed his map and numbered the topics in the order in which he would write about them. As this map is one of Robert's first efforts with *Inspiration*, he has made little use of the categorising functions available. (*Inspiration* software, see page 110)

"Is it to help me see HOW I should answer an essay question?"
(Arguments for and against, or by topic?)

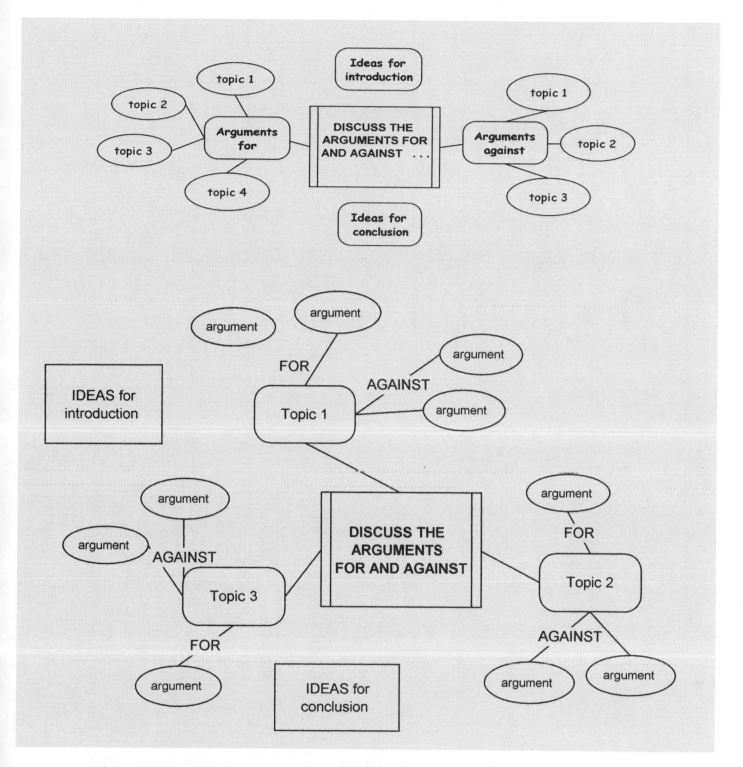

Figure 2.5 It is better to experiment with *HOW* to answer the question before starting on the writing stage – especially for students who are dyslexic and unwilling to restart any essay – writing is such a labour for them, they don't want to 'waste' the great effort they have already made.

"Is it to help me remember a topic?"
(The images, and where they are on the page, help memory)

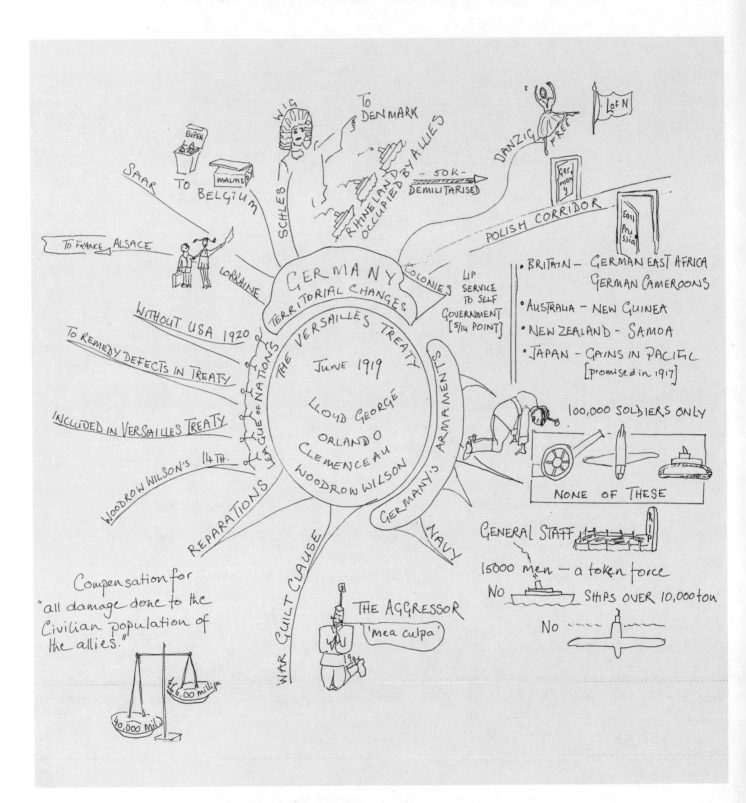

Figure 2.6 Explaining this mind-map to someone else will help the student to remember the terms of the Treaty – as will re-visualising it and describing it from memory.

"Is it to give me an overall view of a subject?"
(Topics seen in relationship to each other chronologically, or by links)

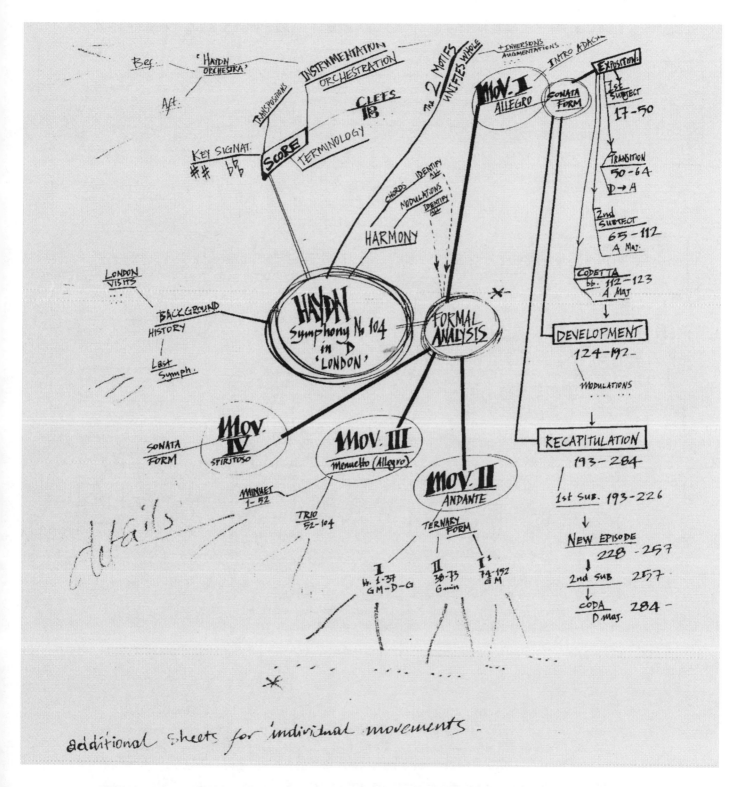

Figure 2.7 This overview of Haydn's Symphony No.104 was drawn by a music teacher who distributed it to his class and asked the pupils to fill in the details of each movement themselves.

"Is it to outline a syllabus for revision?"
(*Processing linear information in a spatial format*)

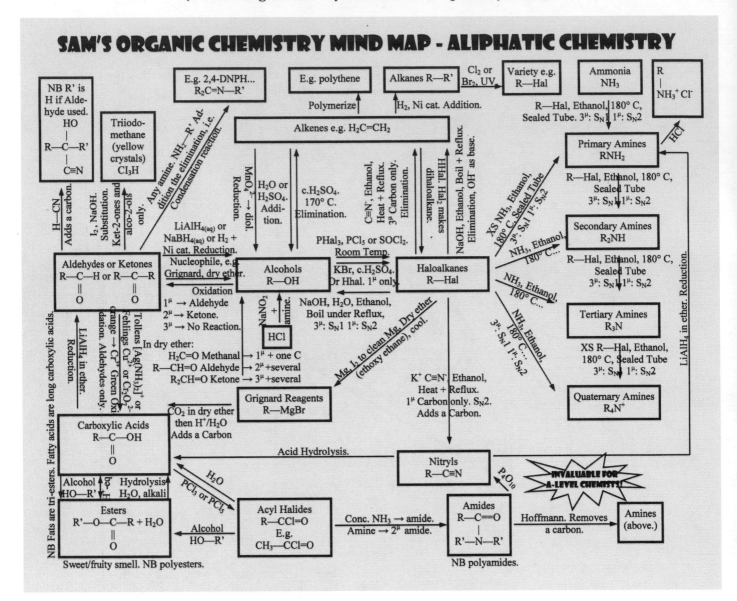

Figure 2.8 (a) Sam followed his chemistry teacher's suggestion that the easiest way to remember pathways of reactions is to visualise them on a map. In the account below he describes the value of visualising, using a computer, working with a friend and creating a personal map. This multisensory method ensured confidence and success in his chemistry exam.

My chemistry teacher suggested that we could most easily remember pathways of reactions by visualising them on maps. In lessons he would draw arrows representing reactions to and from each chemical that we were studying, suggesting that we could eventually combine them into a large map including the entire syllabus for revision.

In time for the first test, I put the information we had so far been given onto my computer so that it could easily be shifted around to make room for more. Charlie (a classmate who always gets full marks in everything) and I

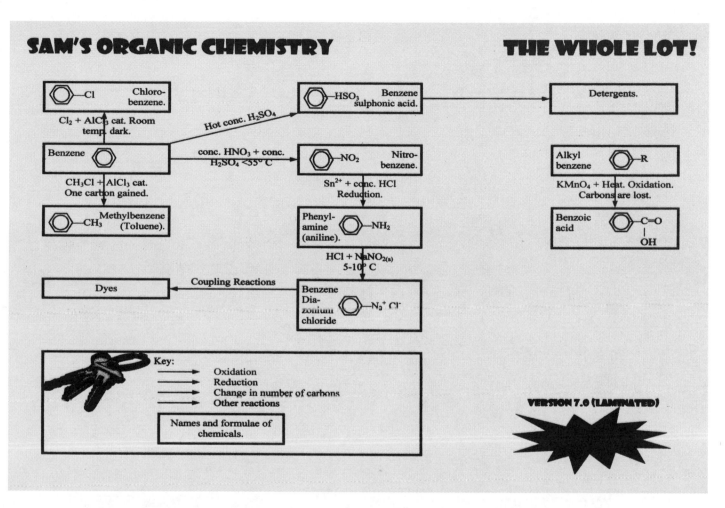

Figure 2.8 (b)

went through the syllabus, ensuring that every point had been covered and correcting errors. The entire CH4 syllabus fitted on two sides of A4.

The map was colour coded: black for reductions, blue for oxidations, green where carbons were lost or gained and so on. Reagents, conditions and types of mechanisms were all written above the arrows. A black and white copy loses some of this clarity but the information is still there.

The map is most useful in a question that goes, 'What steps would you take in converting this acid to this alcohol?' The sequence of reactions needed is often complex and is difficult to work out unless it can somehow be visualised. Imagining each chemical as a place and finding a route from one to the other is far easier and quicker than having to recall lists and tables of reactants and products when several stages are involved.

There were other organic maps. Maybe they were better than mine. However, I never found them as useful, because I fixed the map in my head as I developed it, and looking at someone else's did not help: everything was the other way round and the pathways were not the same, even though the reactions were.

"Is it to revise a whole topic?"
(Information and connections clearly shown on a single page)

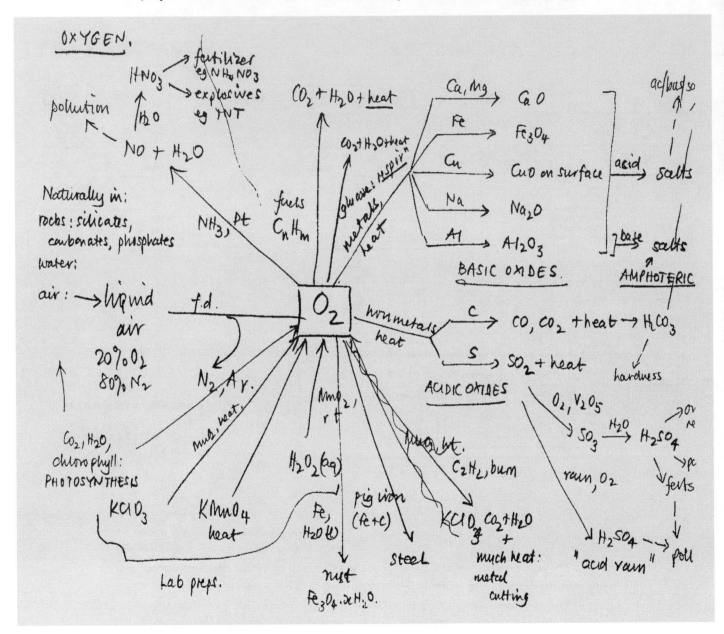

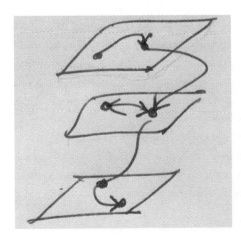

Figure 2.9 (a) The chemistry teacher who drew this map wrote: 'Maps enable relations between different "topics", i.e. put a wholeness into the subject that is absent from linear notes.'

Figure 2.9 (b) They can then be seen three-dimensionally so that links within topics can result in links between them.

"Is it to give an overview of a whole history topic on one sheet?"
(Pictures peg the chronology)

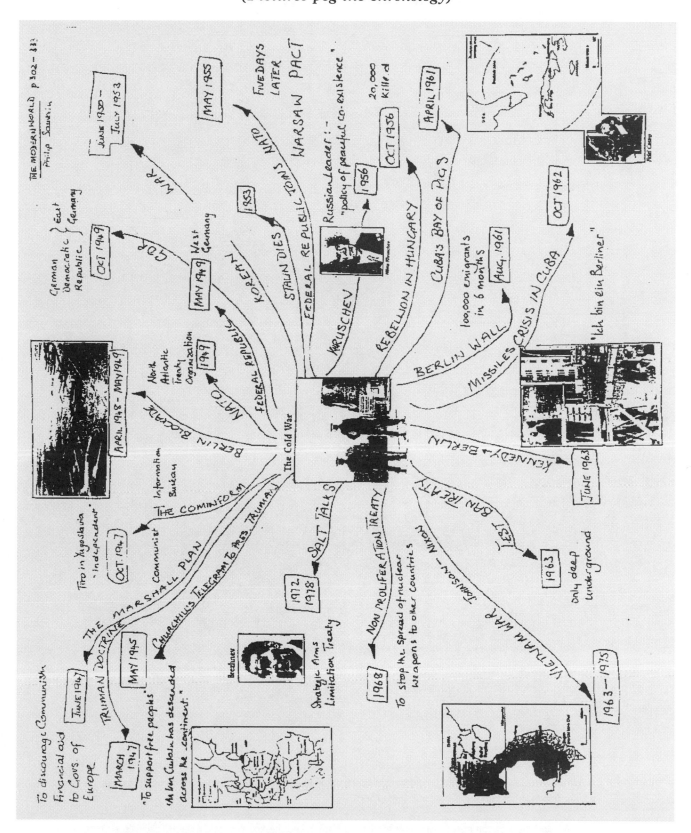

Figure 2.10 Seeing the whole topic on one sheet helps the student to see events in relation to each other. The pictures and symbols photocopied from his textbook provide visual landmarks.

"Is it to provide me with a visual summary of a book or play?"
(Twelve chapters, twelve cards)

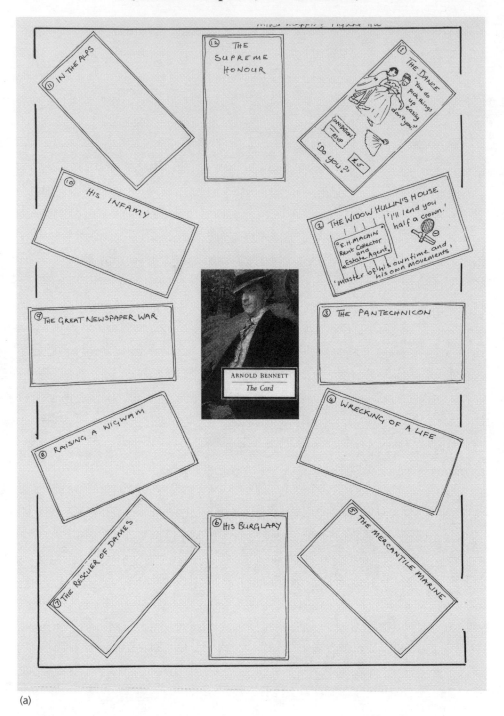

(a)

Figure 2.11 (a) Visualise events and draw images of them on cards, one for each chapter; add short quotations. Sequencing the cards in a circle will give a mental picture of each chapter in relation to the others. Describe what each represents. Be sure to call characters and places by name. Compare 'Knowledge networks' in Chapter 7, page 254.

(b) Using the skeleton map in which his teacher had completed the first two cards, David filled in the rest as he read each chapter. Working at a card in a particular position on the map ensured that, when he had finished, he had a clear memory of where its content came in the story sequence. The cards were useful both as a mind-map and as a pack of 12 to put out in the same circular sequence.

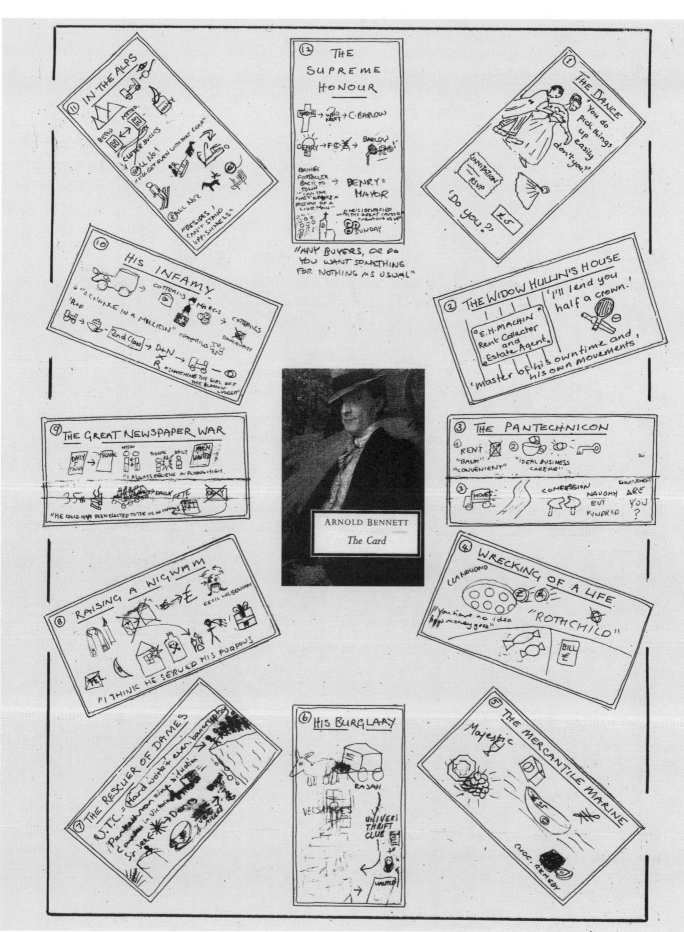

(b)

There follow some examples to show that mind-maps can help with all the core components of academic practice, whether they are receptive, such as listening and noting, revising and summarising – or expressive, such as essay writing or preparing examination answers.

Mind-mapping for making notes from a textbook or a lesson

This is a very good way to start learning to mind-map. Instead of asking a student to 'read the chapter for homework', he could be asked to mind-map it instead (Figure 2.12).

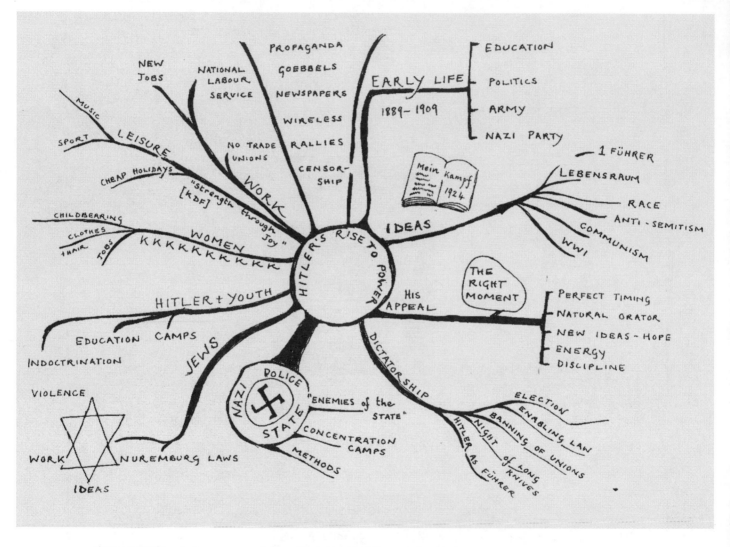

Figure 2.12 This mind-map was made from the summary at the end of a chapter on Hitler's rise to power. Pictures and symbols can be added later to make it easier to commit to memory when the student wants to revise the topic. It will be much easier to re-visualise when it has pictures.

Textbooks are usually neatly divided into chapters, topic headings and subheadings – these can provide the framework for the mind-map, and the student can add the detail with phrases, pictures, symbols, shapes and colours to help commit it to memory (Figure 2.13).

This gives a good focus for reading and, because he is trying to think of appropriate images with which to illustrate his mind-map, the student is encouraged to visualise as he reads. There is no doubt that mind-mapping a chapter involves much more processing of the information than just writing notes or merely reading.

Taking mind-map notes during a lesson is not for beginners. If the student is experienced at mind-mapping and his teacher gives structured lessons, it is an excellent method of recording and organising – topics can be put in order later, new ones inserted, notes added, symbols

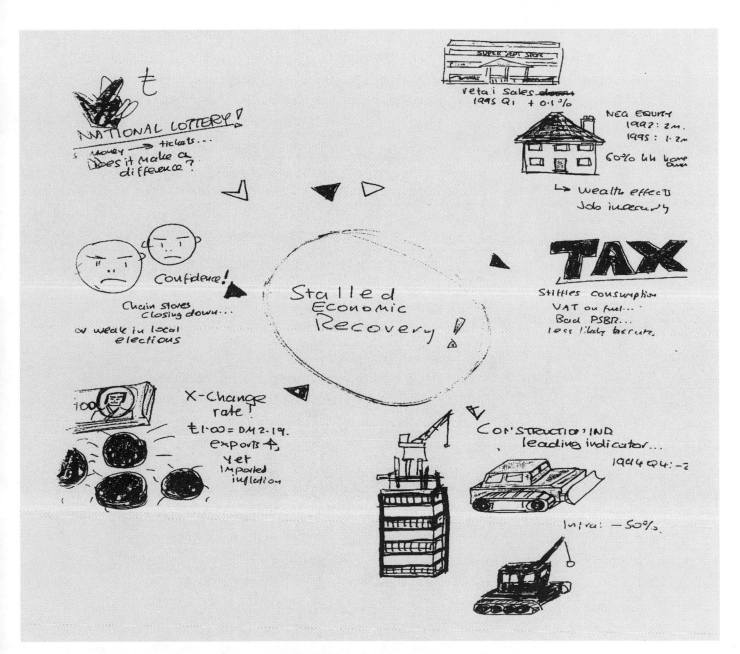

Figure 2.13 A mind-map summary of a chapter on economics. Yoel enjoyed drawing and found that it helped him through a rather boring reading task – and helped him remember what he had read.

incorporated. The nature of the operation encourages the student to summarise, rather than write every word. But this is for experienced mind-mappers. Mind-mapping *from* notes or a book is much more achievable because the time element is removed.

Mind-mapping for summarising

A good exercise both for mind-mapping and for memory is to ask a pupil, or a class, to summarise the lesson or lecture they have just had. This is useful for reinforcing what has just been taught and, if it is a habitual feature of the last five minutes of a lesson, or given as that evening's homework, the fact that the children know that they are going to have to do a mind-map should focus their minds throughout the lesson. Just as important, it also gives excellent practice in mind-mapping (Figure 2.14).

The children could follow this procedure:

- Write the theme of the lesson in the middle of the and draw a circle round it.
- Draw main branches coming from the circle, each with a topic heading printed on it.

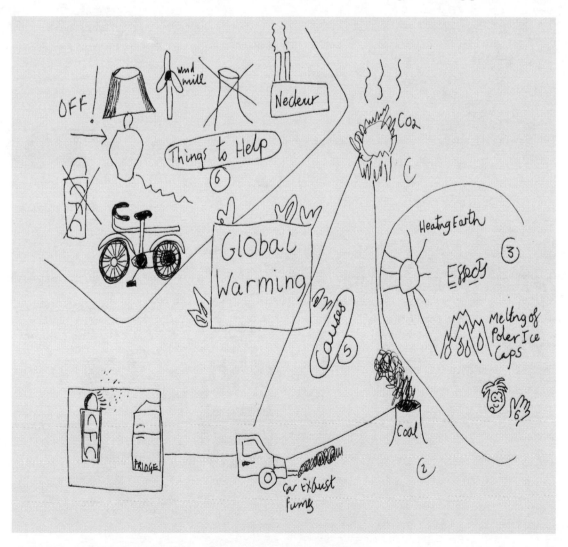

Figure 2.14 A mind-map summary of a revision session on global warming. The processing involved in doing it: the pupil talking to himself: 'What were the main points?', 'How shall I show that?', 'What picture shall I do?', 'Which heading will it come under?' are all valuable for understanding and memory.

- Draw branches for subtopics.
- Draw symbols for main or subtopics.
- Turn the map over and visualise it and be prepared to describe it to the teacher, expanding on the symbols.
- At the beginning of the next lesson, be prepared to describe the mind-mapped lesson in some detail, using the visualised map as a trigger.

This summarising exercise (Figure 2.15) could spark a productive discussion on memory: will the students remember the lesson that they mind-mapped better than other lessons? If so:

- Was this because the end-of-lesson review was good for the memory curve?
- Was it because their creative input into the map helped them to remember it?
- Was it because of the visualising they had to do in order to create symbols and pictures?
- Was it because they knew that they were going to be tested on the lesson and so, during it, were much more focused on how they would represent topics on the map?
- Was it because the material was arranged spatially rather than in a linear format?

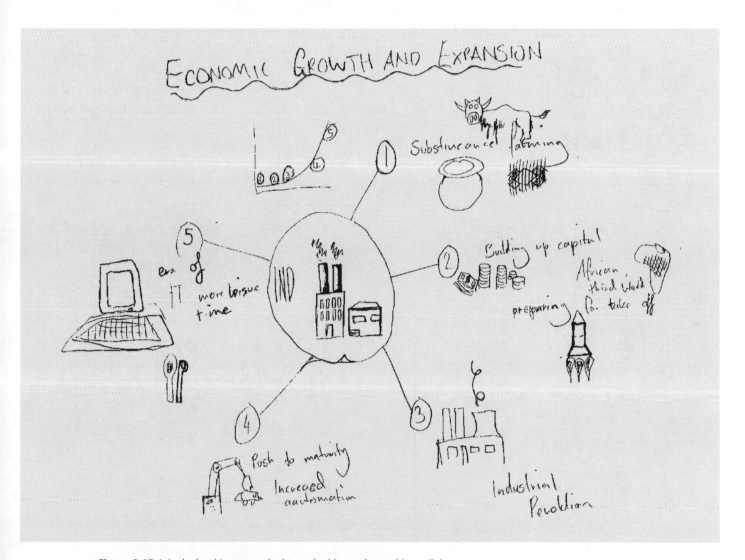

Figure 2.15 Asked what his geography lesson had been about, this pupil drew a mind-map – talking about the lesson while he drew. This made for perfect multisensory activity and memory reinforcement.

Whatever the reason, it is valuable for each child to identify his own most successful memory strategy so that he can use it in the future.

Mind-mapping for summarising a set text

Mind-mapping is a very useful technique for summarising a novel or a play, or indeed any topic where it is helpful to *see* the 'whole picture', whether it is arranged chronologically, thematically or by characters.

It is the making of the map – the selection and rejection, the categorisation, the drawing of symbols, the spacing – that helps memory, as much as the memorable format in which it is done.

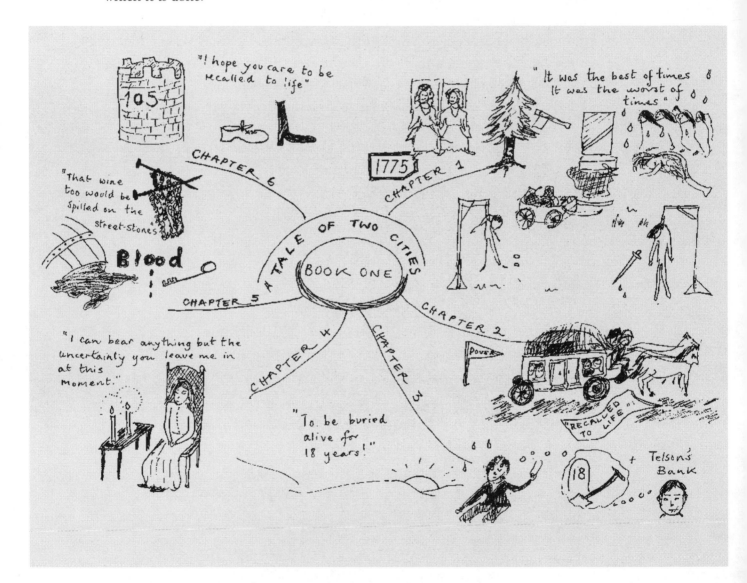

Figure 2.16 Choosing memorable images from each of the opening chapters of *Tale of Two Cities* helps the reader to visualise while he reads and also gives him a chronological record of the novel, laid out in a spatial format, from which he can revise. Pictures can often trigger quotations – just as quotations can spontaneously produce visual images.

Mind-mapping for essay writing

One of the dyslexic's main problems in essay writing is with 'multi-tasking' – doing too many things at once so that the language processing is overloaded. The abilities necessary for writing a good essay can be divided into four groups:

1.   intelligence and creativity
2.   literacy skills
3.   memory skills
4.   organising skills

Each category of skill is important in essay writing. Fortunately, the person who is dyslexic is as likely to possess category 1 abilities as anyone else. It is the lower-level skills in the other three categories that may adversely affect him. They can be dealt with most effectively by a combination of mind-mapping and word processing.

The dyslexic student may well be as creative and intelligent as anyone else in his class, but he is handicapped by his non-automatic literacy, organisation and memory skills. Other

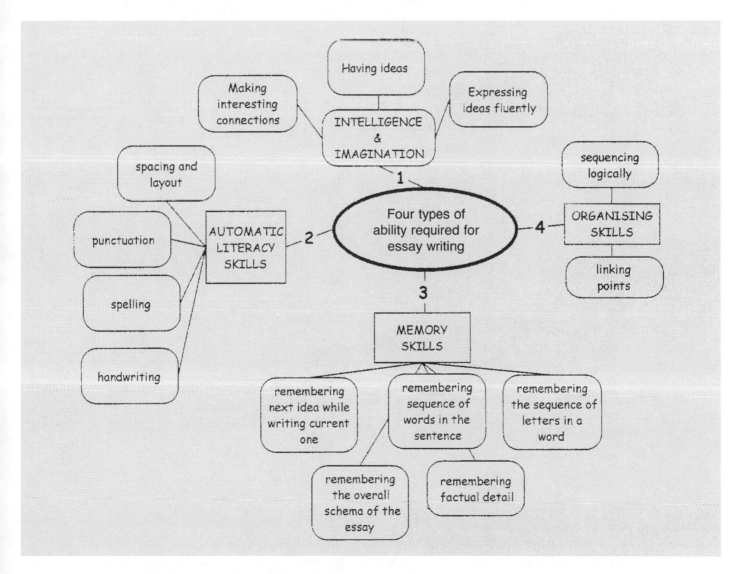

Figure 2.17 Four types of ability required for essay writing.

students can multi-task – think, remember and write at the same time – while he needs to break the operation into smaller steps so that the most important part of the essay writing, the ideas and their expression, does not suffer.

Mind-mapping offers an ideal method of separating activities so that each one can be given its full weight. Ideally, the dyslexic student would follow the procedures described on pages 160–163, planning his essay with mind-maps so that when he comes actually to writing it he can give all his attention to the expression of his ideas. The dyslexic student who is using a word processor will have the best chance of writing fluently – having no immediate worries about handwriting, presentation and spelling to interfere with his fluency.

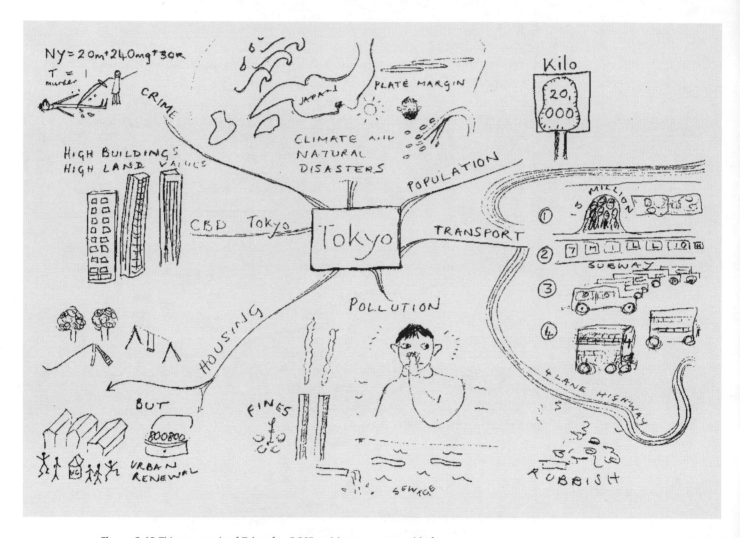

Figure 2.18 This case study of Tokyo for GCSE revision was memorable for the person who did it. He could close his eyes, re-visualise it and talk in some detail about each topic.

Mind-maps for revision

The student's main aim in revising should be to make sure that he understands a topic thoroughly and remembers it well enough to be able to write about it later and in detail. Mind-mapping works for revision because it is an active, multisensory way of revising:

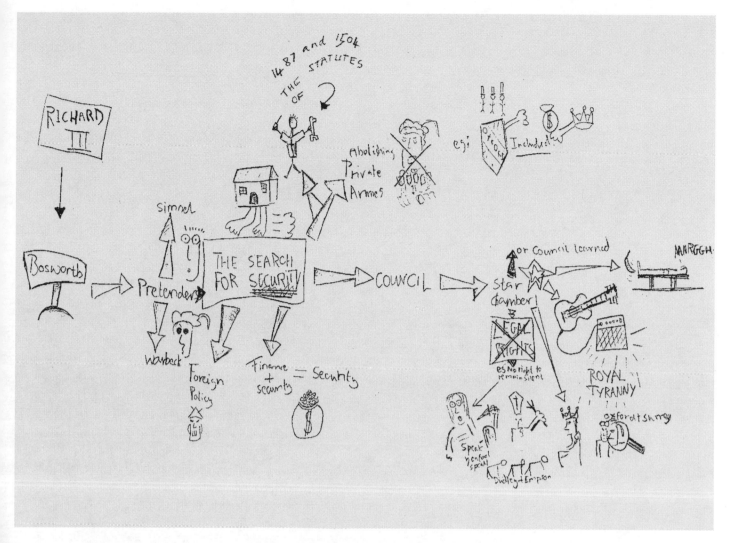

Figure 2.19 The humour and drama in this history revision mind-map made the events much more memorable and the revision session more fun.

- Words and ideas have to be processed and understood to turn them into relevant pictures and symbols.
- Logical categorisation is integral to making the map.
- Categorisation can be done by shape, colour and position.
- A linear sequence is turned into a spatial sequence – which may be much more memorable for the person with dyslexia.
- The input is personal and creative – the student is making the material his own in some way.
- Making the mind-map involves the motor memory – he will remember where he wrote the heading or drew the symbol, and which ideas he linked.
- If more detail is required, there can be a mind-map showing main topics with each subtopic having its own map.

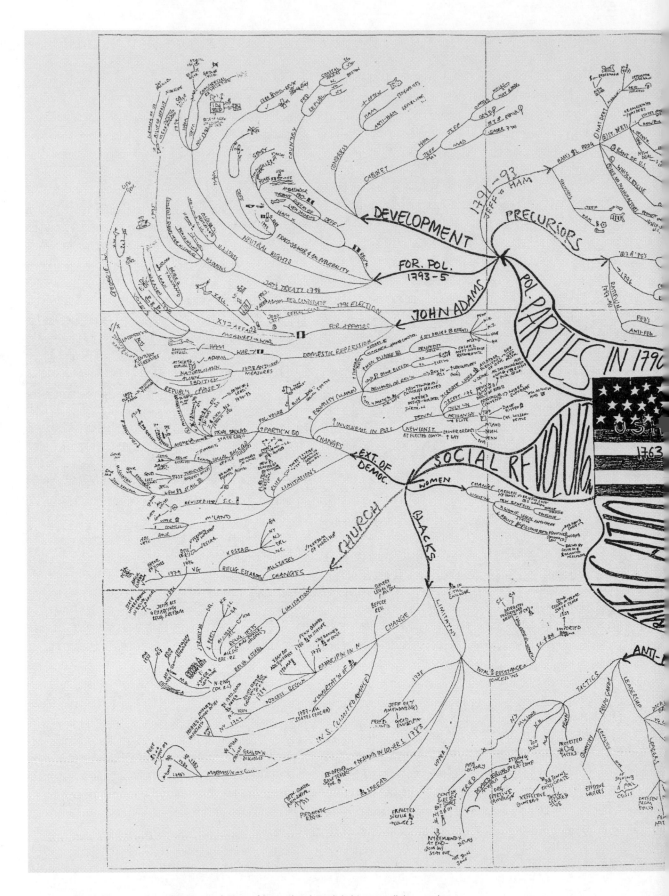

Figure 2.20 Eleanor put this revision mind-map of her A-level English history syllabus on her bedroom wall. It was made up of separate A4 mind-maps drawn either in lessons or as part of her revision programme. Over several weeks, she was able to keep refreshing her memory of individual topics as well as absorbing the overall picture of her period – very good for the 'forgetting curve' aspect of revision.

When he has completed his mind-map, the student should:

- Talk it through, putting pictures back into words, expressing the ideas behind the summaries and the symbols. This is a crucial stage for multisensory integration.
- Put his map away and visualise it, seeing it in his mind's eye.
- Describe what he sees.
- Re-visualise the map once or twice later, at intervals, always talking it through (thus using his own words to describe it), so that he has memorised it well and will be able to call it up again on his 'mental clipboard' in his test or exam.

Skeleton mind-maps

Prepared by a teacher, these can be useful for revision, note-taking and used while students are watching a school video. The main headings ensure that the pupil keeps on track and focuses on the important topics – but there is also room for individual input.

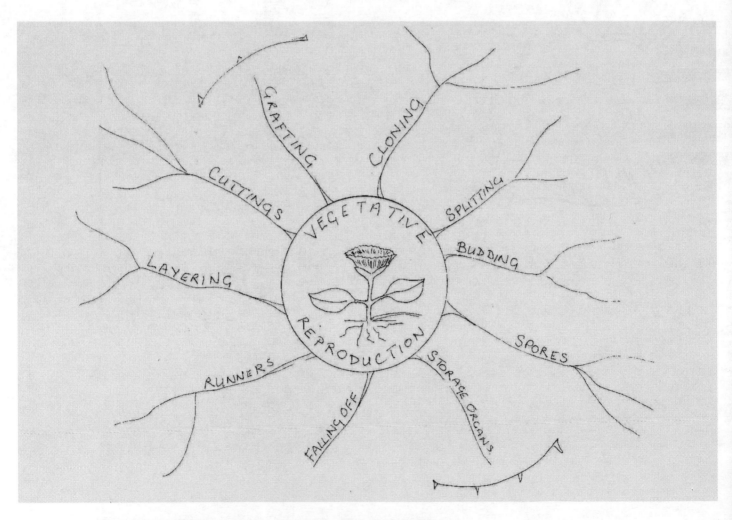

Figure 2.21 This skeleton mind-map was given to a class watching a biology video on vegetative reproduction. Talking through it beforehand focused the class on what to look out for and encouraged them to write single words and phrases rather than try to write copious notes (possibly in the dark!).

Using a computer for mind-mapping

There are many students who, because of their dyslexic or dyspraxic difficulties, find mind-mapping by hand unappealing – being able to produce a well-ordered map with clear handwriting and recognisable symbols may be beyond them. Yet they could be the very people who, because of planning, categorising and short-term memory weaknesses, would benefit most from the technique.

Mind-mapping software is available. 'Inspiration', for example, is very user-friendly. One of the most important features is that the bubbles can be dragged around the screen,

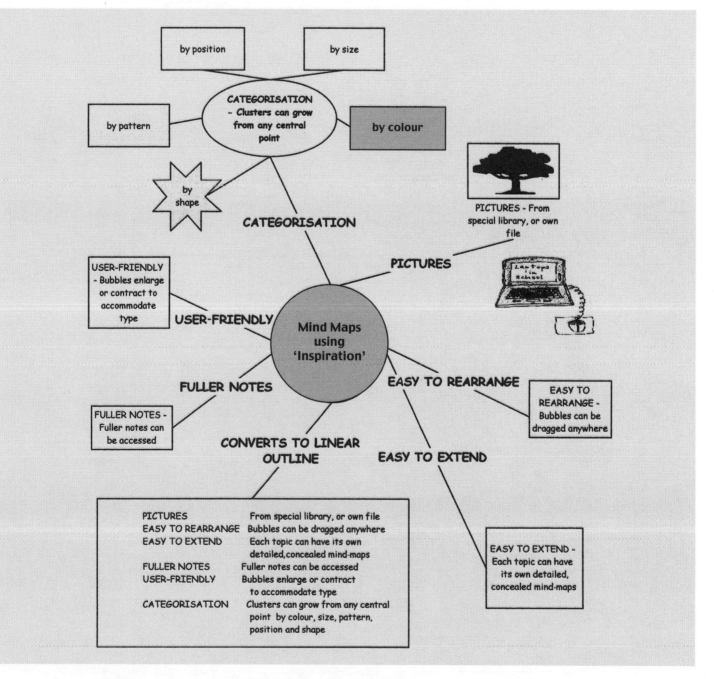

Figure 2.22 Organisation of the mind-map can be converted by the click of the mouse from a spatial one to a linear one, and vice versa. The box at the bottom shows the linear summary of the whole map.

and the shapes and colours, helpful for categorisation, can be changed as the brainstorm is converted into a more organised structure (Figure 2.22).

Some pupils might prefer to reverse the process by collecting the information in outline form – perhaps taking notes from a book – and then converting it into a mind-map where the addition of space, colour, shape and pictures could make it easier to remember and therefore useful for revision.

Chapter 3
Computers

This chapter assumes a best-case scenario where teachers are alert and sympathetic to problems, where schools, parents or local authorities are able to provide computers, and children are motivated enough to learn to touch-type and use computers for most of their work. A great deal of effort or money or both is required to achieve this ideal situation. The fact that it is unachievable for some at the moment seems no reason to stop pushing forward to see what can be achieved now and in the future.

The computer offers all sorts of help for people with dyslexia. For them it is not merely a sophisticated first-aid box – it is also an Aladdin's lamp for those whose talents have been stifled by frustrations with pen and paper. It is the single most important help one can give to a dyslexic secondary school pupil – provided he is taught how to use it and is supported in school. A word processor looks after the lower-level writing skills that are automatic in the non-dyslexic student: fast, legible handwriting and spelling.

NAME   Daniel   SUBJECT   English

```
    The true quality of his work has been difficult to
gauge because of the inhibitions imposed on him by
his handicap. In reading aloud, discussion and con-
versation, his delivery is strong and clear and his
views are perceptive and maturely expressed. On paper,
in writing, the converse is the case: his handwriting
is virtually illegible, errors in spelling and punct-
uation proliferate, vocabulary is kept simple, and
sentence structure too, and the piece is relatively
short. Technology is needed, to help him do himself
justice.
```

Figure 3.1 Where the discrepancy between a pupil's performance in class and his performance on paper is obvious, a sympathetic teacher will recommend word processing.

It enables a student who is dyslexic to express his ideas at last – and yet dyslexic students who use a word processor in secondary school as their main writing tool are the exception rather than the rule.

Sadly, it is true that only a small percentage of children can own a laptop, but why, given that many homes do have desktop computers, are only a small proportion used for word processing and schoolwork? Certainly it costs money and needs parental back-up to get children to stick at formal touch-typing courses or use computer typing programs consistently enough to achieve a typing speed that would induce them to do their schoolwork on a word processor. 'It takes too long!' is the usual complaint from those who have not learnt to touch-type. But there are other reasons.

Word processing for schoolwork

There remain pockets of hostility among teachers and parents to dyslexic pupils using a word processor for schoowork and in the classroom. It stems from a variety of misconceptions, which can be divided into three categories:

1. untrue or irrelevant assumptions
2. queries with some justification
3. practical objections

1. Untrue or irrelevant assumptions

'It is not going to help him to solve his handwriting difficulties.'

Alex (Figure 3.2) will, of course, be allowed to use his computer in exams if he applies for the concession – the teacher is wrong about that.

The misconception that illegible handwriting is usually the result of slack teaching or laziness on the part of the pupil betrays a lack of understanding. Some pupils have genuine hand–eye or language-processing co-ordination difficulties (Figure 3.3).

'He can write perfectly well when he wants to.'

If a pupil produces good writing one day and bad the next, this is an understandable response. But there is a great difference between the writing a dyslexic student can achieve when he is not having to think and remember at the same time and his writing when he is having to hurry to keep up with his thinking.

'He will never learn to spell if he relies on the spell-check all the time.'

The more a student uses a word processor, the better his spelling gets. The printed word helps him to become familiar with how words should look; he can easily read his work back to check it; the spell-check can point out most of his errors as he writes – when he is actively involved in the learning process. He is more likely to take note of the correct spelling at the moment when he is actually wondering about how to spell the word, not a week later when he gets his work back with red lines through it.

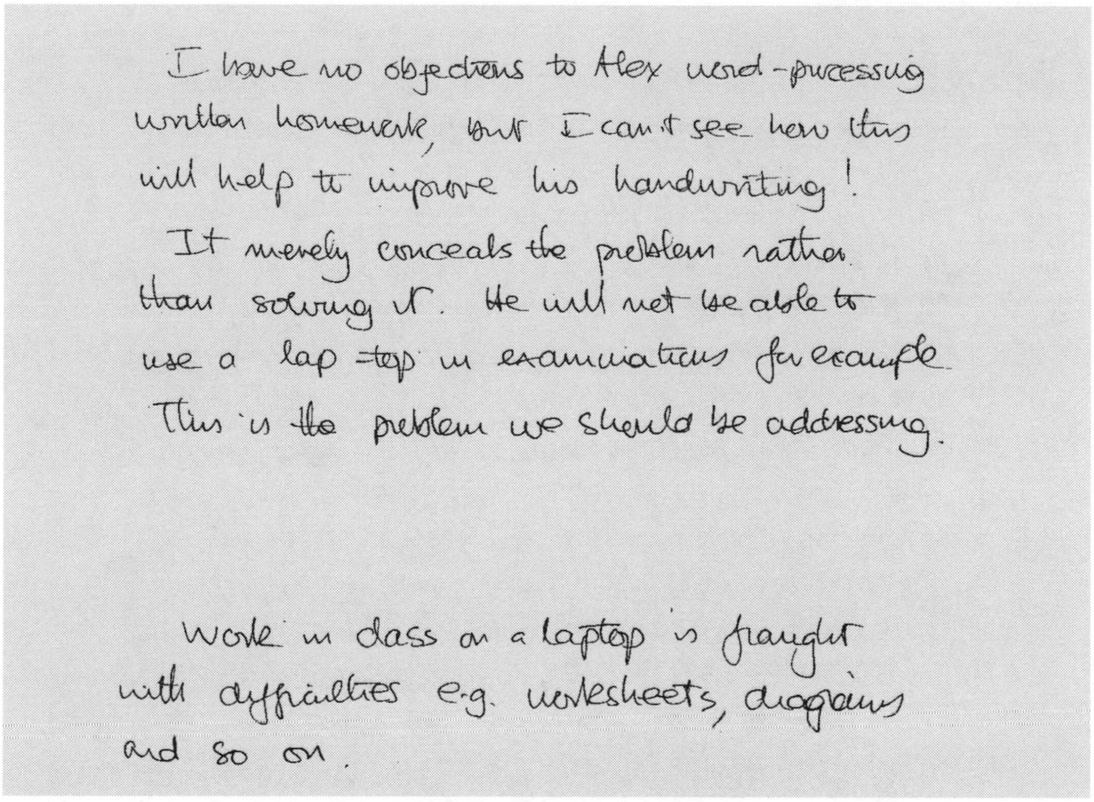

> I have no objections to Alex word-processing written homework, but I can't see how this will help to improve his handwriting! It merely conceals the problem rather than solving it. He will not be able to use a lap-top in examinations for example. This is the problem we should be addressing.
>
> Work in class on a laptop is fraught with difficulties e.g. worksheets, diagrams and so on.

Figure 3.2 A request to allow a dyslexic pupil to do his homework on a word processor met with no objections – but no understanding or approval either. Alex would benefit from more support and encouragement.

'It will give him an unfair advantage.'

If legibility and neatness are what is being tested, then, yes, it certainly will give him an unfair advantage. If the teacher is interested in helping someone with a learning disadvantage to achieve clarity of thought, fluency and the expression of his knowledge, then being able to word-process his work should enable him to compete on level terms.

'He won't be allowed to use a computer in exams.'

Exam boards will 'make every attempt to respond positively to requests for candidates to use computers', subject to certain principles and procedures. Boards want to have evidence from an educational psychologist or suitably qualified teacher that students need to use a word processor for reasons of fluency, speed or legibility, that they usually use a computer for their schoolwork and that they have had practice in using one for internal exams and tests.

In the future pupils may have no option but to use a computer for their exams. In May 2001, the Council for the Curriculum Examinations and Assessment and the examination board Edexcel ran a pilot project to develop electronic GCSE and A-level exams in Northern Ireland to test the practicalities of 'paperless' exams. There are many issues to address: availability of technology in schools, differences in pupils' keyboard skills and

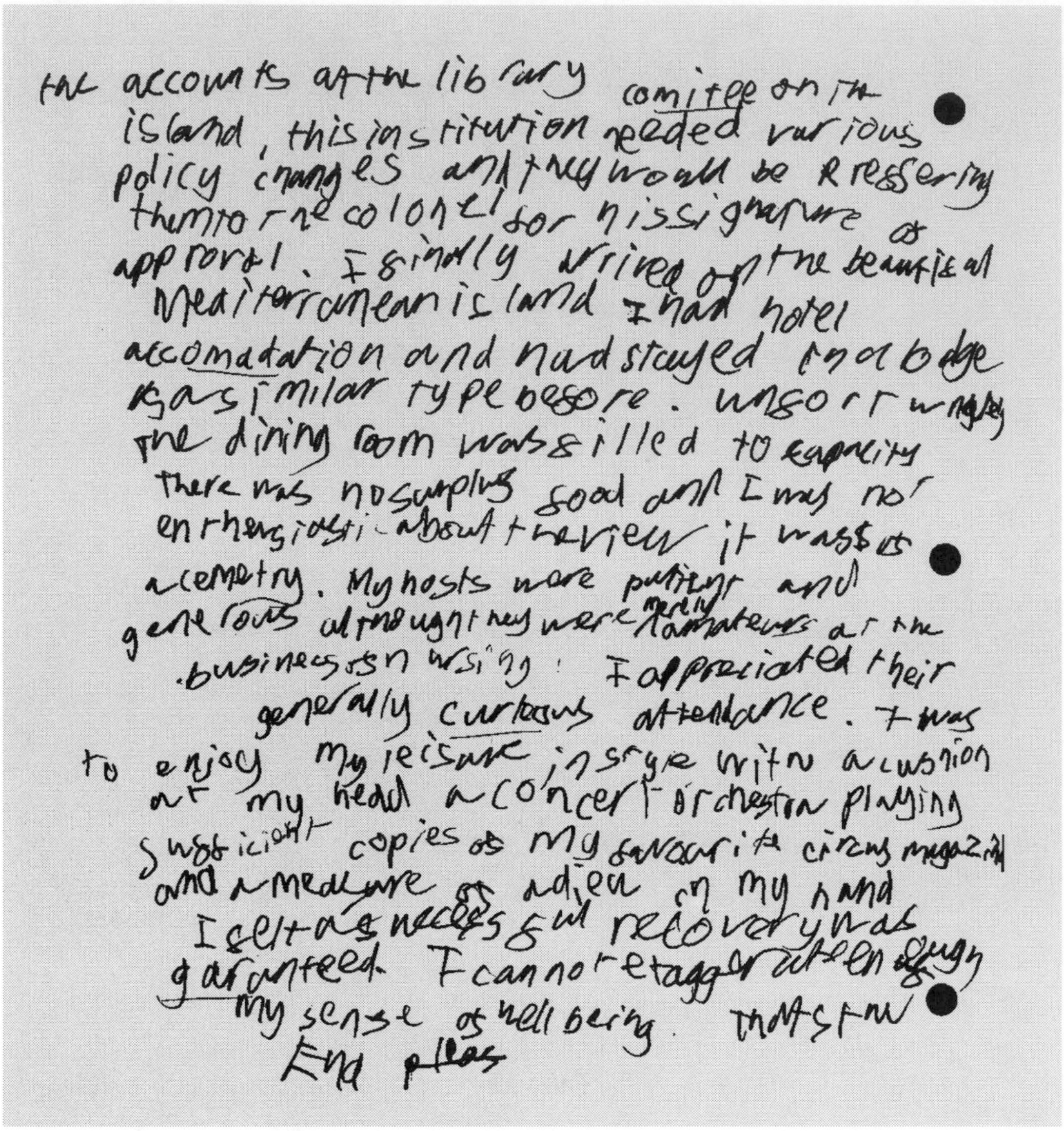

Figure 3.3 This 14-year-old dyspraxic schoolboy is trying to do his best
writing and spelling as he takes down a dictation. You can see his
difficulty with keeping up to the margin and anticipating how much space
he will have at the end of the line.

how to reproduce maths and science symbols that are not on standard computer keyboards.

If this is where the future lies, it is good news for people with dyslexia – provided they have keyboard and computer skills.

'He won't be able to keep up.'

If he learns to touch-type, he will be able to write at anything up to 60 words per minute, which is faster than normal handwriting. A dyslexic GCSE candidate is labouring under a huge disadvantage if he cannot write faster than 12–15 words per minute.

2. Queries with some justification

'His writing style has deteriorated since he started to type.'

This can happen initially. It takes some practice to synchronise thinking and typing successfully. For the dyslexic person who has previously been hampered by handwriting or spelling or memory problems, the floodgates are likely to open and unplanned and un-thought-through work pours out (Figure 3.4).

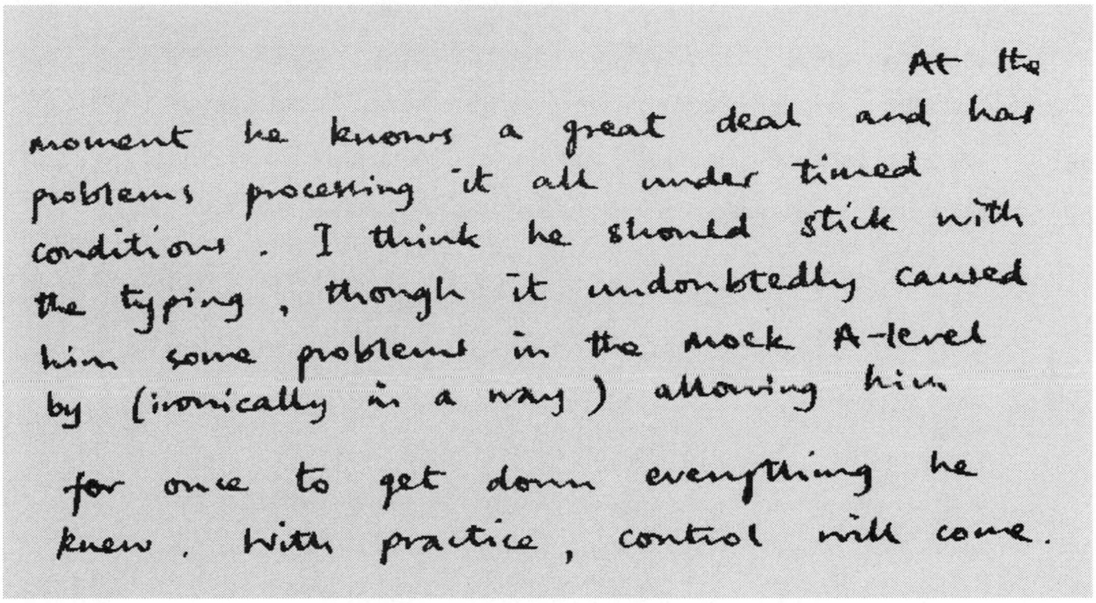

> At the moment he knows a great deal and has problems processing it all under timed conditions. I think he should stick with the typing, though it undoubtedly caused him some problems in the mock A-level by (ironically in a way) allowing him for once to get down everything he knew. With practice, control will come.

Figure 3.4 When first using a computer, there is a temptation, because you know you can move text around, to cut out the planning stage. Jonathan needs to do his thinking and planning before he starts writing down 'all he knows'.

The pupil needs to be trained to plan his work thoroughly before he begins to write and to check it afterwards (Figure 3.5).

'He won't want to draw attention to his dyslexia.'

This is where his teachers' support and encouragement can make all the difference. Given the option of typing or not typing, initially the dyslexic pupil will opt for *not* typing – offering all sorts of excuses. It actually helps for the teacher to insist on typed work (if the pupil has the skills and the equipment) and give praise and continued encouragement for his willingness to co-operate.

'He won't be able to print out his classwork in school.'

A teacher may need to help the dyslexic pupil to set up his laptop to recognise the school printer, or give him the opportunity to print from a disk – without making him feel that he is being a nuisance (see page 89–92).

taxpayer. Also all these immigrants. They can't even speak the language but of course England have to put them up. Why can't India and Africa take them back? And here is a real big nuisance. Why the hell was slavery abolished? Now this blacks things have as much rights as even I do. Now for gods sake, man these things are savages. We should be able to whip them in to line and they should do what they are told. If this carries on much longer we might end up with some black prime Minster. If that happens I personally would start a civil war. A black prime Minster, I know it sounds ridiculous, but it could happen. And another thing, why do women get a vote? A woman's place is in the kitchen not in matters their feeble mind can not handle. I think this is why my wife went off with my butler. If that would have happened 20 years ago she would have been beaten and for a good reason too. Honesty, soon we might have a woman prime Minster. She would probably give the country to Saddam. And who stopped this hitting children in school? Children need disapen and if it takes a bit to do it, then do it. I was hit when I was a child and look how I turned out. Well I am dreadfully sorry but I have to go.

15/20 Quite amusing, but spoiled, as usual, by your total failure to edit your work properly. It is no good merely presenting the homework without adequate punctuation, capital letters in the right places and a general awareness that the whole thing makes sense. I draw an obvious line here. between your dyslexia and your outright sloppiness You are not ignora of commas, full stops, and appropriate capit

Figure 3.5 Asked to write a piece reflecting the views of a racist, this pupil thoroughly enjoyed himself, but failed to edit his work.

'It will distract other pupils.'

During the first lesson a laptop is being used, it may well distract other pupils – but they soon get used to it.

'He won't be able to do diagrams.'

This is a problem area, but there are some solutions:

- Pupils can achieve a high standard through practice and through using software appropriately. If a pupil doesn't attempt any diagrams, he will not get any better at them – a child in the class who has difficulty with drawing will be most helped by a teacher who looks at the problems with him and helps him to solve them.
- Others keep a pad of plain paper in their computer case and use that when the need arises.
- With some computers it is possible to draw on the screen. (See Tablet PCs, page 87)
- Some people find it is easier to draw with a mouse rather than a keypad or button. A mouse can be attached to a laptop.

'He needs to practise drawing by hand because he'll need to do it in the exam.'

True. But the poor copier with hand–eye co-ordination problems may not have time, when taking notes in the class, to do it by hand. In the exams he will need extra time, however he is producing drawings.

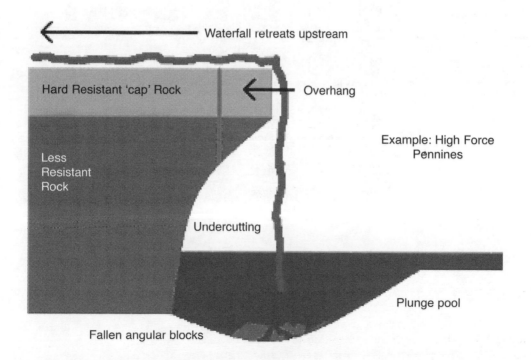

Figure 3.6 Some children enjoy the challenge of doing diagrams on the computer – because of the problem-solving involved, they find they remember the diagram better. This diagram was done with the program 'Paint'.

'If he has a laptop, he may lose it, damage it or have it stolen.

Yes, he may. And that is an alarming possibility – but not sufficient reason for depriving him of what may be his academic lifeline. He needs insurance.

'He spends too much time fiddling with layout.'

Yes, he may at first. It is such a thrill to be able to make work look good at last.

'He will lose his work.'

If he is disorganised, he probably loses his work anyway, even if it is done by hand. But it is true that he may well make errors that result in his losing his work on a computer. He needs to be trained in good habits – always naming his document (*File → Save as → File name*) and then selecting which file he wants to store it in *before* he starts work on it (Figure 3.7).

He should have a routine for backing up work immediately – copying on to disk or another computer, or, if the school has a network, synchronising his work to the school network at the end of each work session.

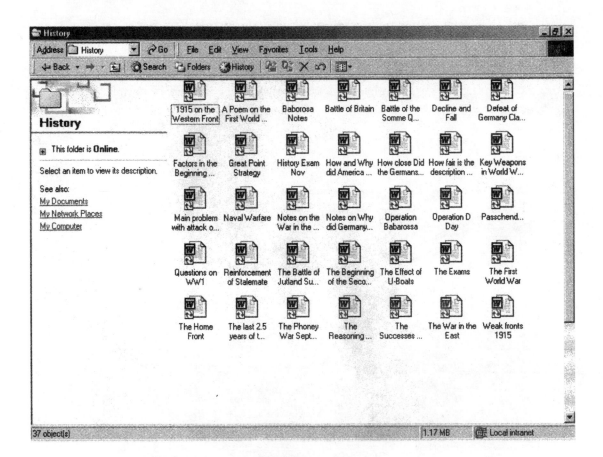

Figure 3.7 Anton has a good routine for keeping his files safe – but careful naming would make this alphabetical list of files easier to use. 'The' is never a good first word!

'He will become dependent on his computer and won't be able to handwrite.'

This is better than being dependent on handwriting that is illegible, too slow and stops him from writing fluently.

3. Practical objections

With a little patience and commitment, these can easily be solved. But somebody with clout needs to be rooting for the person with dyslexia. It is not fair that he should lose his best chance because no one is willing to make a little extra effort to solve his problems (Figure 3.8).

'We haven't enough plugs in the classrooms.'

If his battery is flat, help the child with a computer to secure a seat near to any plug that there is in your classroom. Perhaps more could be organised.

'He'll sometimes need extra technical help with his laptop.'

The school technician is there to help children and teachers to use computers.

'We'll need an extra invigilator if he does his exams in a separate room.'

Yes, you will.

'There are no suitable tables in some of his classrooms.'

Could some be organised?

'He gives classwork in late because he has to print it out.'

But it will probably be much better than if it was handwritten.

'I haven't time to deal with any extra problems. I have 30 other children in the class to think of.'

The special educational needs co-ordinator and school technician could help you to sort out the problems.

'He shouldn't be in a mainstream school if he can't manage without a computer.'

It is all of *us*, in mainstream schools, who must come to terms with computers in the twenty-first century!

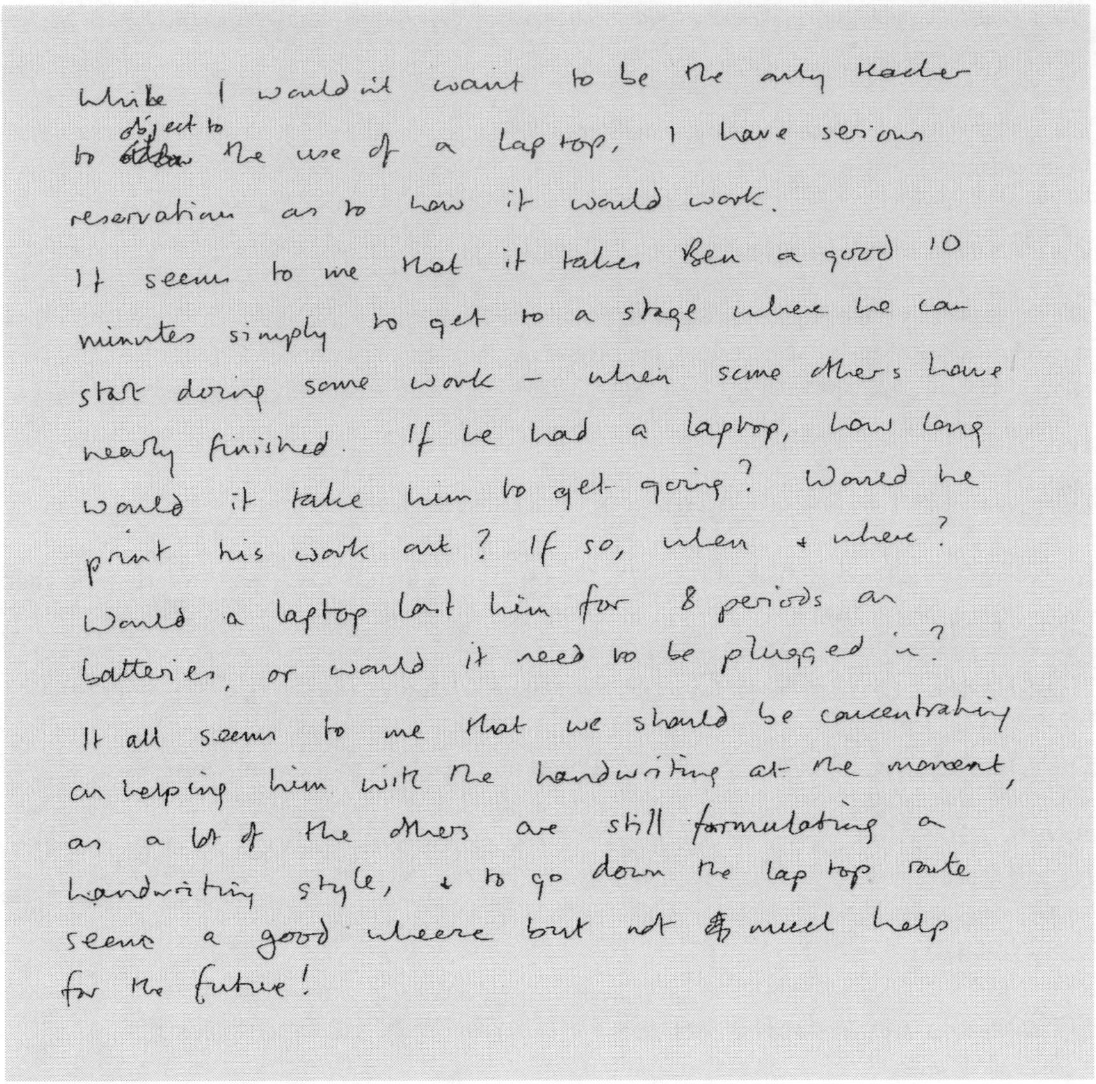

While I wouldn't want to be the only teacher to object to the use of a laptop, I have serious reservation as to how it would work.

It seems to me that it takes Ben a good 10 minutes simply to get to a stage where he can start doing some work – when some others have nearly finished. If he had a laptop, how long would it take him to get going? Would he print his work out? If so, when & where? Would a laptop last him for 8 periods on batteries, or would it need to be plugged in?

It all seems to me that we should be concentrating on helping him with the handwriting at the moment, as a lot of the others are still formulating a handwriting style, & to go down the laptop route seems a good where but not of much help for the future!

Figure 3.8 For the boy in question, these obstacles are minor compared with his own difficulties with handwriting. But they do need to be solved. With good computer skills, he will be better equipped for the world of work than with his inadequate handwriting.

The Code of Practice

The emphasis in the Special Educational Needs Code of Practice is very much in favour of helping the child with special educational needs to cope within mainstream schools. The provision of a computer and training could make all the difference to the child with difficulties.

Extract from the Code of Practice

V1.3 Fundamental Principles
- a child with special educational needs should have their needs met
- the special educational needs of children will normally be met in mainstream schools or settings

- the views of the child should be sought and taken into account
- parents have a vital role to play in supporting their child's education
- children with special educational needs should be offered full access to a broad, balanced and relevant education, including the Foundation Stage Curriculum and the National Curriculum

V1.4 Critical Success Factors

- the culture, practice, management and deployment of resources in school or setting should be designed to ensure all children's needs are met.

Using a computer in school

A 13-year-old boy's list of the ways in which his laptop helps him:

- I found it hard to write in class and so it is nice to have enough time to think about what you are writing and ask the teachers questions.
- It is automatically neater and tidier which means you do not have to rewrite your homework before you hand it in. Also it means that the teachers get a good impression of the work even before they start reading it.
- It is good that you can go back and change things whereas if you had been writing you would have had to rewrite it. This is even more of a chore if you are a slow writer.
- If you are disorganised, it is a help to have all your notes in the same place.
- Certain things are easier on a computer, especially tables and graphs. The table can be used in every subject as you can use it for anything, whereas the graph is more useful for the sciences and geography.

Because as many as 10% of any class of children may have some sort of learning difficulty, it is well worth considering whether any of them might be helped by using a word processor.

This solution becomes less revolutionary with every year that passes; we are only asking students with dyslexia to work in a way that they, and everyone else, will have to work in later.

Touch-typing

It is vital that teachers or parents insist that a dyslexic child learns to touch-type before he starts using a word processor as his writing tool. Otherwise he is exchanging one non-automatic skill – handwriting – for another. However fast he may be able to type with two fingers, so long as he has to look down at the keyboard, part of his mind is involved in searching for the right key. This is bound to interfere with automatic spelling, fluency, remembering what he was going to write next, and certainly with any copying he has to do. The efficient touch-typist doesn't have to think about his writing at all; his fingers become an extension of his mind and he can write as automatically as any non-dyslexic handwrites. He has an added advantage over the handwriter in that he can also keep his eyes on the board, book or teacher if he wants to copy or have eye contact during the lesson.

To convince a reluctant pupil that touch-typing is a more automatic skill than two-finger typing, ask a helpful guinea pig who touch-types to copy something while they touch-type, and chat to them while they do it. They will be able to carry on a reasonable conversation. Next, ask the person who needs convincing, to copy something while he types looking at the keyboard (or handwrites) – and see if he can chat as easily. This simple experiment should convince him that typing-and-looking is not an automatic skill.

Some schools are now offering touch-typing courses as part of the curriculum – every dyslexic pupil should sign on whether he feels like doing it or not! Local courses are usually available within easy reach: children can attend during the school holidays. A good two-week course, comprising a couple of hours' typing each day, would give the student a very good start, particularly if he put in a little practice each evening, and followed it up with consistent use straight afterwards (always resisting the temptation to look down at the keys!). It would be some of the best money and time a parent could invest for a dyslexic child.

Computerised typing courses

There is a great variety of software available, much of it very useful, especially for topping up skills acquired on a course. The danger of just using software unsupervised is that the user can fall into bad habits – poor posture, using the wrong fingers, not bothering to learn numbers, punctuation or accents and not keeping to a strict enough routine to maximise his learning potential.

A possible compromise between the full-blown course and the software option might be an introductory short course to establish good habits, followed by a daily session with the software. However, a highly motivated child, who takes all the advice offered on the program, practises regularly and never looks down, can learn to touch-type from software or from a book.

Assessing which children should be using computers in school

By the time dyslexic children reach secondary school, their handwriting skills are pretty well formed and therefore hard to change. Some handwriting is presentable, some isn't – but in assessing who would benefit from using a computer as their main writing tool there are other considerations.

Writing speed

According to most educational psychologists, a child whose handwriting speed is about 14 words per minute is writing at the minimum speed practicable for coping with GCSEs; around 24 words a minute is reckoned to be the lowest speed for A levels.

Assessing writing speed

The regulations and guidance relating to candidates with special requirements of the *Joint Council for General Qualifications* ask 'Is the candidate's spelling accuracy and/or handwriting so poor as to impair the ability of the examiner to read the candidate's script?' and 'Does the candidate express himself in written form more slowly than is usual for his age, and is there a significant discrepancy between his ability to express himself orally and in writing?'

Testing handwriting speed by asking the pupil to copy or to write simple sentences over and over again may indicate his manual dexterity, but it doesn't take into account one of the main weaknesses of someone with dyslexia: speed of language processing when he is handwriting.

To make a fair assessment for exam purposes, we need to know how fast a pupil can write over a period of time when he is thinking, forming complex sentences and maintaining legibility.

Informally, but just as importantly, there is a need for subject teachers of a pupil with dyslexia to assess whether the pupil is able to write quickly enough for those tasks that he is required to do during his normal school day. Can he get his notes down – either from the board or from dictation? Can he finish classroom work as quickly as his peers? Does he finish his exams? Does his writing hold up when he is working under pressure? If the answer to these questions is 'No', there is a strong case for the pupil learning to type and to use a laptop if his teachers require note-taking or copying – otherwise he is operating at a disadvantage.

Motivation, success, clear notes and self-esteem improve with proficiency.

Assessing fluency

The dyslexic pupil's subject teachers are in a good position to judge whether there is a marked discrepancy between his talking and writing fluency. 'Good in class, poor on paper'

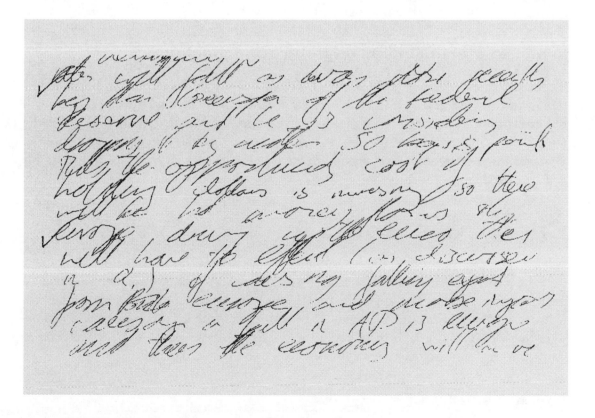

Figure 3.9 James knew all the answers in his economics exam, but teachers despaired of his writing legibly enough for the examiners. If he wrote more slowly, he lost his train of thought.

is the revealing comment that we look out for. This discrepancy usually indicates that his handwriting is not an automatic skill and that he would benefit from word processing.

Assessing pupils' classroom comprehension while note-taking

Some people with dyslexia simply cannot take in meaning or remember what they have written when they are note-taking by hand. This may depend partly on the speed of the teacher's delivery and partly on the pupil's ability to keep up – but, either way, it does handicap the pupil. He needs to have the automaticity provided by efficient word processing that other children can achieve with handwriting.

This comprehension and memory problem may not be detected by the teacher: the handwritten notebooks of a pupil who is dyslexic may look neat and detailed, but they may be masking the most serious of all his difficulties. When the pupil has clearly concentrated throughout the lesson, but has understood or remembered very little, any teacher, and the child himself, could be forgiven for thinking that he is not very motivated or not very bright. His case is worth investigating.

Assessing legibility

The time to assess handwriting legibility is when the pupil has to write and think against the clock. Copying or writing easy material slowly will not give a true impression of the difficulties that dyslexic pupils meet in real-life classrooms or exam situations.

If handwriting is legible but so hard to decipher that the reader has to reread the sentence in order to understand the sense, the flow of the argument or the inference, word processing should be considered (see Figures 3.9 and 3.10).

When to start using a computer for schoolwork?

Ideally, dyslexic children would learn to touch-type before they develop bad typing and posture habits; the earlier they learn, the less resistance they will offer and the quicker they will become fast and accurate typists. Once they have learnt, they should reinforce their skills by using them straight away for schoolwork. Using the laptop all day and every day before the touch-typing is really secure will encourage the typist to go back to typing-and-looking if it is still faster than his touch-typing.

Choosing a laptop for school use

Advice from the members of the school IT department would be most useful. They know how the school works and what the facilities for security and printing are, and they will be much more able and willing to provide back-up for a machine that they know and have recommended than for an unfamiliar one. They will recommend an operating system or software that is compatible with the school system. They will also insist on the installation of up-to-date anti-virus software because viruses can cause serious data loss.

Not too large, not too heavy

A child has to be able to fit the laptop (with padding) into his school bag, along with his books, files and pencil case. Machines with an external disk drive are usually smaller and

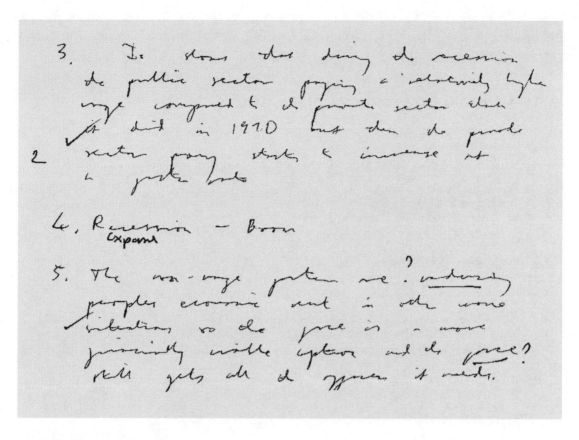

Figure 3.10 Teachers and examiners become exasperated when they have to read and reread examination answers

lighter, and therefore more suitable, providing the child has direct access to a school printer and will not need to use a floppy disk during the school day.

Not only will a child be unwilling to carry a bulky machine that needs its own computer case, but if it is at all obtrusive it could be a security risk as the child travels to and from school.

Reliability

Do some research on this. Computer magazines often review the comparative merits of laptops. Try to make sure that there is back-up support from the supplier and that, in the event of problems, repairs will be local and speedy.

Reasonable battery life

The longer the battery life of the laptop, the more user-friendly it will be. Plugs are not always conveniently placed in classrooms, and carrying power cables and plugs adds to the weight of the school bag.

Insurance

Look into this before launching a child into school with this valuable piece of equipment. Accidental-damage insurance is essential because repair costs can be very high. It may be possible in some cases to add the laptop to general household insurance, although it is unlikely you would get cover for 'accidental loss' (e.g. leaving it on a bus). So security and care are extremely important.

A 15-year-old boy reviews his laptop

Obvious advantages

- Robust, small and light, has no case but fits discreetly into school bag
- Keyboard is a good size for touch-typing
- Touchscreen 256 colour, responsive and clear
- Boots instantly, no saving required to shut down
- Good drawing program for diagrams, especially if familiar with 'MS Paint'
- 132 MHz processor – very fast
- Stable system – never crashes

Battery

- Lithium Ion Backup – CRC2032 – available in book shops £1.10
- Lasts 7 hours (extremely rare, more usual would be 3–5 hours)
- Takes approximately 10 minutes to recharge

Touchscreen pen

- Stored internally
- Replaceable at computer retail outlets, £5 for three pens

Printing

- Infrared connectivity. Hewlett Packard make large IR printer range
- Through PSIWIN or external parallel link for approximately £30

Memory

- 16 MB internal RAM
- 10, 50, 100 MB memory packs available

PC connectivity

- Comes with PSIWIN – desktop link program and RS232 connection cable
- Programs compatible with Windows equivalents through PSIWIN
- PCMCIA card compatible for modems, memory upgrades, etc.

Insurance

- Insurance premiums are high especially for under 18 year olds
- Barclaycard gives free 30-day cover + slightly discounted further insurance

Figure 3.11 This list derives from one boy's experience using a laptop for nearly all his work in school. The aspects selected are ones that matter to him and would matter to most children making similar use of a laptop. He finds these specifications suitable for daily school use, though he is fortunate in having desktop back-up at home.

Tablet PCs

You can draw or write on the screen of a tablet laptop. For routine note-taking, the student will use his usual word processing program and, by clicking 'Insert >Ink drawing' and using a special stylo, he will be able to draw diagrams, graphs or maps wherever necessary (see Figure 3.12).

Should he want to use the computer mainly for drawing and handwriting, he can swivel the screen round and lie it flat over the keyboard. A small on-screen keyboard will enable him to add typed text if necessary and to use keyboard short cuts.

There is also a handwriting recognition facility that is very effective and enables the student to label diagrams, or convert any reasonably clear writing or numbers into printed text.

The following features are particularly useful for the dyslexic student who needs to take notes in lectures or classes:

- The note-taking and drawing facilities are fully integrated. This means that the student can do his drawings during the note-taking session, rather than have to draw them on a separate piece of paper and insert them later. Experience has shown that this extra effort often discourages students from using a computer at all in lessons where drawing is expected.
- The use of colour, for drawing or for highlighting, enlivens notes and makes them more memorable.
- It is possible to edit printed text with handwriting.
- Converting handwriting to neat printed labels is easy.
- Roughly-drawn shapes can be perfected automatically.

Teachers find the tablet laptop is helpful both for themselves and for the students they are teaching:

- Diagrams and drawings can be prepared straight onto the screen in advance, projected, stored and distributed
- Maths teachers can do handwritten calculations on the spot clearly for projection – and there is no need to wipe them off to make room for new ones (so that slow copiers miss the chance to write them down).
- Work that has been written by pupils, and e-mailed to their teachers, can be marked in the traditional way with handwriting – but on the computer – and returned via e-mail

New software that will make the most of these new tablet laptops is being developed at the moment – Microsoft's 'OneNote' came out in the summer of 2003.

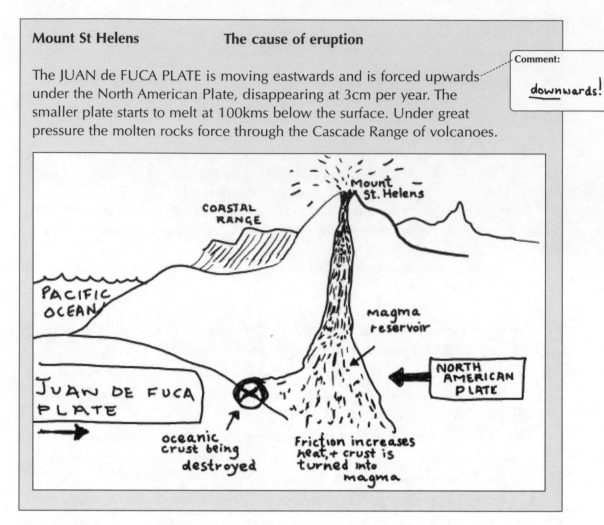

Mount St Helens   **The cause of eruption**

The JUAN de FUCA PLATE is moving eastwards and is forced upwards under the North American Plate, disappearing at 3cm per year. The smaller plate starts to melt at 100kms below the surface. Under great pressure the molten rocks force through the Cascade Range of volcanoes.

Comment:

downwards!

Figure 3.12 These notes and diagram were done in Word on an Acer tablet laptop. To achieve clarity the student enlarged the drawing/writing box while she was working on it. The teacher's comment was in colour.

A low-priced sturdy laptop for classroom use

(www.europe@alphasmart.com)

The dana by Alphasmart is stylish and answers the needs of schoolchildren who want to take notes in the classroom. Costing about £350, it has the following advantages:

- Light (0.91 kg) but sturdy.
- Touch-screen and full-size keyboard.
- Boots up immediately.
- 30 hours of battery life.
- USB cable for synchronising with Mac or Windows computer.
- Spellcheck dictionary.

Laptops in school – a practical survey for teachers

In the classroom be prepared, initially, to help with:

- Power – power points, extension cables, batteries.
- Desk – big enough for laptop and book (would two desks be better/available?).
- Printing – where would be best to do this?
- Being ready – insist on prompt booting up, before lesson starts: subject template with name, title and date on screen; select and 'Save As' immediately.
- Diagrams – anticipate the need for these and agree a system for drawing, using software or drawing straight onto the screen or hand drawing on plain paper.
- Handing in homework – an alternative routine to the rest of the class may be needed – stuck into exercise book or handed in in a file, or e-mailed via the school network.
- Decisions about:

  - whether or not to use the laptop in a particular subject or lesson – always require its use if at all possible
  - guidelines for how you would like work to be presented, if there is no school policy for this

- Good habits – require student to sit correctly, touch-type, use keyboard skills efficiently and independently, and take care of the laptop. No one else should use it or move it.
- Distractions:

  - noises – turn off all sound effects; class should ignore sound of typing
  - novelty – play this down for laptop user and class; it will fade
  - student's fascination with layout, colour, font etc. – value this, but insist on basic format in class; encourage student to enhance his work later (very good for the 'forgetting curve'! (see page 238))
  - greater preoccupation with laptop than with academic topic
  - peers' resentment – one counter argument to this is that the laptop for dyslexic people is the equivalent of spectacles for people with poor eye sight

- Hazards:
  - games – forbid them and enlist parental support
  - electronic interaction between laptops in the classroom – be aware of this possibility; turn it to good account for evaluating, checking and improving each other's work or for working in pairs
  - laptop screens can often be seen by other students but not by teachers – walk frequently behind laptop users!
  - technical difficulties as excuses, usually for work 'lost' while working or not handed in. Be discerning about genuine difficulties (give benefit of doubt).

Practical support – an advocate in the staff room

Members of staff have many queries when students first bring laptops into their classroom. Common questions centre round 'Is it really necessary in his work for me?' and 'How well can I expect him to use it?'. There is sometimes an unvoiced anxiety about how much faster and more knowledgeable the student is likely to be than his teachers. Ideally, students should talk directly to their teachers, but, initially, it is wise to appoint a dispassionate go-between and troubleshooter in the staff room as an additional channel. The topics in the table below are ones to think about.

Student needs:	His teachers need:
• appropriate laptop and software	• information about the specific learning difficulties that make a laptop essential to an individual student
• to touch-type faster than he hand-writes and be able to manage his machine well before he is allowed to take it into lessons	• to anticipate skills in their subjects that a laptop would support
• to take his laptop initially into one or two classes only, where his teachers recognise its value to him and are sympathetic; this will build his confidence	• to know how much to expect in the way of competence and responsible behaviour
• a responsible attitude to home-work, handing in hard copy and discretion in the classroom	• to be patient and inventive with initial snags over printing or handing in homework
• to be familiar with procedures and machines, well in advance of any exams, public or internal	• to be enthusiastic over any improvement the laptop brings
	• to appreciate how important a computer is in exams

If a dyslexic student's difficulties warrant the use of a laptop in class, they will also warrant the practical support of a respected member of staff. His role – mentor as well as advocate – is probably necessary only in the first weeks. Although there may be several laptop users scattered through the school, each needs to follow different routines that fit in with his year group's systems. Students with dyslexia have difficulty observing established routines, let alone working out and following an individual and different system. Many cope in school only by following their classmates to lessons, packing books for home and giving in work when they see others do this.

A typical area of difficulty is likely to be saving and filing. Students should establish a routine that they can manage in a consistent and independent way, something of the sort in the table below, perhaps.

In class and in homework, before typing:

- have a 'writing template' at the ready for all subjects, with automatic name, date and page numbering in header
- insert title as soon as topic is known
- select and 'save as' immediately
- save to a folder called something like 'to finish or print' on the desktop

In class and in homework, having finished typing:

- keep everything in desktop folder called 'to finish or print' until work is completed and/or printed
- only then drag and store documents in subject folders

Hard copies to hand in then file – Keep them in one dedicated 'homework' plastic folder until handed in. On return, having been marked, use same folder to store them until filed, the day they are given back, in subject files. Beware: marked work can go astray.

Back-up files – at least once a week copy new work onto individual subject disks. Label and store in separate 'school' box. Keep this permanently out on worktable at home.

Note: If space has been allocated on the school network, 'synchronise' will automatically back up a student's work. Make sure work is filed where the network will find it.

Apart from saving and filing, some of the following areas may need supervision:

- keyboard skills
- printing
- security
- computer kit
- use in exams
- communications and troubleshooting

The following checklist derives from teachers' experience when integrating the individual use of computers into everyday class work.

Practical support – a teacher's checklist

Keyboard skills – are they good enough? Can he:

- touch-type – shouldn't have a laptop in class if he can't
- do what he needs for each subject, e.g.
    - accents in French
    - sub- and superscript in maths and science
    - bullet points for notes
    - drawing package for diagrams
- use organising, editing and presentation facilities, e.g.
    - headers and footers for running titles, automatic page numbering and dates, key commands, tabs, page break
    - make templates for each subject, use autocorrect, add his own words to a spelling dictionary, use a thesaurus

Printing and filing
Does he know:

- which printers in the school his laptop recognises and when are convenient times to use them?
- that he must print his work regularly and keep it in subject files?

Security
Has he:

- insurance for the laptop if it is his own?
- a convenient safe place to keep it during lunch or games?
- a discreet, protective bag to carry it out of school?
- a private method of identifying it?
- a responsible attitude to caring for it?

Necessary kit
He should have:

- charged batteries, a spare and a system for recharging them
- cable, transformer, plug for mains power
- printer cable if needed (often computers activate compatible printers by infrared or through a network)
- formatted disks, new ink cartridge, plain paper, files for hard copy, a hole punch

Practical support – word processing in public exams

Boxed quotations in this section are taken from the *Joint Council for General Qualifications Examinations and Assessment for GCSE and GCE Regulations and Guidance relating to Candidates with Special Requirements 2002–2003.*

'You may request the use of a word processor where this is the candidate's usual method of communication.'

'In circumstances where special arrangements are needed, awarding bodies will make every attempt to respond positively to requests for candidates to use computers.'

Awarding bodies recognise that candidates using word processors in public exams do so in order to have parity with their peers. This should be an emotional as well as a technical parity. In part, the way to achieve it is to visualise the exam scene well in advance and give candidates practice so that nothing is new except the exam paper.

'The centre (i.e. the school) should ensure that the candidate has experience of and practice in the use of the arrangements requested.'

The exam room scenario

- Ideally in a separate room (with clock).

'Candidates using computers in circumstances where their use may distract other candidates must be accommodated separately.'

- Two desks or a large table: candidates may need more than one desk to hold computer, keyboard and mouse pad, paper for diagrams and planning answers and the question paper – often a double spread.
- Positioning computers: candidates using computers may be embarrassed and others distracted by their clicking keys, intriguing screens and perhaps extra time.
  - No one should be able to read a neighbour's screen. To prevent this, it may be necessary to require candidates to use a small font for typing, enlarging it only to check their work at the end. However, this system might not suit some candidates who count on the benefit of working with large fonts or who check as they write.
  - At the back of the main exam room may be a suitable position for a few candidates. If there are many more, they might sit round the sides of a separate

room facing the wall. In both these cases, screens are easily visible to invigilators. Candidates sitting immediately or diagonally behind one another have too tempting a view of the screens in front of them.

– Mains supply needs to be arranged in advance.

- Sockets, adapters and extension leads: provision for candidates sitting one exam may not be adequate for the numbers using computers in a different subject.
- Invigilators: an extra one will be needed if candidates sit in a separate room. Invigilators must be watchful of computer screens, positioning themselves behind candidates. Ideally, they should have enough technical know-how to save basic technical situations – trouble with disks, memory, 'losing' work and printing problems are typical crises. A standby machine, ready for use, is a comfort to all concerned.
- The computers: it is wise to have a technically competent and sympathetic adult on the alert in the school when candidates are using computers for public exams.

'If it is intended to use the computer other than as a basic word processor, the Head of Centre should consult the awarding body concerned.'

The concept of 'basic word processor' excludes spellcheckers, dictionaries, thesauri, calculators etc.

'Candidates must not be able to gain access to existing files or documents. Where a system operates from floppy disk, the candidate must be supplied with a formatted disk containing only the software required for the examination concerned.'

If a school provides computers that have a prepared 'exam default', candidates should make time in advance of their exams to use the keyboards, word-processing facilities and saving routines. They may need a knowledgeable member of staff to help them. The default should include necessary refinements, such as foreign language accents and sub/superscript where appropriate.

'The candidate must be proficient in the use of the computer and its software.'

Exam routines

Schools' routines will vary, but candidates must be familiar with them if they are not to be distracted by added anxiety during an exam.

- Timing: invigilator and candidate should arrive early enough, before exams start, to deal with unforeseen hitches.
- Before the exam: candidates should boot up, select their word-processing program, put in a disk and 'save to disk', select a font and automatic page numbering. Despite preoccupation with the computer, they should also make sure that they have pens and paper for drawing and planning.
- During the exam:
  - put name and candidate number on every page.
  - number the questions carefully and check that the default setting in Word matches the exam numbering system.
  - start a new page for each question; use 'page break' not 'return' for this.
  - match number of hand-drawn diagrams on paper with number of question.
  - save frequently, even if machine saves automatically.
- After the exam:
  - Printing:

> 'The printing of answers may take place after the time allowed for the examination has expired. The candidate should be present in order to verify that his printing is complete.'

  - nothing should be deleted until exam script is printed.
  - delete script after printing and before next examination.
  - the candidate must be present when printing; he should check that nothing is missing and that handwritten sheets are attached; have hole puncher and treasury tags to hand.
  - Administration:
    - some exam boards require a copy of the official permission sheet to be attached to each script.
    - it is helpful to have a dedicated printer available nearby during the exam period.

Educational software and websites

There is a vast range of educational software to accompany courses, give practice in procedures and to structure revision.

There are three main ways in which the right software or website can be particularly useful for dyslexic learners:

1. A student with a short-term-memory weakness will find a resource that can be returned to again and again (unlike a classroom lesson) and will provide the over-learning necessary for reinforcement.
2. Curriculum material that is explained slightly differently from the way the teacher or textbook presented it, particularly if it is interactive, diagrammatic, pictorial or with working models, can provide a useful additional learning tool.

3. For the weak reader, auditory input is a great bonus – text or labels or explanations read aloud can make all the difference for them.

Computer aids for interactive learning and revision

Among the bewildering wealth of educational websites, a well-developed series of programs that is particularly useful to children with specific learning difficulties is the BBC GCSE Bitesize Revision series (website: www.bbc.co.uk/education/revision). The website runs alongside late-night programmes on television, designed to be video taped and used with related workbooks. 'Bitesize' perfectly characterises the small digestible units into which GCSE subjects have been divided. Within a unit there is usually a summary of the most important facts, well laid out and in a minimum of words, illustrations, sometimes modestly animated, a sample question or two with answers and then a 'testbite'. Testbites can be multiple-choice questions, textboxes to fill in or questions to do on paper. There are tips and warnings and the tone is cheerful and realistic. Figure 3.13 gives the flavour.

The programmes do not go deeply into detail; their strength is in presenting the essentials of a topic in a lively interactive and achievable form. They are designed to engage attention, involve the student and build confidence. Although the approach may not please all GCSE students, it is likely to be particularly helpful to dyslexic students in their attempts to revise. The BBC has recently been awarded funds to develop the 'digital curriculum'. This will consist of courseware across a range of school subjects, including maths and science.

As with websites, so it is with revision CDs. In the search for software to support their subjects, teachers are often involved in an elaborate search and a disappointment at the end. They trawl through a mass of publicity material, order a trial CD, study it and then, as often as not, have to return it as unsuitable. Quite often about 10% of the material would be useful, the rest not at all. Yet interactive practice or a different version is often just what pupils (with or without learning difficulties) need in order to understand or revise a curriculum topic.

It helps to have very specific criteria in mind when searching for software. It also helps to know who among staff in other departments is also searching. This is useful because the source for suitable material in one subject is sometimes a likely source in other subjects. Below is one instance where staff interaction has worked in this way. The need for revision practice that reflected the format of AS French multiple-choice questions led the modern languages department in one school to the product of Multimedia Textbooks Ltd called *It's French, Modern Languages CD-ROM for A-Level* (see box).

It's French

Texts are from up-to-date authentic sources, cater for every interest and deal with topics ranging from regional items and news to environmental and social issues to sport. Short grammar sections help students with points they may have found difficult.

Questions are presented in a variety of options so that the student can work on vocabulary and comprehension techniques, as well as keeping a running total and checking how successful they have been. Question format reflects the style students may encounter in public exams as well as in vocabulary acquisition; they are encouraged to learn from their mistakes in order to improve their scores.

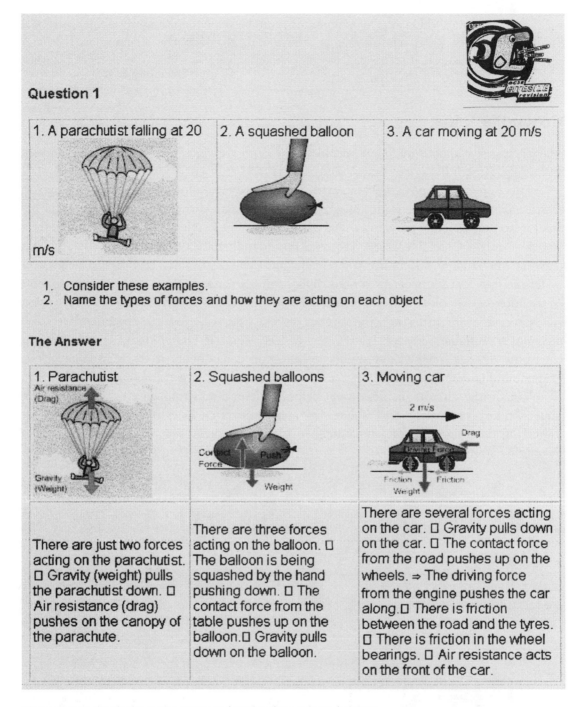

Figure 3.13 In the Physics section Forces and Motion these animated pictures illustrate some basic facts with a question and answers.

This, together with *It's Spanish*, was accessed by modern linguists and the learning support department on the school network; it was found that the CD helped dyslexic boys to revise for their AS French exams, so other MMT products were also investigated. Boys doing history made immediate use of *It's History* for their revision. The biology department trialled the four A-level CD-ROMs for biology, while the mathematics department looked at the CD-ROM *Pure Mathematics* (detailed solutions and explanations where appropriate are provided throughout). There were CDs in the series for economics and business studies. CDs for chemistry and physics were in preparation.

This illustrates the value of communication between departments about software. Similar sharing between schools can also be useful, although the formats, analysis and curriculum information that happen to complement teaching styles in one school do not necessarily suit those in all other schools.

Crocodile Clips

The packages available include *Crocodile Clips Absorb Physics*, *Absorb Chemistry*, *Absorb Technology*, *Absorb Electronics* and *Absorb Mathematics*.

There are several powerful simulation packages, which allow students and teachers to recreate experiments (and explosions!), model mathematical theories, or simulate real life quickly and easily. They provide a useful bridge between the symbolic and the concrete.

Not only is Crocodile Technology very user-friendly for those who have difficulty with drawing (the student selects the components and they neatly join up), it also helps with understanding, for example, represented symbolically, circuits can show the amount of current by the intensity of colour and will or will not work depending on whether the sums are right.

Crocodile Technology covers electronics, programming, microcontrollers and mechanics. Suitable for ages 10–18, and college work, it lets students create and test electronic designs quickly and simply by dragging components from the toolbars. The example in Figure 3.14 shows lamps connected in series and in parallel.

Visualising circuits in this way helps students tremendously in developing an understanding of current and voltage in electronic circuits. Software effects, such as indicating the brightness of lamps, help to clarify the behaviour of the circuit without distracting attention.

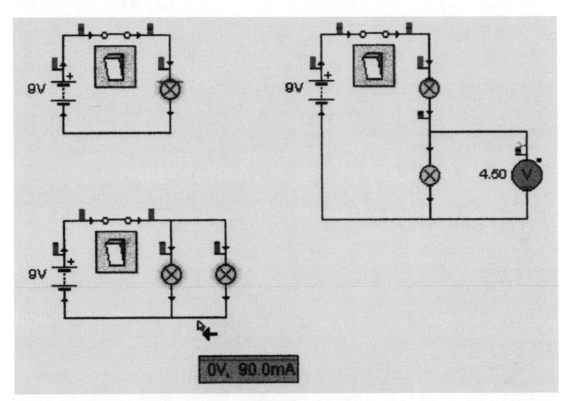

Figure 3.14 The small bars indicate the voltages at different points around the circuit, and the arrows show the flow of current. Meters can be added. In addition, holding the cursor over a particular point in the circuit brings up a tiny information window showing the current and voltage at this point.

The *Crocodile Clips Courseware* has a very useful mathematics presentation. As one student remarked, 'I like being able to replay the course at my own speed. If you haven't understood a lesson, or were fooling around during it, you've missed it for good. But on the computer you can see the course again and again.' This overlearning is particularly valuable for dyslexic students.

Other *Crocodile* simulation packages work in a similar way. There is always something to do, and exploring the behaviour of the simulated elements contributes to a clear understanding of the simulated system. There are various interactive courseware packages, which use simulation as part of a guided learning experience. Details are available from the Crocodile Clips Limited website (www.crocodile-clips.com).

Content-free software

Specific programs that reinforce memory with interactive stimuli are important to dyslexic students, but far more so is content-free software that gives them a flexible facility to process and present their daily work. A comparison between the barely legible confusion in Figure 3.16 following page) and the computer version of the same topic (Figure 3.15 below) illustrates this.

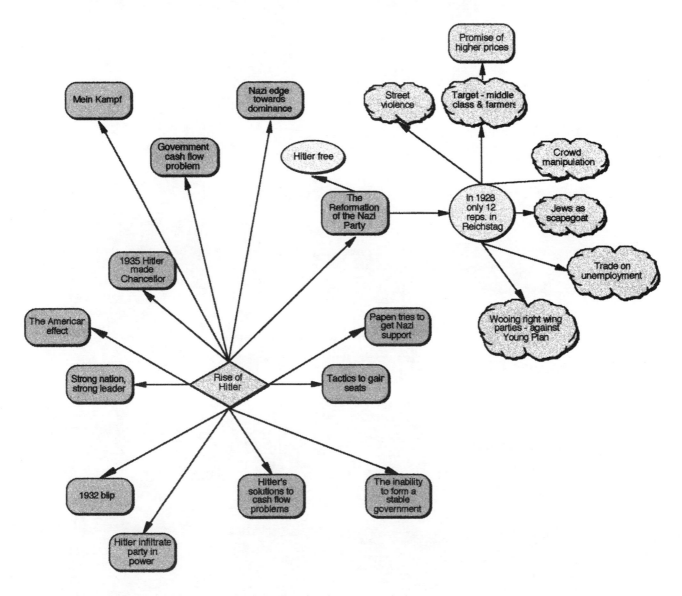

Figure 3.15 As a revision exercise Jonathan redrew his plan using *Inspiration*.

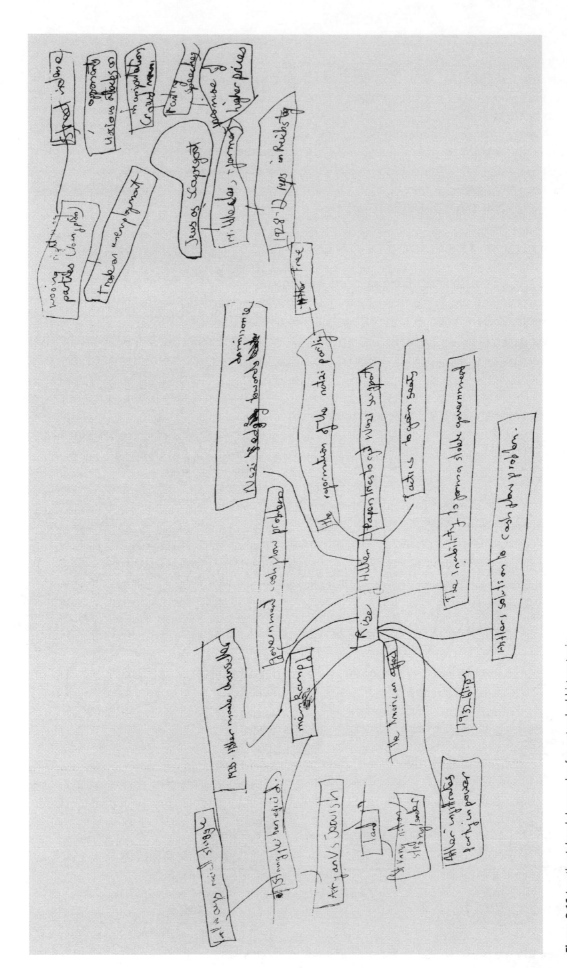

Figure 3.16 Jonathan's hand-drawn plan for a standard history topic.

Technical aids for writing

- A word processor with a dyslexia-friendly spellchecker is important for poor spellers. (Will it recognise and offer correct spelling for a word that *sounds* right but is spelt wrongly? 'jiraf', 'katch', 'persew'?) Fortunately for people with dyslexia, spellcheckers are quite geared to typists putting letters in the wrong order ('thier', 'thuogh').

- Autocorrect (in Word: *Menu bar → Tools → Autocorrect*) is programmed to correct common errors and can be further programmed to correct subject-specific vocabulary (science words, names of historical figures, artists etc.) and extend abbreviations.

- Thesaurus: this is a wonderful bonus for the dyslexic person who may have difficulties with spelling, scanning, the alphabetical sequence and the reading of unfamiliar words, any of which make dictionary work a chore. The ease with which the thesaurus can be accessed (shift F7) positively encourages vocabulary extension and precise use of language. The presentation of a word with several completely different meanings or with subtle shades of meaning makes the distinctions very clear, and the choices invite further discrimination (Figure 3.17).

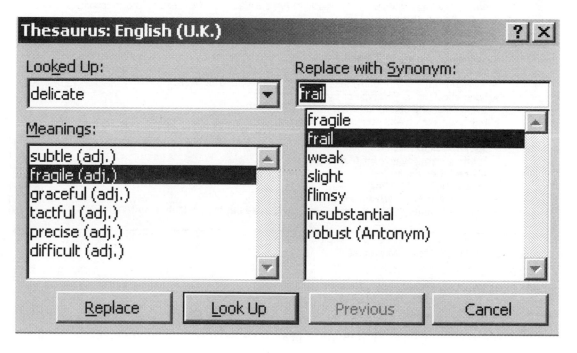

Figure 3.17 Dictionary work can be a pleasure with an inbuilt thesaurus.

- textHELP Read & Write is software made specifically to help dyslexic children. Wrong spellings are highlighted and can be logged, homonyms are pointed out and the computer will highlight and read back text word by word, sentence by sentence or paragraph by paragraph. This is invaluable for pupils with dyslexia who find checking difficult or who cannot *hear* the sense of what they are writing while they are writing. Other features include a thesaurus, word prediction, spoken selection lists for spelling and prediction, and abbreviation expansion. textHELP will read aloud from icons, menus, Help files and the World Wide Web (Figure 3.18).

Search | Site Map | Contact Us

dyslexic.com

Text-Only Version of this Site

Home | **About Dyslexia** | **Software** | **Books, Videos & Music** | **Computers & add-ons** | **Other Gadgets** | **Support & Downloads.**

Home > Software & Books > Accessibility & Tools.

textHELP![TM]

Read & Write V 5:

for Windows 95/98/Me/NT/2000.

We are pleased to be distributors for this exciting product.

What does it do?

In a completely integrated system textHELP! Read & Write offers users all the following for practically any **Windows** **program** your word processor, spreadsheet, DTP, encyclopedia, web page, Help File, educ

- Speech feed back by marked block or as you type letter by letter, word by word or s
- Synchronised speech, highlighting each word as it reads it in theTextreader window;
- Speech from icons, menus, help files and the World Wide Web;
- Spell checking as you type or by marked block;
- Spelt Alike and Sound Alike suggestions for spelling;
- Word suggestion and completion ("word prediction") for slow typists;
- Spoken selection lists for spelling and prediction;
- Speaking Help file;
- Spelling error logging for teachers to refer to;
- Abbreviation Expansion;
- Automatic Word Endings;
- Thesaurus & Word Wizard word finder;
- Help with homophones (words which sound alike but are spelt differently).

Figure 3.18 textHELP addresses many of the literacy problems of the dyslexic student.

- Voice-activated software (*Dragon* NaturallySpeaking): having your spoken words converted to type instantly and then read back word by word, sentence by sentence or paragraph by paragraph must be a dream solution for the dyslexic pupil.

A training session during which the user reads aloud text that appears on the screen is sufficient for the computer to identify the way in which an individual pronounces the sounds of the language. During the first week of use, there will be minor problems of recognition, which the user teaches the software to correct. Thereafter, there is a minimum of inaccuracy and this can be identified either visually or aurally when the machine reads back what has been written. Corrections can be made verbally: 'Correct that.' And then the user repeats the word or spells it. The software not only corrects the mistake but also improves its own recognition of that particular sound pattern.

The software is compatible with most common applications, and the user can control the computer verbally, dictate in more than one language and send e-mails and browse the Web using voice commands.

Foreign languages on computer

Language dictionaries provide an easy access to the grammar, phrases and vocabulary of foreign languages. The arduous looking-up of uncertain or unknown vocabulary is one of the most tedious chores for a dyslexic person. An on-screen dictionary is easy to use – a word is clearly defined, used in context and linked to idioms and verb tables (see Figure 6.26, page 229).

A range of alphabets is available and, for those who have difficulty producing a legible foreign script, it may be worth learning the keyboard.

> Now that he is using a laptop he has grown enormously in confidence and was very pleased to see that he could produce the declension of the Greek definite article faster than those working on paper. His written work is now both fuller and more accurate. He has also been working on word derivation from both languages with the aim of widening his English vocabulary.

Figure 3.19 This school report, the first since Edward start using a laptop, shows how extensively he is using his machine.

PowerPoint

PowerPoint is a useful presentation program for both learning and teaching. It has the advantages given below for everyone but especially for a dyslexic student (provided that it is not just used for written material, e.g. endless bullet points to be copied down).

For learning

- Compiling his presentation from a variety of sources – his notes, the Internet, scanned material – involves selection, rejection, sequencing and the possibility of producing something to be proud of without the labour involved in pen-and-paper work.
- Showing his presentation invites an oral rather than a written commentary.
- To make the slide show, he is processing information – turning words and ideas into pictures, diagrams and maps.
- To give the show, he turns pictures back into words.
- His presentation can be played over and over, so it is useful for revision.
- Confidence is increased because mistakes are not set in stone and can be rectified as they are noticed.

- Making and organising a sequence of slides to illustrate a case study, a process or a history-of-art topic is much more fun than revising from notes or a book – and the resulting presentation is something that can be returned to again and again for improvement or editing.

For teaching

- The teacher can select the best material from a variety of sources and make her own compilation – without worries about copyright.
- She can control the sequence in which images are presented, and the timing.
- She can direct the focus of the class onto a particular image and talk about it while they are actually looking at it (unlike when they are reading from a textbook where they can't read and look at the same time).
- She can keep returning to a slide if she wants to show its relevance in different parts of her presentation.
- Non-linear thinking patterns can be demonstrated and accommodated: one angle/idea can be developed before returning to the same text or image and then pursuing another angle; comparisons can be made.
- The size and quality of a screen shot are a bonus.

Figure 3.20 is an example of an art-history presentation on Holbein's *Ambassadors*. The teacher described the PowerPoint presentation as 'circular' rather than linear – a web of connections being made as the presentation continues and then returns to the main picture.

Discussing Holbein's 'Ambassadors' 1533 — using PowerPoint

This presentation is an exploration of the work itself and an exploration of analytical thinking. The painting itself can be used as a jumping-off point for introducing the artist; the Reformation (the opponents More and Cromwell either side of Henry VIII); who the ambassadors were and the role they played in these politics; the significance of the still-life objects above and the still-life objects below (representing knowledge); the significance of the skull (representing death) and the floor (representing the heavens). Whose side is the artist on? The top-right-hand crucifix offers a hint.

The slides prompt:

- different views of the painting (in historical context, as portrait, as still life, as philosophy)
- focus and deeper views (through the progressive use of close-ups)
- comparisons and connections (through juxtaposition, e.g. with the Cosmati *Pavement*)

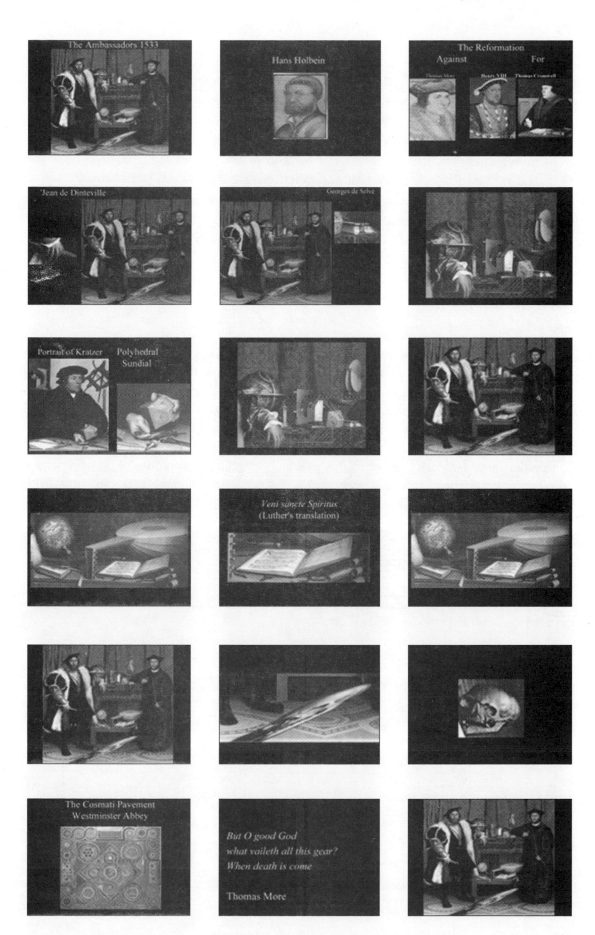

Figure 3.20 The sequence of pictures used in a presentation on Holbein's *Ambassadors.*

Further advantages:

- The sequencing of the slides can clarify the sequencing of an argument (from general to detailed, from certainty to questions); it can also allow the teacher to follow a lesson plan without stopping to consult notes.
- The layout of the slides can make complex situations easier to explain and understand (see *The Reformation – For and Against*).
- Names (*Jean de Dinteville*), or unfamiliar or specialist words (*Polyhedral Sundial*), or keywords (*Reformation*) can be shown to emphasise, clarify and avoid spelling mistakes.
- Text can be juxtaposed with image to clarify one or the other (*Thomas More's poem*.

ChemSketch

Files of pictures and diagrams for school subjects will enable students to incorporate artwork into their documents, e.g. scientific apparatus (Figure 3.22, opposite page).

ChemSketch looks a very useful program for chemistry students – although a great deal of the material in it is only applicable to A level and beyond (Figure 3.21). There are palettes of laboratory kits and apparatus that can be inserted into the student's own notes and experiments. The program also draws molecules quickly and easily. It instantly calculates chemical formulae, molecular weight and percentage composition and predicts several liquid properties, such as density and refractive index. The program customises display properties, e.g. atom numbering. It draws reactions and schematic diagrams and can work with structures, text and graphics simultaneously (see www.acdlabs.com).

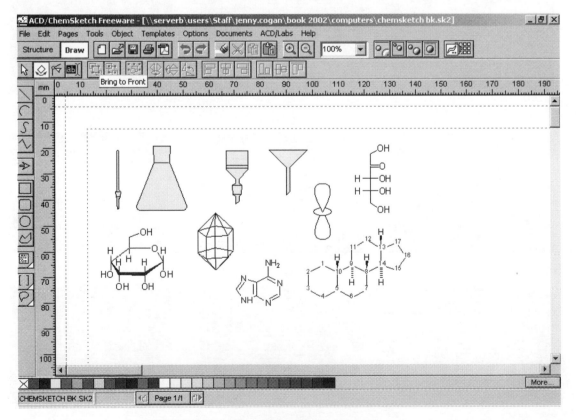

Figure 3.21 Examples of *ACD ChemSketch* graphics, which students can import into their documents. They could make their own template of selected images.

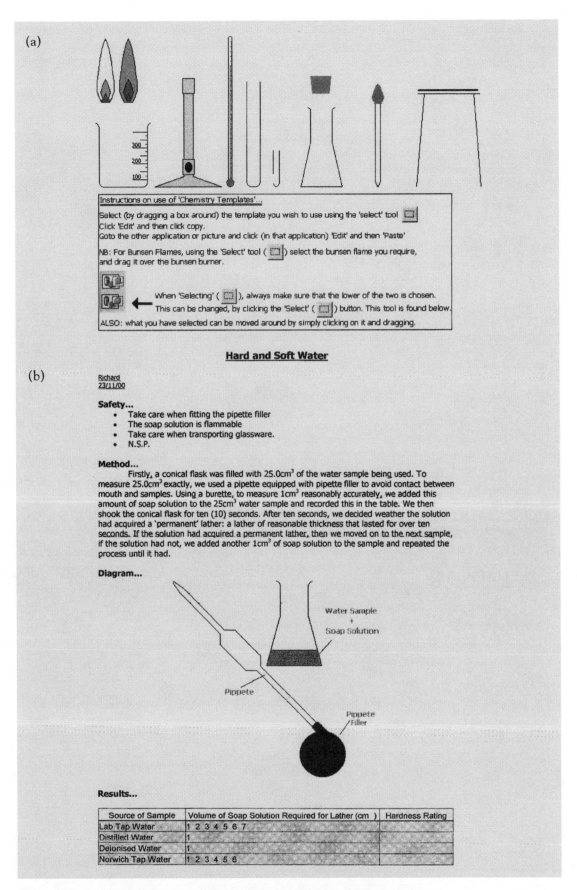

Figure 3.22 (a) Richard, who created a bank of them, copies and pastes drawings into his chemistry notes as he needs them. He finds drawing by hand spoils his work, however much time he spends on it. (b) Richard's use of his own palette of apparatus, text wrapping and tables to present his work.

A drawing package will enable students to do diagrams more easily. Using a mouse is often easier than a touch-pad, and enlarging the screen while working makes for greater accuracy.

Industry through the ages in Wales

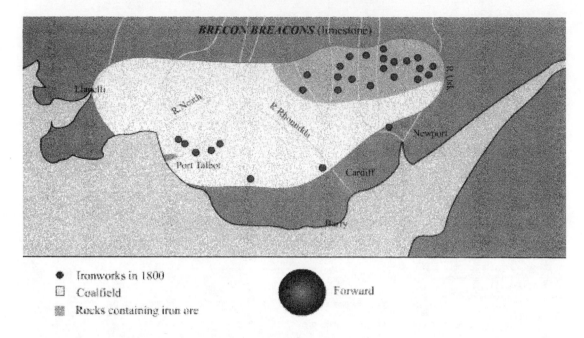

- ● Ironworks in 1800
- ☐ Coalfield
- ▨ Rocks containing iron ore

Forward

Industry through the ages in Wales

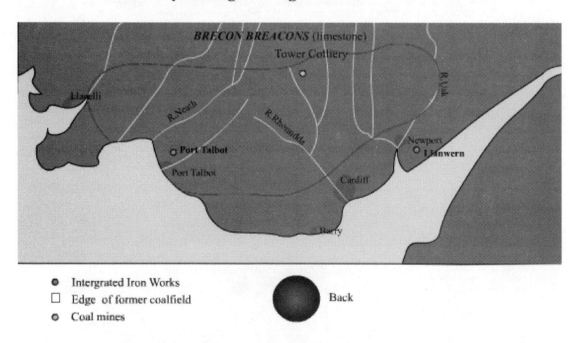

- ● Intergrated Iron Works
- ☐ Edge of former coalfield
- ◉ Coal mines

Back

Figure 3.23 William drew these two geography maps in *Flash*. Here they are printed next to each other – but viewed on the screen a click on the central button enables toggling between the two. *Flash* can be used to create animations – useful in design and technology and in physics. With *Flash* the student is able to achieve a high degree of accuracy, good shapes and natural curves. He can also change parts of the drawing easily, and store the drawings in small files.

Programs for maths

It is usually the case that dyslexic students feel that they cannot do their maths on a computer, even though, when armed with pen and paper instead, they are prone to copying numbers and signs incorrectly, laying out their work badly and failing to draw acceptable graphs and diagrams. Programs to process maths are not so well known as word-processing and drawing packages.

One head of maths introduced a list of pieces of software with the words, 'I don't like to hear people say computers are no good for maths. They are.' His first recommendation was the *Equation Editor*, part of Microsoft Word:

> When typing a document inserting a mathematical character is possible by using the Symbol font: this makes symbols such as $\times$, $\div$, $\geq$, $\approx$, $\neq$, $\sqrt{}$, and the Greek alphabet, lower and upper case available. At the same time we should mention that accented characters, such as è, ã, ö, ç, can be obtained in much the same way, using what is called Normal font. Just click on Insert (on the toolbar), and select Symbol. Then choose the appropriate font.
>
> Using *Equation Editor* can ease the complicated matter of setting correctly formatted mathematics into a document. It allows you to type mixed numbers, such as $3\frac{2}{5}$, radicals, such as $\sqrt[3]{100}$, as well as algebraic fractions, such as $\frac{-b \pm \sqrt{b^2 - 4ac}}{2a}$, automatically setting letters in italics, inserting spaces and adjusting the line spacing appropriately. *Equation Editor* can be accessed via the Insert menu (on the toolbar) followed by Object → Create New → MS Equation. But this process is long-winded and time-consuming. It is much more readily accessed if your set-up allows you to put a button on the toolbar that calls up *Equation Editor* each time you click on it. Facilities available include various brackets (which grow if required to contain large expressions, column vectors or matrices), integral signs (with or without limits), summation signs and notation used in chemical equations. It recognises trigonometric functions, setting them in regular type rather than italic. You can add embellishments to characters, making it easy to include notation such as $\bar{x}$, $\dot{x}$ or $\overrightarrow{AB}$. If doing much work in *Equation Editor*, it is probably wise to view the screen at 150% or 200%.

His next recommendation was *Graphmatica*:

> Excellent software for drawing graphs of functions. It is instant and simple, and graphs are easily imported into a Word document. It is available as 'Shareware'.

He recommended *Autograph* because it does graphs *and* transformations. His next recommendation was *Cabri-Géomètre II* or *Geometer's Sketch Pad*:

> Two delightful programs that can take all the drudgery out of drawing geometrical objects accurately.

Another teacher recommended these for circle theorems.

Armed with software offering these mathematical facilities, there is every reason why dyslexic and dyspraxic students should present their mathematics, not by hand, but on computer.

The final program, *Coypu*, has proved very successful in helping children with specific learning difficulties to understand the relationship between algebraic equations and functions and their geometric representation. It is user-friendly, particularly when the user becomes accustomed to the simple 'set scale' option on the graph menu, so that the graph displays only the required values of *x* and the sensible values of *y*.

Graphs may be drawn in four colours, allowing three or four to be clearly shown together and their points of intersection easily identified.

Used as a teaching aid in conjunction with a smart board, it is first rate and used alone allows children the satisfaction of drawing beautiful, accurate curves, which many could never achieve by hand.

It is also very good for teaching the same skills to non-dyslexic children, although many of these can achieve impressive curves by hand on graph paper.

Inspiration

The beauty of this software is that many of its functions are particularly helpful for dyslexic people:

- A spatial rather than linear layout suits students with dyslexia, who are often divergent thinkers, for example the top-down tree in Figure 3.26.
- The ideas can be moved around the page easily so that random thoughts can be grouped together later.

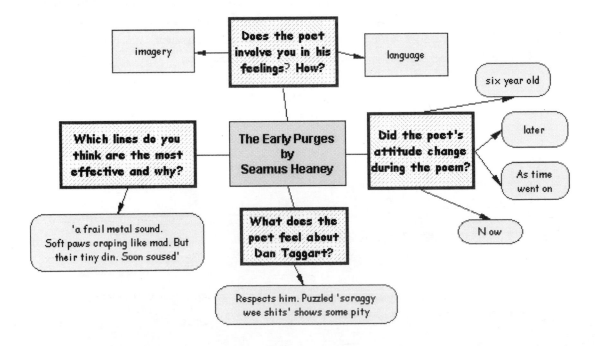

Figure 3.24 This map shows the questions asked by a teacher and the student's plan for answering them. By clicking on the top left-hand corner of each box he can write notes and quotes on each point.

+ **The Early Purges by Seamus Heaney**
  1. + **Did the poet's attitude change during the poem?**
     1. ▭ six year old
        vivid memories, full of pity - frail, tiny
        clear visual impression, bobbing kittens violence of: pitched, slung, ssluice, doused, thrown
     2. ▭ later
        fascinated, frightened - 'suddenly frightened'. Sadly I hung round the yard - watching
     3. ▭ As time went on
        fear came back, impressions stayed with him, not far below surface @trapped', 'snared'
        sickenning tug'
     4. ▭ N ow
        Sounds accepting of country ways, but is he really? acceptable manyly attitude. Says early
        feelings were just 'false sentiments', but his language is emotional full of feeling. Language
        dead in 'but on well run farms pests must be kept down'

  2. + **What does the poet feel about Dan Taggart?**
     1. ▭ Respects him. Puzzled he doesn't feel sad. 'scraggy wee shits' shows mixture of pity
        and cruelty. Follows him round. Tries to believe in his way of looking at the problem.

  3. + **Which lines do you think are the most effective and why?**
     1. ▭ 'a frail metal sound.
        Soft paws craping like mad. But their tiny din. Soon soused'
        Language full of pity, helplessnes, desperation. contrast with actions of Dan.

  4. ▪ **Does the poet involve you in his feelings? How?**
     imagery and language
        He describes things clearly so you can see and hear them 'like wet gloves' 'crisp as old summer
        dung''frail metal sound' You can hear them in the buckeet. He talks about something we have
        ll felt. He leaves you wondering how you ought to feel.

Figure 3.25 Here is the same map arranged in a linear format and including notes hidden on the diagrammatic view. The student clicks on an icon in the toolbar to toggle between the two.

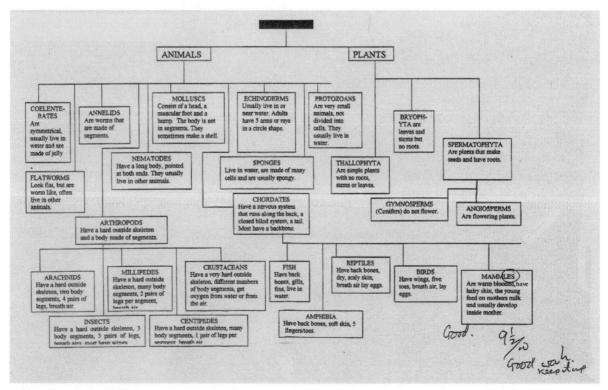

Figure 3.26 This 'top-down' tree for the classification of animals and plants is only one of the possible formats in mind-mapping software.

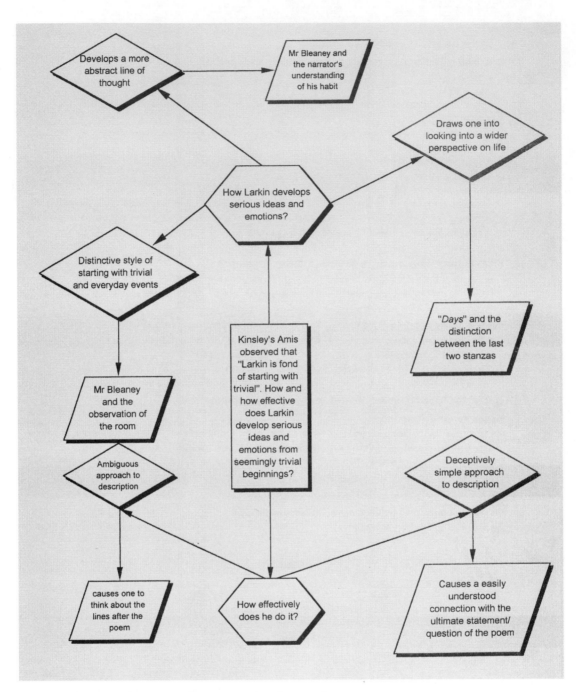

Figure 3.27 Using mind-mapping software *Inspiration*, shapes, colours (particularly colours) and arrows help with categorisation.

- There are numerous easy options for linking and categorising material – shape, colour, style, size. Sorting and prioritising information are both very good exercises in themselves for people with dyslexia.
- Pictures can be imported to make mind-maps visually memorable for revision.
- 'Boxes' for text are easily adapted to hold as much type as necessary.
- Hidden notes and subsidiary mind-maps can be added to any of the topics and revealed or concealed by clicking on a button.
- The whole diagrammatic view of the topic can be converted into a linear presentation at the click of the mouse (Figure 3.25).

Sibelius

This software is a godsend for any dyslexic musicians who have difficulties in producing neat musical notation, have weaknesses in sight-reading or 'visualising' how notes sound.

These comments on *Sibelius* were made by a dyslexic student who is very enthusiastic about composition but finds these practical difficulties very discouraging:

'You can hear as you play.'
'You can visualise the sound as you look at the notes.'
'You can play the piece back and hear it as a whole.'
 'Input from the keyboard is easier than writing.'
'Correcting doesn't make a mess, so presentation is much better.'
'You are allowed to use it for GCSE coursework'
'You can scan a score onto the computer.'
'When you are reading a score, the notes light up as they are played.'
'It is a real learning tool; I can read music much better now.'
'Allows you through experimentation to teach yourself various lessons of harmony and melody.'
(http://www.sibelius.com)

A school network

In a school where there is a network, the special educational needs co-ordinator, in conjunction with the IT services manager, can do a great deal to encourage her pupils and their teachers to use it to their advantage.

The network can provide easy access to:

- guidelines for coursework
- syllabuses
- subject-specific vocabulary
- timetables – both daily and weekly
- essay titles
- reading lists
- teaching or revision notes

Other advantages of a network:

- e-mail can be used for reminding pupils of school assignments, obligations or deadlines
- pupils and teachers can communicate with each other to clarify homework problems
- subject departments' web pages can provide a store of useful back-up information for children whose own notes are unreliable
- departmental links to Internet resources
- each time members of the school log on/off the network, their work is automatically saved and updated; this is a valuable safety net

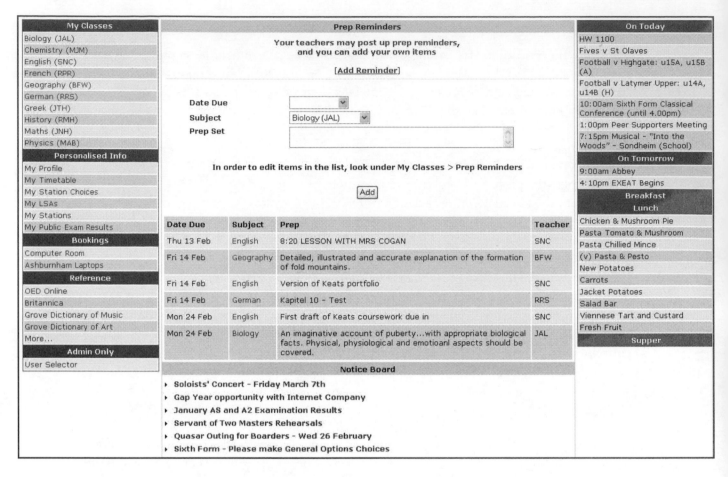

Figure 3.28 A daily on-line reminder of what is on each day in school, which homework has to be done, when coursework should be presented, as well as access to individual timetables, can be added to by subject teachers and the individual whose page it is. This can help a disorganised dyslexic student enormously.

Wireless networking

There is a lot of interest in this area. Wireless networking provides a straightforward way of allowing pupils with laptops to connect to the school network, to print and to save work automatically without the usual connection paraphernalia – which is vulnerable to loss and damage and necessitates each individual being near a connection point. This is an enormous bonus for dyslexic laptop users.

An important advantage of wireless networking for schools in general is that there is no need for a dedicated room for computer classes – any classroom can be used at any time. Schools that are setting up a network from scratch would find costs for wireless networking no more than for conventional cabling.

Pride in their work

Parents and teachers often assume that children who are dyslexic don't mind having a chaotic lifestyle and untidy work. The truth is often the reverse: many feel shame and frustration at their substandard work, and for the dyslexic person who is a perfectionist there is real stress.

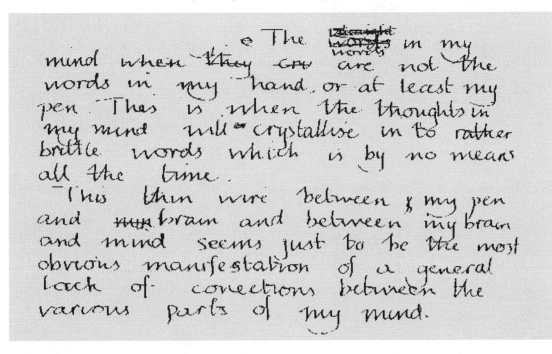

Figure 3.29 Will, a very literary 14-year-old, experienced enormous frustration trying to get his thoughts onto paper. This was his fourth attempt at answering my question 'How does your dyslexia affect your writing?'

Using a computer offers these students the opportunity to present work that is at least legible and correctly spelt, and at best a true reflection of the effort they have put into it (Figure 3.30).

```
                    Word Processing


    As I sit down to write this essay on word pocessing I try hard
    to remember what it was like when I sat with a pen and a piece
    of paper. I ca not remember the difference very well. The big
    difference that remains is the results. Whereas everything that
    I ever wrote before the word processor was incomplete in
    conception I now find myself writing essays that are at least
    mostly true to my orginal idea. It is not that the word processor
    does the thinking for me it is that it somehow allows me to
    better express the ideas which are at the back of my mind.

    Although I have no idea what is going on technically when I use
    this computer I will try and express how it feels. It feels as
    if everything I write has taken a very direct route from my mind,
    it is not perfect, much comes out as I do not want it to but the
    difference between now and before I had this computer is
    stunning.
```

Figure 3.30 This was written by the same boy after three years of using a word processor in school.

Filing

The combination of difficulties that dyslexic children may have – handwriting speed and legibility, spelling, sequencing, short-term memory, spatial layout, organisation – can result in their starting their exam revision at an enormous disadvantage. Their notes may be incomplete, illegible or simply lost.

Organising and saving notes, exercises and essays is easily done on a computer – but a dyslexic student needs to be drilled in good habits at the start of his computer career.

Chapter 4
Note-taking

Some teachers expect their pupils to take copious notes during their lessons; some insist that they write nothing at all. Some teachers just talk, and their pupils try to make a coherent summary; others write explanations and diagrams on the board and expect their pupils to copy them down. Other teachers actually dictate notes. There is a wide range of teaching styles in relation to note-taking.

There is also a wide range in the ability of the pupils to be able to accomplish these tasks. Many children can manage note-taking well – the process of writing and putting the information into their own words helping their understanding and memory. The absolute reverse may be true for a dyslexic pupil because of his technical difficulties in all or some of the following areas:

- copying quickly and accurately from the board
- writing quickly and legibly
- understanding and remembering while writing

A dyslexic pupil who has been writing notes during a lesson may well remember practically nothing of the subject matter and be so preoccupied with remembering the teacher's actual words and with keeping up that he has no time to ask questions and join in discussion (Figure 4.1). This is a serious drawback for someone with dyslexia whose best method of learning could be through talk and participation. Hours of school time can be wasted in what may be an almost fruitless activity for him. His interest and motivation flag.

The irony is that the dyslexic student needs to have clearer notes than his peers, so that main points and categories are easy to scan for. He needs something more than bullet points because it is the example and the detail that often bring the subject matter alive and make it memorable. He finds it hard to remember a string of facts, but where he can visualise and relate to the material he will remember it.

A note for teachers

How central to your teaching is note-taking? If your teaching and the children's learning depend upon it, it is essential for you to look at the underachievers in your classes to see if their weakness stems partly from technical difficulties with handwriting, processing at speed, copying, spelling and short-term memory.

It is very demotivating for students to spend lessons making poor notes, even if they are interested in the subject. These children will need help coping with the note-taking part of your lessons, however inspired your teaching may be.

The questionnaires in Figures 4.1 and 4.2 might form the basis for a discussion about note-taking, both for teachers and for pupils.

Why do you take notes in class?   ✓ or ✗

- Do they help you to understand what the teacher is saying? ☐

- Do they help you to concentrate? ☐

- Do they help you to remember the lesson? ☐

- Are you sure they are accurate? ☐

- Are they a good account of the lesson? ☐

- Are they useful/vital for revision? ☐

Or

- Are they untidy? ☐

- Are they incomplete? ☐

- Are they illegible? ☐

- Are they a poor record of the lesson? ☐

- Are they hopeless to revise from? ☐

- Does taking them stop you from remembering the lesson? ☐

- Does taking them prevent you from asking questions and joining in? ☐

Figure 4.1 Questionnaire for students.

- When you look at a pupil's notes, are you disappointed with their record of your lesson?

- Have you any pupils for whom there is a marked discrepancy between their written work and their oral responses in class?

- Do some children have difficulty copying from the board and listening to an explanation at the same time?

- Are some children too busy catching up on their notes to participate in the lesson?

- Do some children seem to remember less well when they have been taking notes?

- Do you check on pupils' notes and try to suggest alternatives for those who cannot listen, remember, write, organise, précis, understand and participate all at once?

- Do you make sure that poor note-takers have an alternative source of information for essay work and exam revision?

- Do your poor note-takers tend to give up, lose concentration and distract others in the class?

- Would the 'Why do you take notes in class' questionnaire be useful for your pupils?

Figure 4.2 Questionnaire for teachers.

Note-taking practicalities

The problem for the student who is disorganised or has dyslexia or dyspraxia is not merely how to take notes but with what, in what and where to keep them.

Keeping up the supplies

Parents play a pivotal role at this basic level of organisation, even in secondary school. Most will start their children off at the beginning of the term with what they guess is needed, but few may realise the importance of checking supplies and keeping them up throughout the term. The child with organisational weakness is notorious for losing, breaking or lending his kit – even in the first week. Moreover, few teenagers see term-time Saturdays as the ideal opportunity to shop for files, rulers and ink cartridges; nor are they eager to spend their own money in this way. Yet without one crucial item (file paper, laptop battery, pen that works), note-taking, in all subjects, can break down completely and in some may never recover – how then to manage homework, keep track of the topic or revise for exams? The

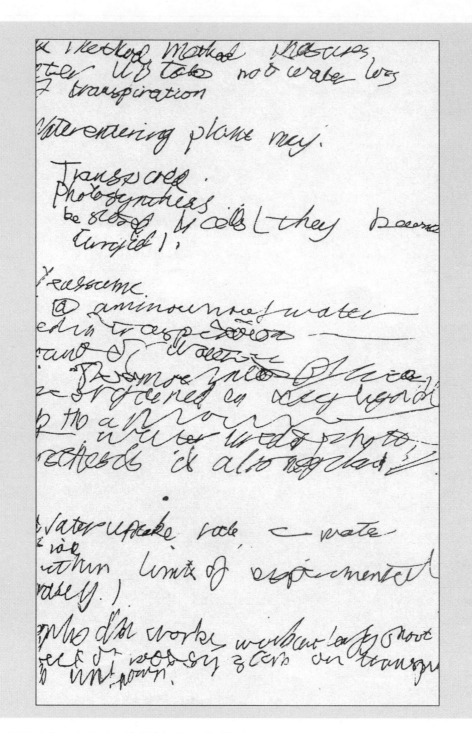

Figure 4.3 On being asked what his biology lesson had been about, the pupil who wrote these notes was unable to remember, saying by way of explanation, 'I never remember a lesson when I've had to write notes.'

consequences are disproportionately disastrous, and the student with dyslexia or dyspraxia is the one least capable of redeeming a situation before it has gone too far.

Teachers of teenagers may well consider this an area that should not have to concern them. However, children with dyslexia live in a state of chaos that is not of their choosing. A sympathetic understanding of this fact should prompt teachers to support their dyslexic pupils, while insisting that nothing gives them the excuse to fall behind with their notes (spare pens and textbook standing by?). The best help lies in teachers finding time to sort out with an individual how he intends to organise himself and then helping him to keep his system going.

Essential gear for taking notes (and for schoolwork in general)

The easiest way to get pupils and their parents to focus on this is to give them a checklist to work from (reissued at half term). As some children with dyslexia may also have dyslexic parents, a list to shop with is an advantage to both (Figure 4.4, page 122).

Filing

Pitfalls

The student with dyslexia or dyspraxia thinks nothing of keeping his notes stuffed randomly into his various pockets. To find one sheet, he may unfold and scatter several others. The one he finds may need ironing (keep iron cool, turn off steam) before he can read or file it. His papers may be stored in heaps under his bed, disintegrating in his bag or crumpled among football boots and crisp packets in the bottom of his school locker. (These lockers are sometimes without shelves or hooks, requiring students to kneel on the floor to delve into the pit of dirty treasures at the bottom. Their unsatisfactory design would appal any bursar, should he inspect them in use. Horizontal rather than vertical lockers would probably work better.)

It is often the case that, even when put away in a conventional ring file, papers (without title or date) drift loose, because the holes tear or the mechanism of the file collapses or because, without a hole punch to hand, they were pushed in loose in the first place. It is hard to respect or learn from such a source. It is also hard to reassemble these papers once they have got out of hand and the curriculum, with its fresh set of notes, has moved on.

One other common pitfall is that of not filing regularly. Papers start to lose their identity if left about for longer than a week. Students may need adult input to keep them to a regular system. An occasional filing homework followed by a teacher check will also help.

Conflicting systems

Sometimes, the disorganised student's preferred filing conflicts with the school's system. This is especially true of dyslexic students who work habitually on word processors. They are unlikely, for instance, to stick notes or homework regularly into an exercise book, although having all their work together securely in one notebook is obviously an excellent notion that probably works very well for others. On the other hand, students with dyslexia who are not word processing as their normal method may want to write all their notes in big hard-backed notebooks, whereas the school expects notes on file paper (easily handed in, extended and rearranged).

If a dyslexic student is taking notes in class on a laptop, while others hand-write, his filing system will also be on the laptop or, if he is fortunate enough to use a computer at home, he will want to download his work into files there. Should he also print hard copies with which to reassure his teacher — how should he keep these and is he likely to maintain this dual system? Any notes handed in and corrected must be kept as hard copy or altered on the screen, otherwise the teacher's efforts to improve them are wasted. Sending and returning by e-mail is an ideal solution.

Note-taking kit – which do *you* need?

- Storage for each subject:
  Exercise books
  Ring binders
  Envelope wallets
  Concertina files
  Box files
  Day file – use in school and transfer notes each evening into subject files
- Dividers
- File paper – lined and plain
- Transparent A4 pockets
- Pencils, rubbers
- Pens (one fine-tipped for annotating texts and handouts)
- Cartridges
- Ink eradicators
- Highlighters
- Rulers – 12" and 6"
- Hole punch
- Hole reinforcers
- Large enough pencil case, or two
- Strong, comfortable backpack or bag – big enough
- Laptop computer – AC adapter, cable connection to school printer, blank disks, spare battery, discreet carry-bag, insurance
- Extension cable
- Tape recorder, dictaphone – batteries, blank tapes, labels
- A3 paper + transparent pockets
- Index Card Box – dividers, lined card and plain
- Felt-tips, pencil crayons
- Multi-coloured biro
- Scissors
- Glue stick
- Card off-cuts
- Paper clips, treasury tags, split pins
- Storage space at home
- Good light in work space

File suggestions:

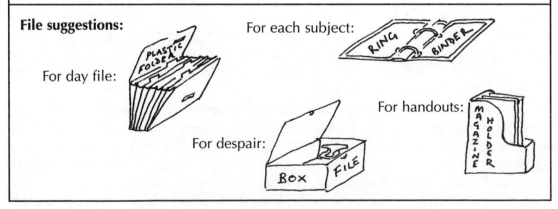

Figure 4.4 Look through this list and decide which items you need. Do you need others that are not listed here?

Find a system that works

Disorganised students must focus on their specific difficulties with filing and solve them; to do so, however, they may need encouragement, suggestions and resources from adults. Although a disorganised student must accommodate his teacher's wishes too, his filing system is most likely to work if he has devised it himself; he alone will know what system he can persevere with and what he can't. Even dropping his papers regularly into subject-labelled box files is better than no system at all. At least everything will be there, including handouts, and in the right order, when it comes to revision. Whatever filing system a student adopts, he should monitor the results and be prepared to try something else if his current system doesn't work. It helps to have an adult with whom to talk this through.

Above all, a student needs to find a way of filing that he can maintain. Filling a gap with photocopied notes from a friend is one thing, but photocopying and returning notes on a regular basis will try the best of friendships – and the organisational skills of both parties.

Far too many secondary school students in general spend precious time taking notes yet end up with incomplete information to work from. Knowing this, teachers could find that any time spent discussing and monitoring the practicalities of note-taking with their classes is time well spent.

'Automaticity'

The ability to perform a task well without thinking about it

The cognitive profile in Figure 4.5 shows the fluctuating levels of competence often associated with specific learning difficulties. It is the range of strength and weakness, rather than where the highs and lows fall on this graph, that is typical of specific learning difficulties.

Weschler Intelligence Scale for Children

Information	8	Picture completion	8
Comprehension	14	Picture arrangement	12
Arithmetic	8	Block design	17
Similarities	17	Object assembly	12
Vocabulary	12	Coding	7
Digit span	8	Mazes	10

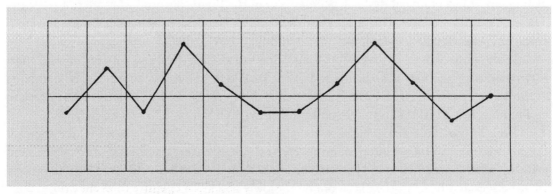

Figure 4.5 The range of cognitive strengths and weaknesses in this typically spiky profile makes multi-tasking in the classroom difficult.

A student with this kind of profile will not be able to perform high-level classroom skills (reading, copying, essay writing, note-taking) with the automatic ease that might be expected from his subskill strengths. These high-level skills that carry classroom work along depend on a fluent, automatic synthesis of several lower-level subskills. Anyone taking notes in a classroom, for instance, probably has to do the activities listed below simultaneously.

Subskills for note-taking:

- listen
- understand
- hold in short-term memory
- select key points
- reject secondary material
- write one point while listening to the next
- arrange on the page
- spell important words – often unfamiliar
- hand-write and punctuate
- process using hand, eye and ear simultaneously
- keep going, fast, for an unspecified length of time

The student with a 'spiky' profile cannot call on this automatic competence. Spelling, remembering, fast writing, layout, each may claim his exclusive attention – blotting out the operation of other skills such as following detail, keeping the big picture in mind or maintaining an appropriate style. His work will falter; he may lose the thread altogether; frustration and anxiety will cloud his concentration. It takes determination and maturity to persevere in the face of such a lack of automaticity.

Research findings confirm this picture

In September 1991, the *New York Times* reported a study that made comparisons between dyslexic and non-dyslexic brains. The study's results, described in the *Proceedings of the National Academy of Sciences*, show that the magnocellular pathways from retina to cortex, the route along which visual information is processed at speed, are 27% smaller and are less well organised in brains of dyslexic people than in the brains of those who are not dyslexic. The result of this reduction in size and organisation is a considerable reduction in speed and efficiency when dyslexic people assimilate information visually.

In the same article, the *New York Times* reported research findings concerning the auditory processing systems in the brains of dyslexic people, which showed that 'fast components of the auditory system were similarly impaired'. Further reference to this area of research can be found in Rack (2001) and Stein and Snowling (2001).

Back in the classroom, what is a secondary school student doing when he takes notes if not attempting to process information received through his eyes and ears? If his visual and auditory systems are smaller and less well organised than those of his classmates, he will process what he sees and hears in the classroom more slowly and less efficiently than they do.

Nicholson and Fawcett (2001) at Sheffield University contribute further evidence for the lack of automatic operation in brains of dyslexic people. Their findings show that the operation of small skills to do with memory, sequencing and the use of language happens, for dyslexic people, at the cortical (i.e. conscious) level, whereas this operation tends to a greater degree to be subconscious, or subcortical, in non-dyslexic people. They describe how processing conducted at a conscious level will be slower, use more blood sugar, tax concentration more severely and the person will tire more quickly than if processing is subconscious. The point is made clear when you think how efficiently we breathe, how effortlessly a professional musician plays scales, how swiftly a good arithmetician calculates, how skilfully a racing driver drives. Co-ordinating a host of subskills to a high level of automaticity still leaves these operators with conscious 'brain space' for further activities, such as thinking, assessing and interpreting, questioning and comparing.

Note-taking is a multi-task

That many students can multi-task well enough to make note-taking worthwhile is remarkable; that dyslexic students can't is almost inevitable. Between these extremes in each classroom, there is every degree of adequate to inadequate note-taking. It is therefore worth a teacher's time to help all his students, not just those with learning difficulties, with their note-taking systems in his particular subject.

Identifying the problems – a teacher's view

The page of notes in Figure 4.6 is the best of a batch taken by six A-level students in an experiment to investigate their individual difficulties when taking notes. The students were art historians. The experiment took place in the spring term before their A-level exams. The topic for note-taking was 'Picasso'. The students were asked to take notes from a short lecture on Picasso and then talk about their particular difficulties in doing so. Ben, who wrote the set of notes in Figure 4.6, has dyslexia. He got a B in his A-level exam.

Ben's notes make it clear, from the start, that his chief difficulty is with spelling. Braque/'brache'/'brach', 'asm'/'ism', 'Cub(e)ism', 'primatuveasm', 'interpentation', 'differacult', 'Gituar' – all illustrate this. What may not be so obvious is the evidence for a common knock-on effect of non-automatic spelling, which drastically reduces the note-taker's interest and understanding of the topic in hand. Ben's problem, as for so many poor spellers, was not simply that he couldn't spell well. More importantly, he couldn't recognise when his spelling was correct. Fearing almost any word he wrote might be wrong and he wouldn't know which, he was more occupied with trying to spell individual words he heard than with taking in meaning as a whole or enjoying an account of Picasso's art. Three attempts at writing the title, 'Picasso', the second one being correct but unrecognised as such, illustrate this problem. The three attempts at a single-word title should also warn that Ben's notes would be lagging behind from the very start of the talk. The subsequent two sets of dates, the first incorrect because only half heard while worrying about spelling 'Picasso', confirm this effect of overload, and illustrate the ongoing inaccuracy and confusion that spelling difficulty may cause.

The tragedy is that a common weakness in one minor skill of note-taking, in this case spelling, may often result in an insufficient record of information, an undeserved dislike of the subject and a reputation for lazy and careless work. As with many dyslexic weaknesses, these consequences in the classroom are disproportionately severe.

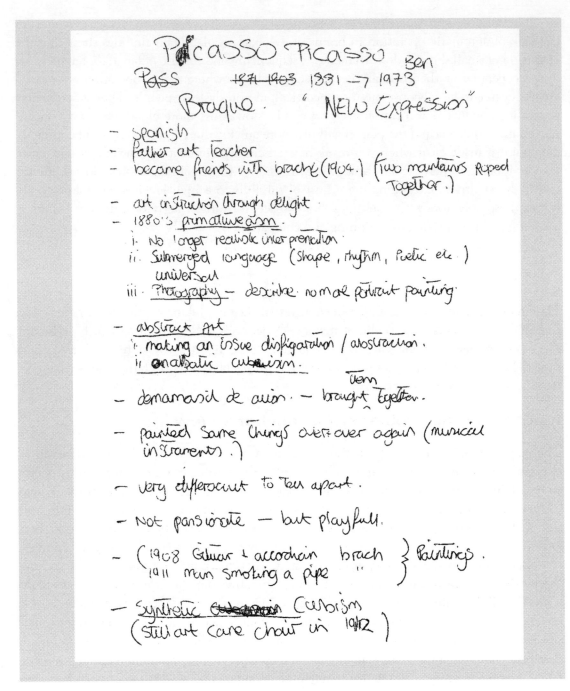

Figure 4.6 Notes written by an A-level student of art history in an experiment to identify problems in note-taking

Identifying the problems – a student's view

In this note-taking experiment, the students were asked to describe their personal difficulties in taking notes from the lecture. Although they mentioned spelling in passing, the aspects of the lecture listed opposite were the ones that, between the six of them, they felt caused the most difficulty.

This lecture had been carefully prepared, and the students' criticisms were startling to the lecturer, especially those centring on fluency and structure. She had given particular thought to both and, in her teaching experience, it had never occurred to her that fluent expression and the *mot juste* might be a drawback. Secondary school teachers in general

---

Summary of students' comments on the Picasso lecture:

The overall reaction was that this was a 'disorganised' talk:

- Unfamiliar topic – no 'landmarks' to take bearings on.

- Unfamiliar vocabulary – technical, foreign, long words.

- No explicit patterns – 'First point... second point... last...'

- No signals – 'This is important...' 'This will amuse you...'

- No visual aids – 'Look, this picture is *Man with Guitar.*'

- No breaks – no chance to interact, physical tension, aching hand.

- Fast, well-expressed delivery – hard to put into own words, no time to become interested, reflect, question, pause or catch up.

---

might teach more effectively if they canvassed students' reactions to their style; it is customary in higher education. As in this case, aspects that they cherish may be the very ones that cause problems for some of their students. Those teachers who rely heavily on note-taking to transfer knowledge to their students may end up questioning this reliance – could there be alternative and better methods, at least for some of the time?

Teach strategies that help with note-taking

Not only is it possible for a teacher to adapt his teaching style, it is also possible for students to learn ways around their difficulties. This is especially successful if strategies are directly related to current work and the whole class can benefit. Here are two suggestions, by way of illustration. It is worth dedicating a lesson to teaching these strategies.

Teach abbreviations

Well-prepared abbreviations make a difference to the note-taking of slow writers and poor spellers, but it may not occur to them to abbreviate words unless they are taught to do so. Their difficulty with writing or spelling seems to make them focus on those skills, rather than on getting round them. If, for instance, it had occurred to Ben to write 'P' for Picasso, 'B' for Braque and 'Prim' for Primativism, and sketch a box for 'Cubism', he might have enjoyed and remembered the lecture, as well as taking more accurate notes about it.

A lesson on abbreviations is helpful for a whole class. Select a suitable textbook page or deliver a very short talk containing relevant technical words and names. Get the class to make a list of words they would like to abbreviate and then discuss alternatives they might use. The lesson could usefully include these pointers:

- Decide abbreviations in advance of note-taking, where possible: very easy when taking notes from a textbook, less so when listening, so develop list from one lesson to the next.
- Keep a 'key' list on A3 fold-out on right-hand side at back of file, as for map symbols in geography. Abbreviations become meaningful if reused.
- Make sure the 'key' words are correctly spelt and keep referring to the list. Don't get into a 'spelt-it-wrong' habit.
- Taking notes on a word processor means the autocorrect facility will give abbreviated words in full.
- Be consistent – use the same abbreviations in all subjects.
- Get to know and use conventional abbreviations, e.g. stat, circs, govt, MP, C20, >, §, &, etc.
- Invent abbreviations for subject-specific words – personal symbols work well, but must be quick.
- Develop 'an ear' for any of these: topic words that repeat, names, technical terms, difficult spellings, very long words, new words it would be an advantage to use.

Figure 4.7 is a sample worksheet using text from David Waugh's geography textbook *The Wider World*. Sheet D in the Worksheet section at the end of this book is a blank version of this page, which can be adapted to teach abbreviations using any text.

Teach signal words

Quite often, 'listening' is a subskill that does not operate automatically for people with dyslexia. Ben's 'primatuveasm', 'interprentation', 'differacult' and 'demanasil de au . . .' are all partly the result of impaired listening. As described by Dr Galaburda (1991) and Professor Tallal (1991), the initial problem is not so much with paying attention or hearing as with discriminating and processing what is heard. However, switching off can often be a secondary consequence for any student who has to make himself listen consciously; the effort becomes too much, especially if he is also falling behind in understanding the topic and taking notes. As a result, school reports for dyslexic students who have an auditory processing problem usually contain complaints about 'lacking concentration' and 'being easily distracted'.

Listening skills worsen when a student with dyslexia either listens in a group – an inevitable part of classroom work – or does not have eye contact with the speaker – head down writing notes. These circumstances lead him to disregard, perhaps not even recognise, the emphasis or direction certain words are signalling, even when accompanied by body language or a change in the speaker's voice. Signal words are often familiar introductory or parenthetic phrases such as 'on the other hand' or 'in addition', easily overlooked in favour of the facts themselves. But most students, once alerted to the idea of signal words in a lecture, lesson or textbook, will start to hear and see them. These words give structure to the content of the lesson, and hearing the signals will make that structure clearer to follow. The resulting notes will be more coherent.

The table on page 130 illustrates categories of common signal words. People with dyslexia may have particular difficulty with the 'sequence' group involving a set order that, although relating information to a time sequence, is often not delivered in chronological order.

Time spent on signal words would be helpful to a whole class in every subject. One way of focusing on these words is to select a suitable textbook page or deliver a very short talk

Abbreviations make note-taking faster
- Which words in this passage would it help to abbreviate and why?
- What symbols might you use for them?
- Could you use these symbols in notes for other subjects?

> **London's Dockland**
>
> During the nineteenth century and up to the early 1950s, London was the busiest port in the world. Because of a series of changes after that, many of them due to improvements in technology, the docks had virtually become abandoned and derelict. By 1981 larger ships could no longer reach the port of London and containerisation did away with the need for large numbers of dockers. One of the first enterprise zones to be created in 1981 was the Isle of Dogs in the heart of London's dockland. By that time the area had very few jobs, the docks had closed, over half the land was derelict, many of the nineteenth-century terraced houses needed urgent repair, transport was poorly developed and there was a lack of basic services, leisure amenities and open spaces. The London Dockland's Development Corporation was set up to try to improve the economic, social and environmental conditions of the area.

Words	Why?	Abbreviation	Use elsewhere
Nineteenth century	Useful convention	C19	✓
London	Repeated 4 times	L	✓
technology	Hard to spell	tek	✓
containerisation	Technical and long	☐	
Enterprise zones	Technical	EZ	
Dock (er/land/s)	Repeated	doc	
terraced	Hard to spell and technical	(symbol)	✓
Leisure amenities	Hard to spell and technical	(symbol)	
London Dockland Development Corporation	Acronym – useful convention	LDDC	
economic	Very common word	econ	✓
Environment(al)	Very common word	Env, envl	✓

Figure 4.7 Practise making abbreviations. Prepare them in advance of note-taking. Use them consistently in any context.

Continuing signals = There are more ideas to come: And, also, too, in addition, similarly, furthermore, one reason… another reason…
Change of direction signals = Watch out, I'm doubling back: However, in contrast, although, the opposite, nevertheless, conversely, on the other hand, yet, but
Sequence signals = There is an order to these ideas: First… second… in the first place, then, before, after, later, until, earlier
Illustration signals = Here's what it means in reality: For example, for instance, to illustrate, such as, in the same way, specifically, just like
Emphasis signals = This is important: Above all, major development, significant factor, primary concern, main idea, remember that, basic concept, important to note

laced with signal words. Get the class to jot down the ones they see or hear and then discuss what signals are given and how they might help with note-taking.

There are two additional advantages to appreciating signal words. The first is that they are just as useful to writing as to listening and reading. Once students are aware of them, they can make deliberate use of signal words to guide readers through their own essays. The second is that they make effective memory pegs when filling in notes after a lesson. Questions such as 'What was *another method?*' or 'What came after *alternatively?*' are likely to trigger the answer.

The table opposite gives a sample worksheet using a paragraph from *Key Science Chemistry* by Eileen Ramsden. Sheet E in the Worksheet section is a blank version of this to be used for teaching signal words in any subject.

Systems for note-taking

Noting one point while listening to the next is the most sophisticated element in note-taking. It requires students to see the importance of each point in relation to a whole that they have yet to hear completed. Each note written is an act of faith, and often the student's mind is partly taken up with the wish to change what he has just written – while simultaneously putting down the next point and listening to the one beyond. (Try worrying about spelling and layout in the midst of that, remembering the previous point or asking a question!)

One common fault that exacerbates the difficulty is that of writing too much. The wish to record everything in case it turns out to be important and the challenge of summarising a well-expressed idea press the note-taker to try to scribble everything down.

Many students, not just those with dyslexia, need practice in selecting and summarising important ideas from books or the spoken word.

As the spoken word comes in an auditory sequence – present only for a fleeting second – its meaning is dependent on the listener's memory or anticipation of groups of other words. It is by far the hardest method of communication to take notes from. Practice in a situation

---

Signal Words will help with organising notes

To practise recognising signal words in chemistry:
- Which words give structure to the information?
- How would they affect note-taking?

Composite materials

The reason why unreinforced concrete has low tensile strength is that it contains microscopic pores. To reduce porosity and increase tensile strength, *one solution* is to drive air out of the powder by vibrating it *before* mixing with water. *Another method* is to add, to the cement–water mixture, materials, *e.g.* sulphur or resin, which will fill the pores. *Alternatively*, a water-soluble polymer can be added to the cement–water mixture to fill the spaces left between cement particles. *Other* filler materials, *e.g.* glass fibre, silicon carbide, aluminium oxide particles or fibres, have been used in the polymer–cement mixture.'

Words	Effect on note-taking
The reason why	Be sure to include this
One solution	Expect more than one solution
Before	Make sequence in procedure clear/look out for any method implying 'after'
Another method	Link with note on 'one solution'
e.g. (twice)	Decide whether examples are important here
Alternatively	Note what is different about this solution/link with 'one solution' and 'another method'
Other	Extension of previous method, new method or just further examples of fillers?

---

where the notes taken, despite being on a current topic, are not at all important will encourage students to take risks and experiment. Some suggestions are given below.

Keywords

A class should experiment with identifying keywords and then have time to discuss them. This will sharpen their ability to choose well. They should see how much detail they can remember by going through their selected keywords. Will they act as an efficient trigger for that information after a few days or weeks? Identifying keywords means rejecting all but the very few words that carry essential meaning; it's a form of auditory skimming and takes practice and confidence. Pupils may find that they are selecting certain parts of speech – nouns and verbs will probably predominate – and should listen for syntax as well as for content. Taking keyword notes can involve a writer in thinking of his own summary word to stand for a sentence or two, as well as making a selection of the speaker's words. All of this, needless to say, is a great deal easier when taking keyword notes from a book.

Highlighting

This popular form of note-taking is limited to books and papers owned by the note-taker. Occasionally, the font may be too small for accurate marking. The minimal physical activity and swift progress that make highlighting popular are also a drawback – students may be involved in comparatively little multisensory processing and it is possible to highlight a text while half thinking of something else. In this relaxed state, students often highlight too much of the text or miss key points.

In a chapter in *Dyslexia: Integrating Theory and Practice* Virginia Kelly describes an exercise to improve highlighting technique, see the table below.

Two-step highlighting:

Whenever practicable, make an enlarged copy of the text

1. Do initial highlighting

2. Using a second colour, go over sheet again highlighting as few words as possible

•   Both versions may be useful:
      Reduced sheet – as memory triggers
      Expanded sheet – for revision of detail

•   Final step – discuss distinctions between the sets of highlighted words (vital
               if process of note-taking is to be understood and improved)

Exercises in highlighting and selecting keywords give students a chance to think about their note-taking skills in general and improve them.

Mind-mapping

Mind-mapping during a lesson or lecture

Taking mind-map notes during a lesson is not for beginners. If the student is an experienced mind-mapper and his teacher gives structured lessons, it is an excellent method of recording and organising: a branch created for each new topic, subtopics inserted, notes added, symbols incorporated. The nature of the operation encourages the student to summarise, rather than write every word. The map format allows the mapper to return to a topic (as a teacher often does), to link topics visually, to 'see' the sequence and to view the 'whole picture' of the subject on one page – all of which may suit a pupil with dyslexia much better than linear notes. Certainly, the end product will be more memorable for many dyslexic students.

However, it is a sophisticated operation that suits some pupils, some teaching styles and some subjects better than others. The method is perfect for some dyslexic students and is therefore well worth teaching and encouraging (Figure 4.8).

Mind-mapping from notes or a textbook

This is much more achievable because the time element is removed. It is therefore a good place to start with mind-mapping (see pages 58–59).

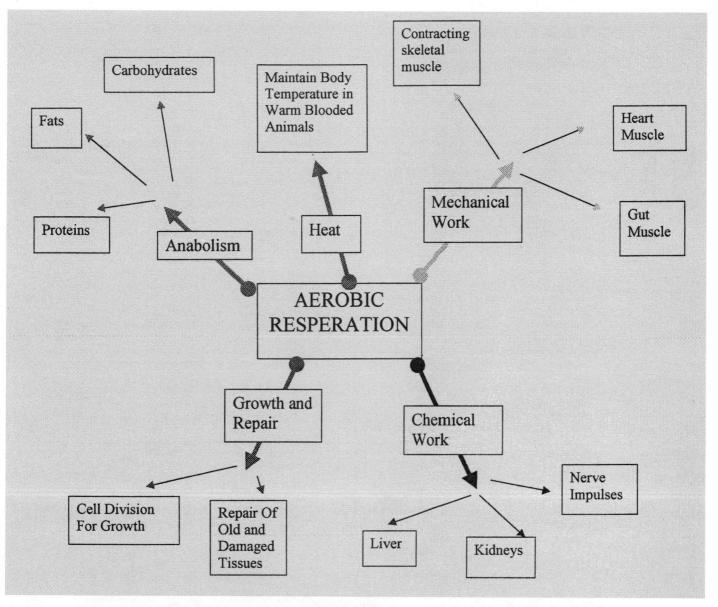

Figure 4.8 Aerobic respiration: Tom was able to mind-map these notes on his laptop in class as easily and as quickly as others wrote them linearly by hand. This was partly due to the clear structure of his teacher's lesson and partly to his own high level of computer skills.

Making notes of notes or notes from a textbook – tasks often set for revision or homework – can be done almost without thinking. The resulting notes are often just a more boring version of the original – all the interesting (and therefore memorable) bits removed. Mind-mapping, on the other hand, involves a great deal of processing – the reader has to visualise, categorise and organise. When he has finished, he has a map that he can visualise when he needs to recall the information (see Figure 4.9).

Making questions, not notes, from a textbook

As the pupil reads each paragraph in his textbook he should ask himself, 'What questions are answered here?' and write them down (Figure 4.10).

(a)

The *Mary Rose*

The *Mary Rose* was finally raised from the floor of the Solent on 11 October 1982 by the giant crane Tog Mor. The ship was brought back to a dry dock in Portsmouth Naval Base so the long process of conservation could begin. Initially this involves spraying the ship with chilled water and maintaining a low temperature and high humidity in the specially constructed ship hall. Eventually chemicals will be added to the water which will preserve and stabilise the ship's timbers. Only then will the sprays be turned off.

The remains of the ship's galley, or kitchen, were found, along with many cooking utensils. The bones of cattle were discovered stored in casks, showing that animals were butchered to provide standard portions, or rations, to feed the ship's crew. Items of woollen and leather clothing representing both fashionable and working garments, were also recovered. After careful study it is possible for experts to say exactly how these were made. The size and shape of the garments also tell us something about the physical stature of the men on board. The study of their skeletons indicates a great deal about the men who served aboard the Mary Rose. Their average height was 1.71 metres but some were over 1.85 metres tall. Most were between 18 and 23 years of age, but

there were also some young teenagers who were 13 or 14 years old, and some older men as well. Many of them had suffered from malnutrition in their early youth. The barber/surgeon's chest contained medicines and surgical equipment, as well as a large barber's bowl. The surgeon had to meet all the needs of the 450 men who normally served on board the ship. One pot of ointment contains the fingerprint of the barber/surgeon still intact.

A large collection of carpenter's tools were found in a cabin on the main deck, including planes, augers and mallets of various kinds. These would have been used to repair the ship and modify the fittings in the cabins and the storage compartments. A number of musical instruments, including fiddles, pipes and drum, have been found on board and replicas have been made and played. Games including dice, backgammon and Nine Men's Morris were also found preserved in the fine silt of the Solent.

The most spectacular objects are perhaps the weapons, which range from the heavy bronze and iron guns to the longbows and arrows used by the archers. Because all this material was discovered when the ship was at action stations, we are able to study how the ship prepared for battle.

(b)

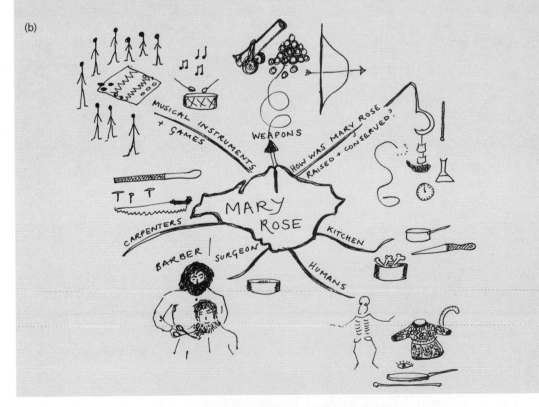

Figure 4.9 (a) This is part of a chapter on the *Mary Rose* that David had to read in preparation for a test. He decided to mind-map it to help him remember the facts. (b) Visualising and then drawing the symbols and pictures helped David to revise very effectively. In the test he was able to re-visualise the map and mention all the points he had thought about while he drew it.

QUESTIONS	**Energy flow inside an Eco System**
1) What energy do producers use to make organic matter?	Energy enters on Eco systems in the form of sunlight. Producers use this energy during PHS to make organic matter (for example cellulose, protein, glucose).
2) Give an example of organic matter.	
3) What kind of energy is released from organic matter during respiration?	This organic matter then contains chemical energy which can be released during respiration. When one organism eats another, the chemical energy of the eaten one is transferred. Hence energy can be said to flow through a food chain.
4) What happens to the energy when the organism is eaten?	
5) What percentage of energy passes between each level.	However energy is lost at each level and only 10% passes between each level.

Figure 4.10 The questions can be short factual questions, as above, or more complex questions where it is the implications of the material that need to be probed.

Making questions is one of the most valuable revision techniques on several counts:

- The student will have to understand and process the material very thoroughly in order to produce relevant questions that will elicit a full reply.
- The student will have a list of questions to answer at the end of his reading session and again before any examination or test. This builds in the concept of reviewing.
- Tackling the questions will tell him how much he really does remember – whereas just reading the notes can make a student feel that he *knows* the material when in fact he is only *recognising* it.
- Answering the questions, especially aloud or on paper, will give him practice in expressing himself on the particular topic, using his own words and the appropriate phraseology and vocabulary – a much more useful exercise as a preparation for writing than just reading through the notes.
- The student who uses the technique is aware, even when he first writes his notes, that they are going to be turned into questions – this helps give the notes a relevance and focus from the start. This will encourage active reading.

The Cornell system for taking notes

The main feature of the Cornell system is that the way the notes are laid out initially should invite further work at a later stage. It works well whether they are notes taken in class, notes from a book or notes for revision, and it can be done both by a pupil who is writing his notes on a computer or by one who is writing by hand.

Instead of having a narrow margin on the left side of the page, there should be a wide margin (perhaps 7 cm) that, in the future, could accommodate summary headings for each paragraph, pictures, questions to test his knowledge of the passage at a later date or symbols to remind the pupil of the main point (Figure 4.11).

Philip (the Fair) 1285 - 1314

(Documentary evidence)
Boox: Daniel Waley: General
J.R. Strayer: France: Philip the Fair
Lot and Fawtier: the Capetians
Elizabeth Hallam: thematic

Philips Character: 'The culmination of the
                medieval French monarchy' (Strayer)

Bernard Saisset: 'The king is like an owl, the
                most beautiful of birds, but worth nothing.'
                Not alone in this, most commented that he
                was aloof.

Geoffrey of Paris found fault with Philip the Fair:
- Allowed himself to fall under sway of his
  advisors
- St Denisian writers (Capetian hagiographers)
- -Ivo of St Denis felt he was 99% great – but
  too gentle . . . .

However:
1. He arrested the Pope
2. Burned leaders of the Templars
3. Castrated daughter's lovers

We can use documentary evidence to work out
whether Philip or his advisors were responsible.

He spent loads of time hunting (all the meetings
were at huntey places). As he got older his interest
in hunting lessened.

He gained an interest in works of piety (devotion
to Christianity in his case). We know this because
he endowed monasteries (lots of 'em).

Near his death concerned for his own soul –
French kings have a tendency to worry about this.

Figure 4.11 Part of a page of notes taken in class on a word processor.
The left-hand margin has been used at a later date for picture symbols
to make the page easier to remember and to encourage the note-taker
to visualise.

This way of organising notes makes sense for any student who is intending to use them in the future for revision. There is only a minority of students for whom just reading through their notes is an efficient way of revising – most need to process the material in some way. For someone with dyslexia who needs to review his work two or three times for it to be secure in his long-term memory, the sequence could be as follows:

1.　Write the notes.
2.　Later . . . formulate the questions, summaries or symbols.
3.　Later . . . test yourself or be tested.
4.　Then return to the questions again before the examination, or attempt to re-visualise the page and talk about it.

Tables/Charts

Before a well-trained dyslexic student takes notes from a book or lesson, he will choose a suitable format. This format mirrors the approach he needs to take to the information he is recording. He asks himself, 'What am I taking these notes for?' The answer will prompt the use of one format rather than another. If, for instance, he wants to record information, he may select the Cornell format. If he has an essay title to research he may prefer to mind-map.

If he is looking for material to construct both sides of an argument or to make a comparison, he may like to use a table or chart. The simpler the table format, the better; a generic structure of three columns with appropriate headings is adaptable and quick to draw up by hand, as in Figure 4.12(a).

FOR	AGAINST	INTERESTING

Figure 4.12 (a) A basic table for organising notes. This format has the advantage of discouraging long-winded note-taking.

Even easier is a table using 'Tables and Borders' in the Word menu. The table over the page, Figure 4.12(b) is one for 'What are the arguments for and against taking notes on a computer?'

Virginia Kelly lists Edward De Bono's suggested headings – PMI for Plus, Minus and Interesting, TAN for Then and Now, SAD for Similarities and Differences – to stress the flexibility of this approach to note-taking. An additional advantage is that a table restricts any tendency to write full sentences.

Copying

So many notes are taken in this form. So many dyslexic learners cannot do it either neatly or quickly. Nor can they follow the meaning, still less an explanation, while copying. This form of note-taking is another instance of a multi-task. It trades on a cluster of low-level skills, some of which may not be automatic, overloading the dyslexic brain and causing one or more of the component skills to break down (Figure 4.13).

For	Against	Interesting
• Automatic note-taking formats, e.g. bullet points, Cornell, automatic hierarchies • Variety of fonts and size • Easily edited • Expandable • No worry about spelling or no mess • Automatic writing means more brain space for thinking • Re-sequencing for order of importance • Can programme automatic expansion of abbreviations • Can look at board or teacher while taking notes	• Cost/availability of computer • Need for automatic typing skills • May be the only one in the class	• Colour • Clarity • Speed • Flexibility • Safe filing • Later reworking no mess

Figure 4.12 (b) This spatial layout gives visual emphasis to the strengths and weaknesses of each case.

Teach techniques to help with copying

As copying is a skill learned in childhood, secondary schoolteachers have reasonably assumed that their students will be proficient at it. However, a proportion of every class will have difficulties, so certain skills in copying are worth identifying and teaching.

As always, a multisensory approach to the problem is effective – engaging voice to support memory and finger to guide eye. Even more helpful is to teach the habit of recognising a difficulty, looking for ways round it, then using the methods that work.

Subvocalising

If visual and spatial skills are weak and working memory limited or unreliable, saying the words to be copied, while looking at them, and again while writing them, will improve accuracy and fluency. This improvement will, in turn, raise a student's confidence in his copying, and reinforce the strategy.

As it is impractical to speak aloud in class or in examinations, students learn to subvocalise – i.e. speak under their breath – provided they move lips and tongue. Muscles in the mouth have contributory memory and the rhythm of the spoken words or syllables further increases the impact on working memory. Together, eye, mouth and ear transfer more words, from board to pen, with greater speed and accuracy than eye alone will do. There is a danger of teachers interfering with this strategy if they are explaining while students are speaking to themselves – students may hear neither voice properly. Copying will also be easier if teachers talk about the lines that they have just written on the board, not the one they are in the middle of writing.

Subskills for copying from the board:	Automaticity required in:
• Find and focus on the particular words to copy from the board – unfamiliar content, hand-written	• Visual perception and spatial skills
• Decide how many words, syllables, letters to store in short-term memory	• Segmentation, sequencing, relating parts to whole, syntax
• Note layout, spelling, punctuation	• Visual perception and memory
• File in short-term memory and look away from board	• Working memory – storing
• Find and focus on last words copied onto page of notes	• Spatial recall
• Recall text from the board	• Working memory – recall
• Arrange new material, hand-write, spell, punctuate, while remembering	• Spatial and motor skills, hand/eye co-ordination, auditory, visual and semantic memory.
• Rediscover place on board	• Visual perception
-----------------------	-----------------------
• Repeat fluently, legibly. Understand and remember the ideas	• Speed of processing

Figure 4.13 A breakdown of the activities and subskills necessary for efficient copying.

Finger guide

Where spatial difficulties impede copying, one solution is to keep a non-writing finger pointing at the spot on the page to which the eye should return from the board. Repeatedly 'finding the place' and refocusing on the interrupted writing can cause a dyslexic copier to drop a long way behind the rest of the class. Patiently allowing more time sometimes helps slow writers not merely to catch up but also to speed up. The opportunity to try a helpful strategy can bring confidence and improved speed in its wake.

Near copying from a book

Using a finger guide or piece of card, this time on the text to be copied, is helpful; so again is subvocalising. The position of the text to be copied in relation to the writing paper or computer screen is worth considering. Arrange this in advance of copying – having broken the spine of a book that will not stay open and having bought a copy-holding attachment for computers.

Word processing

This is by far the best way to solve copying problems, provided the student can touch type. With his eye focused on the board or book, while his fingers type, he will copy with a degree of accuracy far greater than if he is constantly looking away and trying to remember the words to be copied. Instead of his usual position trailing laboriously behind, he will not merely be up with the class, he is likely to be ahead of it. Automatic 'writing' will free him up to listen as he types. Typing gives a greater chance to understand the lesson and even join in a discussion – probably his best way of learning.

Figure 4.14 shows the contrast between one boy's actual French – these are his answers in a test – and his ability to copy it fairly accurately, accents included (even if some are wrong), from the board, so long as he uses his laptop and his touch-typing skills. The gulf between the two pieces of work illustrates how vital automatic copying is if there is to be any hope of a dyslexic student like Nicholas learning French. Without a laptop his copying was nearly as inaccurate as his test answers; he could learn nothing from the board.

Part of Nicholas's French test:	Nicholas copying from the board:

Journal en France

Mardi:	Je me suis levé à cinq heures j'ai voyagé en bateau à Caen. Je suis arrivé au château vers quatre heures et demi.
Mercredi:	nous avons visité un musée du cidre. nous sommes allés á un autre musé-du fromage. On a joué au foot derriére les dortoirs du soir.
Jeudi:	Quelques garçons se sont levés de bonne heure (early) pour aller á la boulangerie. On est allé á un collége á Falaise pour assister á des cours. Aprés on regardé le grand château.
Vendredi:	noue avons conduit à Bayeux pour voir...

Figure 4.14 A hand-written French test contrasting with typed diary entries copied from the board illustrates how useful a laptop and good typing skills can be in helping a dyslexic student to make progress in learning foreign languages.

More extreme measures

When all else fails, and copying remains a necessary part of the learning, it is important to keep trying for a solution. Teachers could:

- give their notes as a handout for dyslexic students (or all their students) to make their own with additional comments, questions, diagrams and colour.

- organise the regular copying of a good set of notes. This will require a reliable system for giving and returning the notes and a place to copy (one that does not require a student to produce money each time).

- recommend an additional textbook with page references for the current topic. Dyslexic students who urgently need a textbook version of their lessons often either cannot find their way to a matching section in the book or find that the match between lesson and text is too tenuous for them to benefit from looking it up. They try it once and then settle for the impression that their textbook is 'not much use'. Teachers can give valuable help by supervising pupils while they get to know their way round the book and come to make use of its support.

- give careful, detailed directions to a website.

- be prepared to have their lessons recorded – if the student is, in turn, prepared to listen to the tape and take notes from it in his own time. Many dyslexic students wait for home-time to digest topics that they have been taught at school. Tape recordings are valuable to these students, particularly if the teacher takes charge of the recorder, selecting crucial bits of the lesson and changing the tape when necessary.

- suggest the student simply listens to the lesson or dictation and follows what is on the board, without the distraction of writing. The extract below is taken from a biology teacher's note to the tutor of a boy in year 10. It confirms that 'just listening' can suit some learners.

To Tutor
From Biology Teacher
Re: Edward in Year 10

Thanks for your note. As you know I've been having problems with Edward too – principally his lack of organisation and inability to write notes in class at anywhere near an appropriate speed... The note-taking remains a problem and I imagine that he will have many problems in exams writing at speed. This will definitely put him at a disadvantage.

At my suggestion, in today's lesson he took no notes at all and simply listened and participated. The change was immediate. Where before he would be running 5 minutes behind the rest of the class he was now well ahead and was invariably the first one to put up his hand; with the right answer to boot!

I have suggested that he adopt this strategy in future biology lessons and arrange to copy a 'good student's notes'.

In any event he will, I feel, require extra time next year in the GCSEs.

With dyslexic students principally, but not exclusively, in mind, the table below is a checklist from the teacher's perspective.

Can you avoid these?	These are helpful:
• writing illegibly on the board	• taking notes in regularly and giving practical advice on improving them
• rubbing the top lines off to make room for more writing, so the spatial sequence is confused	• allowing class time to experiment with note-taking formats
• giving an explanation while writing, back to the class, a slightly different version on the board	• welcoming laptops as useful to note-taking
• giving homework in a hurry at the end of a lesson while some students are still finishing notes	• making sure that the note-taking that helps most members of a class doesn't destroy your subject for the one or two who do not have automatic note-taking skills

Audio-tapes

Any students who enjoy listening and speaking or have poor short-term memories or slow hand–eye co-ordination, or who have none of these but understand the value of multisensory learning, should include the use of audio-tapes among their note-taking strategies. They adapt well to a variety of situations. A suitable tape-recorder or CD player, together with batteries/cables, blank tapes and a consistent labelling routine, need to be readily available.

Taking notes from audio-tapes

High school and university students in America who are dyslexic qualify to have their textbooks or course packs read onto tape. These audio-tapes put students in a position to follow the text while listening, to replay the information as often as they need and to take notes from the tapes at their own speed.

In Britain, teachers, relatives, friends or students themselves can transfer curriculum material from page or lesson to audio-tape and thereby access the same advantages. Once prepared by teachers in school, such tapes become a permanent department resource, copiable for any student who would find them useful. Listening Books Young People's Library (Figure 4.15) has put current GCSE history books on audio-tape as part of their general catalogue.

The idea that listening is somehow not as good as reading has been put to flight by an explosion of commercial books on tape at every level of adult sophistication. To combine listening, reading and note-taking, at a personal speed, could turn study into pleasure for a surprising number of students, dyslexic or not.

Figure 4.15 Listening Books Young People's Library has begun to record curriculum material, but any teacher, family member or friend can make recordings that help with note-taking.

Taking notes on audiotapes

This is an excellent strategy for anyone who, for whatever reason, wishes to avoid writing. A student can improve his class notes or make notes on a book by dictating, again at his own speed, onto tape. Tapes are a good place to collect references, quotations and ideas for course work or a dissertation. All they require is meticulous attention to labelling and storage to make them a sympathetic resource for subsequent writing and revision.

Taking notes from videos

The problem with taking notes from videos

Videos make excellent teaching material. They are, however, hostage to a cultural attitude that classes all videos as entertainment, an easy option and a reason to relax. This attitude discourages vigorous mental processing or alert note-taking. The need to pull classroom blinds and turn off the light adds further good reason to abandon serious note-taking and lean back. Finally, the flow of interesting action makes students resent any teacher-imposed interruption for writing or reflection.

One solution is to preview keywords and topics on a skeleton mind-map, before a class settles down to watch. Students can reasonably be asked to recognise and tick these previewed topics as they appear on the video. There is no set sequence to a mind-map, so topics can receive several ticks in random order as the video unfolds.

Figure 4.16 is an example of a skeleton mind-map for students to tick while they watch a video on the Cold War. It is worth spending preview time saying and spelling keywords – in this case unfamiliar names – and touching on their relevance, so that hearing them on the video later causes recognition rather than an impulse to ignore. As a result of this preview focus, students are more likely to use the right vocabulary when they talk or write about the subject later.

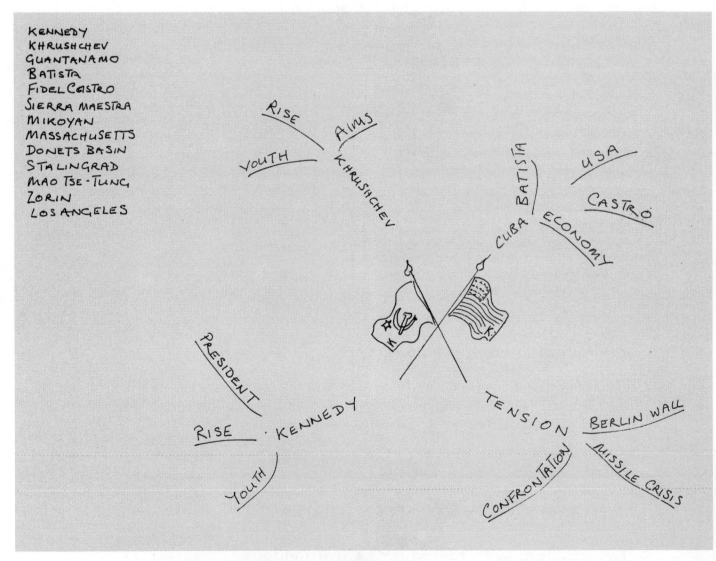

Figure 4.16 Give pupils a skeleton map to tick as they watch a video. Preview names with them before watching. Fill in details on the map during discussion afterwards. A3 plain paper is ideal for this note-taking format.

Creating a preview mind-map before watching the video follows an established principle for remembering, namely the technique of laying down mental velcro on which to stick a second layer of information and detail at a later date. This provides the first step of a 'forgetting curve' routine. Recognising previously mapped topics on the video and then reviewing them in detail, either at the end of the same session or at the start of the next, acts as the second and third steps of the 'forgetting curve'.

One way of reviewing a video is to copy the skeleton mind-map, on which students have ticked topics during the showing, onto the classroom board. As students remember bits of the video and volunteer details to add to each branch on the class map, there is time for all to fill in their own personally drawn version. Fresh copies of the skeleton, on A3 plain paper, would invite full coloured in-fill and give plenty of space to include symbols and images. In the creation of such a mind-map, students re-visualise much of the video, extract and categorise information and express it in their own words and images. This sociable and multisensory review is excellent for memory and capitalises on a classroom activity that already starts with an unusual expectation of pleasure!

Laptops and note-taking

Taking notes on a computer during lessons at school or lectures at college presupposes owning or having the use of a laptop. This is a very large investment for a family, taking into account that they will also have to buy a printer and make sure that the person with dyslexia learns to touch-type. Security from damage and theft is obviously a problem too.

The Prime Minister is keen that every family should have a computer – for a family with a dyslexic pupil, a laptop would be the best choice. It can be used wherever the pupil is – in school as well as at home. Sharing a family computer often means that the child cannot use it when he needs to or has to use it in a room where it may be difficult to work.

Some local authorities provide laptops for those pupils whose Statement recommends it, but at the moment (2003) there is very uneven provision throughout the country. Some schools and authorities either do not have the funds or do not recognise the value of a laptop to a pupil with dyslexia; some provide the machine, but not the touch-typing training that should go with it. Educational psychologists are, however, becoming increasingly aware of the enormous advantage of a laptop and touch-typing training for dyslexic students and recommend both on their Statements.

The national picture is improving all the time, but for a secondary schoolchild tackling his GCSE or A/S or A-level courses *now*, next year may be too late. This may be the moment when his handwriting and literacy difficulties, and his copying and note-taking problems, may make him lose motivation because of his lack of success.

English, history, geography, economics, general studies, religious studies and history of art are subjects where the value of the laptop is most obvious. Essay writing and note-taking are necessary skills in these subjects, and for this reason many pupils with dyslexia avoid them, choosing mathematics and science subjects wherever possible within the curriculum. These choices are being made all the time, often for negative reasons, but they may not be the right choices, and they do not solve the problems pupils are having with writing and note-taking – skills that they may need as students in later life.

Using a laptop will not solve all note-taking problems but will help with some of them.

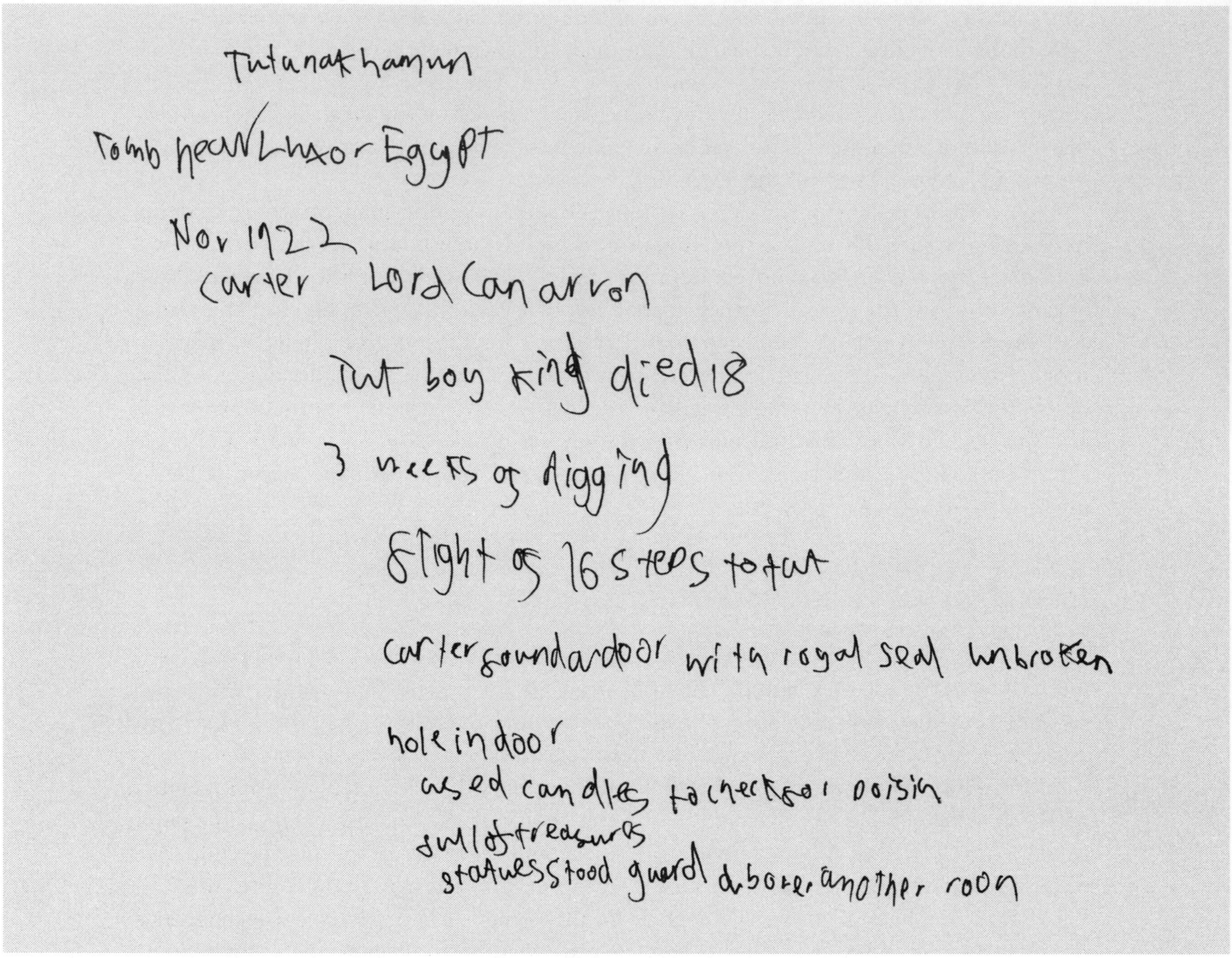

Figure 4.17 'I'll be on a level playing field at last!' was this dyspraxic pupil's comment just before using his laptop in the classroom for the first time.

Speed

Dyslexic pupils who have hand–eye co-ordination and spelling problems tend to write too slowly to be effective note-takers. Their notes will be incomplete, and they will constantly lag behind what the teacher is talking about. Touch-typing will enable them to double or treble their speed (Figure 4.17).

Pupils with short-term memory difficulties will tend to write too fast – trying to get down every word the teacher says before they forget. They can't trust themselves to be able to listen, remember, summarise and then write. Their notes will probably be untidy, unstructured, incomplete and unusable (Figure 4.18).

Legibility

With a word processor, words will at least be legible, even if they are wrongly spelt. And you can't forget to dot an 'i' or cross a 't' when you are typing!

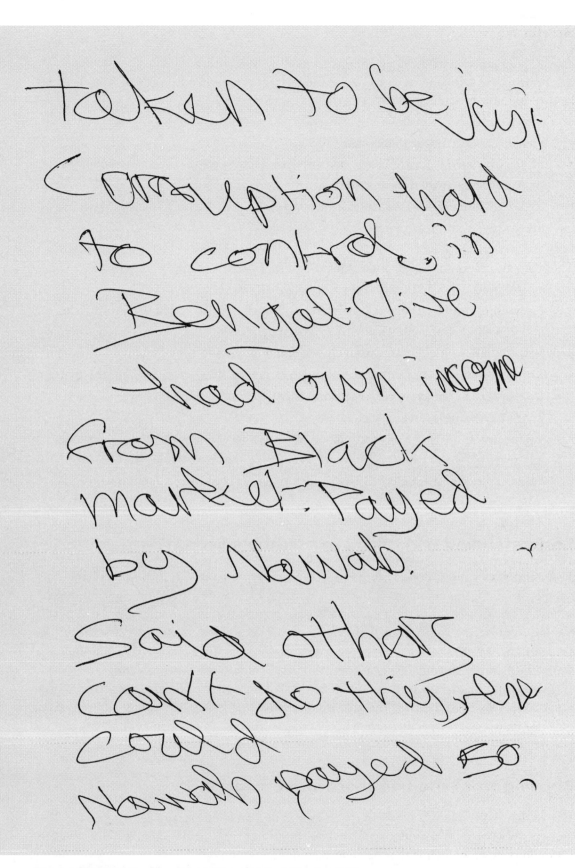

Figure 4.18 One of 12 pages of notes taken during a history lesson. To Ben, what the teacher was saying was just a string of words, and he wrote down as many as he could remember – but he couldn't take in the meaning while he was writing and knew practically nothing about Clive of India after the lesson.

Spelling

There are obvious short-term advantages to spelling in having a spellchecker built into the word-processing software, but experience shows that using a word processor can also bring long-term improvements to a dyslexic student's spelling:

- Fingers can learn to spell automatically.
- Having the word corrected at the moment when he is wondering about its spelling, rather than a week later when the teacher marks the work, is a more effective way of learning it.
- Repeatedly seeing the image of the correct word on his screen, rather than his own misspelling, reinforces correct spelling.

There are also more subtle advantages for the poor speller:

- As spelling can be corrected later, with or without a spellchecker, speed of writing and flow of ideas for someone with dyslexia need not be affected by anxieties about how to spell.
- Knowing that the word processor will earmark any spelling errors for him, the dyslexic student, instead of avoiding using words that he cannot spell, will have the confidence to risk using a wider vocabulary.
- 'Autocorrect' on 'Word' is programmed to correct most common spelling mistakes and reversals – and can be set to correct any word that a particular student with dyslexia tends to misspell. It is especially useful for unfamiliar or foreign words and subject-specific vocabulary.

Understanding and taking part in the lesson

The child who cannot cope with hand-written notes will get very little out of the class; unable to follow the argument while he is writing, he will not, therefore, be able to contribute to any discussion of the topic. In any case, poor note-takers usually spend every pause for discussion trying to catch up with their notes. The problem is often most severe in science lessons, where the teacher is giving a crucial explanation (rather than information) while children are writing. Using a laptop efficiently eliminates this problem.

Touch-typing makes writing an automatic skill for dyslexic students – as hand writing is for non-dyslexic students. If the skill is automatic, this lessens the amount of processing that the brain has to do to achieve what should be the purely mechanical part of the task, making it possible for the student to listen better.

Copying from the board or from a book

The student with dyslexia who can touch-type is at a great advantage because he can keep his eyes on what he is copying, which makes for greater speed and accuracy. This solves the common copying problems that beset such students:

- Getting material from the board before the teacher wipes it off to make room for more writing or diagrams.

- Copying inaccurately and frequently losing his place.
- Copying homework details from the board.

Reluctance to read through and correct hand-written notes

Very often students with dyslexia have difficulty making sense of their own notes. Omissions, poor handwriting and not having heard what the teacher was talking about while they were writing make it an unrewarding experience. However, these are the very students who need to check their notes, for accuracy, and to reinforce their memory.

Word-processed notes can be read easily, corrected, augmented, reduced, reorganised – each of which is useful in involving the student in processing the information.

Organising, filing, dating, categorising notes

Keeping control of notes, especially those on sheets of paper, is more than many students with dyslexia can manage. Notes are very vulnerable to loss and deterioration in the time between writing them and filing them – especially when they are undated and mixed with notes from other subjects and photocopied sheets. They become crumpled, difficult to identify and often lost (Figure 4.19).

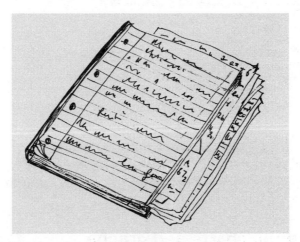

Figure 4.19 A common filing method: notes stuffed into the back of a pupil's pad.

Word-processed notes lend themselves to easy filing and retrieval. They can be automatically named and dated when the pupil uses a template, and automatic saving is an integral part of most word-processing packages. Backing up notes on disk, another computer or the school network is a necessary discipline (Figure 4.20).

Presentation of work

Hand–eye co-ordination, and spatial and sequencing difficulties, will contribute to the poor presentation of hand-written notes. This can be intensely frustrating for the student with dyslexia who, as any other pupil, would like to produce a piece of work that he can be proud of.

A pupil using a word processor can choose the overall look of his notes either before he starts or after he has written them – a font and font size that he finds easy to read, line spacing, paragraphing style; having these choices encourages him to take more pride in his notes.

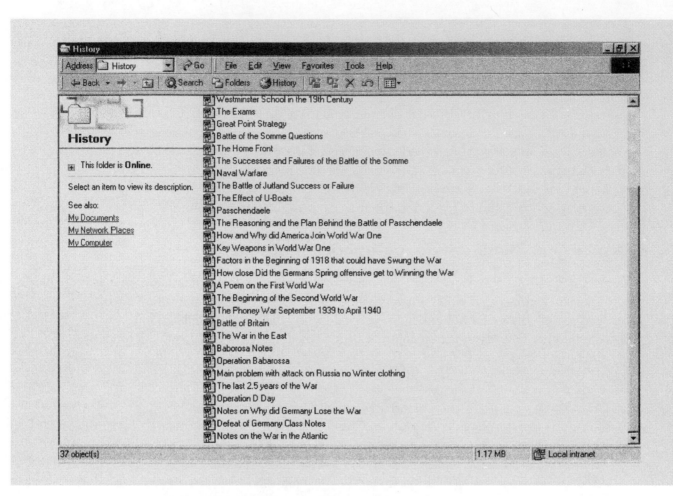

Figure 4.20 Screenshot of a pupil's history file. This filing facility can transform a dyslexic pupil's control over his daily life. To file his work in the order in which he wrote it the student should click 'View' → 'List'→ 'Arrange icons' → 'By date'. To see which was the date on which he did his work he should click on 'View' → 'Details'. Even if *he* has forgotten to date his work, his computer hasn't.

Drawing diagrams, charts and graphs

The number of drawings required in note-taking in some subjects can act as a deterrent to a pupil using a word processor in those lessons. In fact, the pupil who has difficulties with drawing may, after practice, find that he can draw quite efficiently with a drawing or 'paint' package on his word processor. (See also notes on Tablet laptops, page 87.)

Pupils have also commented that, because they are problem-solving while they draw on a computer ('How could I draw that shape?', 'How can I do the shading?', 'I need to alter the size', 'Where can I fit the label?'), they actually *remember* the diagram better than if they had copied it by hand. However, it does take time and practice to achieve the expertise – but it is well worth it, particularly for the poor drawer (Figure 4.21).

Graphs and charts and colour are all available to help with note-taking (Figure 4.22).

A logical structure for notes

Imposing a logical structure on a lesson's notes can be hard to achieve on the hoof. 'It's impossible to sort out what is a main heading and what is a subheading when I'm rushing to keep up. I can't tell how they should have been laid out until the lesson is finished!' A student with dyslexia often likes to see the whole picture before organising the parts.

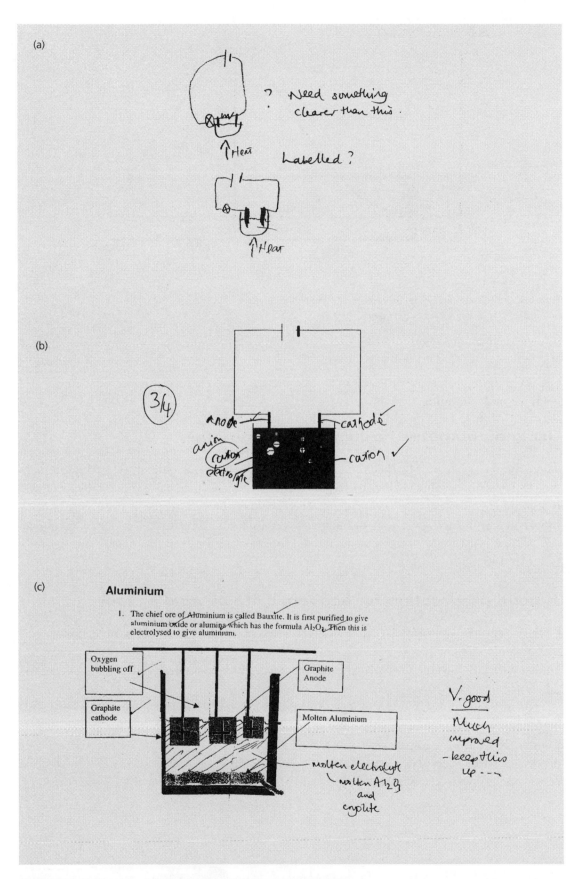

Figure 4.21 (a) Like many dyspraxic children, this 14-year-old has great difficulty doing diagrams and labelling quickly by hand. (b) His first attempt at drawing on a computer in a chemistry lesson. (c) This time he has discovered how to put in labels and is getting more adventurous with his shapes.

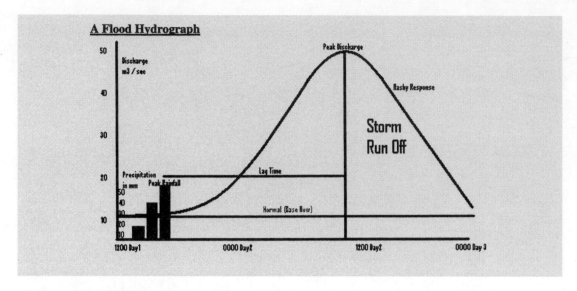

Figure 4.22 Pupils can enjoy the challenge of achieving good diagrams and get quicker and quicker at doing them.

Arranging notes after the lesson can be a very useful exercise – good for memory and good for understanding.

Using a computer for mind-mapping notes

There are many people who, because of their dyslexic or dyspraxic difficulties, find mind-mapping by hand unappealing: being able to produce a well-ordered map with clear handwriting and recognisable symbols may be beyond them. They could be the very people who, because of planning, categorising and short-term memory weaknesses, would benefit most from the technique.

There is a variety of software available. 'Inspiration', for example, is very user-friendly (see Mind-mapping, page 69).

A good preparation for academic life beyond school

College lectures or tutorials can involve a student in an hour's solid note-taking – if the dyslexic student has not been given the skills to cope, he is going to be handicapped unnecessarily. Being able to touch-type and use a word processor effectively could make all the difference.

Many young people learn to type after they have left school. It is often the very children who have been least academically successful who learn word-processing skills in order to improve their job prospects – if only they had done it before secondary school where they needed to write every day, many of them (especially those with dyslexia) would have done better and enjoyed school more. They would also be well prepared for the job market.

Chapter 5
Essay writing

In formal education, essay writing is central to GCSE and A-level work, especially in the arts subjects. Pupils complain that there is a great deal of emphasis on what the essay should contain, but not much on how to structure it. Teachers are usually naturals at essay writing, and some pupils are too. But for a small percentage of every class, particularly those students who are dyslexic, essay writing needs to be taught.

Unfortunately, the lower-level language skills required for essay writing are precisely those that are weak in the student who is dyslexic or dyspraxic: short-term memory, spelling, fast, legible writing, sequencing, punctuating and checking. Teachers, and the pupils themselves, are inevitably frustrated by the mismatch between oral and written ability – the child who is perceptive and interested in class but who cannot get his ideas onto the page is certainly a candidate for practical help with identifying his underlying problems and suggesting ways of dealing with them.

The difference between the dyslexic pupil and his peers (who may have other difficulties, such as limited understanding, language, motivation, confidence) is that the writing skills of someone with dyslexia are not automatic. When he is forming letters, spacing, spelling, remembering, sequencing and punctuating, his ideas and their expression suffer; when he is thinking, remembering and making interesting connections, the technical part of his writing can disintegrate. Either way, the teacher is disappointed, and the pupil rapidly becomes demotivated. Both decide that essay-writing subjects are not for him. This is not a sufficient reason for opting for the sciences, because the problems can, and should, be dealt with.

Identifying the difficulties: the underachiever's list

The first step in dealing with writing problems is to identify which writing skills are not automatic – a good start for this is through a questionnaire formed from expectations in the National Curriculum. Here, for instance, are the expectations for level 7 of Attainment Target 3 in Key Stage 3 'Writing' in English:

> **Pupils' writing is confident and shows appropriate choices of style. In narrative writing characters and settings are developed and, in non-fiction, ideas are organised and coherent. Grammatical features and vocabulary are accurately and effectively used. Spelling is correct, including that of complex irregular words, and work is legible and attractively presented. Paragraphing and correct punctuation are used to make the sequence of events or ideas coherent and clear to the reader.**

Having turned these criteria into a series of questions (Figure 5.1), each member of a class can make his own response. The subsequent discussion may air not simply the difficulties anyone with dyslexia or dyspraxia may be experiencing, but those of others in the group – much to the relief of any dyslexic students, who usually feel that they are the only ones with writing problems.

Thinking about Writing

**Requirements for Writing
at Keystage 3 Attainment Target 3 Level 7**

When I am writing:

- Am I confident that I can find the words to say what I mean?

- Can I make characters live and grow in my stories?

- Can I make the reader feel he is 'there'?

- Do I know what it means to 'vary my style'?

- Do I organise my ideas clearly enough for a reader to follow them?

- Do I understand about grammar, and do I recognise when mine is not correct? Do I know how to put it right?

- Can I call up just the right word when I need it?

- Can I spell reliably – both regular and irregular words?

- Is my handwriting easy to read? Is it attractive?

- Do I organise my paragraphs so that the order of my ideas is clear to the reader?

- Does my punctuation help a reader to follow my meaning?

Figure 5.1 This questionnaire can be used in class to help students focus on their individual strengths and weaknesses in writing. It makes a basis for discussion (see Sheet F in the Worksheet section).

A questionnaire on the basis of the final Attainment Target Level would challenge anyone who feels that there is no problem with the requirements of Level 7:

Pupils' writing has shape and impact and shows control of a range of styles maintaining the interest of the reader throughout. Narratives use structure as well as vocabulary for a range of imaginative effects, and non-fiction is

coherent, reasoned and persuasive. A variety of grammatical constructions and punctuation is used accurately and appropriately and with sensitivity. Paragraphs are well constructed and linked in order to clarify the organisation of the writing as a whole.

Although answers to these questionnaires preoccupy teachers, their pupils may have quite a different set of anxieties. They are probably thinking:

- **'I never seem to answer the question.'**
- **'I don't like planning.'**
- **'I don't know how to begin.'**
- **'I can't finish in time.'**
- **'I know what I want to say, but I don't know how to say it.'**
- **'I forget what I am saying in the middle.'**
- **'I like thinking and talking about this, but I hate writing about it.'**

As many exam candidates have these concerns uppermost in their minds, it is best to address them.

'I never seem to answer the question'

The first of these anxieties is the one that provokes the most frequent criticism from exam boards. Examiners complain annually that too many candidates, although clearly knowing a great deal about a given topic, still fail to answer the question: 'The Marathon Trap' as one classics teacher describes it. 'They see the word "Marathon" and launch into telling the tale. However, the question usually asks either "Why did the Athenians win?" or "Why did the Persians lose?" and the story of the battle, splendid as it may be, is by no means the whole answer to either.'

Alice, a dyslexic sixth former, was asked, in the run-up to her A-level exams, how she would set about analysing the wording of a question in her English language paper. 'Oh, I don't really bother with the wording,' she replied. 'I don't really look at it at all. I just read the passage and then start writing.' It is as though she feared the question might frustrate her fixed intention to tell what she knew. Yet examiners usually intend their questions to be both an invitation and a guide.

Failing to answer the question is characteristic of dyslexic pupils, but it is common in the scripts of other pupils too. With the hope of steering away from such an elephant trap, teachers urge their pupils to 'analyse the question' before they attempt an answer. Many pupils need guidance on how to make that analysis.

Most exam questions require candidates to respond in two ways. They ask for information, on the one hand, and use of that information in some form, on the other. Marks are awarded proportionally to each response. Figures 5.2–5.5 describe a system for analysis, called 'Question the Question', that has this typical pattern in mind.

Figures 5.4 and 5.5 give questions for analysis and a checklist. A 'right or wrong' approach is less productive than an emphasis on deconstructing each question from three different angles. This is partly because an understanding of the question is essential, but partly because it often takes time to recognise all the implications of a question. A formal

Question the Question

1	Topic Area	Underline the words that indicate the subject matter.
2.	Limiting Words	Highlight the words that control the slant required on the topic area.
3.	Directive	Circle the words that suggest the structure into which your answer should fit, the use you are to make of what you know.

Illustration Question
Taken from English GCSE OCR
Non-Fiction and Media Texts

'"Following Fashion is a Waste of Money."
Argue your own point of view on this subject.'

Question the Question

1.	Topic Area	<u>Following Fashion</u>
2.	Limiting Words	Waste of Money, own view
3.	Directives	Argue

Figure 5.2 'Question the Question': a routine for analysing an essay question. (See Sheet G in the Worksheet section.)

routine for question analysis will check the impulse to plunge straight into the writing that both overconfidence and nervous self-doubt provoke. Even then the writer may find he understands the requirements of a question only when he is finally reaching his conclusion – which may therefore not express his final thoughts at all! Making a plan before writing the essay is a second device that anticipates this danger.

Analysing an Essay Question

Examiners' most common criticism of the essays they mark at GCSE and A Level is that candidates have not answered the question.

There are basically two kinds of essay question: one asks you to give information, and the other asks you to use it. Most exam questions combine the two. You should ask yourself:

'Am I being asked for a straightforward presentation of facts (describe, outline, trace) or am I being asked to process information in some way (assess, discuss, evaluate)? Am I being asked to do a bit of both?'

Examples of common directives and their meanings:

Describe: Offer a detailed account

Trace: Note turning points and stages

Contrast: Show differences between

Compare: Explore both similarities and differences

Summarise: Identify key ideas, present concisely

Discuss: Consider all sides of the argument

The point of this work on question analysis is to save you from writing everything you know about a topic, regardless of the question, or from reproducing a good essay you have previously written that is not strictly the answer to your current question.

Figure 5.3 'Question the Question': some signposts. (See Sheet H in the Worksheet section.)

Question the Question – trials

History Advanced Level
(OCR Paper 16 The Normans in England)

'How accurate is the judgement that throughout his reign
Edward the Confessor was a puppet of the House of Godwin?'

Topic area:

Limiting words:

Directive:

Religious Studies GCSE
(MEG Paper 6 Judaism)

'Describe two ways in which Jews may celebrate the Sabbath in the home
and explain the importance of these celebrations.'

Topic area:

Limiting words:

Directive:

Geography Year 8
(ISEB Geomorphological Processes)

'With reference to examples you have studied, show how man can reduce
either coastal erosion and its effects or coastal flooding and its effects.'

Topic area:

Limiting words:

Directive:

Figure 5.4 'Question the Question': three sample questions to practise
questioning the question. No previous knowledge of the subject is necessary.
(See Sheet I in the Worksheet section.)

Question the Question – analysis of trials

'How accurate is the judgement that throughout his reign
Edward the Confessor was a puppet of the House of Godwin?'

Topic area:	Edward the Confessor, the House of Godwin
Limiting words:	Judgement, throughout reign, puppet
Directive:	How accurate?

'Describe two ways in which Jews may celebrate the Sabbath in the home
and explain the importance of these celebrations.'

Topic area:	Jews, the Sabbath
Limiting words:	Two ways, celebrate, in the home, importance
Directive:	Describe, explain

'With reference to examples you have studied, show how man can reduce
either coastal erosion and its effects or coastal flooding and its effects.'

Topic area:	Coastal erosion, coastal flooding, effects
Limiting words:	Either/or, examples studied, man, reduce
Directive:	With reference to, show how

Figure 5.5 'Question the Question': there is no definitive analysis. It
is the process that is useful. (See Sheet J in the Worksheet section.)

'I don't like planning'

Mind-mapping for essay planning

One of the most successful techniques for tackling overload is mind-mapping. It deals with all the problem areas and can transform every aspect of the finished essay. Teachers tend not to use it, because they themselves have found their own methods successful and want to pass them onto their pupils, but there is no doubt that many underachievers would benefit from a new approach. Inherent in the technique is the breaking-down of the task into smaller, more manageable, steps. Separate the tasks and the student can give each stage his full attention. He is always reluctant to do this, feeling it will prolong the agony or, in an exam, take up precious writing time.

An exercise in planning an essay by mind-mapping

Stage 1: focus and analysis

- Put the essay title in the middle of the page. Draw a circle round it
- Analyse the question (see 'Question the Question', page 156).

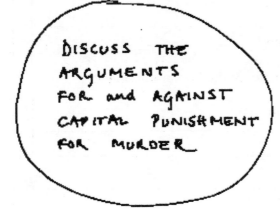

Figure 5.6 Highlighting the words that indicate which is the topic area, the limiting words and how the question should be answered, can be done in different colours. This will focus the pupil's mind before he brainstorms.

Stage 2: brainstorm

Brainstorming is most often done orally and in groups, but it *can* be done alone and on paper. The technique is ideal for the person with dyslexia because, while he brainstorms, he need have no worries about presentation, sequence or categorisation.

Lines are drawn out from the central circle, and from these lines topics or ideas can spring (Figure 5.7). Headings should be very brief – not too much writing – and for this brainstorming stage there should be no attempt at structure, so that the mind can run free, making associations, including both obvious and less obvious ideas, impressions or arguments, following hunches or prejudices and thinking of examples.

A structure, at this thinking stage, can prove a straitjacket for those who cannot think and write at the same time. Unless the material has been worked over many times before, most essays will benefit from brainstorming first.

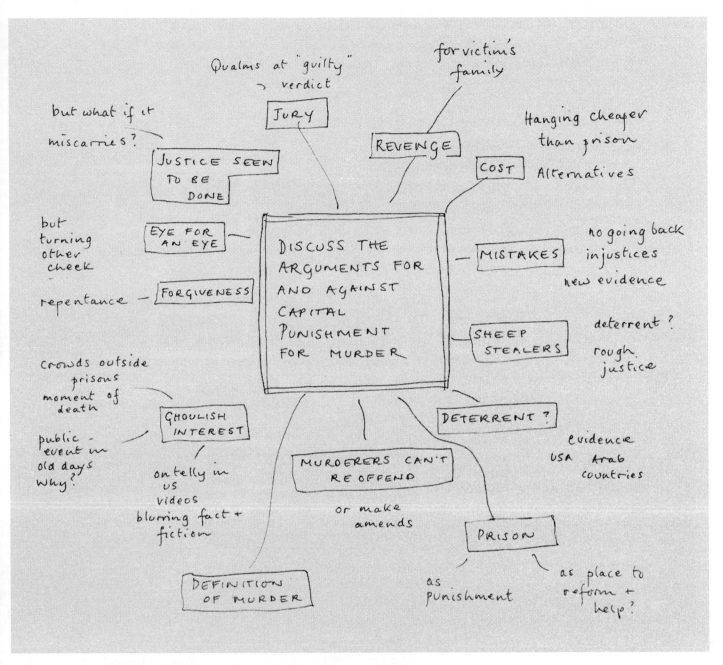

Figure 5.7 A brainstorm: ideas, images, opinions, arguments, memories, quotes and topics can all be jotted down in single words or short phrases. This is in no way an essay plan.

Essays in some subjects, such as English and history, will almost always profit by a brainstorm, particularly if the emphasis of the question is slightly different from one previously tackled.

Stage 3: selecting and rejecting

Using highlighters, select those topics to be included and group them by colour. This visual categorisation lightens the memory load. Numbering the branches is another way of grouping topics.

Stage 4: structuring – a new mind-map or mind-maps

Write the essay title in the centre of the page again, and draw a shape around it. Decide how to handle the question:

- Decide how many main topics are to be included, and then draw and label a short main branch for each.
- Provide evidence or arguments for and against each main topic.
- Make a box at the top of the page for ideas for the 'Introduction' (not to be attempted until you have done your thinking about your essay).
- Make a box at the bottom of the page for 'Ideas for Conclusion'.
- Number the paragraphs in the order that seems most appropriate to the argument or discussion.

Either a 'for or against' argument (Figure 5.8) or a theme-based discussion (Figure 5.9) can be used.

The structures of these two essay plans are fundamentally different. It is much more satisfactory to experiment with the structure of the essay *before* embarking on the actual writing; only a very determined dyslexic student would start again after writing more than a side, however unsatisfactory he decided his first approach to be.

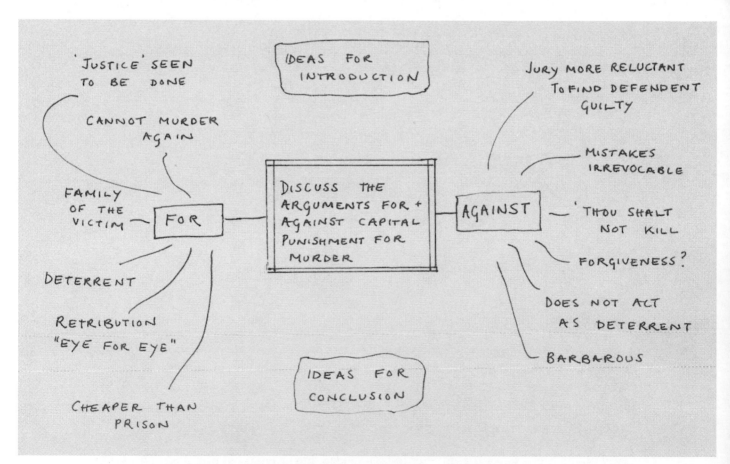

Figure 5.8 Most children go straight for the 'for and against' format in an argumentative essay. Experimenting with their evidence and views for a few minutes on the mind-map might lead them to change their approach and go for a more thematic essay.

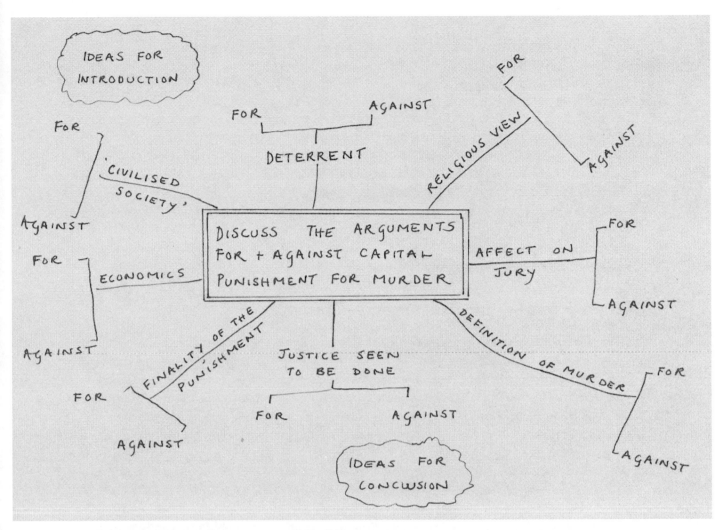

Figure 5.9 On this topic a theme-based discussion might be a more economical way of handling the argument – avoiding repetition of topics.

The point about this visuo-spatial display of the bones of the essay is that the pattern is easy to see, the essay is viewed as a whole and, because of the way that it is laid out, discussion of each theme is invited. The essay will be balanced and the sequence will be clear.

While deciding how to approach the question or which theme to pick up from each topic, the 'Introduction' and 'Conclusion' almost write themselves – instead of acting either as a block to starting at all or a straitjacket to prevent further thinking.

Stage 5: writing

With the mind-map in front of him, the pupil can begin to write. The limitations of his short-term memory, his sequencing ability, and his spelling and handwriting will not have interfered with the most important aspect of his writing – the thinking behind it.

When he begins to write, he can give far more of his attention to *how* he is expressing himself. This splitting of the stages of writing into distinct steps is the crucial one for dyslexic people.

Sometimes students who are using a word processor feel that, because they can move their words, sentences and paragraphs around at will, there is not the same need for planning. Certainly it is a great boon for minor corrections and insertions, but it is just as important for the word-processing dyslexic student to stand back at the start, take an overall look at the subject by brainstorming, decide how to handle it and then begin.

Stage 6: checking the work

Reading aloud is the best way of checking work – the pupil can *hear* the mismatch between what he is seeing and what he meant to write or hoped to convey. He can also learn to punctuate by ear: listening carefully to the rise and fall of his voice, the short and long pauses, will help him to recognise where punctuation is needed. This may need a surprising amount of practice for a dyslexic student.

If the pupil needs to do a separate check for spelling, reading it backwards is a good way of spotting errors – then the words have to be recognised in their own right. Read in context, the dyslexic person tends to see the word he expects to see. A lapse of time between writing and checking is also likely to make checking more fruitful.

Using a model for structuring an essay

A prescribed format for an essay will differ from subject to subject. In English literature essays, each topic or argument would be backed up by some examples and some quotations; in history, main points would require examples and evidence; in geography or economics, a proposition would need case studies and data. It sounds deadeningly formulaic to suggest that an all-purpose model will fit any topic, but there is no doubt that using such a model can ensure that all the necessary ingredients are included – and from there pupils can develop their personal ideas and approach. At GCSE level and below, pupils might use the model as their essay plan, whereas older students would use it as a starting point or brainstorm from which they would develop their theme.

Many teachers give just this sort of guidance, but in linear form. Half the class take note, but the other half never seem to follow instructions – probably the pupils who are dyslexic. For them, perhaps, the spatial layout of a prototype will stick in the mind better, if their difficulty is with sequence; in an exam they may well remember, in their mind's eye, the more visual representation of the essay plan, particularly if originally they drew it up themselves. A good task for these children would be for them to create their own map of the essential ingredients required in each type of essay, colour-coding the different elements. In this way, they will also *see* the balance of the essay and *see* the best way to make links.

Dyslexic pupils' comments on mind-mapping for brainstorming and planning

'It's much easier to get started on your essay. A quick scribbled mind-map seems to trigger an "ON" switch in my brain and start me thinking.'

'The title is right in the middle of the page, so you can't forget it or wander off the point.'

'They're good for paragraph planning and order.'

'It stops you repeating yourself.'

'It's easier to picture the whole essay.'

'It makes you choose keywords.'

'It makes you see links between points.'

'They help you to think, make you want to explore ideas.'

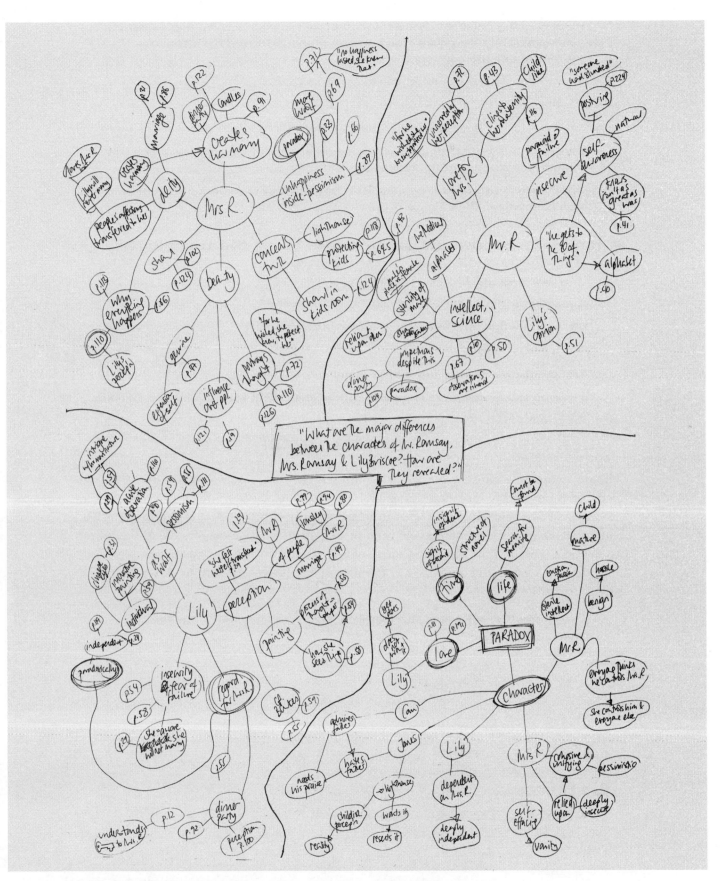

Figure 5.10 These maps show Eleanor's research for her essay. You can see how much thinking is going on. Having brainstormed her three characters, she finds that she now wants to base her essay on the theme of 'paradox'. Final writing was much helped by including page references as she mapped.

'Mind-mapping gives you something to do when you're collecting evidence from several history books. You can group points from different books together under the same branch.'

'I don't have to worry about spelling and handwriting.'

'It seems to stimulate my brain.'

'You don't forget ideas so easily. You can write them when you think of them.'

'It's a good way of sorting ideas you've researched for an essay, especially if you put in the page references at the same time.'

'Main themes often emerge only after you have been working on a mind-map for a little while.' (See Figure 5.10.)

A teacher's comments about pupils using the technique

'They seem to get to the structure more quickly.'

'The structure is a more integral part of the essay.'

'The introduction is usually much more relevant.'

'There's less waffle.'

'Argumentative essays are more balanced.'

'It seems to steady pupils in exams so that they don't rush in without thinking.'

'I don't know how to begin'

Almost anything dreadful can happen in the first sentence of an essay. Properly, its role should be to catch the reader's attention, preferably with a crisp reference to the question. However, the writer of that sentence may find that he is not considering its effect on his reader at all, but, rather, is using it to wind himself into thinking about what he might write in the rest of his essay. As a result it is often irrelevant, confused or spectacularly badly expressed.

Here in Figure 5.11 is Alice's opening sentence in response to an A-level English language question:

'Show how the writers of the following two passages use language to achieve their ends.'

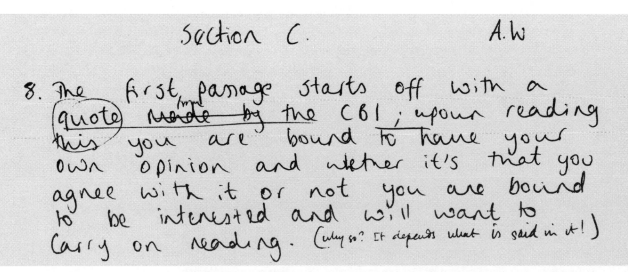

Section C.   A.W

8. The first passage starts off with a ~~quote~~ ~~made by~~ the CBI ; upoun reading ~~this~~ you are bound to have your own opinion and whether it's that you agree with it or not you are bound to be interested and will want to carry on reading. (why so? It depends what is said in it!)

Figure 5.11 The problem of getting started.

Having got that off her chest, the rest of her essay is quite sensible and clear, but the cost in torturing herself with anxiety, squandering precious minutes and disaffecting her examiner was far too high.

An essay is best seen as a vehicle for thought, but the relationship between thinking and writing is complex. For the lucky few, mind and pen work in harmony together, creating and sequencing ideas that are instantly dressed in suitable words – the mind shaping the whole while the pen writes the detail. However, most writers need to separate thinking and writing, at least some of the time. For those to whom writing does not come easily, the thinking process needs to be over, at least in the main, before the writing begins. If the essay is the thinking process itself, it is in danger – particularly if the writer has dyslexia – of being disorganised, repetitive, unbalanced and too short or too long. Starting well for any writer depends on having a sense of the essay as a whole, including the conclusion; knowing where to end will ease the problem of knowing where to begin. It will also avoid either repetition or inconsistency between the two.

There are two chief difficulties about starting. The one described above is to do with the relationship between writing and thinking; the other is to do with starting to think in the first place. Pupils burdened with underlying difficulties in literacy, sequencing and memory are accustomed to failing in attempts to match their thoughts with lucid writing. As a result they frequently suffer from a severe thinking block when they see that essay writing lies ahead. Their mental tension often manifests itself physically in legs twisted round the chair, hunched shoulders, head supported awkwardly on one arm, eyes squinting sideways, white finger tips gripping the pen.

Creative writing is particularly susceptible to 'thinking block', because there is the added expectation that both ideas and expression should be interestingly original. If the essay is to be a narrative, there are several well-known ways of breaking through this initial blockage.

Responding to 'wh' words as starters – where? who? what? when? why? – although a rather mechanical and superficial approach to a creative task, will at least prompt the writer to think out his basic story and provide a key fact round which to build each of five preliminary paragraphs. The story may yet catch fire from these dry sticks.

A similar system – that of dipping into a sensory bucket filled with personal memories – may stimulate a more lively and original response when descriptive writing is called for.

A way of getting started

As a result of their special difficulties, dyslexic students tend to worry about the formal aspects of essay writing, instead of putting first things first – namely what they actually want to write about.

For the writing of creative essays, a sensory mind-map can be a very effective starting point, because it draws from their own personal experience and distracts their attention from the areas that they find difficult – sequencing, spelling and handwriting.

This technique encourages the free play of a range of mental activities; by relaxing critical control, it links the imagination and the random chain of memory so that both are used to the full. By drawing on images, sounds and feelings from the personal memory store, the student can create a background to the story that will make it convincing and enjoyable.

A strategy of this kind enables a dyslexic pupil, or indeed any pupil, to get started on any creative essay required of them in school or for public exams, e.g. in the 1999 GCSE English language paper pupils were asked to write a creative piece on 'A journey' inspired by a short story by Nadine Gordimer, which described an African journey. Instead of approaching this topic in a logical, sequential or chronological manner, which most students would find straightforward, the pupil in question got herself going by putting together the mind-map in Figure 5.12. This is loosely built on her recall of impressions of a journey or

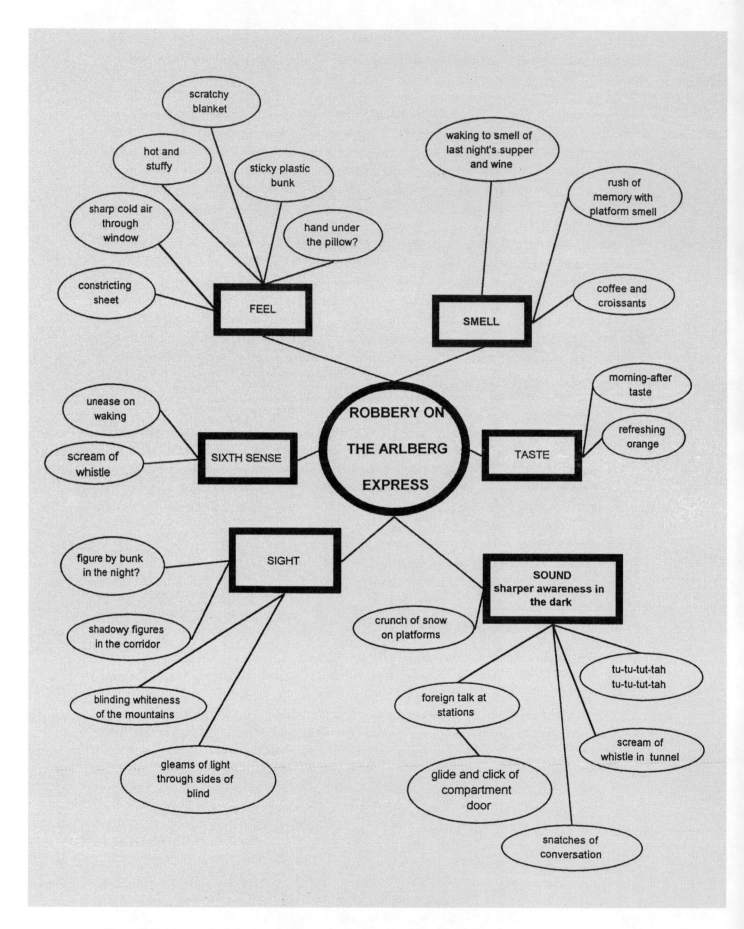

Figure 5.12 A 'sensory' mind map – drawing on images, sounds and feelings to stimulate creative writing. This mind map was made using *Inspiration* mind-mapping software

journeys that she had actually taken, no doubt supplemented by fictional details as well. Obviously, this map is in no sense an essay plan, and the short story will need a plot and shaping and structuring. But the reluctance to start the essay will have been offset by the excitement of recapturing glimpses of the pupil's own past and inventing others. The formal problems of expression and presentation will no longer seem so daunting.

Triggering personal memories makes the pupil want to tell his story. Vivid writing that really engages the reader usually stems from a writer who has dipped into his own sensory memory making first himself, and then the reader, feel that they are *there*.

Another way of coping with the start is not to start with it. This may be the traditional way of presenting a story:

- The beginning (introduction)
- What happens first (the action rises)
- The main event (the exciting bit)
- What happens next (the action winds down)
- The conclusion (ending and final comments)

However, the following may well be a better way to go about planning and even writing it:

- Main event
- Conclusion
- Rising action
- Winding down
- Introduction

An initial focus on the central event of the story saves the writer from facing, cold, the inhibiting challenge of a perfect opening. Figure 5.13 is a guide to this idea.

Planning and writing a story

The order

Writing a story in this order:
1. Main event
2. Conclusion
3. Rising action
4. Winding down
5. Introduction

has several advantages:

- it takes the pressure off the introduction
- gives prime attention to the most important bit of the story
- forces the writer to visualise the whole before writing a part
- gets all the parts into proportion with each other
- stresses the idea of links between sections of the narrative

Planning and Writing a Story

If it is difficult to start a story using this conventional structure:

- The Beginning

- What Happens First

- The Main Event

- What Happens Next

- The Conclusion

try a different approach. Invent the parts of your story in this order – write key phrases in the boxes:

The Main Event (the exciting bit)

Conclusion (ending and final comments)

What Happens First (the action rises)

What Happens after the Main Event (the action winds down)

The Beginning (the introduction)

Figure 5.13 Planning and writing a story – no need to start at the beginning.

The plan

You may think out your story using the sequence grid in Figure 5.13 or you may find that mind-mapping is the most flexible way to think out this working sequence: a map can be created in any order and re-sequenced in a second map or the parts numbered or colour-coded just before writing. At this stage, think out the narrative links that will join each section.

The writing

Having thought the story through in sections out of order, the writer can continue to work in these sections, concentrating fully on his powers of story-telling to bring life to each. Finally, he can reorder events in a variety of possible sequences, joining his already written sections with the narrative links thought out at the planning stage and reducing emphasis on the introduction still further. If this seems too inorganic a way to work, some writers may find that planning out of order and then renumbering the steps is enough to set them going on a fluent narrative.

Word processing

The editing facility on a computer makes word processing the best means for writing, linking and improving a sequence of paragraphs.

This way of planning and writing a story involves the writer in visualising the whole piece before he attempts to write it for his reader. If such planning takes place, the start will find its level as one segment among several that make up the whole. Finally, this method avoids the situation in which the writer is just reaching the exciting bit when he is told to put down his pen.

There are obvious but important points to make about word processing: the writer who is typing will have no technical problem if he experiments with the order in which he writes the sections of his story. Although the order of planning suggested here is only slightly unconventional, there is in fact no limit to the idiosyncrasy of order in which a writer can put his ideas down on a word processor. He can break off from one idea, returning or jumping ahead to others. He can cluster details round one, leaving another no more than a bare phrase. He can revisit to prune or embellish, and he can adjust the order and balance of events as often as his creative impulse prompts. Using mind-mapping software, e.g. *Inspiration*, a writer can type phrases or whole paragraphs when they occur to him and attach them as notes to main topic branches, to be pasted into the narrative sequence at the writing stage.

The mere realisation of all this may be enough to release a swirl of good ideas previously dammed by a log-jam of non-automatic writing skills that require simultaneous management. Thus, a writing block can often be cleared simply by the writer realising he is in a position to deal with each element of his essay on its own.

'I can't finish in time'

Many pupils, but especially pupils with dyslexia, have difficulty with timing essays. Dyslexic teenagers often cannot gauge the length of a unit of time – an hour, ten minutes, a week. They cannot judge what activities there is time to complete in a morning or a half-hour, or how best to sequence them. Often they tell time on a clock face, but cannot tell its significance in the context of their life. Quite often they cannot tell the time reliably in the first place – especially on a traditional clock face – the one most likely to hang in an exam room. As a consequence of all this, they may easily miscalculate how long it would or should take them to write an essay.

In exams, this hazy sense of time becomes a serious problem. Once engaged in a complex activity such as writing an essay, dyslexic students are unlikely to keep up a useful sense of time passing or be able to see the essay they are writing in the context of a whole exam paper or mark scheme. 'I can't finish in time' stands for a whole raft of problems with time, including its opposite – finishing far too quickly.

Problems with writing to time in exams also affect writing in everyday school life and result in a variety of attempted solutions. One student may simply 'forget' to write anything at all. Another may attempt to cram thinking, planning and writing into a 20-minute lunch break, while yet another expects to give up the whole weekend to writing one essay.

This last solution may result in work that delights student and teacher, but it is dangerous training for exams. Writers with a poor time sense are better served by a system of preparing a topic at leisure and then answering a question on it in strictly timed circumstances, at least for some of their weekly essays in a GCSE or sixth-form course. Dyslexic students have more than normal difficulty in selecting and prioritising their ideas and need to practise against the clock. However, practice in timed writing from memory often comes too late in a sixth-form course for students with learning difficulties to establish a confident thinking/planning/writing routine that fits their allotted time and suits their particular strengths.

There is a further reason to compare timed and untimed essay writing early in a new course. It may be that the inability to match potential when writing under timed conditions is the first recognisable sign that a motivated and hitherto successful student has a specific learning difficulty. Identification well into GCSE or sixth-form courses may mean it is too late for the student to solve his writing problem by word processing, at least in the impending exams. It is, however, never finally too late to learn touch-typing, even if the dyslexic student is about to leave school. At whatever point his learning difficulties are identified, confident word-processing skills are likely to be his best support equally in tertiary education or in the workplace.

If pupils with a poor sense of time have not worked out and practised their solution to timed essay writing beforehand, exam conditions and stress may well cause serious underachievement. Despite having a clock in view and knowing exactly when they must stop writing one answer and move on to the next, dyslexic students become engrossed in a task and oblivious of time's meaning, even though they look at it on the clock face. They are liable to carry on with one question long into the chunk of time reserved for the next. Inevitably they run out of time. Joe, aged 12$\frac{1}{2}$, commented: 'I have never finished my story in an English exam.' On the other hand, Alex, in his mock GCSE English exam, wrote six frantic essays in response to six questions from which he should have chosen just one. He had no sense of inappropriate timing to prompt him to reread the instructions.

Henry, now reading history at university, makes a good illustration of a pupil whose handwriting difficulties, although familiar to all his teachers, were not recognised as a serious impediment until he wrote timed essays at the end of his first sixth-form year. Figure 5.14 is a specimen of his handwriting under timed conditions at that point.

Not only was it clear from these essays that no examiner would be able to read his writing beyond the first few paragraphs, but Henry himself made the following comments:

Figure 5.14 Part of an essay on Frederick William of Prussia showing the effect time pressure can have on the hand writing of a sixth former with specific learning difficulties and a great deal to say. Note his history teacher's kindly protest – a public examiner might not be so forbearing.

'Writing slows me up and worries me, so I don't know how long I should be taking.'

'Writing is difficult. It distracts me when I am trying to think.'

'It's tiring.'

'My writing is out of time with my thoughts.'

All of these difficulties contributed to his lack of control over the timing of his essays and veiled his considerable talent as a historian.

Henry was assessed by an educational psychologist who confirmed a childhood diagnosis of dyslexia and hypotonia. He learned to mind-map. Figure 5.15 shows both his scruffy presentation and the mass of connections he was making as he thought through the topic.

Despite the weak muscle tone characteristic of hypotonia, he learned to touch-type and brought a basic word processor into school, using it in his final sixth-form year for all his note-taking and essay writing. Exam boards granted him the concession to use a word processor for his A-level exams.

His first experience of the benefit of word processing in an exam was wholly to do with timing. He emerged from typing a two-and-a-half-hour English literature paper saying: 'I wrote the two essays straight off and found I had only used up an hour. It dawned on me that I could go back and add a whole lot more. I could change the order. I could tinker with everything. It was brilliant.'

The box below shows the content of a letter from Henry's Head of history, written shortly after he had started to word process his essays.

You mentioned some time ago an essay Henry wrote for me. I forgot to tell you how good I thought it. He has w-processed it pretty efficiently, but as an essay I thought the tightness of the paragraph arguments was much better than anything I've had from him before.

I intend to urge him to take this essay with him to his Oxford interview. He could produce it if appropriate to show what progress he has made with the w-processor already and, should they read it, they'll see how he is coming on intellectually...

I will suggest that he takes it in a folder, so that he doesn't produce it in the usual distressed condition.

The reason for quoting this letter is to show how the combination of mind-mapping and word processing not merely disposed of Henry's writing difficulty but improved the quality and concise nature of his writing. The wry last sentence is a reminder that the problem itself remains; the art is in finding ways round it.

The first step in tackling a timing problem is for teacher and student to work out what precisely causes mistiming. As good timing is crucial to success in exams, it is worth having them particularly in mind when investigating likely causes. Is a particular student slow to choose one question out of several? Does he spend time panicking over the choice? Does he find the mechanics of writing so stressful that he cannot get started? Does he start

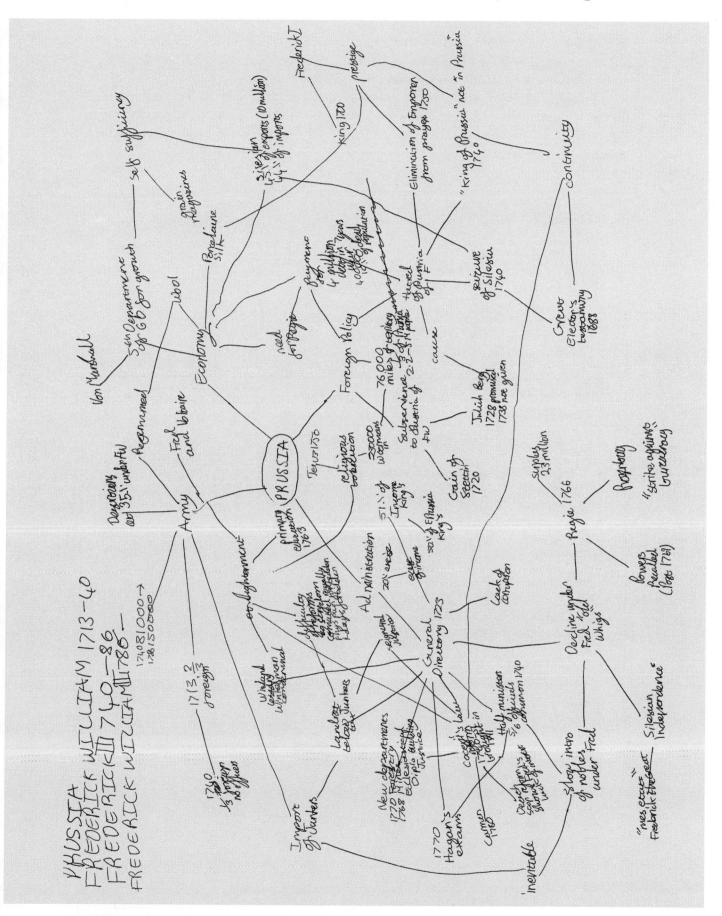

Figure 5.15 Mind-mapping made it possible for Henry to put down a web of connections as he thought about Frederick William of Prussia.

writing impulsively and then run out of ideas? Is he confused by the way ideas crop up and are then forgotten unless he writes them into his essay immediately? Is word-finding a problem? Is his handwriting laborious and slow?

These possibilities, singly or in combination, will all affect essay timing and may well be worth a general discussion in class as well as on an individual basis. The questionnaire in Figure 5.16 sets out some of the likely problems. Filling it in encourages all pupils to think about their exam technique.

Mistiming Essays

Understanding:
- Am I slow to assess what I know in answer to exam questions – and to make a choice?

- Do I waste time panicking or daydreaming?

- Does stress block my thinking?

Remembering:
- Does worry about time make me forget?

- Do my ideas wander from the main point?

- Does writing one idea make me forget the others?

- Do I forget what I am saying in the middle?

Organising:
- Does a muddle of ideas prevent me from writing?

- Do I have so much to say I cannot select ideas and put them in order?

- Do I rush in and then run out of things to write?

- Do I have good ideas out of place and struggle to fit them into my essay?

Writing:
- Is my handwriting hard work, slow, messy?

- Is it fast, needing many corrections, illegible?

- Does worry about spelling restrict my vocabulary?

- Do I hate checking?

Figure 5.16 Filling in this questionnaire will focus pupils' attention on exam skills (see Sheet K in the Worksheet section.)

2

Section A

Answer **one** *question from this section.*

All questions carry 50 marks each.

1   Write a critical appreciation of the following poem. Among other things you might like to consider:

-    the mood and meanings of the poem;
-    the poet's use of imagery;
-    the effects of verse form and punctuation;

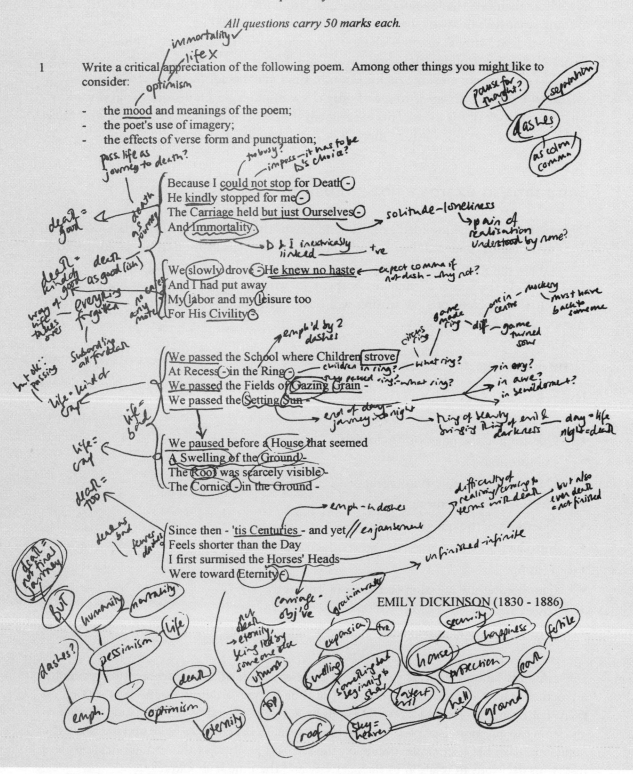

Because I could not stop for Death
He kindly stopped for me
The Carriage held but just Ourselves
And Immortality.

We slowly drove He knew no haste
And I had put away
My labor and my leisure too
For His Civility

We passed the School where Children strove
At Recess in the Ring
We passed the Fields of Gazing Grain
We passed the Setting Sun

We paused before a House that seemed
A Swelling of the Ground
The Roof was scarcely visible
The Cornice in the Ground

Since then - 'tis Centuries - and yet
Feels shorter than the Day
I first surmised the Horses' Heads
Were toward Eternity

EMILY DICKINSON (1830 - 1886)

Figure 5.17 This shows Eleanor's annotations and mind-mapping on her actual A-level exam paper (she brought it out of the exam with her by mistake). Like many of her friends taking the same exam, she initially felt the mood of the poem was pessimistic. In mapping her evidence, however, she changed her opinion, and in the subsequent essay she made the case for optimism.

In an exam, minutes spent brainstorming a question and making a plan, before starting to write, will save rather than lose time, but few students believe this. Nor do they readily accept how planning an answer can sharpen and focus their argument (Figure 5.17). Yet a preplanned paragraph is more likely to be swiftly written and securely linked into the essay as a whole than one that evolves spontaneously from the nib of a pen while the writer tries to think what he will say next (and whether he has already said it).

A student who is anxious about time management should try timing each step separately – choice of question, brainstorm, mind-map plan, a typical central paragraph, introduction, the conclusion. As his sense of time may be adrift, work with a stopwatch will show him that he needs to spend only a few minutes on brainstorming and working out the sequence of his ideas. This experiment leads naturally into considering how time ought to be apportioned when there is a fixed length of time available in which to complete an essay.

Extra time in exams – how to use it

Dyslexic pupils can be awarded extra time in exams. It is important to emphasise to them that the time is awarded because of their particular difficulties: their need to read instructions, questions and extracts slowly and carefully and their need to plan and to check their work. If the extra 15 minutes is spent in writing fast and furiously until the last moment, the problem of slow writing will have been addressed – but the other, equally important, weaknesses will not.

Time-keeping for exams essays

This procedure works well for everyone:

- Questioning the question (to focus)
- Brainstorming
- Questioning the question (again)
- Planning and structuring
- Questioning the question (again)
- Introduction
- Writing
- Questioning the question (is the essay still on track?)
- Checking
- Writing the conclusion

Depicting the amount of time available for the essay by drawing and segmenting a circle is a practical way of discussing the allotment of time for the activities essential in writing an essay. For example, after teachers and pupils have discussed and tested how long it takes to 'question the question' (see page 156), to brainstorm, to structure, to write and to check, the pupil can make his own circle, decide on the size and position of the various elements and justify his decisions in relation to each activity and the time it should take.

The teacher may prefer to be more prescriptive – using a cut-up model of the circle with its constituents, he can simply ask the dyslexic pupil to assemble the parts in the order he thinks appropriate to the task in hand. It may seem an infantile pursuit for a serious-minded

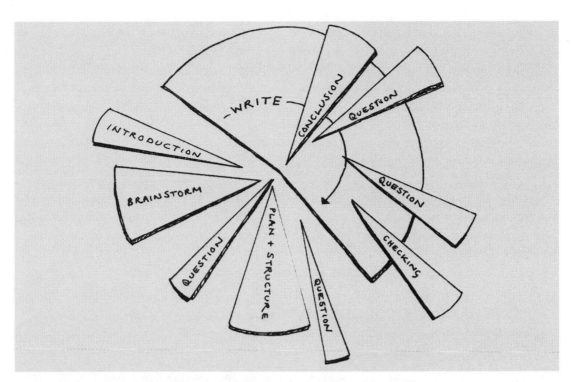

Figure 5.18 Putting together this segmented cardboard circle gives rise to comments like 'Where do we start?', 'Why are there four QUESTION segments?', 'Where would you put them, and why?' and 'Where would you put INTRODUCTION?' 'Would you do checking before you wrote the CONCLUSION? If so, why?'

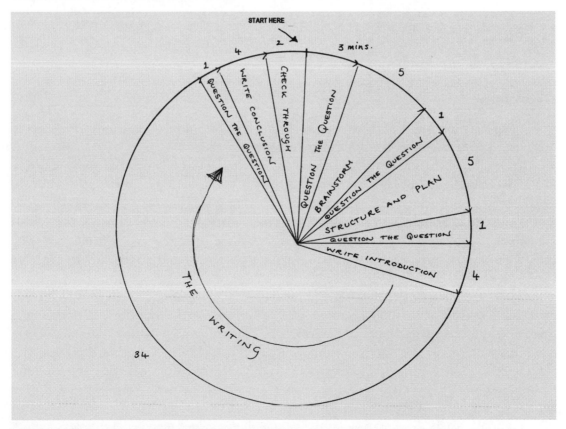

Figure 5.19 The circle represents the amount of time available for writing the essay (perhaps an hour). The segments indicate the activities necessary in the process of writing an essay, the order in which they should be done and the proportion of time that might be spent on each activity. (See Sheet L to cut up in the Worksheet section.)

A-level student, but it always produces a smile, an eagerness to get their hands on the pieces and a useful discussion about how to write a good essay (Figure 5.18).

The example in Figure 5.19 is a time schedule done by a pupil for an A-level history exam essay. The discussion before she made the plan was very revealing – it was clear that in previous examinations she had always felt that she had no time for planning, and under the pressure of the occasion rushed onto paper whatever she knew on a topic. She was led by the information at the top of her mind rather than by considering which information would give substance to her arguments.

Central to this planning technique is the constant referral back to the question. Sometimes it is only after brainstorming that the thrust of the question becomes clear – and this crucially affects how it should be answered. The final look at the question before writing the conclusion encourages one to tie up loose ends and show the relevance of one's evidence in relation to the question.

After testing the method in mock exams, pupils have made the following comments:

'I got into the subject straight away instead of winding myself up for a page and a half.'

'I didn't have to write so much.'

'I didn't have so many odd points to tack on at the end.'

'I had time to read it through.'

'I got a much better mark.'

'I know what I want to say, but I don't know how to say it'

Discrepancy

Calling up the right words to order is a profound and persistent problem lying at the roots of dyslexia; to some degree, it is a problem for other pupils too.

The bad spelling and constrained writing that are typical of a dyslexic student's essay is usually an outward display of an inward difficulty with the nature of the written word, i.e. the way sounds are represented by letters, the way words are built up in syllables, the way they carry unwritten associations and the way meaning is conveyed by syntax as well as by single words. As dyslexic people do not process these aspects of language automatically, they have to construct written expression more consciously and often with less success than other people.

To do the other business of essay writing (to research, assemble thoughts, sequence paragraphs, make links, handle grammar, spell, hand-write and punctuate), all at the same time, often proves too much for a dyslexic writer. The least automatic of these skills breaks down. In such 'multi-tasking' the effort required to hold it all together is too great, the adult appreciation too small. After a while, the dyslexic student grows reluctant (in some cases, quite unable) to write essays, or at any rate writes the minimum he can get away with.

Yet from a teacher's point of view this writer is often a valued member of the class, joining in with articulate comments and displaying a lively interest in everything to do with the subject in hand. Orally he seems to have no problem at all. School reports make the point:

> **Richard is full of bright and unusual ideas, but rarely transfers them onto paper.**

Occasionally a student's oral prowess is a bit overdone:

> **Alex always has plenty to say – not always at the right moment. However, there is no doubt that he is a capable scientist.**

Articulate or silent in class, minimalist or verbose on paper, students with language-processing difficulties need practical help from subject teachers if their writing is to flourish. The first step is to recognise the fundamental difficulty with words that probably underlies an apparent reluctance or ineptitude when it comes to written work.

Subject-specific vocabulary

Luckily, focusing on subject-specific words will benefit everyone in a class, not just the underachievers. This is because a student's ability to write about a school subject depends significantly on his command of its technical language. Yet too many schoolchildren are embarrassed to admit that they cannot always pick up new terms and how to use them from the way their teacher happens to teach.

If a student can't pronounce a keyword or spell it, or if he doesn't quite understand its meaning, the idea for which it stands may take on an unnecessary taint of mystery and sophistication; the student will fear both the word and the concept it stands for. Faced in the sixth form with an English essay on 'prescriptivism', Kate's understanding of the subject and how to write about it was blocked by her inability to *pronounce* the word. Although her teacher had said it more than once in class (rather fast), Kate had never had cause to say it herself, much less write it. Until she had said each syllable separately and noted the meaning of the Latin 'pre' and 'script', she could not recognise that the word was merely a technical term standing for pedantic formality in the use of language. This 'Renunciation of Probate' might be a good instance:

> **NOW I do hereby declare that I have not intermeddled in the Estate of the said deceased and will not hereafter intermeddle therein with intent to defraud creditors and I do hereby renounce all my right and title to the probate and execution of the said Will of the estate of the said deceased.**

In Kate's case, mastery of a single word led directly to a competent piece of writing.

Unfortunately for secondary school students, the best way of mastering words is often seen as childish, and many teenagers are embarrassed to use it. This best way is to look, say, spell aloud and write, all as simultaneously as possible, thereby giving maximum multisensory impact to the initial learning. The need to practise unfamiliar words by naming and spelling them aloud can, alas, be falsely taken as a sign of immaturity or stupidity. However, speaking new words aloud as a preparation for writing is valuable to all and teachers can make the method acceptable by using it in a regular, matter-of-fact manner as one of their own usual teaching habits.

Students can develop this way of bridging the gap between receptive and expressive language by working aloud, backwards and forwards, from word to definition. This is useful to reading as well as to talking and writing, and is especially valuable in subjects where technical terminology is extensive, geography for instance. In the end, success will justify the means, for no teacher can be content to leave her classes only partly in possession of the language they need in order to read, talk or write about her subject.

If the case has been successfully made here for the crucial importance of subject-specific vocabulary, teachers might ask themselves how responsible they feel for teaching the language of their particular subject in a conscious and deliberate fashion. If children are to expect and be expected to use appropriate technical language, they would benefit from a whole school policy in this area. It helps all of them, for instance, if subject vocabulary and definitions are collected and accessed on the school's web pages, and if expectations and methods for teaching/learning/testing new vocabulary are uniform for all subjects. Here are three suggestions for teaching subject vocabulary:

Collect words – Teach pupils to keep a list in their current file

- They should refer to it when they write. Spell aloud while writing.

- They should expect and be expected to use the right word correctly spelt.

Preview – Teach important words before you use them:

- Say them deliberately – don't drop your voice on the last syllable.
  (a) Keep them written up on the board.
  (b) Discuss their make-up – syllables, affixes, derivations.

- Attach them where possible to a 'family' by meaning and/or spelling pattern

---

Polythene:

Derivation: poly = many
                  mer = meros = a part + ethylene

Family: polymers, polypropene, polystyrene, polyurethane

- Get underachievers to say them – using as pretext the discussion mentioned above or by asking the class to invent contexts for them or by any other means.

Spelling – Pupils will avoid writing words they fear they can't spell.

Unlearning misspellings is difficult and boring. Where possible, teach poor spellers that their best chance is to learn from the start like this:

Step 1 Looking at the word all the time:

- Say the whole word aloud (or mutter) and listen to yourself.

- Spell it aloud (or at least say each letter under your breath).

Step 2 From memory:

- Mutter the whole word.

- Try to 'see' it on your mental screen: its shape may help.

- Write it, saying the syllables or letters aloud.

Step 3 Saying the word:

- Take the trouble to look back and check.

This method forms the habit of supporting a weak visual memory with auditory and kinaesthetic input.

The memory trace from Step 1 will help to 'fix' Step 2.

Step 3 is an essential habit for any weak speller.

Style

One of the writing skills for English, listed at the start of this chapter, is the ability to 'show appropriate choices of style'. This ability is fundamental in other subjects as well as within English. The style for a geography essay is not the same as the style for history. An English essay writing style is not appropriate in biology or geography. The structural bones should show in writing for the sciences; they should be cloaked in literary writing. In an English essay, much use of the passive tense is a stylistic weakness but it is standard in the format for writing up experiments in science.

Many people have an intuitive awareness of the nuances of style, whereas others, including those with dyslexia, can be successfully taught to recognise and cultivate the relevant characteristics. Dyslexic writers typically use only one style of expression: they write more or less as they speak. Where their contemporaries who read fluently pick up stylistic features from their reading, dyslexic readers have enough to do coping with the content. For someone who reads by sounding out individual words (often incorrectly) inside his head, 'style' may be a concept too far.

A young child with dyslexia, for instance, can often relate the events in a nursery rhyme, but not reproduce its verse-form style, whereas a dyslexic teenager, while noticing the all-pervading presence of fog in the opening page of Dickens' *Bleak House*:

'Fog everywhere. Fog up the river, where it flows among green aits and meadows; fog down the river, where it rolls defiled among the tiers of shipping, and waterside pollutions of a great (and dirty) city. Fog on the Essex marshes, fog on the Kentish heights. Fog creeping into the cabooses of collier-brigs, fog lying out on the yards, and hovering in the rigging of great ships; fog drooping on the gunwales of barges and small boats. Fog in the eyes and throats of ancient Greenwich pensioners, wheezing by the firesides of their wards; fog. . .'

may yet not register how the simple repetition of the word 'fog' conveys that emphasis – unless his attention is drawn to it. Even less is he likely to transfer this basic rhetorical device to his own writing at a suitable moment.

Luckily, appropriate writing styles are within the reach of dyslexic children, provided that they are taught to build up the little skills that go into making style appropriate and learn to recognise significant elements in their own, probably idiosyncratic, writing. Once again, it is fortunate for the whole class that a few members may need lessons in the mechanics of suitable writing style. There will always be others who write adequately but whose style for a particular subject would be improved by deliberate explanation and practice. Even the most successful stylists will hone their skills by analysing them.

The list in Figure 5.20 is intended to help teachers pinpoint a few teachable elements of style that may characterise writing in their particular subject.

'I forget what I am saying in the middle'

Most people at some time lose their thread in the middle of a piece of writing. 'What was I saying?' can apply to a sequence of complex ideas, to the rest of an unfinished sentence or even to part of a word. Few people have totally efficient memories, but what makes it worse for people with dyslexia is knowing, before they even start, that short-term memory loss is likely to interfere with their writing. They know it may happen several times in the course of writing one essay. It may even happen, not while the brain is temporarily holding a memory, but actually in the midst of recalling something: 'What was I in the middle of remembering just then?'

This memory weakness can give rise to a variety of results. As it reduces the writer's self-confidence, it can sometimes account for brief or graceless writing. On the other hand, it can result in a garrulous ramble of words while the writer tries to reconnect with his line of argument. It may result in repetition or the essay may drift permanently off course. Whatever the outcome, the writer loses control of his writing, and that is unsatisfactory for his reader and demotivating for himself.

A practical classroom solution – mind-map essay plans

Supporting an unreliable memory may be only one of the reasons why essay planning is essential, but it is an important one. The multiplicity of demands in sustained writing makes thinking things out in advance an obviously sensible move for even the most proficient writer. Essay planning is not just for people with specific learning difficulties.

A mind-map plan provides the strongest support to a treacherous memory. There are no pages to turn or miss; a quick glance surveys the whole. The essay topic is in the centre of

---

Essay Writing Styles – teachable elements

- **The length of the essay:**
  It encourages the reluctant writer to be able to gauge how far he has got.

- **The order of important ideas:**
  Should the writer save the best point to the end or lead off with it?
  Should all points be given equal weight?

- **Paragraph patterns – for example:**
  1. Make a point, show relevance to the theme, give an example.
  2. Write four sentences, each making a new point.
  3. Some other format specific to your subject?

- **Paragraph links:**
  Are these important? If so, can you teach some linking phrases?

- **The beginning and the end:**
  What is their aim? What should they contain? How long should they be?

- **Tone and pace:**
  Should this be factual and swift, explanatory, analytical, contemplative, illustrated and detailed? Should it be descriptive or argumentative? Can you give vocabulary guidance, e.g. 'might' and 'could' imply doubt?

- **Vocabulary:**
  Teach and expect the technical language for your subject.
  Teach your pupils how to make this vocabulary work in a sentence.

- **Technicalities:**
  Word processing or handwriting, presenting titles and references, underlining, indenting, spacing, including graphs and diagrams.

- **Sample essays in your subject:**
  Both good and bad, these will illuminate style if you read them and discuss them with the class. The less successful writer will not intuitively learn how to improve his style simply by reading books.

Practice in each of the above areas – separately – will help a writer to adapt his style appropriately.

Figure 5.20 A teacher's checklist. Which of these elements of style can you teach in your particular subject? Are there others?

the page. It cannot be overlooked, and every thought radiates out from it. Details are visually subordinated to main ideas that catch the eye at a glance. Links between ideas can be drawn in; an order of writing can be made obvious by numbering, clustering or colour. The introduction and conclusion to an essay can be modified as the writer's ideas develop.

The creative nature of a mind-map stimulates personal memories and connections. In a visual framework, there is flexibility and space to categorise these, however illogical the sequence in which they occur to the writer. When completed, the map provides a valuable chance for a writer to use visual and spatial channels for refreshing his memory and checking the direction of his argument. Supporting sequential and linear verbal skills through these alternative channels relieves much of the strain on working memory and frees 'brain space' to concentrate on writing well.

Speaking helps remembering

The method suggested here may not come easily to a teenager in the classroom. Nevertheless, saying a sentence, silently, but with lips forming the words, acts as a rehearsal for the line to be written next. Once rehearsed, the memory is less likely to lose a sentence while the writer is preoccupied with writing it. Saying a sentence and hearing it inside the head will also act as a check on suitable expression. 'Does it sound right?' is a useful question for all writers to ask themselves.

Using tapes

Speaking into a tape recorder can help deal with an essay, particularly a longer piece or coursework, where the memory load is too great for anyone to manage without some sort of external holding and prompting mechanism.

This method is unsuited to the classroom, but it is very useful for homework. If pupils take incomplete or muddled notes and find them hard to work from, they can try gathering information for an essay onto a tape, so long as they understand that labelling is crucial to the method. Provided they include source references on the tape, they can find quotations, draw diagrams and describe case studies etc. later, at the writing stage. Spoken notes can be brief and colloquial. They can be cancelled or rerecorded. They can be played back repeatedly.

At the essay-planning stage, it is still best to draw a mind-map, thus transferring an auditory sequence into a visual one that can be surveyed as a whole. Replay taped notes to act as prompts while mapping. At the writing stage, the student who has serious difficulty with retaining the detail and expression of what he wants to say can, with a mind-map as guide, compose each paragraph onto tape and then take his own words down as dictation, polishing as he goes.

Anyone whose working memory and/or literacy skills are weak will be helped by this system of breaking up a major task and dealing with each step separately, particularly if the manner of it involves good mapping, speaking and listening to support weaknesses in remembering and writing.

'I like thinking and talking about this, but I hate writing about it'

Topics 1–6 are the reasons for this! Dyslexic students are often interested and interesting about the essay topic and have as much as anyone else to say about it. They need to be encouraged to *talk* about it and follow some of the suggestions here. It is vital that teachers encourage and value oral contributions.

Chapter 6
Languages

Learning languages

This chapter could be called, 'What to do with your weakest language pupils, when all else has failed'. There is usually a proportion of every class who:

- can't make the transition from the English sounds that letters represent to the sounds of another language
- can't remember vocabulary for longer than 24 hours
- can't remember verb conjugations
- take ages to sort out tenses
- don't 'hear' accents
- don't remember gender
- have very heavily corrected work
- can't sort out the right order of a sentence

It is in language lessons in secondary school that children with dyslexic problems usually show up most clearly. Those who have had difficulties learning to read, write and spell in their own language are very likely to encounter the same problems when they try to learn a foreign language in the classroom. It is not too surprising that someone who can't spell well in English is likely to make spelling mistakes in foreign languages and lose marks and motivation. But there is much more to it than that. These pupils forget not only the spellings, but also the meanings, the endings, the tenses, the grammar and the accents. They may start with success and enthusiasm but gradually find that repeated failure makes language learning their most hated school subject.

The cognitive weaknesses shown in a typical dyslexic profile can be directly related to the skills needed for language learning.

Typical dyslexic profile – marked strengths and weaknesses

The profile in Figure 6.1 shows the IQ scores of a dyslexic child who has been assessed because of his underperformance in school. His scores for Comprehension, Similarities, Vocabulary and Block Design are high – he may well be a child strong on reasoning with good conceptual abilities, and he can understand and enjoy the logic of grammar and will respond well to ideas about adapting his own learning style. All his low scores relate to skills – auditory perception and memory (Information, Arithmetic and Digit Span), visual perception, memory, sequencing and hand–eye co-ordination (Picture Completion and Arrangement, Coding, Mazes). These low scores will mean that acquiring the nuts and bolts of language learning will never be easy, however bright or motivated the child may be.

Looking at the graph, or at the educational psychologist's report, is less confusing than looking at the pupil. When you look at the real child in the classroom there seem to be many ordinary reasons why he is not learning well – lack of concentration, laziness, disorganisation, lack of motivation, carelessness, poor behaviour – which may all apply, but are probably secondary to the underlying difficulties.

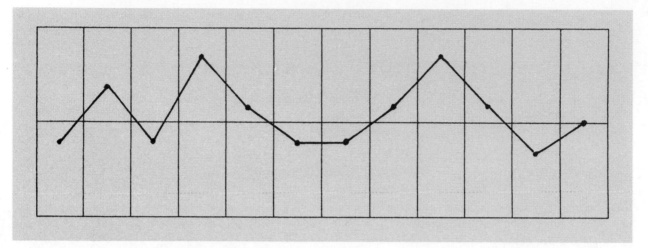

Figure 6.1 Weschler Intelligence Scale for Children (WISC). Peaks and troughs are usually evident in a dyslexic child's cognitive profile.

As well as finding the initial learning hard, these pupils are going to slip further and further behind in a subject where the steady accumulation of vocabulary and grammar is vital. Mastering even the basics can take ages. There is far less incentive to learn something if experience tells you that it will take you a much longer time than your peers and that you will probably forget it almost at once anyway.

There are solutions. These solutions are easiest to apply to a whole class of children rather than to some children within each class. The 'bottom' language sets would be a good place to start with multisensory teaching methods. Here, the approach likely to meet with most success is metacognitive: each child with his teacher should discover how he learns best and use these learning strategies where necessary, rather than plugging the 'work harder', 'more-of-the-same' approach. Language learning need not be a nightmare for pupils with mild dyslexia.

For the child with severe dyslexia, there is no doubt that studying the written component of an additional language imposes a very heavy burden of time and effort, which might be better spent on other subjects. It is unfair to expect a severely dyslexic child, who has great difficulties in his own language, to struggle alongside classmates who have no difficulties at all, unless both the teacher and the pupil are totally committed to using multisensory methods in a structured and cumulative programme.

This chapter examines how a typical dyslexic weakness can affect the specific tasks required of pupils who are learning languages – and suggests the adaptations in teaching and learning that could make all the difference to the performance of both the teacher and his pupil. The principle of multisensory learning is at the heart of each example.

Cognitive weaknesses affecting aspects of language learning

Auditory and visual perception difficulties

- hearing and seeing crucial differences in sounds and accents
- spelling correctly
- accurate reading
- hearing stress
- scanning text for endings
- looking things up in the dictionary
- being able to break up words into syllables
- hearing where one word ends and the next begins
- seeing errors in work when checking
- accurate copying

Auditory and visual memory and sequencing

- learning conjugations, declensions, vocabulary
- remembering the sentence while juggling with the sequence – while writing, translating or reading:

E	portu	Dubri	ad	flumen	Tamesin	iter	celeriter	fecimus
4	5	6	7	8	9	2	3	1
from	the port	of Dubri	to the	River	Thames	the journey	quickly	we made

Or

Je	ne	vous	les	ai	pas	donnés
1	3	7	6	2	4	5
I	not	to you	them	have	not	given

- sorting the concept of tense – and the language we use in connection with grammar
- structuring and sequencing ideas in an essay

Hand–eye co-ordination

- fast, accurate copying
- clear layout
- legibility
- effective note-taking
- orientation of accents

This direct correlation between cognitive weakness and specific difficulty explains the striking underperformance of dyslexic students tackling languages in the classroom. Not all dyslexic children will have all these weaknesses, and some teachers use teaching methods that put these children at far less of a disadvantage. Whether the weakness is auditory or visual, the solution is to integrate hearing, seeing, saying and writing so that the input and output are multisensory.

Sound–symbol correlation

Making the transition from reading the English sounds that vowel and consonant combinations represent, to recognising and saying the sounds of the language that they are learning is, for some children, a step too far. One solution is to make 'tracking' sheets with which the pupil can practise simultaneously seeing, saying and hearing each sound pattern until recognition becomes automatic.

The sheet in Figure 6.2 is made up of a selection of sounds that a particular pupil pronounced wrongly. Rather than practising all the sound patterns in the same learning session, it seems to be more beneficial to choose two confusable patterns, e.g. *de* and *des*, *un* and *une*, *le* and *les* or *eu* and *eau*, and concentrate on those for a few days until the linking of sound and symbol (ear, eye and tongue) becomes automatic, and then move on to another pair. This basic language work should be backed up at once by using the words and sound patterns in context.

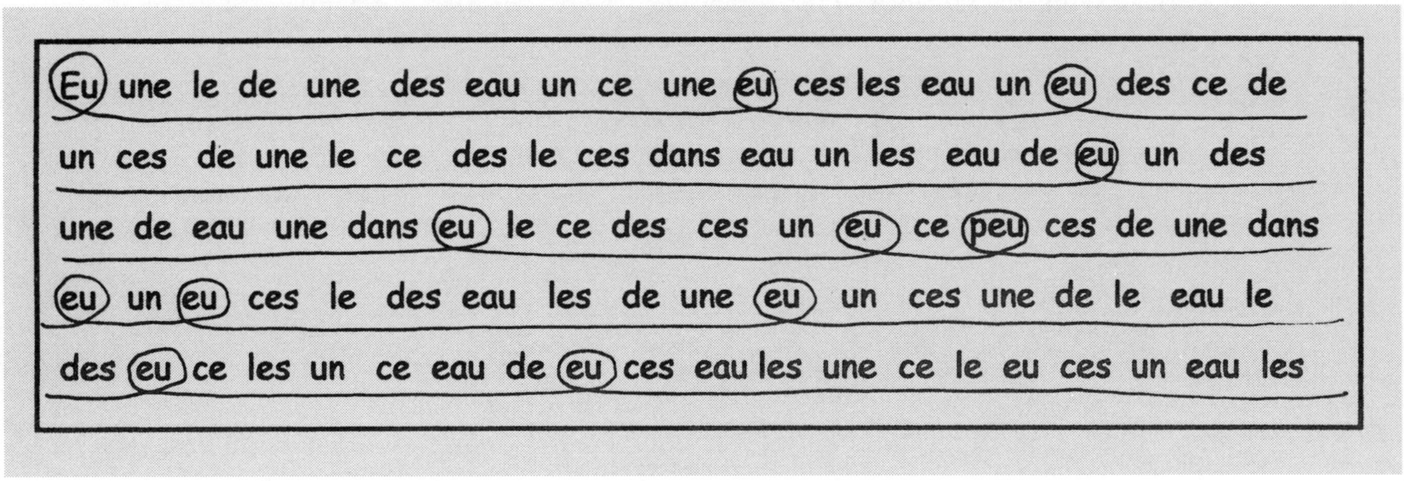

Figure 6.2 The student should focus on the letter pattern he is looking for, mark it and say the sound aloud. (See Sheet M in the Worksheet section.)

As repetition is crucial in acquiring automaticity, it is a good idea to make a sheet that can be used over and over again: either laminate a two-sided sheet (different sounds on each side) or put it inside a plastic envelope so that the pupil can track with an overhead pen and then wipe it clean afterwards, ready to be used again. A collection of these tracking sheets could cover all the sound patterns.

Following this exercise by making up a story or rhyme, or even a list of words containing the sounds that have been practised, and putting them on tape would reinforce the work done by tracking. Again, the student should look at the text while listening to the tape, and then read the text aloud with the tape or with the teacher. Using a highlighter to mark the sounds in question will focus the student's attention and sharpen his ear to the sound.

Vocabulary learning

Although only 25% of the GCSE language exams depend on written accuracy, all aspects – listening, reading, oral and written – of the exam depend on having a good basic vocabulary in the target language.

Nobody enjoys looking words up in the dictionary, but for a learner with dyslexia it takes twice as long. As sequencing for alphabetical order, scanning for the word and then copying it accurately are all difficulties, he tends not to bother and to use a limited vocabulary or guesswork. Yet he is the very pupil who needs to have a good vocabulary in his long-term memory to allow him to take any pleasure from language work.

In schools, too many children try to learn vocabulary silently from a page in a textbook. They learn it the night before a test, do reasonably well in the test and then forget most of it.

Assessing which pupils have difficulties learning vocabulary

- Set a class a list of ten *new* words to learn during the lesson.
- Give a written test (English into target language) at the end of the lesson.
- Take in the test. (Do not tell them that you are going to test the class again.)
- Give the same test a few days later. This will reveal whose learning methods were least effective for them.
- Another test after two weeks will show whether this type of learning task was an effective use of time for these children.

In this way, a teacher will be able to see who, in spite of learning under supervision, cannot remember the words, the spellings or the gender. Unless work is done under supervision, it is hard to know who has difficulties or who has simply not put in the time.

There will be a proportion of underachievers in every language class who will find language learning difficult and who would benefit from multisensory learning – linking writing directly to speaking, listening and hearing.

Getting pupils to focus on how they learn

This experiment could generate a constructive discussion on how children learn. Those in the class who remember little of what they learnt certainly need to adopt a different learning method. A dyslexic student, for example, finds it harder to remember vocabulary used randomly in the classroom and for homework. For him, a structured programme of vocabulary learning (see next page) in conjunction with oral and aural reinforcement in the classroom is ideal.

Even if the evidence is all to the contrary, dyslexic pupils are very reluctant to admit that their learning method is wrong. They would rather admit that they hadn't spent long enough, didn't bother at all or even that they are 'no good at languages'. The crucial question to ask any student with dyslexia before he embarks on a learning task is:

How **are you going to do it?**

Learning a list of vocabulary

Ideally, seeing the words and saying, hearing and writing them should make learning far more effective. The pupil with either auditory or visual perception weaknesses will be helped by using all channels simultaneously; his strengths will support his weaknesses. Faced with a list of vocabulary:

head	la cabeza
ear	la oreja
hair	el pelo
mouth	la boca
nose	la nariz
tooth	el diente

the pupil should follow this procedure:

- Look carefully at the Spanish word and say it aloud: 'la cabeza = head'
- Try to think of some way of remembering the words, for example:
  - Looking for derivatives, or linking with other languages: 'la oreja – like oreille', 'la boca – like la bouche', etc.
  - Making mnemonic links (visual if possible): a head shaped like a cab, hair made out of orange peel, a book in the mouth. Drawing or thinking of a picture is the element that makes the difference for some dyslexic learners.

Figure 6.3 eye = el ojo.

- Cover the Spanish word and say it from memory.
- Write it and then go on to the next word.
- Cover it and say it from memory.
- Write it.
- When testing, cover the column of foreign words and work down the list asking 'the head?', 'the ear'?, 'the eye?' and always say the answer out loud.

Tackling the list in this way, the memory in the eye, the tongue, the ear and the hand are all working together. Speaking the word aloud means that the pupil has to notice and respond to the syllables and the spelling – which he might gloss over if he is only *glancing* at the word. People with dyslexia simply do not notice the spelling, the accent, the syllables or the endings, unless they have to SAY the word.

The more connections dyslexic learners can make between their own language and the foreign language they are learning, the more confident they become. The mind-map 'Translate the spelling – translate the word' in Figure 6.4 shows some of the common transliterations between French and English. Recognising them will expand French vocabulary without the need to learn by rote.

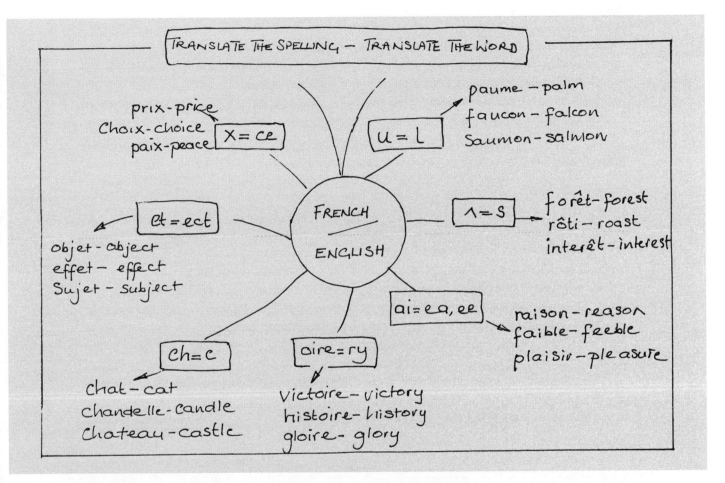

Figure 6.4 A mind-map to show connections between French and English spellings, useful to students who find rote learning hard but who learn easily through understanding a pattern.

Learning Latin vocabulary and verbs

In Latin, there are strong arguments in favour of the pupil *saying* all the principal parts, the nominative and genitive, or the masculine, feminine and neuter, of the vocabulary they are learning. When they are made aware of the 'memory' in their tongue and lips, pupils are more likely to tap into this method. The old-fashioned, rhythmic linking (*amo, amare, amavi, amatum*) also seems to work well for students with dyslexia and gives them a packet of information all at once. Pupils are occasionally persuaded to make the effort to learn in this harder but more effective way when they notice that there are often direct clues to meaning in the perfect and the supine:

Accipio, accipere, accepi, acceptum – to receive, accept

Ago, agere, egi, actum – to do, act, carry out

Sterno, sternere, stravi, stratum – spread out, lay flat, overthrow
Opprimo, opprimere, oppressi, oppressum – overwhelm, crush
Fingo, fingere, finxi, fictum – imagine, invent
Findo, findere, fidi, fissum – to split

Being tested by friend or family

When they are practising for a school test, pupils much prefer it if the tester says the foreign word and they themselves say the English. This is certainly much the easiest way round but is far less effective as a way of learning – it is about auditory recognition not about being able to remember and generate the word themselves. They are also wasting the opportunity of having to say the word aloud, which reinforces the memory in the tongue and lips and ear.

How we learn our own language

As children, we learn the vocabulary of our own language in context – in the case of nouns, we see the object, hear the word and then say it. Repetition makes that word part of our automatic vocabulary, stored in our long-term memory. It is the instinct of every mother to point to something, say the word, ask her child to repeat the word and then ask 'what's this?' again and again until that word is part of the child's expressive vocabulary.

Dyslexic children have no problems with learning their own language in this way – there is so much multisensory input and repetition – but it is when they are dealing with the written word that the difficulties show themselves. They learn the symbolic written language *after* they have learnt the spoken language and have to start all over again, pulling words apart and relating the letters to the sounds.

As secondary school pupils have to *write* the foreign language as well as speak it, it makes sense for them to learn the written form at the same time as they learn the spoken word. The ideal is that they should see it, say it, hear it and write it simultaneously, and then use it.

Learning through actions

In the same way, linking the action to the verb is much more memorable than looking at the word on the page: smiling, while saying *sourir*, getting up while saying *je me lève* or saying *je tousse* between coughs are all actions that could be done in the classroom. Others might be better done alone.

Learning through pictures

Learning with pictures, certainly in the early stages of building up a vocabulary of nouns, verbs, adjectives and adverbs, mimics the way children learn their own language. To look at a picture (Figure 6.5), say the word and write it is a much more direct route into memory for a student with dyslexia (and probably everyone else in the class too) than reading the English word, relating this to the object in question and then reading the French word.

Figure 6.6 shows the failure of a dyslexic learner to memorise Latin vocabulary for a test. His method was visual: having looked at the parallel lists for a while, he covered over the English, looked at the Latin and tried to say the English in his head. Despite painstaking effort, this method got him only 9/30 in his test.

se dépêcher

Figure 6.5 This picture also exploits the auditory link between the word for fishing, 'la pêche', and the verb to hurry, 'se dépêcher'.

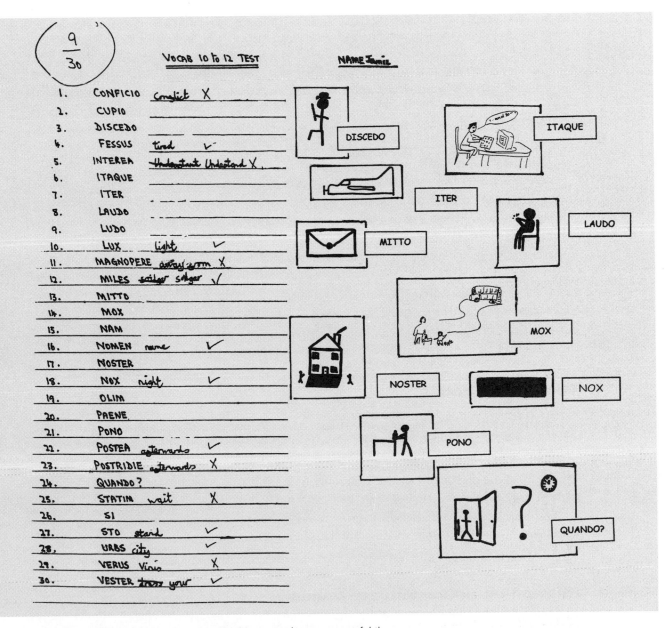

Figure 6.6 Learning Latin by drawing pictures was much more successful than just looking at the words in a list. James' original mark in his Latin vocabulary test was 9/30, but he got full marks in his re-test, having drawn pictures.

The pictures down the side of the test are drawings he subsequently made to help him learn for a re-test. He drew the pictures rapidly on cards, saying the Latin word as he drew and writing it on the back of the drawing. These he kept to use as a revision activity, looking at each picture and saying the Latin. He did not say the English words at any time, but kept tracing the direct pathway between each image and its Latin name. He made no mistake with these words in his re-test – and remembered them thereafter.

Students who have difficulty with rote learning would have a better chance with a list like this if it was shorter and if they did not necessarily learn the words in alphabetical order. Alternative methods of learning might be to draw pictures as James did, categorise the words in some way or string some of them together in a silly story: 'At once Tim (*statim*) and the soldier whose name (*nomen*) was Miles (*miles*) sat down to play their favourite old game (*ludo*); Tim versus (*versus*) Miles. When Tim confessed to being tired (*fessus*), they left on roller discs (*discedo*) for the suburbs of the city (*urbs*).

Topic-based pictures

Collecting them takes time initially, but a bank of topic-based pictures will prove a very useful resource for anyone teaching languages to dyslexic pupils. They can be hand-drawn or cut out from picture dictionaries, clip art or language textbooks. Once collected and categorised ('school', 'holidays', 'food', 'travel' etc.) they can, of course, be used again and again. The sets can be photocopied onto card so that individual pupils can borrow copies of the master pack. The teacher can put the relevant sheet on an overhead projector and, with the class, rehearse the foreign words aloud.

For homework the children can practise saying the word aloud while looking at the picture, perhaps think of mnemonic links and then cut out the pictures and labels and try to match the right word with the right picture, saying the word aloud again as they do so. They should do this several times at intervals and then keep their pack of pictures and labels for future revision (Figure 6.7).

Picture dictionaries are a useful source of pictures – cutting out the pictures, making the labels for them and storing them in topic packs. Testing the pupils could consist of asking them to write the appropriate foreign word under the picture while saying it, or getting into pairs to test each other with the pack of pictures. The latter has the advantage of being more fun and ensuring that the children do *say* the words aloud.

Vocabulary books

When dyslexic pupils build up a vocabulary book of their own, there are likely to be miscopyings, an unclear image of the word, erratic definite or indefinite articles (if any), a justifiable lack of confidence in what has been written and no space for practising writing the word. Checking each word in the dictionary to see if it is accurately spelt and defined, and with the right gender, is time-consuming – and rarely done (Figure 6.8).

Checking individual handwritten vocabulary books so that the pupils don't learn the wrong words is an important task for teachers, but it is frustrating correcting a dyslexic pupil's book that is often full of errors and has no space for clear corrections.

Custom-made vocabulary tables

Building up a collection of vocabulary spreadsheets or tables on a computer to match the school textbook or course is a useful way of making a reliable list for pupils to work from.

une boite   un classeur   un crayon   un livre

une trousse   une calcatrice   une règle   une fenêtre

une chaise   une platine-laser   une gomme   une porte

un cartable   un magnétophone   un bic   un ordinateur

Figure 6.7 A bank of pictures with separate labels is a useful resource.

This could be done by the teacher and be made available to pupils or, if pupils have their own computers, collecting their vocabulary on a spreadsheet is a very efficient method of recording words that need to be learnt. Some of the exam boards actually provide very useful vocabulary tables on the Web ready for downloading (www.ocr.org.uk).

Unfortunately, using Excel spreadsheets has two drawbacks: 'Word' shortcuts for accents do not at present work within Excel – a new set of rather cumbersome shortcuts have

A page from Richard's French vocabulary book

je m'entends bien avec

je ne mentends pas bien avec

(*) embêtant
gâté
se disputer   spoik
                     to argue
(*) je me dispute avec } I argue with
(*) mon père ~~~~~   } my father
un avantage   advantage
un inconvenient ~ disadvantage

je
  le correspondent   pen pal
  en plein air   open air

mettre une lettre à la poste - to post a lette
un paquet   ~   a package
(*) Ca fait - that costs
(*) La boit a lettre - letterbox
La ~~qui~~ kiosque téléphonique
est-ce que je peux -
Composer le numéro - dial the #
(*) les rensengements - info
(*) la banlieu - suburb
est-ce que je dois - must I /do / have to

Figure 6.8 (a), (b) Two pupils' vocabulary books: problems of space, alignment, clarity, hearing and copying accurately are obvious. Pupils probably don't feel completely confident even in those words that are actually correct.

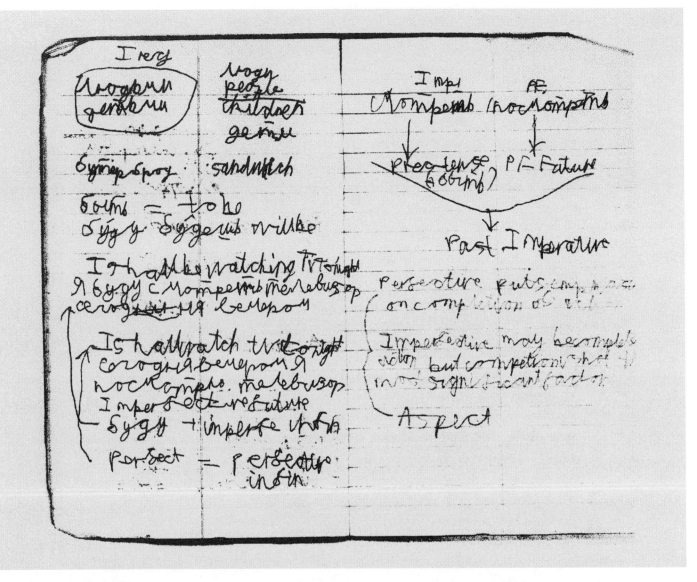

Figure 6.8 (b)

to be learnt – and the foreign spellchecker, so useful for checking accuracy, does not work either. One solution is to use a table within 'Word' – this enables the pupil to access the accents, use the spellchecker (pretty important for dyslexic pupils) and still have the advantages of a spreadsheet.

Advantages of using tables within 'Word' for vocabulary

- Word-processed work is easy to correct
- Clear image for pupils to learn from
- Columns for pupils to write or type into
- Space available for pupils to draw a picture or mnemonic link
- Facility to hide the answer column while self-testing
- Facility to hide the words already learnt – and 'unhide' for revision
- Option to work either on the screen or on paper

Topic	Spanish	English	Picture	✓ or ✗	3rd review	2nd review	1st review

Sorting it

The vocab can be set up in any order but sorted later (Table → Sort → topic or language or whatever heading you invent):

- Words arranged alphabetically – lists could be used as a dictionary (or use Control → F).
- Target language → English or vice versa.
- Vocabulary needing more work could be put at the top of the list (sort on ✓ or X).
- Vocabulary from set books could be arranged chapter by chapter.
- Teachers could arrange words for particular exercises, e.g. verbs conjugated with *être* grouped together, topic vocabulary, words of the same gender, declension, verbs of the same conjugation or sharing the same rules.
- Just rearranging the order of words in a list is useful for those pupils who remember the word because of its neighbours in the list and then are all at sea when they see the word in isolation.

Building up the list, categorising the words within it and then testing are all active and useful learning tasks.

Pupils can use one of these sheets (see Figure 6.9) for homework – drawing a picture in the picture box, perhaps with some mnemonic link and then doing timed reviews of the words in columns 1, 2 and then 3. The sheets can be folded to hide the answers, and then unfolded for checking (Figure 6.10). The extra columns can be used for further reviews. Some children will find it much more effective to look at the picture rather than look at the English word to help them to remember the French.

The 'forgetting curve'

The 'forgetting curve' is a crucial element in all learning, particularly for pupils who are dyslexic (Figure 6.11). They need to take it into account and take practical steps to counteract it.

Most students would agree that, of 20 words learnt on Monday in one learning session, only a very small proportion will be remembered by the following Monday. That learning session is therefore almost a waste of time unless it is topped up by further reviews. Psychologists tell us that reviewing information at intervals is the secret to transferring it from short to long-term memory. (See Chapter 7, page 238, and *Your Memory: a User's Guide* (Baddeley, 1982)).

	French	English	Picture	3rd Review	2nd Review	1st Review
1	le tablier	apron				
2	le pull	pullover				
3	la ceinture	belt				
4	la botte	boot				
5	la casquette	cap				
6	la robe	dress				
7	le gant	glove				
8	le sac	handbag				
9	le chapeau	hat				
10	la veste	jacket				
11	le jean	jeans				
12	la chaussure	shoe				
13	la jupe	skirt				
14	une écharpe	scarf				
15	la chausette	sock				
16	la cravate	tie				
17	le collant	tights				
18	la chemise	shirt				

Figure 6.9 This pupil has used mnemonic links in her pictures to help her remember her vocabulary: A# knitted into a scarf, un tablier on a table, a vest worn *over* a shirt.

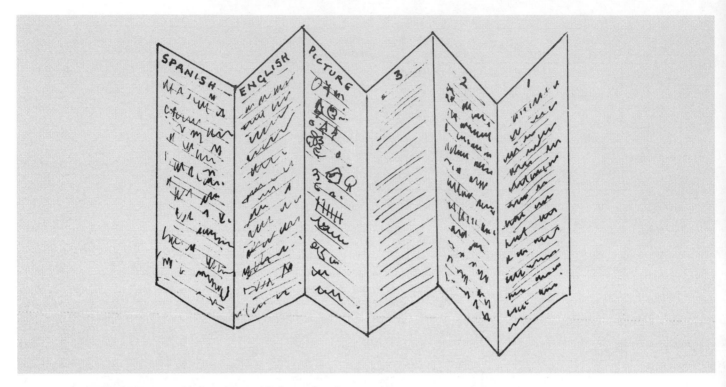

Figure 6.10 A4 vocabulary sheets with the word and its meaning printed in the first columns can be folded in this way. The format encourages the pupil to write the words out while he tests himself and provides additional columns for reviewing.

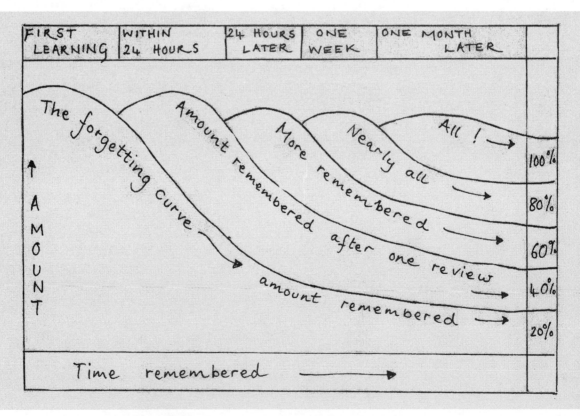

Figure 6.11 The 'forgetting curve'. It is a more efficient use of time to review vocabulary etc., while the memory trace is still strong. Leaving revision until the first learning is almost forgotten means a great deal more work is needed to revive the trace.

Although most teachers work to a schedule that maximises memory efficiency – lesson, homework, class session, test – it is important that pupils themselves are made aware of the dramatic difference that reviewed multisensory learning makes. Once aware, they can generalise from successful learning experiences and use the same system for all their learning.

Vocabulary learning provides a perfect model for setting up a class experiment about learning effectiveness: not only 'How to learn it?' but also 'How often to review it?' and 'At what intervals?' This will help everyone, but it is vital for dyslexic students to be helped to find their best way of transferring learnt work from short- to long-term memory.

Recording vocabulary onto tape

By using audiotapes, the pupil's speaking and listening can be linked directly into the initial learning of vocabulary. Recording vocabulary and phrases is something that pupils enjoy. Two voices on the tape make it more lively – teacher or friend for the English words, pupils the foreign word. Making the tape and discussing why it is an effective learning method is a useful lesson in itself. A rehearsal is important, to make sure that there are no misreadings or mispronunciations:

- The pupil rehearses by saying the English, then the foreign word aloud, thinking of mnemonic links, noting gender.
- He switches on the tape recorder.
- He or his teacher says the English word into the microphone.
- He leaves a pause long enough to give the answer when he is practising with the tape later.
- Then he says the foreign word.
- . . . and so on, saying all the words in the list.

When he comes to revise he should do the following:

- The first time he plays the tape back he should look at the list while he says the foreign word in the gap on the tape.
- Play it again, but this time he should not look at the list but try to fill the pause before he hears his own voice on the tape.
- When he has played the tape several times he will 'hear' the word hanging in the pregnant pause before it is spoken and be able to respond without thinking.
- The final stage in this operation is for the student to be able to *write* the word in the pause while he speaks it.

One of the advantages of using tape is that it is an ideal medium for revision; it is stored all ready for future reinforcement (Figure 6.12). Labelling and storing the tapes are important parts of the exercise!

Learning phrases from tape

By putting phrases or grammatical examples onto tape, and hearing them again and again, the listener learns not only the words auditorily but also their order. For many people with dyslexia the grammatical sequence that *sounds* right is much more reliable than one that *looks* right. (This is why dyslexic students should always check their work by reading it aloud – or, if they are in the exam room, by subvocalising.) Hearing the way the grammar works in

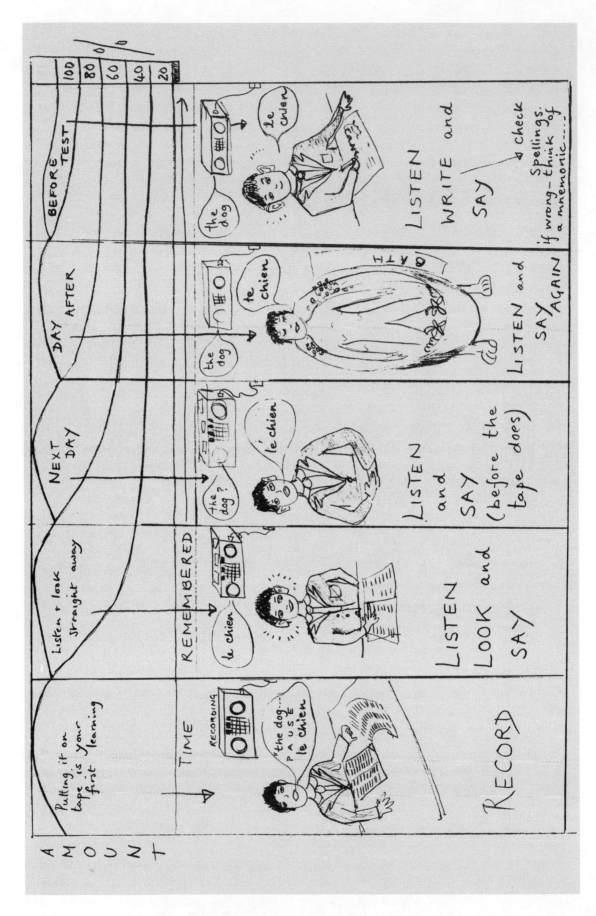

Figure 6.12 A child using a tape recorder in conjunction with the 'forgetting curve' to help him learn his words or phrases.

the particular instance on the tape will also help the pupil to develop an ear for the syntax generally.

The same procedure of rehearsing before recording, and looking carefully at the written phrase while speaking and listening, is particularly important while learning sentences and phrases. Dyslexic students may have difficulty knowing where one word ends and another begins, so seeing the visual presentation helps enormously.

How are you today? – Pause – 'Comment vas-tu aujourd'hui?'

Working with a dictionary

Scanning, sequencing, visual or auditory short-term memory and accurate copying are all areas of difficulty for dyslexic students – and, unfortunately, all are necessary skills for dictionary work. Looking words up is therefore time-consuming and very demotivating. Vocabulary that is stored in the dyslexic person's long-term memory will be more quickly and accurately retrieved – so effective vocabulary learning is vital for him.

Ideas to help with dictionary work

- Buy a dictionary with clearly laid out pages, reasonably large print and spaces between entries. The dictionary should not be so thick or tightly bound that it automatically closes when you take your hand off it.
- Alphabetical finger marks or 'ears' on the pages will speed up finding the right letter. Pupils can mark the outside of pages themselves with coloured stripes and letters – Figure 6.13(a) – to help them find their way around.

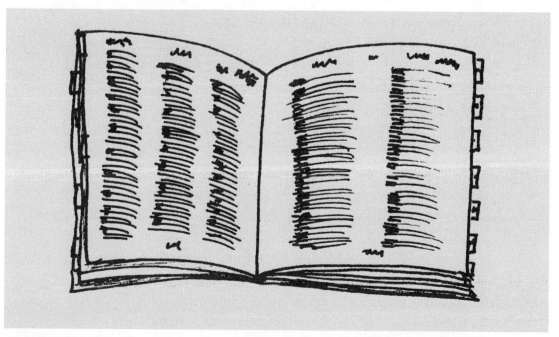

Figure 6.13 (a)

- A bookmark with the alphabet printed on it will help the student to find first the letter and then the word he is looking for. This is particularly helpful with Russian, Greek or other unfamiliar alphabets (Figure 6.13b).

The experience of many pupils is that having looked up a word in the dictionary is no guarantee of remembering it accurately in the long or even the short term. In fact, the act of looking up the word and writing it down makes the pupil feel 'now I needn't remember it'!

How to help the student remember the words he looks up

- Whenever he has to look up a word, the student should highlight it (Figure 6.14). This will draw his eye to the word every time he opens the dictionary at that page, thus reinforcing his memory of the word. This is less arduous than copying it into a vocabulary book (perhaps inaccurately).
- Highlighted words can then be put in a list or onto tape.
- It is particularly useful to use an audiotape when the student is working through a set text – these are words he knows he will definitely need to know in the future. They are worth learning. If he simply writes the translation directly onto the text, when he comes to revise for his exam he will not have to search his memory for the right word and so his translating session will be too passive.

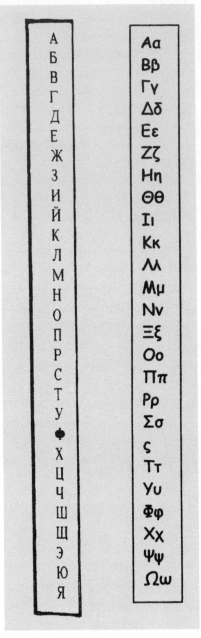

Figure 6.13(b)

- There are good foreign language dictionaries for students with dyslexia who work on computers. They are so easy and quick to use that they actually encourage vocabulary extension and reduce the problems imposed by poor scanning and sequencing. Idioms, grammar, model letters and verb tables make these dictionaries a rich resource – even if they do make it much harder for the teacher to know what is the pupil's own work and what is lifted straight from the dictionary (see page 229)!
- Pocket translators are worth investigating. In particular, Franklin Electronic Publishers sell an English Dictionary/Thesaurus DMQ 440 with a 'Bookman Rom' card slot that allows a user to add foreign language dictionaries. 'Professeur d'Anglais', for instance, translates and spells 200,000 French and English words and

383　English ~ French

flamingo → flu

flamingo NOUN
le *flamant rose*

flan NOUN
1 la *tarte* (sweet) ◇ *a raspberry flan* une tarte aux framboises
2 la *quiche* (savoury) ◇ *a cheese and onion flan* une quiche au fromage et aux oignons

flannel NOUN
le *gant de toilette* (for face)

to **flap** VERB
battre de ◇ *The bird flapped its wings.* L'oiseau battait des ailes.

flash NOUN
see also flash VERB
le *flash*
(les *flashes* PL)
◇ *Has your camera got a flash?* Est-ce que ton appareil photo a un flash?
• **a flash of lightning** un éclair
• **in a flash** en un clin d'œil

to **flash** VERB
see also flash NOUN
1 *clignoter* ◇ *The police car's blue light was flashing.* Le gyrophare de la voiture de police clignotait.
2 *projeter* ◇ *They flashed a torch in his face.* Ils lui ont projeté la lumière d'une torche en plein visage.
• **She flashed her headlights.** Elle a fait un appel de phares.

flat ADJECTIVE
see also flat NOUN
1 *plat* ◇ *a flat roof* un toit plat ◇ *flat shoes* des chaussures plates
2 *crevé* (tyre) ◇ *I've got a flat tyre.* J'ai un pneu crevé.

flat NOUN
see also flat ADJECTIVE
l' *appartement* MASC ◇ *She lives in a flat.* Elle habite un appartement.

to **flatter** VERB
flatter

flavour NOUN
1 le *goût* (taste) ◇ *This cheese has a very strong flavour.* Ce fromage a un goût très fort.
2 le *parfum* (variety) ◇ *Which flavour of ice cream would you like?* Quel parfum de glace est-ce que tu veux?

flavouring NOUN
le *parfum*

flew VERB *see* **fly**

flexible ADJECTIVE
flexible ◇ *flexible working hours* les horaires flexibles

to **flick** VERB
appuyer sur ◇ *She flicked the switch to turn the light on.* Elle a appuyé sur le

bouton pour allumer la lumière.
• **to flick through a book** feuilleter un livre

to **flicker** VERB
trembloter ◇ *The light flickered.* La lumière a trembloté.

flight NOUN
le *vol* ◇ *What time is the flight to Paris?* À quelle heure est le vol pour Paris?
• **a flight of stairs** un escalier

to **fling** VERB
jeter ◇ *He flung the dictionary onto the floor* Il a jeté le dictionnaire par terre.

to **float** VERB
flotter ◇ *A leaf was floating on the water.* Une feuille flottait sur l'eau.

flock NOUN
• **a flock of sheep** un troupeau de moutons
• **a flock of birds** un vol d'oiseaux

flood NOUN
see also flood VERB
1 l' *inondation* FEM ◇ *The rain has caused many floods.* La pluie a provoqué de nombreuses inondations.
2 le *flot* ◇ *He received a flood of letters.* Il a reçu un flot de lettres.

to **flood** VERB
see also flood NOUN
inonder ◇ *The river has flooded the village.* La rivière a inondé le village.

flooding NOUN
les *inondations* FEM PL

floor NOUN
1 le *sol* ◇ *a tiled floor* un sol carrelé
• **on the floor** par terre
2 l' *étage* MASC (storey) ◇ *the first floor* le premier étage
• **the ground floor** le rez-de-chaussée
• **on the third floor** au troisième étage

floppy disk NOUN
la *disquette*

florist NOUN
le/la *fleuriste*

flour NOUN
la *farine*

to **flow** VERB
1 *couler* (river)
2 *s'écouler* (flow out) ◇ *Water was flowing from the pipe.* De l'eau s'écoulait du tuyau.

flower NOUN
see also flower VERB
la *fleur*

to **flower** VERB
see also flower NOUN
fleurir

flown VERB *see* **fly**
flu NOUN

F

Figure 6.14 A dictionary with highlighted words is useful for a quick revision of words that the student actually needs. It can also be used as a vocab book for testing. (This page is taken from Collins' *Easy Learning French Dictionary*, which has most of the criteria to make it user-friendly, including colour, for dyslexic students up to GCSE standard.)

phrases. The card includes a useful verb-tense guide for each verb in its vocabulary, a facility to create personal word lists and seven language-learning games. This small, robust device has a clear display and is a single alternative to dictionaries in book form for several languages including English.

- For those children doing their work on a word processor, the Language facility in 'Word' will check their grammar and spelling for them (up to a point). Some teachers may feel that using this aid for school homework is 'cheating'. Others feel it is more beneficial to the pupil and teacher to have the pupil's work corrected for him within seconds of writing it – rather than a few days later when the teacher is able to correct it and the pupil may have lost interest in the exercise.

Gender

When learning vocabulary, most pupils with dyslexia don't even bother to try to learn the gender of the word. They don't see the definite or indefinite article, they don't notice the ending of the word, which might give the clue, and they are mostly unaware that there are any rules about gender (except that in French most words ending in 'e' are feminine). In spite of the fact that not knowing the gender of the word inhibits them from saying anything at all and makes them lose marks in every piece of work they do, learning the gender of a word seems to be the last straw.

Teaching some of the rules of gender is a useful starting point. One student, asked to learn the rules for his homework, turned a rather forbidding list of rules into a mind-map. To help him to learn which endings were usually masculine, he wrote an ending on each branch of a mind-map and then chose words with those endings and then drew a picture to remind himself of each example and its ending. The exceptions to the rules are made very clear in an extra box. Having done this, he then turned the page over and visualised the mind-map, describing it aloud as he did so. He was able to remember the rules without any difficulty (Figure 6.15).

Saying the word and its article aloud while learning will not only link the 'le' with the 'fermier' auditorily but will also focus the learner's attention on the ending of the word: to say it, he has to notice that there is an '-ier' ending (not *la* fermiè*re*) – a clue to gender which affects pronunciation. Just looking at the word does not focus the attention in the same way – especially not for the child with visual weaknesses. (See Sheets N and O and P in the Worksheet section.)

Almost any strategy for remembering gender is better than none

- When a pupil has to learn a list of words, he could group them according to gender either in a picture (Figure 6.16) or in a list.
- He could colour code the words or colour code the pictures, e.g. blue for a boy, pink for a girl.
- He could link the word with a gender-specific (blanc/blanche) adjective (Figure 6.17).

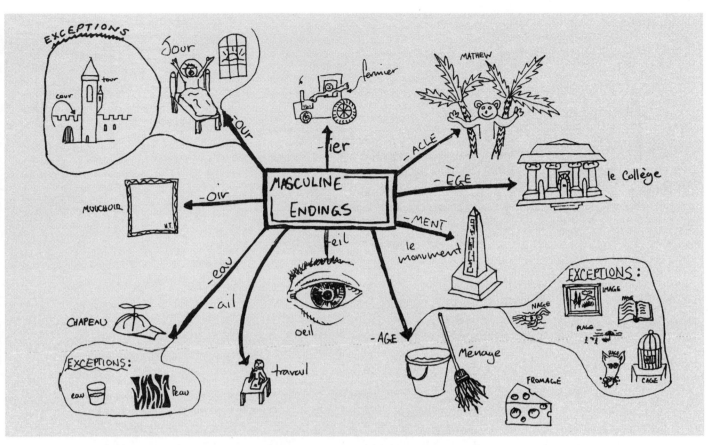

Figure 6.15 The pictures are personal to the person who drew them, and therefore memorable (in this mind-map Henry has shown his friend Matthew Akle as a monkey, saying that he was a good climber). (See N and O in the Worksheet section.) Each child could make up his own pictures to help him remember the gender rules.

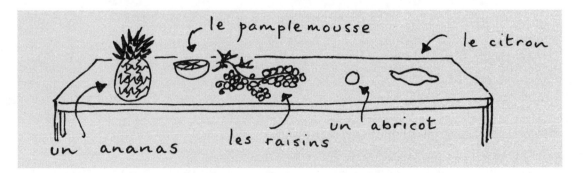

Figure 6.16 Noticing that nearly all the words for fruits in French are feminine, this pupil selected the only fruits that are masculine, visualised them on his own kitchen table and drew them. In this way he was able to visualise the picture each time he needed to check on the gender of a fruit.

- He could draw or visualise the word in a masculine or feminine situation – a blue umbrella (parapluie) held by a man or a coat-hanger (un cintre) with some trousers on it.

Ignoring the gender problem will not make it go away.

Figure 6.17 Attaching an adjective to every noun can give a package of information – noun, adjective, gender and order of words.

Verbs

Here very basic difficulties in understanding occur. To begin with, the study of language has generated a technical vocabulary of its own. There is a special symbolic language for language learning, as there is in maths. It gets in the way of understanding, particularly because some familiar words are used in a special sense – 'imperfect', 'present', 'tense'. There are questions that pupils are embarrassed to ask – and the more time passes, the more difficult it becomes for them to ask:

What is a verb?   What is the first person singular?
What is conjugate?   What is the perfect?
What is the infinitive?   What is tense?
Which bit is the ending?

On the other hand, if teachers did not use this specialised vocabulary to explain and categorise the make-up of foreign verbs, students would have to rely solely on rote memory to learn them. Any method is better than this for dyslexic linguists.

Activities in the following pages may help students with the formation of French verbs and the technical words that describe them. Teachers can apply this multisensory and personal style to verbs in other languages. Though initial processing involving thinking, making, seeing and saying may take longer, it will make a strong impact on memory and the resultant products – verb wheel, checklist, pocket card, tracking sheet, audiotape – are all ideal for 'forgetting curve' reviews.

Without multisensory teaching, it is commonplace for dyslexic children to study French for at least six years and still not be able to recognise, speak or write the correct form of regular (let alone irregular) foreign verb tenses. Could anything more clearly indicate a misfit between teaching and learning styles?

Learning verb endings

Phonological Processing

- Dyslexic learners do not easily see or hear segments within a word. They are not therefore alert to the arrangement of 'stem' and 'ending' characteristic of verb formation in inflected foreign languages.

Sequencing and Memory

- Not recognising any pattern, students with dyslexia see each part of each verb as just a string of letters to be learned and reproduced in isolation: the load on memory and sequencing is too great.

Visual and Auditory Perception

- In French, for example, some verb endings don't sound at all (je paye, tu payes, ils payent) or sound the same but are spelt differently (je payais, il payait, ils payaient). Differences in pronunciation or spelling are often slight (vous payiez) but significant (the 'i' denotes the imperfect tense).

Hand–eye Co-ordination

- Dyslexic learners cannot be counted on to copy or spell accurately. Writing is not therefore a reliable aid to memory. It is often the reverse.

The strategies below will help:

- **To reduce memory load** – recognise, name and categorise all segments of a verb: pronoun, stem, ending, auxiliary, past participle. Look for patterns.
- **To enlist cognitive strength** – understand the repetitive and cumulative structures in forming verbs. (In French, the imperfect endings, ais, ais, ait, ions, iez, aient, are used again with the future stem to form the conditional tense, je viendrais, tu viendrais etc.) They need to be learned only once.
- **To use memory in lips and tongue, ears and eyes** – repeat whole tenses aloud, stressing the rhythm while identifying the endings on the page.
- **To learn the order** – spell endings rhythmically aloud: 'e-es-e/ons-ez-ent'.
- **To monitor spelling** – say the verb, thinking 'Does it sound right?' while writing.
- **Repeat the learning** – keep topping it up. Keep referring to a check sheet. Keep getting the verbs right.

Forming regular verb tenses

Keep using the checklist until you can visualise it in your head. Drawing pictures on it will help you to visualise the page. Keep saying the endings aloud.

Ask yourself:
- Am I using an 'er', 'ir' or 're' verb?
- Which tense do I need?
- Is it regular?
- Which person?

To form the **PRESENT** in regular 'er' verbs:
Take the infinitive
Remove 'er'
Add the endings

e	ons
es	ez
e	ent

parler
travailler
penser
marcher
cultiver

To form the **PRESENT** in regular 'ir' verbs:
Take the infinitive
Remove 'ir'
Add the endings

is	issons
is	issez
it	issent

finir
cueillir
mentir
se guérir
rougir

To form the **PRESENT** in regular 're' verbs:
Take the infinitive
Remove 're'
Add the endings

s	ons
s	ez
-	ent

entendre
répondre
défendre
rompre
descendre

To form the **PERFECT** in all verbs:
Take the present tense of avoir
(sometimes être)
Add the past participle of the verb

ai + joué	avons +
as +	avez +
a +	ont +

eu   reçu
été   dit
allé   mis
ri   fait
pris   vécu

To form the **IMPERFECT** in regular verbs:
Take 'nous' form of present tense
Remove 'ons'
Add the endings

ais	ions
ais	iez
ait	aient

Nous
choisiss/*ons*
....
Je
Choisiss/*ais*

To form the **FUTURE** in regular verbs:
Take the infinitive
Add the endings
(Remove 'e' from 're' infinitives)

ai	ons
as	ez
a	ont

Vendr/*e*
....
Je vendr*ai*

Forming advanced verb tenses

Keep saying the endings aloud until you can visualise the page and say the endings from memory. Keep using this checklist when you write.

To form the **PAST HISTORIC** in all 'er' verbs: Remove 'er' from the infinitive Add the endings	ai âmes as âtes a èrent
To form the **PAST HISTORIC** in regular 'ir' and 're' verbs: Remove 'ir' or 're' from the infinitive Add the endings	is îmes is îtes it irent
To form the **PAST HISTORIC** in many, but not all, 'oir' verbs: Remove 'oir' Add the endings	us ûmes us ûtes ut urent
To form the **PLUPERFECT** in all verbs: Take the imperfect tense of avoir (Sometimes être) Add the past participle of the verb	avais + dit avions + dit avais + aviez + avait + avaient +

To form the **CONDITIONAL** in all verbs:
 	
Take the future stem
(in regular verbs that is the infinitive)
Add imperfect tense endings
	fer + ais fer + ions
	      + ais + iez
	      + ait + aient

To form **FUTURE PERFECT** in all verbs: Take the future of avoir (sometimes être) Add the past participle of the verb	aurai + vu aurons + vu auras + aurez + aura + auront +

Learning verbs

Dyslexic students are often hampered in language learning by not having grasped fundamentals at the time they were taught. Multi-sensory methods may clear the way. Here are strategies to help with sorting and remembering:

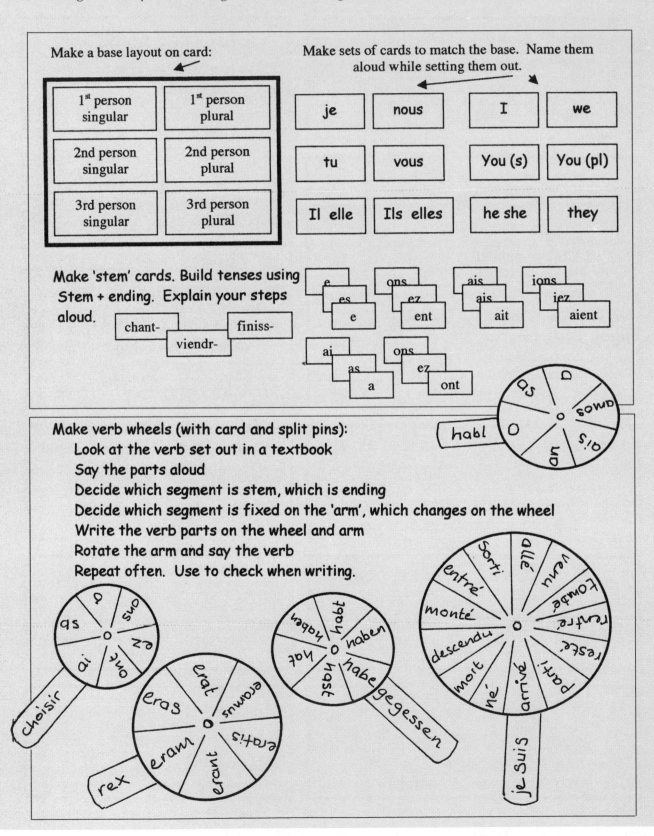

Make a base layout on card:

1st person singular	1st person plural
2nd person singular	2nd person plural
3rd person singular	3rd person plural

Make sets of cards to match the base. Name them aloud while setting them out.

je	nous	I	we
tu	vous	You (s)	You (pl)
Il elle	Ils elles	he she	they

Make 'stem' cards. Build tenses using Stem + ending. Explain your steps aloud.

chant- viendr- finiss-

e es e ons ez ent ais ais ait ions iez aient

ai as a ons ez ont

Make verb wheels (with card and split pins):
Look at the verb set out in a textbook
Say the parts aloud
Decide which segment is stem, which is ending
Decide which segment is fixed on the 'arm', which changes on the wheel
Write the verb parts on the wheel and arm
Rotate the arm and say the verb
Repeat often. Use to check when writing.

habl

choisir

rex

je suis

Learning irregular verbs

Pocket cards
· Write the verb on a small card.
· Keep it in your pocket for a week.
· Take it out often and say the verb aloud, write it or test a friend.

ich bin	wir sind
du bist	ihr seid
er ist	sie sind

The difficulties are:
· Recognising tense, person, meaning
· Pronouncing especially vowel sounds
· Spelling French sounds, silent parts
· Segmenting stem and endings
· Sequencing the parts in order
· Recalling quickly

The solutions are:
Multisensory: Speak while looking, write while speaking, visualise while sequencing.

Processing: Ask yourself which of your learning methods will work best here – use that method.

Separating the task into steps – *make a verb card *keep it in your pocket *take it out and say it, write it, test a friend on it *file it for later review.

Repeating the Learning – Where will you keep the card, tracking sheet or tape for later use? When will you use it?

Make a tape of irregular verbs, in German for example:
· Say: 'Present tense of 'to be''
· Leave a pause, then say the verb.
·' ich bin, du bist, er ist,' etc.
Hear & stress the rhythm.
· Replay the tape and say the verb in the pause.
· Hear your own voice saying it.

Tracking sheets are helpful both to make and to use
To make – scatter parts of a verb in its conventional order along a line of meaningless words in the target language:
Latin: *sum es est sumus estis sunt*
Foro candidatus sum nos favemus mercator es optimam quod diem est multi cum Sumus amicis discum parabat maxima estis vidi omnes postquam sunt villam
To use – Say each part in order aloud, search for it and circle it.

Tenses

Dyslexic students, who often have a poor sense of time anyway (a fact that those of us who haven't got this problem find hard to accept), can have an added problem when it comes to learning verb tenses.

They may have only a foggy notion of the terms 'present', 'imperfect', 'perfect' and 'future'. Loosely talking about the 'past tense' is a clue to their confusion. Without an understanding of tense, learning another language is going to be an uphill struggle (Figure 6.18).

These students can be greatly helped by first distinguishing the tenses in their own language. They can sort out a heap of cards with verbs written on them, by placing each one under the appropriate column heading. Two tenses would be enough to start with and when these are secure, others can be added (Figure 6.19).

Once the pupil can do this and justify each decision out loud by using the terminology, e.g. 'this is in the imperfect tense because it is a continuous action in the past', he will be ready to do the same exercise in the target language (Figure 6.20).

This exercise can also be done on a worksheet, but, as with all language work, using cards seems to encourage pupils to say the words aloud and also to talk about what they are doing and why (see Sheets Q and R in the Worksheet section.)

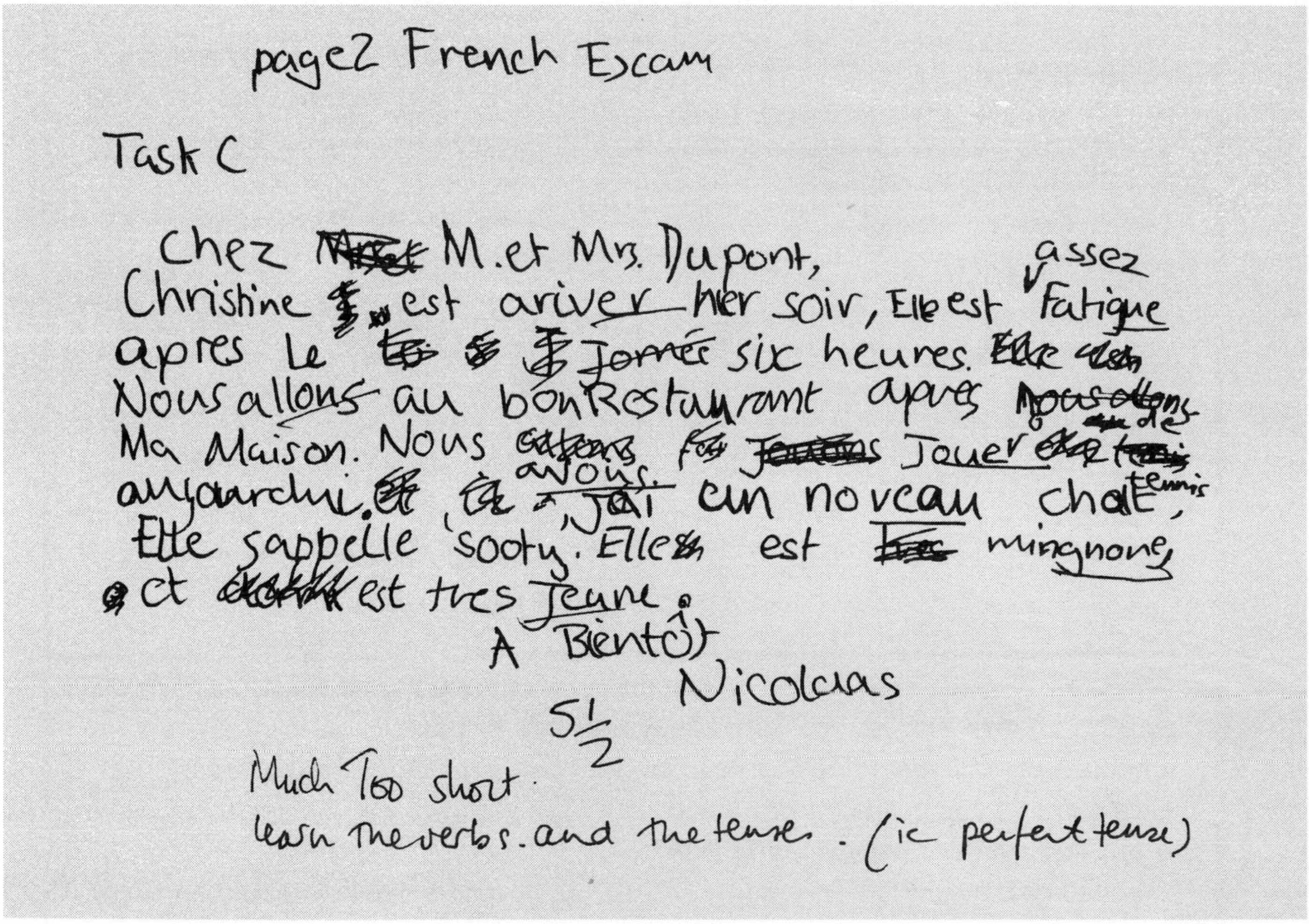
page2 French Excam

Task C

Chez M. et Mrs. Dupont,
Christine est ariver hier soir, Elle est assez Fatigue
apres le Jornée six heures.
Nous allons au bon Restaurant apres de
Ma Maison. Nous Jouer de tennis
aujourdui. avons J'ai un noveau chat,
Elle sappelle 'sooty'. Elle est mingnone,
et est tres Jeune.
A Bientôt
Nicolas

5 1/2
Much Too short.
learn the verbs. and the tenses. (ie perfect tense)

Figure 6.18 Nic had problems of capitalisation, sequencing, accents and spelling, as well as verbs. It was demoralising trying to cope without this basic knowledge.

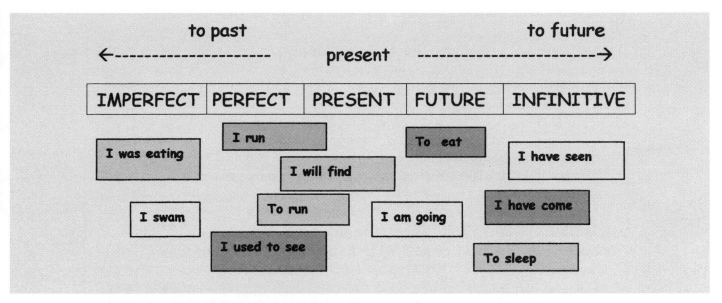

Figure 6.19 Sorting cards is a practical and palatable way of learning and revising tenses. It is a good idea to start with the pupil's own language before moving on to the target language. (See Sheets Q and R in Worksheet section).

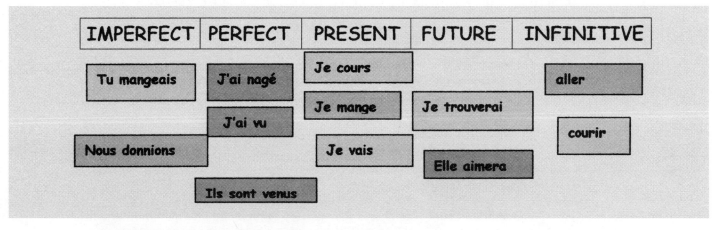

Figure 6.20 When the tenses are clear in English, the target language can be attempted. This example shows several tenses, but it is a good idea to start on two tenses at a time because this will simplify the task and build confidence.

Some pupils say that, after doing this exercise, they can 'see' where each tense is, spatially, on the table or the page, and this helps them to identify the correct tense when they are constructing their own sentences. Others colour code the different tenses. This sorting exercise is effective for pupils with dyslexia because it involves multisensory learning:

- Seeing the words
- Saying the words aloud
- Categorising by physically moving the cards around
- Expressing ideas aloud
- Memorising concept of time spatially

To practise identifying tenses as a task in itself

Pupils can take a piece of written French, German, Spanish etc. and colour code or track for the endings of the verbs. For the person who is dyslexic this is helpful because it develops scanning skills, encourages the pupil to recognise and focus on the verbs and to separate stems from endings (Figure 6.21).

El barco se acercaba al puerto. El capitán, de pie sobre el puente, contemplaba el subir y bajar de las olas cuando, de pronto, vio dos pequeños objetos en la lejanía que parecían nadar.

Al principio, pensó que serían peces, pero en seguida cambió de opinión. No había peces tan grandes en aquella parte del mar. Decidió acercarse por curiosidad.

Los objetos pequeños resultaron ser dos niños. Los marineros les recogieron en el barco y les dieron café caliente y ropa seca. Cuando se sintieron un poco mejor, explicaron al capitán cómo habían estado jugando en una pequeña barca de goma cerca de la playa cuando se levantó un fuerte viento que les ajeló de la costa. Al principio, no se preocuparon, pero, cuando desapareció la costa se su vista, sintieron miedo y saltaron al mar con la intención de nadar a tierra. Tres horas habían luchado con las olas y todo habría sido en vano sin la curiosidad del capitán.

Figure 6.21 Scanning for and marking verb endings is very useful training for the eye. Dyslexic students may have a particular difficulty breaking words up into stem and suffix – a skill that is vital in language learning.

Mind-mapping the tenses

As hearing is 'sequencing in time', children with auditory sequencing and memory difficulties may find it helpful to lay out the tenses spatially so that they can see the sequence – 'sequencing in space' (see Mind-mapping, page 43).

Mind-mapping the tenses helps some dyslexic pupils to remember which tense is which by its position on the page and subsequently to 'see' the characteristics of each tense in their mind's eye. Pictures and mnemonic links help initially until the knowledge is lodged in the long-term memory (Figure 6.22).

Making the mind-map, drawing pictures or symbols, thinking of mnemonics and using colour represent the thorough processing that helps the dyslexic student to remember the verbs, the tenses and their endings. Re-visualising the map and describing it aloud several times will reinforce the memory trace so that, when the information is needed in the future, the spatial display can easily be called up on the pupil's 'mental clipboard'.

Grammar

It is important to differentiate between children who have specific difficulties with the sub-skills of lanaguage learning and those who cannot learn easily for other reasons. Sometimes they are lumped together, to the disadvantage of both. A bright dyslexic pupil will appreciate

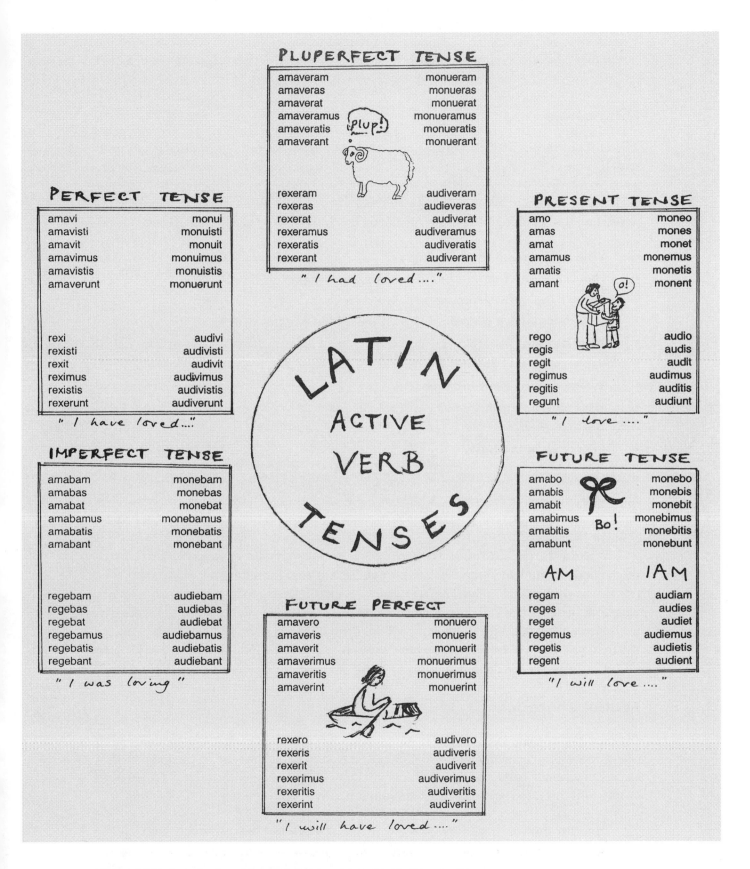

PLUPERFECT TENSE

amaveram	monueram
amaveras	monueras
amaverat	monuerat
amaveramus	monueramus
amaveratis	monueratis
amaverant	monuerant
rexeram	audiveram
rexeras	audieveras
rexerat	audiverat
rexeramus	audiveramus
rexeratis	audiveratis
rexerant	audiverant

"*I had loved....*"

PERFECT TENSE

amavi	monui
amavisti	monuisti
amavit	monuit
amavimus	monuimus
amavistis	monuistis
amaverunt	monuerunt
rexi	audivi
rexisti	audivisti
rexit	audivit
reximus	audivimus
rexistis	audivistis
rexerunt	audiverunt

"*I have loved...*"

PRESENT TENSE

amo	moneo
amas	mones
amat	monet
amamus	monemus
amatis	monetis
amant	monent
rego	audio
regis	audis
regit	audit
regimus	audimus
regitis	auditis
regunt	audiunt

"*I love....*"

IMPERFECT TENSE

amabam	monebam
amabas	monebas
amabat	monebat
amabamus	monebamus
amabatis	monebatis
amabant	monebant
regebam	audiebam
regebas	audiebas
regebat	audiebat
regebamus	audiebamus
regebatis	audiebatis
regebant	audiebant

"*I was loving*"

FUTURE TENSE

amabo	monebo
amabis	monebis
amabit	monebit
amabimus	monebimus
amabitis	monebitis
amabunt	monebunt
AM	**IAM**
regam	audiam
reges	audies
reget	audiet
regemus	audiemus
regetis	audietis
regent	audient

"*I will love....*"

FUTURE PERFECT

amavero	monuero
amaveris	monueris
amaverit	monuerit
amaverimus	monuerimus
amaveritis	monuerimus
amaverint	monuerint
rexero	audivero
rexeris	audiveris
rexerit	audiverit
rexerimus	audiverimus
rexeritis	audiveritis
rexerint	audiverint

"*I will have loved.....*"

LATIN ACTIVE VERB TENSES

Figure 6.22 Latin tenses map. Mnemonic links have been added to this map: the boy saying 'o' as he receives a present, the bow to show that the future tenses of the first two conjugations end in 'bo'; the prominent 'am' and 'iam' to remind the pupil of the third and fourth conjugation endings, the future perfect ending in 'ro', the pluperfect ram called 'plup' etc. (See Sheets T and U in the Worksheet section.)

a structured approach to the grammar of a language, providing he is familiar with the terminology. Ideally, he should be taught in small logical steps, with much reinforcement and practice in both the receptive and the expressive spoken and written language.

Difficulties

The chaotic written work that characterises dyslexic pupils' experienced by attempts to write sentences in a new language is often largely the result of the overload imposed on the memory while it is trying to put the whole thing together. Until there is automaticity, each aspect of translating a sentence has to be worked out. There are too many considerations to think of when translating this sentence: 'Where are Adam's shoes?' 'I have given them to him' (Figure 6.23).

- 'What's the word for "where?"'
- 'Has it got an accent; if so, which way does it go?'
- 'What's the verb, which person, which tense?'
- 'What's the word for "shoes"? Is it masculine or feminine?'
- 'How do I say "Adam's"'?'
- 'What order do I put the words in?'
- 'Which are the right pronouns?'
- 'Which verb, which tense?'
- 'Agreement?'
- 'I can't be bothered!'

For a child with short-term memory, sequencing, spelling and handwriting difficulties, writing each sentence is a marathon. While piecing it together, his efforts to remember vocabulary and grammar rules are punctuated by arduous looking-up in the dictionary. (See Sheet S in the Worksheet section.)

Whether he has auditory or visual problems, his solution must be to speak, hear and see the sequences simultaneously. The auditory element is vital for telling the pupil whether or not the sentence *sounds* right. This is probably his most reliable guide – in our own language we check our grammar by how it sounds, rather than by referring to a rule. In the same way, for some people, seeing it on the page will tell them if it *looks* right. Others, floundering for the right grammatical sequence, may have to resort to saying the English sentence as Hercule Poirot or Inspector Clouseau might say it: 'He them to him has given.'

Model sentences

An effective strategy for grammar learning is to prepare a sheet of model sentences, each one demonstrating a grammatical rule or convention to be memorised by the pupil so that he has an example to refer to, to help him 'hear' and 'see' correct grammar. He will then have examples in his mind against which he can test his own constructions:

> 'He was having lunch when Paul arrived – *Il déjeunait quand Paul est arrivé*'

> 'She completely forgot to call me – *Elle a complètement oublié de m'appeler*'

> 'He will never see her again – *Il ne la verra plus jamais*'

Transferring a list of these model sentences onto tape (see page 203) is an excellent way of encouraging simultaneous speaking, listening and looking. It is much the most painless and

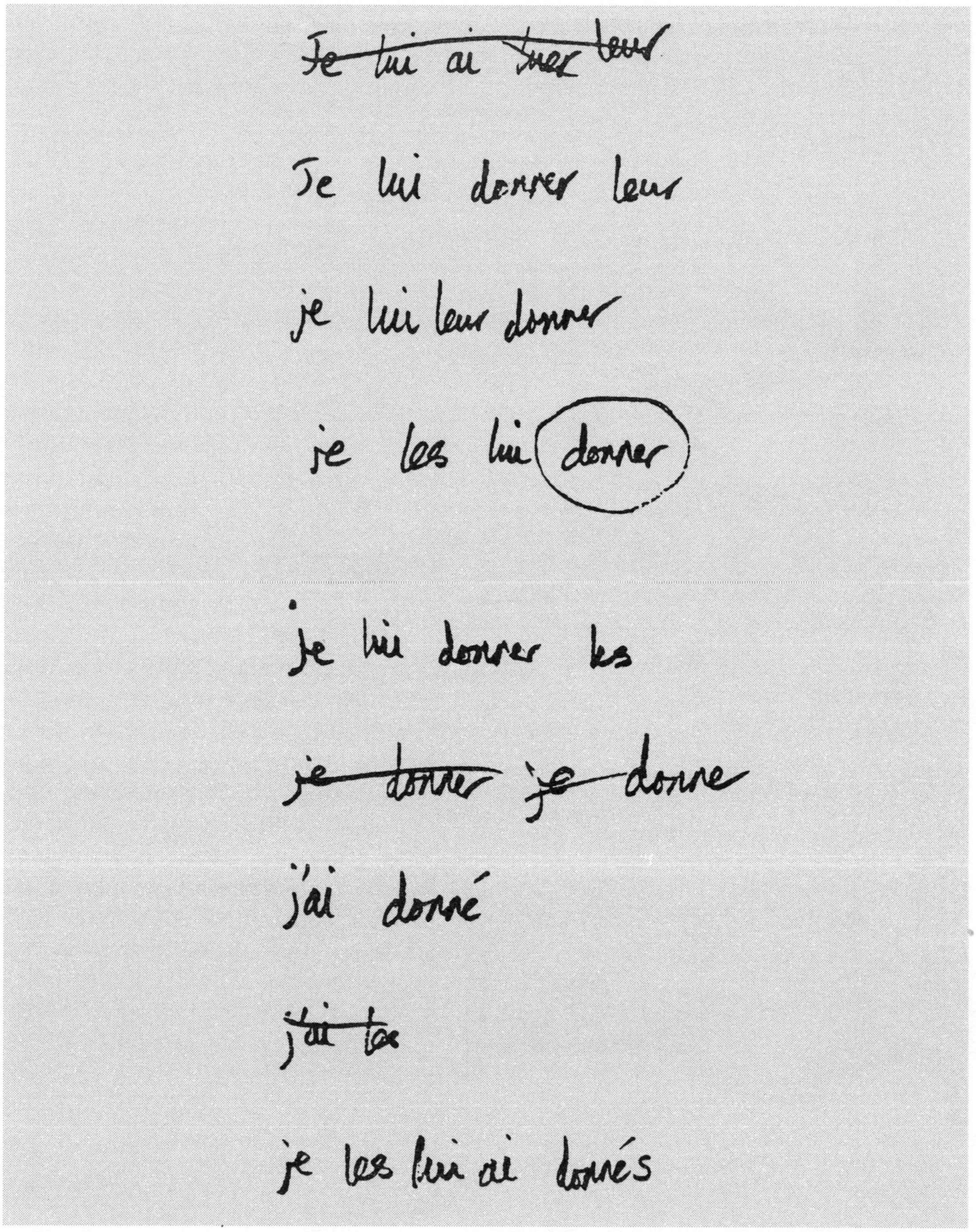

Je lui ai ~~mes~~ ~~leur~~

Je lui donner leur

je lui leur donner

je les lui (donner)

je lui donner les

~~je donner~~ ~~je~~ donne

j'ai donné

~~j'ai tes~~

je les lui ai donnés

Figure 6.23 Nine attempts to write the French for 'I have given them to him' – only finally achieved with help. The pupil knew the theory but couldn't manage the sequencing and the overload.

effective way for dyslexic pupils to get a feel for the correct grammar. Listening to correct phrases is the surest way to develop an ear for what sounds right.

Books on tape

As a general rule, the more a dyslexic person can listen to the spoken language while looking at the text, the faster he will learn. He will develop an eye and ear for correct usage, his weaker faculty being supported by his stronger. Use of the book and the tape of a fairly simple and familiar story, perhaps with pictures, would enable the pupil to make sense of what he was hearing and seeing (Figure 6.24). Timing and tone of voice are a great help for comprehension – and enjoyment.

Il y avait une fois en Saxe une ville qui s'appelait Hamelin. C'était une bonne petite ville, bien entourée de bonnes murailles, avec de bonnes tours bien solides, par peur des brigands qui couraient sans cesse le pays en ce temps-là. Au milieu de la ville passait le fleuve Weser, avec un beau pont dessus ; et non loin de là s'élevait la cathédrale, dont les bourgeois étaient très fiers à cause de sa flèche aussi mince qu'une épée et de la foule de saints en pierre qui habitaient sous les porches et dans tous les coins.

Peter Cornélius, le maître d'école, en avait compté six cent vingt-sept rien que sur la tour du Nord ; mais monsieur le bourgmestre disait toujours qu'il y en avait bien plus que ça et que d'ailleurs Peter Cornélius n'était qu'un âne...

Figure 6.24 *The Pied Piper*. This French version comes with an audio-tape. (*Le jouer de flute de Hamelin*, Castor Poche Flammarion, 1990).

The use of the past historic in literature is a frustration for those of us who want to use this method in the earlier stages of French learning. We want our pupils to have practice recognising the perfect tense! It is probably worth explaining the tense rather than abandoning a very useful teaching tool.

Textbooks with accompanying tapes are a very useful resource, but the child with difficulties will appreciate it if the tape is played on a machine that can slow down the speed of delivery without distorting the sound.

Using cards to learn grammar

Another way to help a dyslexic pupil to lessen the overload that he experiences when he tries to write clearly and remember the vocabulary, the correct sequence, the spelling and the grammatical rules is to break the task into stages.

If he is learning, for example, how to form a sentence containing negatives, then that is the part of the exercise he should be able to concentrate on, without the distraction of unfamiliar vocabulary, tenses, agreements etc. By sequencing a selection of cards with parts of speech written on them, he can practise placing the cards until he gets the sentence right – without the frustration of writing it over and over again, correcting repeatedly, until the 'shape' of the sentence is visually unrecognisable.

Initially the pupil could be provided only with the correct cards for his needs:

I have not given the apples

Je n'ai pas donné les pommes

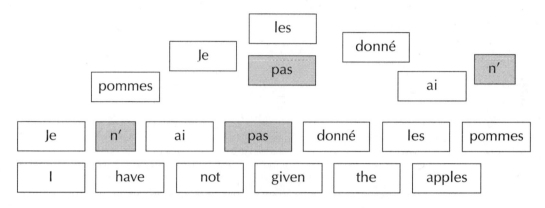

When he is more confident, he could be asked to select the correct ones from among several possible cards.

Anyone who has used this method for teaching grammar will have noticed that, while people are doing something with their hands – in this case picking up the cards and moving them around – they tend to read the words aloud while they are doing it. This is just what we want.

Colour coding different parts of speech – dark for negatives, perhaps – can help the visual memory; the kinaesthetic and spatial element of moving the cards into position will help some dyslexic pupils:

In the same way, using cards to reinforce the categorisation of parts of speech will help all pupils, particularly if they say the words aloud as they are dealing with them, e.g. the rules of order for object pronouns is always a problem area that can be clarified by using cards:

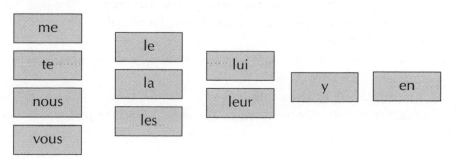

Some pupils will remember the shape of the formation, others will remember the order by the rhythm of:

me te nous vous

le la les

lui leur

y

en

Asking a pupil to form up cards into a chart can also be a useful exercise – saying the words, placing the cards and justifying the format:

'These are all masculine; these are all the plurals; these all mean "their".'

As it is multisensory and interactive, this is a more effective way of learning than just looking at the words on the page:

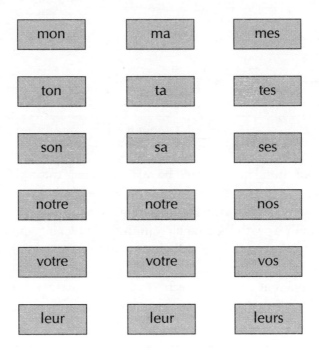

mon	ma	mes
ton	ta	tes
son	sa	ses
notre	notre	nos
votre	votre	vos
leur	leur	leurs

Listening comprehension

The most effective way to help a dyslexic person to understand the foreign language he is listening to – apart from his spending time with people who are speaking it all the time – is to equip him with matching tape and text and to make sure that he listens to the tape *while looking at* the written word.

At first the foreign words will seem too fast to follow – one word running into another – but as he listens again and again, and because he can see the words as separate on the page, his comprehension will gradually improve. He will begin to be able to understand without looking at the text. Frequent repetition and a variety of passages will consolidate his knowledge.

When the pupil is very familiar with the tape, he should be asked to read the text aloud so that he is linking the memory in his eye and ear to that in his mouth and tongue (integrating cognitive channels).

Preparing for an oral exam

Working with tape

The child who has already done much of his language learning using tape (see page 203) will be well prepared for the oral examination. He will be able to understand, and respond orally, he will have had practice in pronunciation and his vocabulary and phrases should be as much a part of his spoken vocabulary as of his written.

When preparing questions and answers to put on tape:

Question → Pause in which to answer later → Answer

This will provide good practice, and the constant repetition will produce the automaticity with which we respond to simple questions in our own language.

Mind-mapping is a good way to collect topic vocabulary and phrases in preparation for an oral exam. It not only gives a focus to the task but also makes it much easier for the student to remember what it is that he *does* know. In the stress of the exam he can visualise his mind-map: the pictures, symbols and clear layout will remind him of the phrases and words that he has learnt.

Preparing and learning a speech

The principle of breaking a task into steps and concentrating on each separately works well when preparing a set speech for the oral part of GCSE and A-level exams. These steps should involve all the senses from the start if there is to be a fluent rendering at the end.

Mind-map

Mind-mapping the topic, as for an essay, gives a visual, spatial dimension. At this stage, the student who is dyslexic should also be speaking and listening to himself while he maps. He should keep asking, 'Does that sound right?'

Type the speech correctly

With the intention of learning the speech by heart, he should type it up from his mind-map in a large clear font. Students often make the mistake of thinking that, as no one else will see the text, it doesn't have to be correctly written. This is a dangerous attitude on two counts. If it is written wrongly, it may well be pronounced wrongly. Knowing this is a possibility will undercut the confidence of the speaker, both when he tries to learn the speech and when he finally delivers it.

Use audiotapes

As this piece is to be spoken in the exam, practice in speaking it is essential. Yet students often avoid this step. One system is to record the speech, not fast, onto an audiotape. Time it and correct it until it is a suitable length. Then practise saying the speech with the taped voice. To begin with, follow the text as well. Finally, practise the speech without the tape. Be sure always to speak aloud rather than subvocalise.

Pictures as notes

As students are usually allowed to have a few notes with them in the oral exam, their motivation to learn a speech by heart is reduced. However, stress and interpolations from the examiner on the day will take their toll, so it is best both to know the speech by heart and to have notes that work well for the occasion. Linear notes may not be as helpful as some reminder of the original mind-map. Picture symbols drawn in a circle to represent the main points of the talk can be seen at a glance and can be used out of order if necessary. Drawing the symbols on a suitable card and practising speaking from the card are multisensory activities to build memory and confidence.

Students sometimes think taking these steps is too elaborate a preparation for just one part of the oral exam, but there are good reasons for taking such trouble:

- The oral may come early in the sequence of public exams – doing very well in it, particularly if you don't usually, has an outstandingly positive effect on one's confidence and motivation to prepare for later exams. The reverse is also true.
- Writing correct French, reading aloud, listening critically to check accent and pronunciation, and learning several sentences by heart all work to fine-tune the hand, the eye, the ear and the tongue. The practice involved here is the best kind of preparation for all other aspects of the French exam.

Writing essays and letters

When composing an essay in, say, French, the writer is thinking, 'What can I think of to say in English?' 'What are the words/spellings/tense/order in French?' 'What good French expressions can I include?', 'How do I organise all this?' and attempting to write accurate French – all at the same time. Whoever may achieve this, dyslexic students will not. They need to break essay writing into a sequence of smaller steps when writing in their native tongue; how much more so in a foreign language? Once again, mind-mapping is an excellent tool for this. It provides the opportunity for the writer to build up the elements of good paragraphs, using English and French, as his ideas and corrections occur, and in any random order. He need not organise the final sequence of paragraphs until just before he begins to write. At this stage he should plan what phrases he could use to link them. With content and structure largely thought out, the writer is now in a position to concentrate on the fine detail of good expression as he starts to write. This area of careful accuracy is one that most often lets a dyslexic student down when writing in a foreign language (Figure 6.25).

Set texts

Those rare dyslexic schoolchildren or students who are taking languages beyond GCSE will have to study set texts – understand them, be able to translate them and be able to write about them. Listening to the unabridged tape of the novel or play in its original language

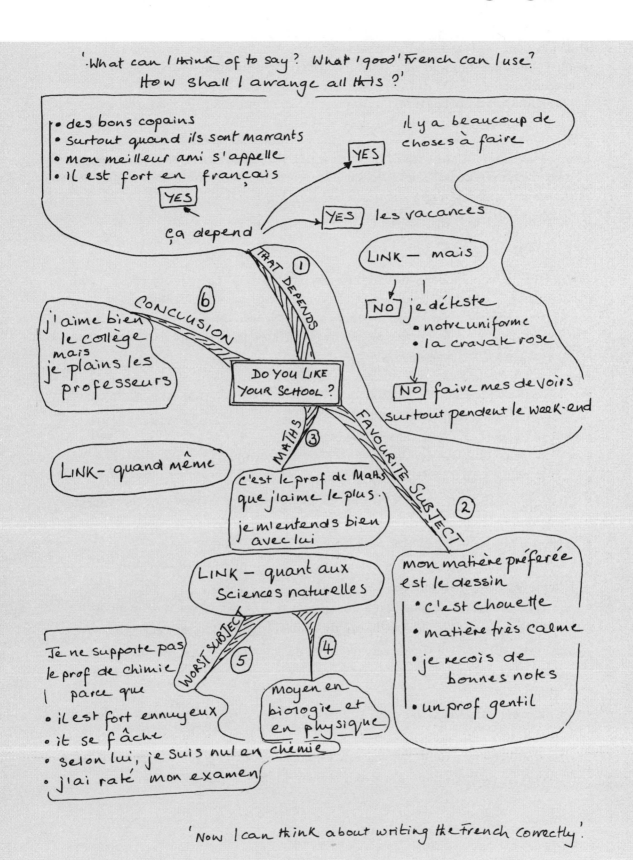

'What can I think of to say? What 'good' French can I use? How shall I arrange all this?'

des bons copains
surtout quand ils sont marrants
mon meilleur ami s'appelle
il est fort en français
YES

il y a beaucoup de choses à faire
YES

ça depend
YES les vacances

LINK — mais
NO je déteste
notre uniforme
la cravate rose
NO faire mes devoirs
surtout pendent le week-end

THAT DEPENDS 1
CONCLUSION 6
j'aime bien le collège mais je plains les professeurs
LINK — quand même

DO YOU LIKE YOUR SCHOOL?

MATHS 3
C'est le prof de Maths que j'aime le plus. je m'entends bien avec lui

FAVOURITE SUBJECT 2
mon matière préférée est le dessin
c'est chouette
matière très calme
je reçois de bonnes notes
un prof gentil

LINK — quant aux Sciences naturelles

WORST SUBJECT 5
Je ne supporte pas le prof de chimie parce que
il est fort ennuyeux
it se fâche
selon lui, je suis nul en chimie
j'ai raté mon examen

4
moyen en biologie et en physique

'Now I can think about writing the French correctly.'

Figure 6.25 Mind-map preparation for a question entitled 'Do you like your school?'. With the essay title in the centre, the writer puts down in English his main points and in French any supporting ideas and phrases. He numbers the order of his paragraphs and provides linking words. Now he is ready to start writing his essay, concentrating on accurate language.

while following the text provides the student with a rich input: seeing and hearing the words simultaneously help oral and aural skills and word recognition; tone of voice and timing help comprehension.

Building up vocabulary from the set texts that are being studied needs to be approached systematically from the start. Rather than writing the translation on the text – so that the student never has to wonder about the meaning of words and phrases when he reads them again – the dyslexic student would find that actively collecting a separate list of vocabulary on tape, in an exercise book or on computer sheets (and having it checked for accuracy by a teacher) and then learning it out of context would be much more productive.

Using a computer for language work

Dyslexic pupils who are happy to use their computers for all the arts subjects, and perhaps the sciences too, often baulk at using them for language work. 'It's too much of an effort doing the accents', 'The sentences are short; there's no need'.

In fact there are compelling reasons why the dyslexic pupil should use a word processor for language work:

- He can say the sentence that sounds right aloud, type it down quickly while he remembers it and then edit the details.
- Typed work is easy to read back aloud for checking.
- Correcting doesn't make a mess, so he is more likely to do it.
- Mistakes look wrong.
- He can use the Language tool within 'Word' for spelling and grammar checking or an inbuilt foreign language dictionary (Figure 6.26).
- He will be able to correct his work more easily.
- Touch typists can copy without taking their eyes off the board or page; this will improve accuracy (Figure 6.27).
- Accents are easy to organise on a word processor – in 'Word' Insert → Symbol → normal text – and children will learn them quickly and be putting in accents automatically after two or three exercises. They have the option of choosing their own shortcuts, ones that might be easier for them to use and remember than the defaults within 'Word'.
- Collecting vocabulary on a table (see page 196) is a very convenient way to learn it, store it, review it and practise writing it. The visual image of the typed word is clear for learning – type can be enlarged for easy reading or words can be typed in different colours for categorisation. It is worth keeping a template for this available.

sharp / ʃɑːp /

I *noun* **dièse *m*.**

II *adjective*

1   (good for cutting) [*knife, razor*] **tranchant**; [*edge*] **coupant**; [*blade, scissors*] **bien aiguisé**; [*saw*] **bien affûté**;

2   (pointed) [*tooth, fingernail*] **acéré**; [*end, needie, rock, peak*] **Pointu**; [*pencil*] **bien taillé**; [*point*] **acéré, fin**; [*features*] **anguleux/-euse**; [*nose, chin*] **pointu.**

3   (abrupt) [*angle*] **aigu/-uë**; [*bend, turning*] **brusque, serré**; [*movement, reflex*] **brusque**; [*drop, incline*] **fort**; economy, finance [*fall, rise, change*] **brusque, brutal**;

4   (acidic) [*taste, smell*] **âcre**; [*fruit*] **acide**;

5   (piercing) [*pain*] **vif/vive**; [*cry*] **aigu/-uë**; [*blow*] **sévère**; [*frost*] **fort, intense**; [*cold, wind*] **vif/vive, pénétrant**;

6   figurative (aggressive) [*tongue*] **acéré**; [*tone, reply, rebuke*] **acerbe**; [*disagreement*] **vif/vive**;

7   (alert) [*person*] **vif/vive, dégourdi**; [*mind, intelligence*] **vif/vive**; [*eyesight, eye*] **perçant**; [*hearing, ear*] **fin**; **to have a sharp wit avoir de la repartie**; **to keep a sharp lookout rester sur le qui-vive (for pour)**; **to have a sharp eye for sth** figurative **avoir l'œil pour qch**;

8   (clever) pejorative [*businessman, person*] **malin/-igne**; **sharp operator filou *m***;

9   (clearly defined) [*image, outline, picture, sound*] **net/nette**; [*contrast*] **prononcé**; [*difference, distinction*] **net/nette**; **to bring sth into sharp focus** literal **cadrer qch avec netteté**; figurative **faire passer qcl au premier plan**;

10   [!]GB [*suit*] **tape-à-l'œil (*inv*)** pejorative; **to be a sharp dresser prendre grand soin de son apparence**;

11   [!]US (stylish) **chic (*inv*)**;

12   music **dièse**; (too high) **aigu/-uë.**

III *adverb*

1   (abruptly) [*stop, pull up*] **net**; **to turn sharp left/right tourner brusquement vers la gauche/la droite**;

(promptly) **at 9 o'clock sharp à ncuf heures pile[',] *or* précises**;

music [*sing, play*] **trop haut.**

Idioms
to be at the sharp end être en première ligne;
to look sharp[!] se dépêcher;
you're so sharp you'll cut yourself tu te crois vraiment très malin/-igne.

Figure 6.26 The user can just tap in a word and the French equivalent comes up on the screen – broken down into different shades of meaning and illustrated in context. Colour coding and layout make the dictionary easy to use. ©Oxford University Press (1994–1996), ©Hachette Livre (1994–1996).

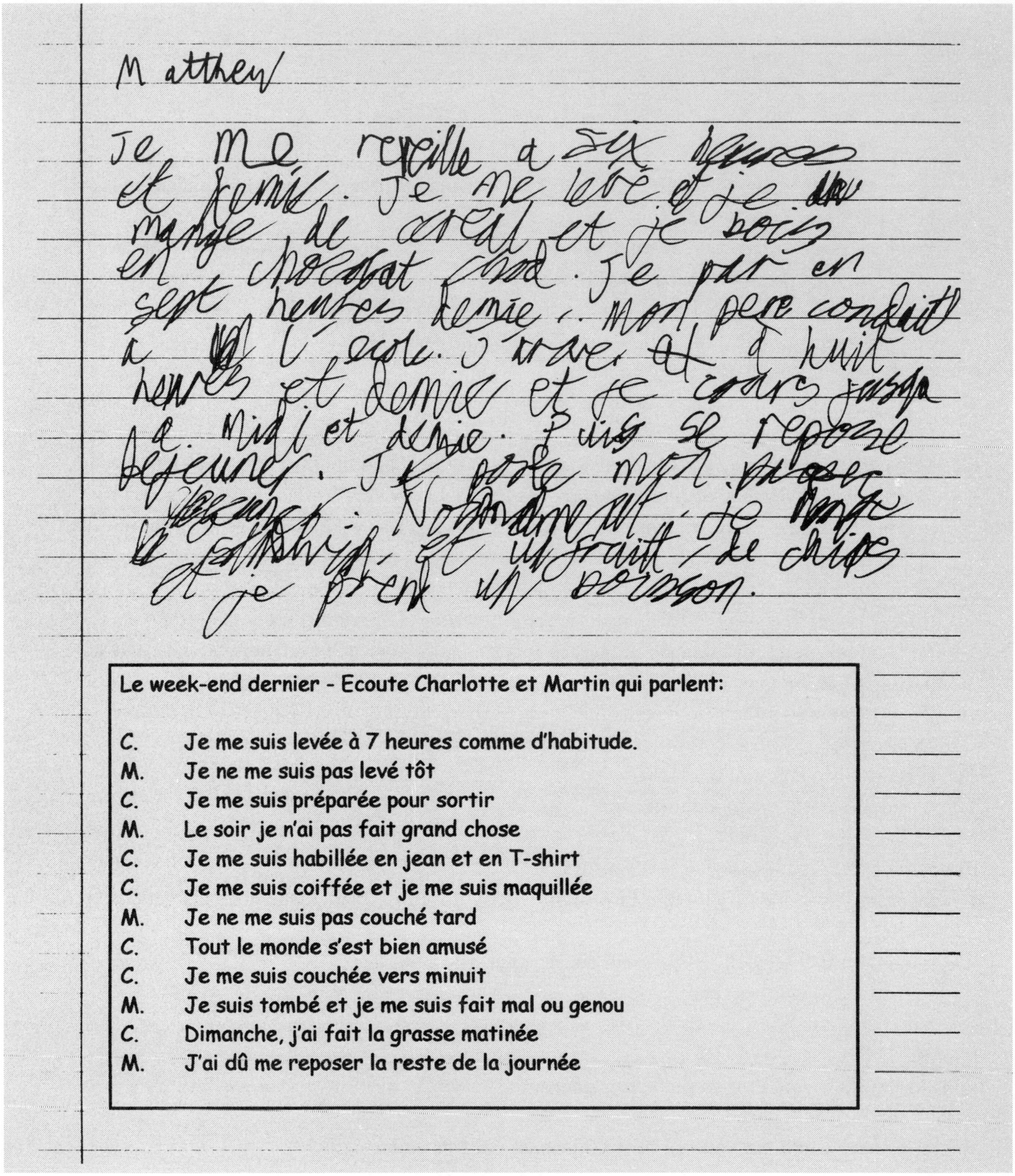

> Matthew
>
> Je me reveille a six heures et demie. Je me lève et je mange de cereal et je bois en sept chocolat chaud. Je pars en heures demie... Mon pere conduit a l'ecole. J'arrive et t huit heures et demie et je cours jusqa a midi et demie. Puis se repose dejeuner. Je prend mon... Normalement je mange et je prend un fruit. Je chips et je prend un boisson.

> **Le week-end dernier - Ecoute Charlotte et Martin qui parlent:**
>
> C.   Je me suis levée à 7 heures comme d'habitude.
> M.   Je ne me suis pas levé tôt
> C.   Je me suis préparée pour sortir
> M.   Le soir je n'ai pas fait grand chose
> C.   Je me suis habillée en jean et en T-shirt
> C.   Je me suis coiffée et je me suis maquillée
> M.   Je ne me suis pas couché tard
> C.   Tout le monde s'est bien amusé
> C.   Je me suis couchée vers minuit
> M.   Je suis tombé et je me suis fait mal ou genou
> C.   Dimanche, j'ai fait la grasse matinée
> M.   J'ai dû me reposer la reste de la journée

Figure 6.27 Accuracy (only one mistake here), and of course legibility, are much easier to achieve when a dyslexic pupil can keep his eyes on whatever it is he is copying.

Chapter 7
Revision

Looking ahead

The home scene

Students need to handle the home scene tactfully if it is to be calm and supportive. Parents have their own priorities and other family members to consider. If, for instance, students would prefer to revise rather than visit relations or go on family holidays in the spring break before GCSE or A-level exams, they should warn their parents.

Parents worry about revision. Students can sometimes turn this to good account by involving them – parents could, for instance, be asked in the evening to test revision done during the day or listen together to audiotapes of a set book or record textbook chapters for them onto tape.

Students can minimise their parents' anxious involvement with the revision process by keeping control of the situation. They can appreciate an offer of help while directing the activity themselves. If students choose the subject for parental help, the form it takes and revise the topic before being tested on it, they will show that they know what they are about and are revising successfully. The resulting collaborative work is likely to be very useful, even enjoyable.

Parents interfere less if they can see a regular routine of work operating – preferably one that takes place in the daytime. They will probably be willing to support a working routine with regular meals and transport to outdoor exercise and meetings with friends. They may be glad to replenish supplies of revision materials such as A3 plain paper, small cards, coloured felt tips, computer ink cartridges, blank tapes and access to books on tape. (If students rely on public libraries as the source for these tapes, they may need to anticipate revision dates and order them well in advance.)

A student's workplace is important, particularly as there will be years of revision ahead. The basics are a big table, good light, power points if using a computer and tape machine, and enough space to have revision books and papers spread around. Is privacy, or the kitchen table with useful family and comforting pets about, preferable? Music (avoid meaningful vocals) can shut distractions out; television is not likely to.

External help with revision

Revision courses for public exams

These are expensive. If there is a serious difficulty in a particular subject and funds are available, a revision course, for a few concentrated days during the holidays, could take care of the problem. Courses in anticipation of exams are better than ones geared to resitting exams after failure. Good revision courses survey the whole syllabus, focus on exam questions and demand strenuous interactivity from their students. They usually teach students in small groups. This is of particular value to dyslexic students, who need to be at the centre of the action with the teacher's attention focused on them in order to learn really well. They are all too often operating at the margins of a larger class in school.

Courses fill up quickly and need to be booked well in advance. Students should check that the course they select is centred on the syllabus they are studying; they need to know their Exam Board for this.

BBC Bitesize Revision

These programmes make a valuable multisensory addition to revision material. They are two-hour sessions broadcast on BBC 2 late at night or very early in the morning, and they are designed to be recorded for use when convenient. They concentrate on known areas of weakness and are supported with CD-ROMs and workbooks available at good bookshops. In addition, the website (www.bbc.co.uk/education/revision) includes interactive tests with feedback and an e-mail service that responds to revision queries within 72 hours. BBC Education Information on 020 8746 1111 will give current details. Although geared to GCSE students, much of the material is useful for students revising in lower years. Some AS and A2 revision material is also available. Once again, students need to organise themselves in advance if they intend to video these programmes.

Collecting up revision resources

Nothing destroys a student's good intentions faster than settling down to work and finding he doesn't know his syllabus or he hasn't got the right book. Dyslexic students are the ones most likely to have mislaid a syllabus, failed to photocopy missing notes and to need a different textbook from the standard issue. Teachers can help, in advance of a revision period, by supervising their students' resources – course syllabus, practice questions and exam papers, suitable textbooks, websites and a complete set of notes. Being willing to set and give feedback on individual practice questions during study leave and before public exams can make the difference of a grade; it encourages motivation and expertise. Again children with specific learning difficulties benefit most because slow processing in class and homework means that they often have not had as much practice as their peers.

Capitalise on past experience of revision and exams

Students remember the 'feel' of their last set of exams but often not the details that produced it – particularly if the 'feel' is negative. However, recalling what happened last time is likely to improve the quality of their next revision effort. Figure 7.1 shows a GCSE candidate putting down his immediate impressions of revision and mock exams, before hearing his results. Three months later when planning study leave for the summer exams he looked back at this mind-map and incorporated its various leads into his final revision.

Figure 7.2 is an exam debriefing form for students to fill in as soon after their exams as possible. (See Sheet V in the Worksheet section.)

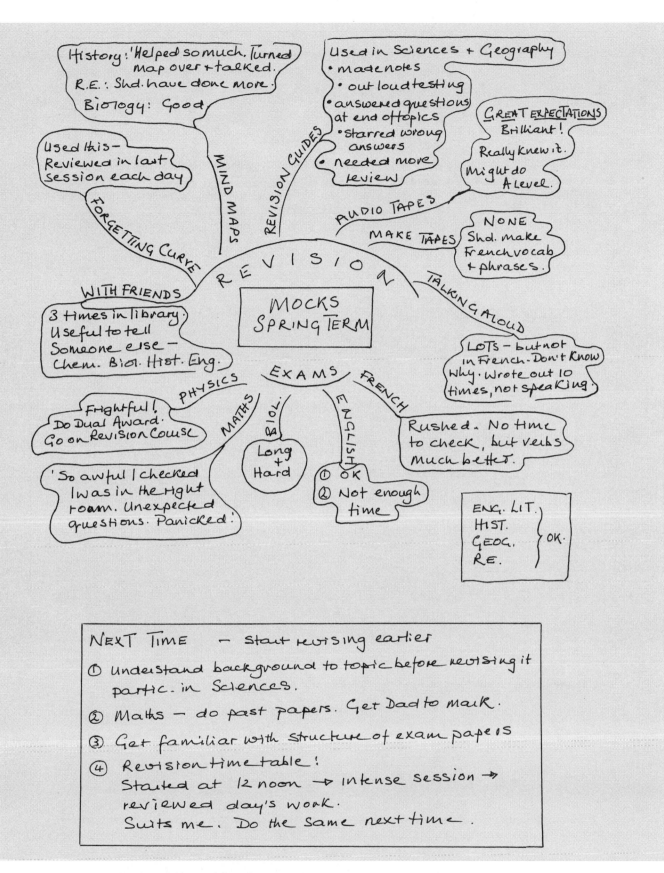

Figure 7.1 A GCSE candidate mind-mapping his revision and mock exams. Here a teacher is mind-mapping while a boy talks through his mock-GCSE experiences – a useful guide for study leave and the actual exams in the summer term.

What happened in the exams?

The best moment to do an exam debriefing is as soon as possible after the event, when the memory (and perhaps the pain) is still fresh. There is a lot to learn from previous experiences. It is useful for pupils to fill in and then file a debriefing sheet so that it can be produced before the next exam preparation. Detailed and focused questions – and answers – are most helpful.

	Did you plan your answers?	Did you finish?	Best revision method?	Were your notes good enough?	Did you make any silly mistakes?	Did you use a word processor?	Resolutions for next time?	Marks?
English								
History								
Maths								
French								
Biology								
Geography								
Chemistry								
Physics								

Figure 7.2 Some people might prefer to fill in a table rather than a mind-map.

Timetabling

Most students, estimating time available for revision, feel a twinge of panic that there isn't long enough to do it properly, but a dyslexic student's sense of time may be fundamentally distorted. He may not know when his exams are (although the information has been posted for weeks) or how long the preceding holiday period is. He may have no sense of how long a topic will take to revise, or even any sense of how long an hour or a morning is. All students must look ahead and tackle time, but dyslexic students depend on their teachers for quite detailed guidance in planning their revision timetable. There are basic concepts to convey.

What time is there for revision – in a day?

To establish how many hours in the day are *potentially* available for revision – far more than students imagine – they could look at units of time parcelled out in a chart as in Table 7.1. It offers 11 working hours to select from.

Before breakfast	6.30am–8.00am	One and a half hours
Breakfast	8.00am–9.00am	
Morning	9.00am–1.00pm	Four hours
Lunch	1.00pm–2.00pm	
Afternoon	2.00pm–4.00pm	Two hours
Tea	4.00pm–5.00pm	
Early evening	5.00pm–7.00pm	Two hours
Supper	7.00pm–8.30pm	
Late evening	8.30pm–10.00pm	One and a half hours

Table 7.1 Time available for revision in a day

Although the early-morning slot may seem ludicrous to a teenager and the late-evening one pitifully short, Table 7.1 will serve as a model for students to rearrange as they prefer. The intention is to think out how many hours a day they ought to work and which parts of the 24 hours suit them best.

What time is there for revision – in a week?

The next step is to think out time patterns for different days of the week – one student may choose not to work on Saturday evening or any time on Sunday. Another may usually play football on a Tuesday afternoon in the holidays; another may have touch-typing lessons each morning for a week. Previewing the weeks of study leave or holiday ahead will help towards realistic revision plans (Table 7.2). (See Sheet W in the Worksheet section.)

What time is there for revision – in a whole holiday?

Finally, students need some picture of the whole time-span available for revision. This is best presented spatially, so they can measure a holiday or study leave period at a glance, rather than roving back and forth along a vertical or horizontal sequence, where a sense of the whole may never be grasped. In the chart of a winter break shown in Table 7.3, a student who was unlikely to revise on the days shaded on the chart would have a maximum of 12 days left for revision.

	Mon	Tues	Wed	Thurs	Fri	Sat	Sun
Before breakfast							
Breakfast							
Morning							
Lunch							
Afternoon							
Tea							
Early evening							
Supper							
Late evening							

Table 7.2 Time for revision in a week

				Fri 18 Dec. End of term	Sat 19 Dec.	Sun 20 Dec.
Mon 21 Dec.	Tues 22 Dec.	Wed 23 Dec.	Thur 24 Dec. Christmas Eve	Fri 25 Dec. Christmas Day	Sat 26 Dec.	Sun 27 Dec.
Mon 28 Dec.	Tues 29 Dec.	Wed 30 Dec.	Thur 31 Dec. New Year's Eve.	Fri 1 Jan. New Year's Day	Sat 2 Jan.	Sun 3 Jan.
Mon 4 Jan. Term starts						

Table 7.3 Revision time over a holiday

Such a clear picture may be unpleasant, but it will encourage exam candidates to tailor their revision realistically.

Students may not be aware that how they 'see time' affects the way they draw time charts – days across and weeks down as above, or vice versa? If the version above is uncomfortable to work with, Table 7.4 (with days vertical and weeks horizontal) may be better.

	First week	Second week	Third week	Fourth week
Monday		21 Dec.	28 Dec.	4 Jan. Spring term starts
Tuesday		22 Dec.	29 Dec.	
Wednesday		23 Dec.	30 Dec.	
Thursday		24 Dec. Christmas Eve	31 Dec. New Year's Eve	
Friday	18 Dec. Autumn term ends	25 Dec. Christmas Day	1 Jan. New Year's Day	
Saturday	19 Dec.	26 Dec.	2 Jan.	
Sunday	20 Dec.	27 Dec.	3 Jan	

Table 7.4 Time chart

If blank time charts were posted on the school intranet, they would be available and useful to everyone.

Managing revision sessions

Many students mistakenly believe that good revision is defined by the number of hours spent doing it. But 'I'm going to do x hours a day' easily becomes unproductive and competitive and often leads to pointless feelings of guilt and failure. A personal rhythm of work sessions, centred more on active mental processing than on hours spent at a desk, will be more effective both for learning and for self-confidence.

Primacy and recency theory

Psychologists tell us that learning is at its best at the beginning and end of any working session, provided that the end of that session is fixed in advance. It therefore makes sense to create beginnings and endings, and revise in a series of quite short sessions, for example 20 minutes for a list of foreign vocabulary, 40 minutes to review a geography case study, an hour for the build-up to the Second World War. Students should adapt the length of these working sessions to their personal level of concentration for a particular topic.

To create the end of one session and the start of a new one, there needs to be a break of a few minutes in between – to move about, eat or chat. Whether to return to the same topic, review past revision or move on to something new depends again on the individual – his global view of the work to cover, his tolerance for the subject and how he has planned to incorporate 'learning curve' reviews into his day.

Tony Buzan gives an account of primacy and recency theory in his book *Use Your Head*. Figure 7.3 is his diagram showing the time pattern that best correlates with effective learning. It illustrates how mental efficiency declines over long periods of uninterrupted learning.

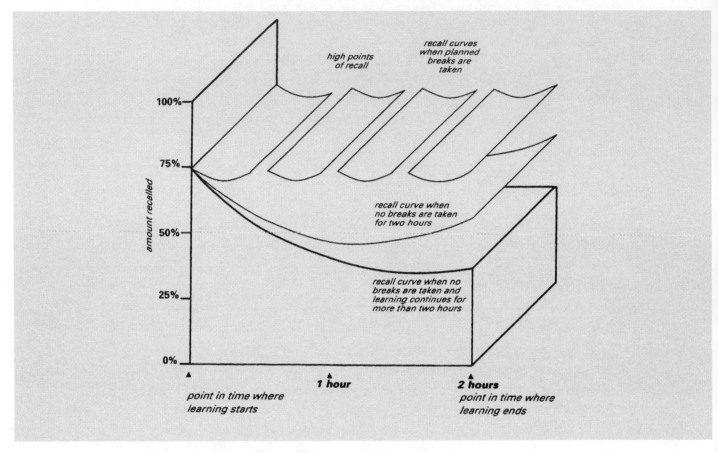

Figure 7.3 Recall is most effective at the beginning and end of each learning session – if the length of a session is fixed in advance. It makes little sense, therefore, to learn in one long uninterrupted session with only one beginning and one end. Settling down to revise for 'the morning' or 'the evening', without planning beforehand when to stop and without taking breaks, may seem serious and impressive but is actually the least productive use of revision time.

The 'forgetting curve'

When you are revising, you need to know how to transfer knowledge from your short-term to your long-term memory. This important skill is a problem for all students – especially if the reading matter, data or foreign vocabulary bores them – but it affects almost every aspect of the dyslexic student's schoolwork.

Most students (whether or not they are dyslexic) would agree that, if they read a chapter, learn some definitions or memorise a diagram and then don't look at them again for several weeks, they will remember only about 20% of what they learnt (Figure 7.4).

Faced with this evidence, students are tempted to do as much of their revision as they can *just* before the exam so they can use what they have learnt before the memory trace fails. Anyone who has been present at an exam will remember the heap of discarded notes and revision material outside the door, discarded by those who are relying on last-minute cramming.

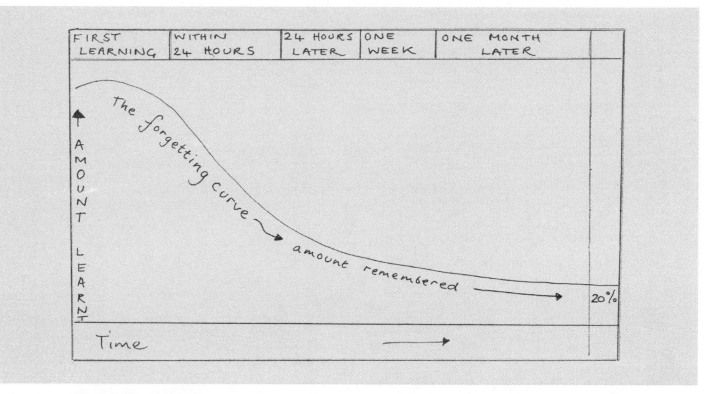

Figure 7.4 First revision phase.

Taking the 'forgetting curve' diagram apart (see Figure 7.8), one can see that the optimum moment to reinforce any revision is when the memory trace is still strong (as soon as possible) – because the information is still fresh, it will need very little work to reinforce the work already done (Figure 7.5).

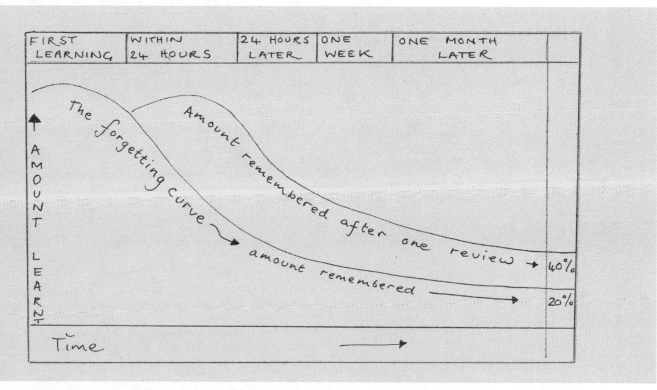

Figure 7.5 The 'forgetting curve' after second revision session.

This second session strengthens the trace sufficiently to allow more time to elapse before the next revisiting of the material (24–48 hours later) (Figure 7.6), and yet more time can be allowed before the next revision session (Figure 7.7) until the material is firmly in long-term memory (Figure 7.8).

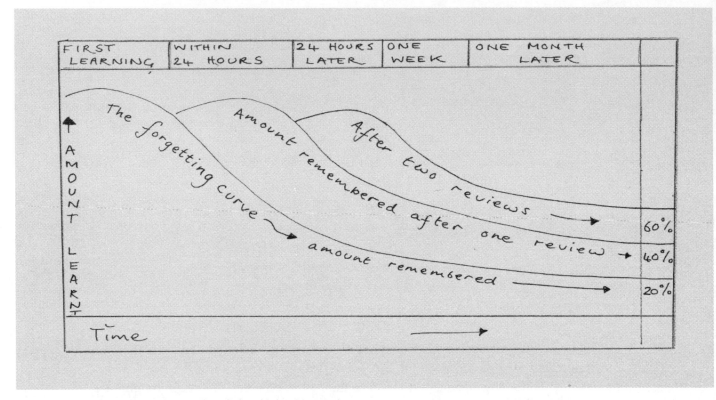

Figure 7.6 60% remembered after third revision session.

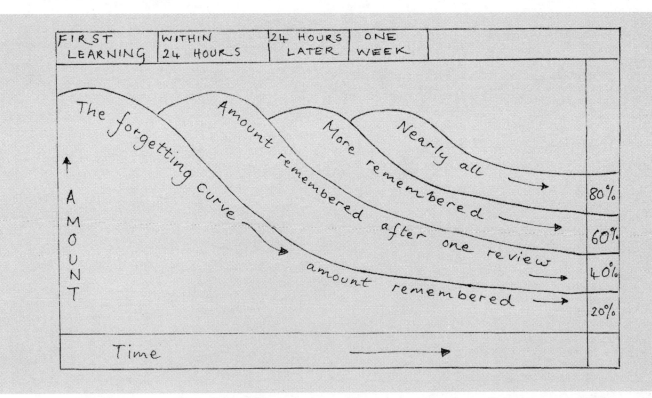

Figure 7.7 Four sessions result in 80% retention.

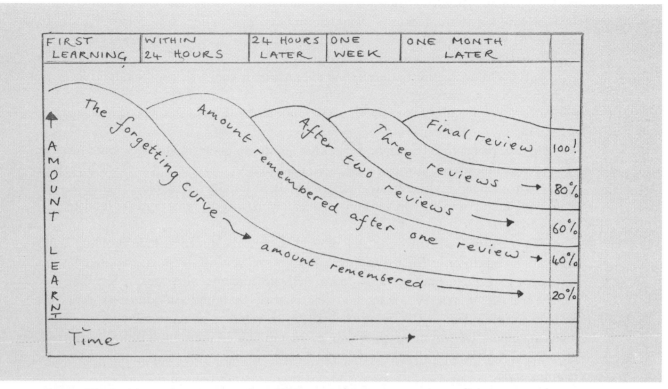

Figure 7.8 Last revision session – 100% recall just before examination.

Allowing a great deal of time to elapse after an early revision session puts the revised knowledge at risk and means that proportionately more time has to be spent on retrieving what has been learnt than if it had been reviewed soon afterwards. Capitalising on work already done in this way, the revision sessions become shorter but the retention time longer.

For dyslexic pupils who have short-term memory problems, particularly for rote learning – vocabulary, formulae, dates, names and sequences (as opposed to ideas or concepts) – the keys to transferring it from short- to long-term memory are reviewing and processing information.

Good teaching does build in the concept of the 'forgetting curve': lesson, discussion, homework, test. But students themselves need to understand the value of these procedures – why they are doing them and how they themselves could turn the 'forgetting curve' to good use in their own work and revision.

A good moment to experiment with the 'forgetting curve' is when a test or exam is coming up – something you want to do well in. With a piece of revision work in mind, you could look at the 'forgetting curve' and decide how you are going to plan your revision schedule in relation to it.

Many dyslexic students would say that they just don't have time to keep revisiting the topic in this way. The truth is that there is no point in doing revision that isn't reviewed and therefore doesn't stick – *that* is the real waste of time.

Multisensory learning

When asked *how* he intends to revise a topic, a student usually looks slightly surprised at the question and then replies, 'By going through my notes'. This may be adequate for pupils with excellent notes, good understanding and a first-rate memory. For students who are dyslexic, something more is needed – they must make the material 'their own' in some way to make it secure in long-term memory. Vigorous, internal processing of whatever has to be understood and learnt will involve multisensory activities: changing cognitive channels.

Receiving information in one mode (language, for example) and expressing it again in another (images) will result in transferring information from working to long-term memory. Both the use of a variety of sensory channels and the creative effort itself involved in this transferral from one modality to another will result in the learner maximising his chance of understanding and remembering.

He may prefer to talk, listen, debate, list questions, draw timelines or mind-maps or posters, visualise, invent mnemonic pegs, use his hands to make verb wheels, deal cards or type. He may prefer different modes and combinations for different revision topics, but the lively work involved in changing channel, preferably to a stronger one, remains fundamental to successful recall.

The tough work involved in this transfer sharpens a student's understanding of his material: he has to prioritise the information to fit his new format and generate language or images to express new versions. Many dyslexic students who cannot learn by rote benefit crucially from a revision method that improves their understanding – as would any student to some degree. Changing channels is therefore a basic method for successful revision, especially for those to whom understanding is their most reliable route to memory, or for those who may have been taught initially in a mode unsuited to their learning style.

However, students shrink from such strenuous work and prefer to 'look over' their notes instead. Although they may not recognise the value of changing modalities, they can certainly see that reproducing the content of their notes in a different form would require creative effort. If they have no experience to prove that such an effort would be worthwhile, cannot gauge how long it would take them to do it and have no friend working in such an unconventional way, they will probably not want to revise differently from everyone else.

Teachers can help here by teaching the rationale for changing channels and also by making practical suggestions about how to do it in their own subject. Many students, not just those with learning difficulties, would benefit.

It is worth having a trial of a selection of multisensory activities when teaching a specific topic, in order to investigate whether these or more conventional methods work best for long-term recall:

- Lists of questions to answer out loud, with notes or textbook page references for checking.
- Mind-maps to fill out with further branches, symbols and colour, to re-visualise and describe aloud from memory.
- Models to reassemble, naming the parts and functions aloud.
- Tapes to interact with – listening, speaking and writing.
- Sets of cards to categorise, pair or set out, speaking aloud during each of these activities.
- Packets of labels to identify parts of diagrams – naming each aloud and describing its function.
- Notes set out in the Cornell mode to revisit with symbols, questions or summaries.
- Essay titles to mind-map while listening to taped set texts.

- Sets of pictures to match with foreign words or phrases.
- Time-lines with space to draw symbols that represent events.

Revision products as homework during the year

The run-up to exams might be revolutionised if, during the year, students in their initial learning were able to make and keep a variety of materials for each subject, with an eye to their reuse later for revision.

As this kind of work invites original and personal involvement, it is ideal to set as homework. Individual products can be further refined and shared in class, with a view to both immediate learning and later revision.

To assess this, there needs to be both immediate and delayed testing carried out in class and without prior warning. This kind of experiment will also raise the question of why different methods suit different children and lead to a more precise recognition of individual learning styles within the group.

For pupils who are dyslexic in particular, this approach compares very favourably with another well-known method of revising – 'drumming things in' – which can work, but is mind numbing and soul destroying. It involves reinforcing the same memory trace over and over again, instead of making new connections in the brain, which will provide a network of knowledge that is much more reliable, flexible and useful. Therefore, every time he settles down to revision, a dyslexic student must ask himself, 'How am I going to do this?'

Multisensory methods

The choice of a revision method depends on the form of 'vision' in the first place. If a topic was learned in a multisensory way, there will be products – tapes, cards, pictures, mind-maps, diagrams, posters – ready to revise from. In this case, revision is likely to be swift, successful and moderately entertaining. If the topic was originally learned in written formats, in notes, essays or from a textbook, it will take time to recreate in more multisensory ways, i.e. to include as much as possible of speaking, visualising, questioning and making.

A revision 'product'

Any student, but especially the dyslexic student, should aim at producing something – a map, a quiz, questions, a tape, a diagram, an essay plan, a mind-map, a summary – during his revision session. As well as involving the crucial 'change of modality', there are practical reasons why he should aim to do this:

- It gives him something interesting to do – active rather than passive revision will stick in the memory better.
- It gives focus and purpose while he is revising.
- Building up a revision file or box gives a sense of satisfaction and something to show for what he has done. (Figures 7.9 and 7.10).
- It leaves him with something he can test himself on later (a day later, a term later, even a year later for those on two-year courses). Questions rather than notes is an excellent example of this.

A box of revision cards
A practical way of fighting the 'forgetting curve'

NUMBERED DIVIDERS
(Each number represents day of the month)

INDEX CARDS
(Some lined, some unlined)

INDEX CARD BOX

QUOTES FROM MACBETH: his conscience [*Revise on April 6,8,11*]

Macbeth (1.7) - that but this blow
Might be the be-all and the end-all!
Macbeth (1.7) We will proceed no further in this business.
He hath honoured me of late, and I have bought
Golden opinions from all sorts of people
Macbeth (1.7) I dare do all that may become a man;
Who dares do more is none.
Macbeth (1.7)   If we should fail?
Lady Macbeth   We fail!
But screw your courage to the sticking place,
And we'll not fail.
Macbeth (II.2) Listening to their fear I could not say 'Amen'
When they did say 'God bless us.'
Macbeth (II,2) I am afraid to think what I have done.

FRENCH	ENGLISH	TEST YOURSELF 2	TEST YOURSELF 1
La viande	meat		
Le bœuf	beef		
Le jambon	ham		
L'agneau	lamb		
La mouton	mutton		
La saucisse	sausage		
Le poulet	chicken		
Le poisson	fish		
Le pâté	pâté		
La banane	banana		

Volcanic Hazards April 9,11,14

① What are the 4 primary effects of volcanoes?
② What is the difference between primary + secondary effects of volcanoes?
③ List the 3 main secondary effects of volcanoes.
④ What is the most dangerous primary effect?

April 6,8,10
anther
stigma
style
ovary
ovule
filament
petal
sepal
receptacle
PARTS OF PLANT

April 7,9,11
• JEWS
• GAYS
• CRIMINALS
• WORK SHY
S.S.
DEATH HEADS
NAZI POLICE
Local Units
GESTAPO
FORM D II
CONCENTRATION CAMPS

MACBETH
FRENCH PHRASES
LISTEN TO TAPES

What to do
When you have done a piece of revision file your diagram, mind-map, summary, questions, tape, vocab, quotes, etc in your revision box noting on the cards the dates when you will use them again

After testing yourself for the first time (by re-drawing the diagram, re visualising the mind-map and talking through it, answering the questions, writing out an essay plan from memory, rehearsing vocabulary or quotations), file the card on the date when you feel you should next review it.

When you think the information is solid, you can either leave the cards in place – so that on the same day of the following month you will see them again and check on your knowledge – or file the cards you've learnt in subject bundles, ready for a test just before the exam.

Figure 7.9 A box of revision cards: a practical way of fighting the 'forgetting curve'.

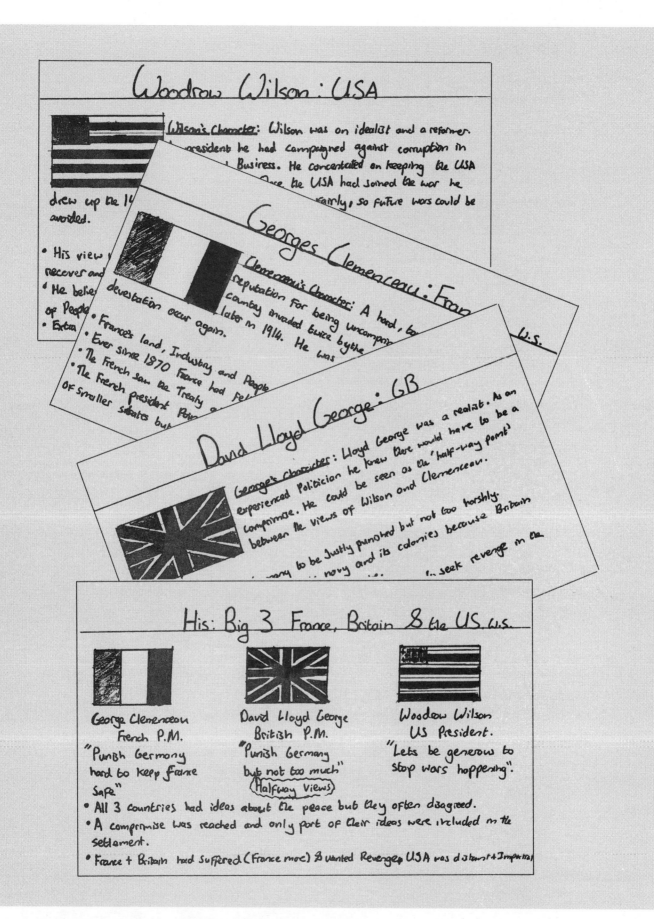

Figure 7.10 Versailles Treaty – The Big Three. Will's revision cards for his
Forgetting Curve Box.

Making questions from notes or a textbook

As the pupil reads each paragraph in his textbook he should ask himself, 'What questions are answered here?' and write them down (Figure 7.11).

VOLCANIC HAZARDS

Primary Effects - are the volcano's immediate effects when it erupts, and can cause damage in a short time.

1. Lava Flows - hot molten rock (magma) from Earth's upper mantle, emitted through the crater.

2. Pyroclastic Flows - a mixture rocks, ash and lava, fuelled by a cushion of extremely hot gas.

3. Ash Falls - fragments of magma from explosions.

4. Volcanic Gases - H_2O, CO, CO_2, SO_2, H, Helium.

Secondary Effects - these take longer to develop and thus occur longer after the start of the eruption, and often last longer than some of the Primary Effects.

1. Lahars - large avalanches of debris and material travelling up to 22m/s.

2. Landslides - occur after a violent eruption or slope deformation.

3. Tsunamis - giant waves, simply the intense energy from the eruption transmitted through the water.

The most dangerous hazard of the primary effects is *undoubtedly* pyroclastic flows. ash and lava is l fast - up to 100m materials ride on tear down the mour everything in its

Volcanic Hazards

① What are the four Primary Effects of volcanoes?

② What is the difference between Primary and Secondary Effects (of a volcano)?

③ List the 3 main Secondary Effects of a volcano.

④ What is the most dangerous Primary Effect? Why?

⑤ How far can a large ash-fall travel, and what widespread effect could it have?

⑥ What sorts of damage, if any, can lava flows cause? Why do they rarely cost human lives?

⑦ What is the most common Secondary Effect? Why is it so dangerous.

Figure 7.11 Ed has turned his geography notes on volcanoes into a series of questions – much more effective for revision than just writing them out again.

This exercise is one of the most valuable revision techniques on several counts:

- The student will have to understand and process the material very thoroughly in order to produce relevant questions that will elicit a full reply.
- The student will have a list of questions to answer at the end of his reading session and again before any exam or test. This builds in the concept of reviewing.
- Tackling the questions will tell him how much he really does remember, whereas just reading the notes can make a student feel that he *knows* the material when in fact he is only *recognising* it.
- Answering the questions, especially aloud or on paper, will give him practice in expressing himself on the particular topic, using his own words and the appropriate phraseology and vocabulary – a much more useful exercise as a preparation for writing than just reading through the notes.
- The student who uses the techniques is aware, even when he first writes his notes, that they are going to be turned into questions – this helps give the notes a relevance and focus from the start. In the same way, it will encourage active reading.

Getting it off the page

Dyslexic students, and others too no doubt, face serious difficulties when trying to revise detailed information from their textbook or class notes. Their literacy skills and working memory may not be up to the technical vocabulary or the quantity of abstract information. The print and diagrams may be too small (and, if hand-written, too messy) for their visual perception and spatial memory. They need study methods that lift the information off the page and integrate the functions of both hemispheres of the brain in learning it.

Figure 7.12 illustrates one such method. Here functions in both hemispheres of the learner's brain combine to recreate the words of a poem in a personal image. The creative activity involved in visualising the poem, together with the actual image generated by such activity, are both powerful agents for memory. The learner may easily recall the idea of the poem 'Love without hope', but he may also find that phrases from the poem have become integrated with details of his picture. So, as he re-visualises the angle of the tall hat he drew, the phrase 'swept off his tall hat' may come with the image. Similarly the words 'imprisoned larks escape and fly' may be integrated with his recall of the larks fluttering out as little hearts with wings. The very words he would normally find so hard to remember become an echo of the image he has made for them.

A multisensory approach to revising a biology topic: 'the brain'

In this example, cognitive functions are being integrated in an effort to visualise and remember parts of the brain – the shapes, positions, names and functions. Typically in formal education, much of the initial learning, in this case about the brain, will be presented in words, supported by a clinical diagram, on the pages of a textbook (Figure 7.13).

Enlarge text and diagrams

This is the sort of textbook page that can cause problems to students with specific learning difficulties. The page is a valuable summary of divisions of the brain, with terms,

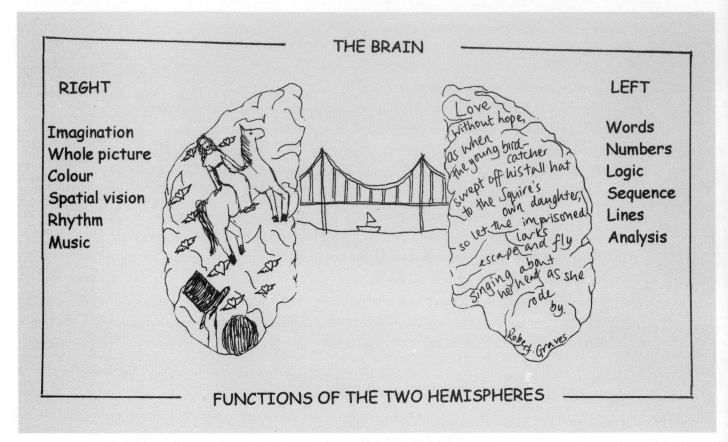

Figure 7.12 Integrating the language functions of the left hemisphere with the image-making functions of the right hemisphere improves understanding and memory (this image looks at the brain from the front).

descriptions and functions clearly set out. However, dyslexic readers would have difficulty decoding small print on a dark background and would probably not be able to revise such concentrated information simply by reading it, despite having studied the brain previously. Using a photocopier to enlarge the page to A3 size and to take out the background colour would, as a start, give them a friendlier text and diagram to work from.

Make models

Despite specific problems with written language, these same students still need to access textbook information and make it their own in order to consolidate their understanding. Probably the ideal way in this case would be to hold parts of the brain in one's hand while reading the book, but, as this is not practicable, a cardboard model can serve; students should make their own. To make the model, start with an enlarged version of the brain diagram, glued or photocopied onto card. Colour and cut out the separate parts. To reinforce memory, fit the pieces onto an outline of the brain, naming each and describing its place in relation to other parts. A kinaesthetic method like this will help more students than just those with dyslexia to remember the layout of the human brain.

Models are useful for revising many biology topics – animal and plant cells, parts of a plant, the eye, heart, liver, the classification of species etc. – but they make for good revision in most other subjects too. Random examples might be the Battle of Hastings in history, architectural features in classical civilisation and the principle of density in physics.

THE CENTRAL NERVOUS SYSTEM
Divisions of the brain

	DESCRIPTION	FUNCTION
Medulla	Most inferior portion of the brain stem; continuous with spinal cord;	Contains vital centers (within its reticular formation) that regulate heartbeat, respiration, and blood pressure; contains reflex centers that control swallowing, coughing, sneezing and vomiting; relays messages to the other parts of the brain
Pons	Consists mainly of nerve tracts passing between the medulla and other parts of the brain; forms a bulge on the anterior surface of the brain stem; contains respiratory centers	Connects various parts of the brain; helps regulate respiration
Midbrain	Just superior to the pons; cavity is the cerebral aqueduct	Regulates visual and auditory reflexes
Diencephalon	Thalamus contains many important nuclei	Main relay center between spinal cord and cerebrum; incoming messages are sorted and partially interpreted here before being relayed to the appropriate centers in the cerebrum
	Hypothalamus	Contains centers for control of body temperature, appetite and water balance, helps control autonomic system; involved in some emotional and sexual responses
Cerebellum	Located at back of brain under cerebral hemispheres; surface convoluted; greyish in colour.	Responsible for smooth, coordinated movement; maintains posture and muscle tone; helps maintain equilibrium
Cerebrum	Largest, most prominent part of the brain; longitudinal fissure divides the cerebrum into right and left hemispheres, each containing a lateral ventricle;	Centre of intellect, memory, language and consciousness; receives and interprets sensory information from all sense organs; controls motor functions
Cerebral cortex	Convoluted, outer layer of grey matter covering the cerebrum	
White matter	Consists of fibres connecting the two hemispheres; basal ganglia located within the white matter	

THE CENTRAL NERVOUS SYSTEM

Cerebrum
Diencephalon { Thalamus / Hypothalamus
Pineal body
Midbrain
Cerebellum
Fourth ventricle
Pons
Medulla
Spinal cord
Corpus callosum
Fornix
Optic chiasma
Pituitary

Figure 7.13 A textbook page setting out the main parts of the brain and their functions. The original background colour was darkish rust. The diagram (superimposed here) was small.

Not everyone's visuospatial memory is well developed, so some people (often those with dyslexia, but others too) cannot, for instance, remember maps or draw them. Yet maps are important in many areas, e.g. understanding historical events or visualising the country whose language and culture is being studied. They are obviously crucial to geography. Ways of 'getting a map off the page' are therefore important. To take one instance, a revision activity to learn the map of South America might be to colour and cut out each individual country, see its colour and shape in isolation and place it on an outline of the whole continent, like a piece in a jigsaw puzzle. This processing through colour and kinaesthetic activity will enable students to visualise and draw the map, where simply looking at it on the page would not. Verbalising comparisons with familiar objects will also help in remembering maps. Students could say: 'the jigsaw piece of Chile looks like a chilli', 'A map of England and Scotland is like a triangle tipped slightly to the left.' This way of learning works through integrating functions – visual, kinaesthetic and verbal – in both hemispheres of the brain.

Visualise

To continue with the revision example of the brain, visualisation is a way of linking operations and technical terms, particularly if the learner includes story detail, puns or mnemonics. As memory responds to the ridiculous, this kind of picture making, to define, for example, the site and functions of the diencephalon, will be memorable (Figure 7.14).

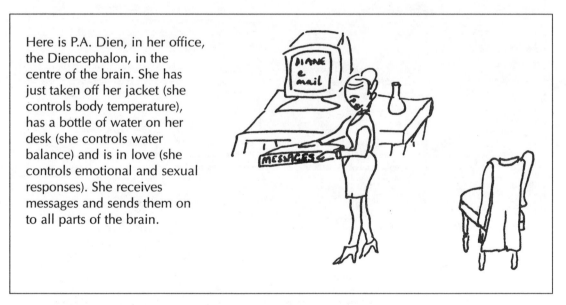

Here is P.A. Dien, in her office, the Diencephalon, in the centre of the brain. She has just taken off her jacket (she controls body temperature), has a bottle of water on her desk (she controls water balance) and is in love (she controls emotional and sexual responses). She receives messages and sends them on to all parts of the brain.

Figure 7.14 Visualising to remember the position and function of the diencephalon.

In the same way, memory responds to images that are crude (Figure 7.15).

Use cards to categorise and express information

Many exam candidates know the facts but cannot write about them in appropriate language. Speaking in technical language will help them to write in it, so revision methods that invite speech are important. A pack of revision playing cards about the brain can be used in a

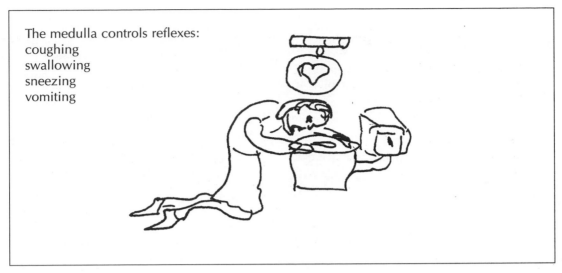

The medulla controls reflexes:
coughing
swallowing
sneezing
vomiting

Figure 7.15 The brain easily remembers crude or humorous images – this unfortunate person has celebrated too well after winning her medal.

variety of revision activities: face up (shuffling and sorting), face down (turning and matching name), description and function cards (categorising by size or colour of card), playing Pelmanism with friends who also need to revise the brain:

Some with names on:

> Cerebrum

Some with descriptions:

> Largest, most prominent part of brain; consists of two hemispheres

Some with functions:

> Centre of intellect, memory, language and consciousness; receives and interprets sensory information; controls motor functions

During these activities, read the cards aloud or say what you are looking for before turning a card face up. Merely looking at the words will not do – the language must be spoken if it is to be recalled when writing in an exam. Figure 7.16 is a summary page to show the three revision methods just described.

Labelling diagrams

The knowledge required to label pictures and diagrams is frequently tested in exams, especially in science and geography. Labelling is a factual part of a question where students could aim to count on full marks. A quick, multisensory method to revise for this is to make a set of labels, one for each part in the diagram. You can place these repeatedly on the diagram, saying the name aloud each time (Figure 7.17).

Text

Cerebrum – largest, most prominent part of the brain: longitudinal fissure divides the cerebrum into right and left hemispheres.

Cerebellum – located at back of brain under cerebal hemispheres; surface convoluted; greyish in colour.

Centre of intellect, memory, language and consciousness; receives and interprets sensory information; controls motor functions.

Responsible for smooth, co-ordinated movement, maintains posture and muscle tone; helps maintain equilibrium.

1. Make a model

Brain outline – enlarge to A3 size and mount on card

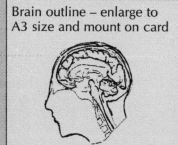

Cut out 'jigsaw' pieces to place on brain outline

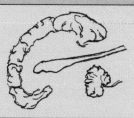

2. Visualise, make a story

Prof Cerebrum in his Clinic

Consciousness
Language
Intellect
Memory
Interpret sensory Infr
Control motor function

Bella the ballerina dancing the cerebellum

Smooth co-ordinated movements
posture
Muscle tone
equilibrium

3. Make cards to group
- **read cards aloud**
- **which cards go together?**
- **use often**

cerebellum

cerebrum

Centre of intellect, memory, language and consciousness; receives and interprets sensory ation; controls functions

Responsible for smooth, coordinated movement, maintains posture and muscle tone; helps maintain equilibrium

At back of brain under cerebral hemispheres; surface convoluted; greyish in colour

Largest part of brain; consists of two hemispheres

Figure 7.16 Three ways to revise parts of the brain: visualise, make models, make cards.

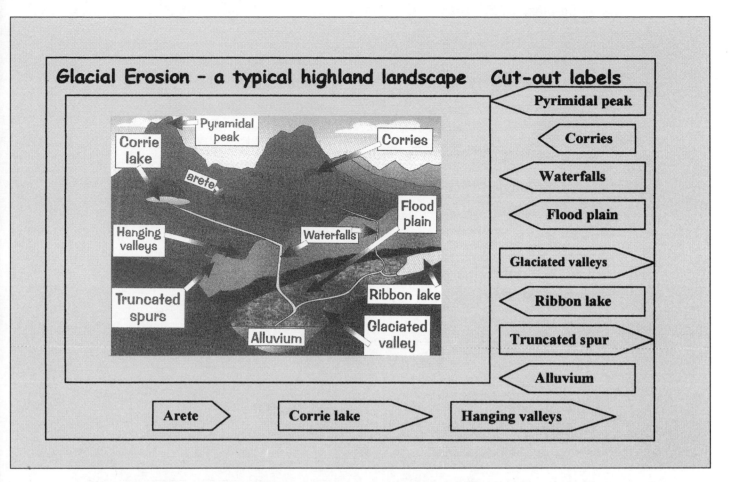

Figure 7.17 A revision product in geography consisting of a photocopied diagram taken from GCSE *Geography: The Revision Guide,* together with a set of labels ready to cut out (both mounted on card for longer life). Pupils who make their own version (deleting the diagram's labels) relearn the diagram as they make it. They can use the diagram and labels for further quick revision.

Following on this rather gentler form of review, put an A4 copy of the diagram in a transparent plastic wallet and then practise writing labels on the diagram through the wallet, using a dry-wipe pen. Again this has the advantage of repetition. It is much more of a challenge than selecting the right label from a set, because pupils will have to recall and spell each one. As before, it is essential to name the part out loud every time.

Making cue cards for sequences

These are cards, each one with a separate instruction on it, kept in the correct order (with a treasury tag?) and used as a drill exercise or to cue the steps in problem-solving or in an exposition.

Cue cards are particularly useful for revising maths, where sequencing is both an important mathematical skill and a common dyslexic weakness, especially under the time stress of an exam. Assembling a set of cards that traces each separate step in a problem-solving sequence is a good revision activity. Talking through the set or using it to cue responses to a practice question, without time pressure, will help to fix the sequence in long-term memory. Figure 7.18 illustrates this idea for revision.

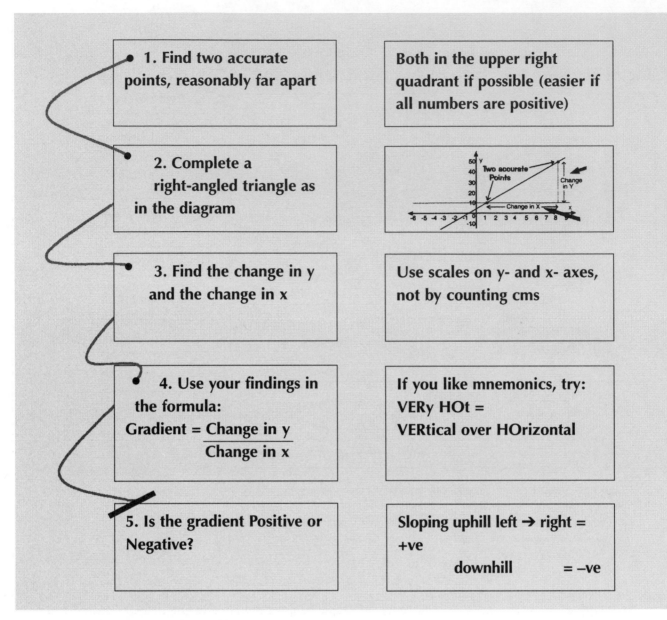

Figure 7.18 A set of cue cards for five steps in working out the gradient of a straight line. Write helpful notes on the reverse of the cards.

Forming knowledge networks

The slow and partial recall that is characteristic of dyslexia frequently causes underachievement in exams. How often does a dyslexic candidate remember just what he could have written, 10 minutes (or two days) after the exam ended? Non-dyslexics may fail to do themselves justice in the same way.

This is a problem of capricious recall, not of ignorance. 'I can't rely on my brain,' complained one infuriated exam candidate. If recall during an exam is to be more reliable, revision should focus on storing information in a memorable format where key points are summarised and linked together. This is because recall works in the brain through a system of links. Emphasising those links in revision means that, when an idea surfaces in an exam, any further information networked with it will surface too.

To make a knowledge network, collect information on a single topic and put a summary or symbol for each key idea on a separate card. Arrange the cards, as logically as possible, in a circle. The last card will thus lie beside the first. The circular format transforms a list of facts into a knowledge network that has neither a beginning nor an end. A knowledge network about the digestive process, for instance, might look like Figure 7.19.

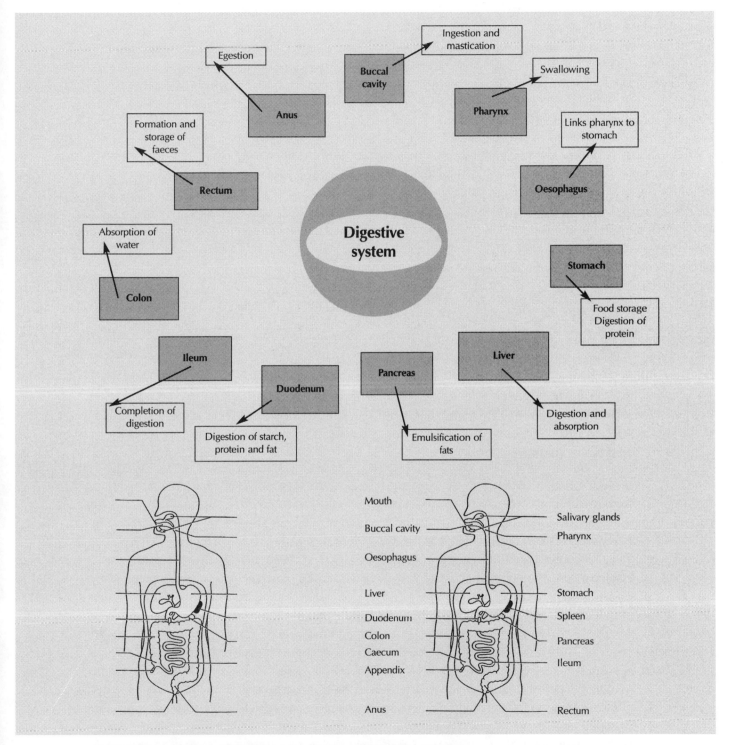

Figure 7.19 A knowledge network about the digestive system: cards representing parts and their functions are laid out in a circle. The labelled diagram acts as a reference guide. The unlabelled version can be used to practise naming. Enlarge the diagram and put it inside a transparent wallet. Using a dry-wipe pen, write the labels on the wallet; the diagram can then be reused.

The inner ring of cards names the parts. An outer ring links functions to parts and follows the process of digestion round the circle – memory is all about connections.

Preparing a network is excellent learning. For further revision, review the information laid out in the network using the following routine. Start anywhere in the circle:

- Moving either clockwise or anti-clockwise, read the information on each card aloud.
- Do it again.
- Next, read the cards aloud, but, this time, turn each one face down after reading.
- Now turn any card in the circle and read it. Try to remember the facts (out loud) on the card either above or below it. Then turn that card up to check.
- Keep travelling in the same direction for the remainder of the circle, speaking, then turning each card to check.
- Repeat the procedure by reading aloud and turning each card face down again.
- If the contents of a card are forgotten, just turn the card and read it aloud.
- Try starting in different parts of the network and moving in either direction round the circle.
- Quite soon, remembering one fact from the network will be enough to trigger the remainder.

At the original 'making' stage, it is important to extract all key information from lesson notes and books. Abbreviations, symbols and drawings are all useful in making the cards. Several smaller networks – probably not more than 20 cards – on one topic work better than one large one. As revision using a knowledge network follows both an original learning session and the making of the network cards, much of the information will have been absorbed already. The network circle provides a framework in which to re-visualise the information – condensed and linked – confidently in an exam.

Picture networks

As knowledge networks will improve recall in exams and the dyslexic memory is more likely to remember pictures than words, a valuable revision exercise is to combine the two, especially if there is a sequence to be learned as well. English literature candidates can become very confident in the sequence of events in set plays or novels using this method. Some revision guides are helpful because they portray the main events of a play, e.g. by Shakespeare, in a series of pictures. You can revise using these pictures as visual pegs ranged in a circle.

To make a picture network, photocopy and enlarge the pictures in the study guide and photocopy or paste them onto card. Cut the pictured events into separate pieces and set them out in a circle, explaining aloud the details relevant to each picture (Figure 7.20). If students practise the cards as a knowledge network, they will soon recall the order of events – what happened before as well as after – starting from any point in the play. This method works even better when students sketch their own pictures. Shuffling the picture cards and reassembling the circle while explaining the sequence of events can be a puzzle-type exercise to share with a friend.

Figure 7.20 A sheet of pictures taken from a Letts Study Guide for *Romeo and Juliet* summarising events in the play. Mount the guide page on card. Cut the sequence into separate images and practise putting them out in a circle in the order of the play. Talk about each one.

Rhythm, rhyme and music

All these three have a powerful impact on memory – once learnt, never forgotten. Combine the three, preferably with movement, and you have the perfect medium for rote learning (Figure 7.21).

AULD LANG SYNE

PHOTOSYNTHESIS
(Tune: "Auld Lang Syne")

When sunlight bathes the chloroplast, and photons are absorbed
The energy's transduced so fast that food is quickly stored,
Photosynthetic greenery traps light the spectrum through
Then dark pathway machinery fixes the CO_2.

Two chlorophylls (*a, b* to you) are cleverly deployed
In photosystems I and II, within the thylakoid
System I takes energy, at 700 (red)
While system II (with pigment *b*) takes 680 instead.

At manganese on centre II, see oxygen displace
As water's split, and protons too, leave membrane inner face
Electrons that we thus produce, cross, 'photo-fortified'
Plastoquinone then to reduce, upon the other side.

Meanwhile at I, chlorophyll *a* is photo-oxidised
(At 'positive holes', formed that way, electrons are much prized),
Electrons that we thus eject reduce NADP
With ferredoxin we suspect, as intermediary.

That hole in I we now negate, plastoquinol moves in
With *b* and *f* to mediate, and plastocyanin,
That redox loop, potential large, runs exergonically
With membrane-separated charge, and thence to ATP.

That Z track by electron pair, reduced NADP,
Plucked oxygen from water's care, and made some ATP.
Now we've got power to reduce, and ATP to spare,
Food in the dark we can produce, from CO_2 in air.

Ribulose diphosphate takes, a mole of CO_2
Gives two 3-phosphoglycerates, (if Calvin's story's true)
NADPH now provides, reducing power to make
Two phosphoglyceraldehydes (as ATP we break).

There now occurs a jolly jig (the details we'll ignore)
With carbon chains both small and big, to ribulose once more,
Each time round, as CO_2, is fixed we've chains to spare
And we can make hexoses new, from triose phosphate pair.

Other routes involve C_4, or pyruvate to fat,
NADPH as before, is vital still for that,
ATP still provides the drive, the moral still is this—
The one thing that keeps life alive is photosynthesis.

Figure 7.21 This extract from Professor Harold Baum's collection in his *Biochemist's Songbook* (Taylor & Francis) has an accompanying tape and diagrams. The level is about right for first year medical students, but a less detailed version would be a godsend for GCSE and A-level students and fun to do.

Getting a class to set their history or chemistry to rap would make an interesting homework, as would composing a ballad, limerick or the words to a well-known tune:

a pint of good water

weighs a pound and a quarter

is rather out of date now, but remembered since childhood.

Rhythmic chanting of conjugations, principal parts and declensions is a time-honoured method of coping with rote learning. It works, especially for children with strong auditory skills. Speaking aloud with rhythm and expression will be the best way to learn phrases in foreign languages, poetry, parts in plays, arguments for debates and school presentations.

A timeline

Being a good historian is not about just being able to remember dates and names, but having that information provides a vital framework on which to pin events.

A dyslexic person may have a problem holding a sequence in his mind – it can be letters in a word, words in a sentence or the order of events in his day. The events in a historical period present the same difficulty. The dyslexic pupil may be potentially the best historian in the class – full of interest, understanding and insight – but if he cannot remember dates and sequences he is severely hampered.

Making his own revision timeline in order to revise the period of history he is studying works well for a variety of reasons.

Rationale

Sequencing

For many people, presenting events in a visual sequence – 'sequencing in space' – is much more memorable than remembering a list of facts and dates. It fixes the time of the event visually and, just as importantly, its relationship to other events.

The whole picture

It is well known that dyslexic people like to see the whole picture and then relate the parts to it. (You see visual information all at once, whereas auditory information comes bit by bit.) A timeline with the major events marked can help to create the 'picture' that the dyslexic person needs: the sequence of past events in relation to each other.

Processing and making information 'his own'

Creating the line himself will encourage the pupil to visualise events in order to invent his own layout, symbols, drawings and mnemonics.

Pictures and symbols

These will certainly make the timeline more memorable – the pictures themselves will help the student to visualise the timelines and also the internal talk that accompanies the pictures (Figure 7.22): "How shall I remember that the Treaty of Sèvres was with Turkey?' 'Where are the Aaland Islands?' 'How shall I show the Beer Hall Putsch?'

Linking the unknown to the known

Each slot could have an 'Already known' band that includes both personal and cross-curricular information, e.g. 'Grannie was born', '*Titanic* sank'. Each student should try to think of at least one landmark to make the period familiar territory for him. This will help to create a network of information, each strand of which will help to build up a picture of time across the subject range and place the period or topic within a wider perspective.

How to present the line

Many people 'see' events going from left to right across a page, but most timelines in books are presented in a vertical list – more because it is easier to fit in the writing that goes with

		GRANNIE BORN			PHILIP LARKIN BORN		
W O R L D E V E N T S	WILSON [14 POINTS] CLEMENCEAU LLOYD GEORGE in power END OF WAR	(JAN) PARIS TALKS (JUNE) VERSAILLES GERMANY (SEPT) ST GERMAIN AUSTRIA NEUILLY BULGARIA	TRIANON HUNGARY TURKEY SÈVRES	WASHINGTON	CONFERENCES	FRENCH OCCUPATION RUHR LAUSANNE WITH TURKEY	
	1918	1919	1920	1921	1922	1923	
L of N			US SENATE SAYS "NO!" TO AMERICA JOINING 45 MEMBER STATES "EUROPEAN CLUB"	AALAND ISLANDS LAPLAND SWEDEN FINLAND SUCCESS! UPPER SILESIA - SUCCESS!	RAPALLO [APRIL] GERMANY + SOVIET UNION LoN OUTCASTS RESCUE PLAN for AUSTRIAN ECONOMY	CORFU INCIDENT UN FAILED TO AGREE DISPUTE OVER MEMEL	
G E R M A N Y	WAR MEDALS FOR BRAVERY AS MESSENGER KAPP PUTSCH	HITLER JOINED GERMAN WORKERS PARTY	NAME CHANGED - NAZI	STORM TROOPERS : SA		BEER HALL PUTSCH HYPERINFLATION	

Figure 7.22 The spatial arrangement and the processing involved in categorising and summarising the information will make this timeline memorable for the person who made it. For some students, the addition of pictures will provide landmarks and make it easier to re-visualise.

each event than to make it visually memorable for the students. A problem with timelines is in deciding how much space to allow for each unit of time – in some years something happens every month, in others, nothing much. As a general rule, keeping the space/time ratio consistent is best, if possible.

Making a timeline

How do you 'see' time? To draw a timeline you must consider whether you would like to present it as going from left to right (or right to left), from up to down (or down to up) or in some other way (Figure 7.23).

- Making topic bands run concurrently across (or down) the page is a good way to categorise events and to see them in relation to each other. They can be made separately, on the same scale, and joined when they are completed. Putting the strips up on your wall is a good way of familiarising yourself with the sequence and relationship of events of the period, giving the whole picture of main events. The familiar landmarks in the bedroom can also provide incidental reference points: 'The Wall Street Crash is nearer the door than the New Economic Policy, so it must be earlier'.

- Look on the Internet for history timelines – not as good for revision as making your own, but you could print them and then add to them with facts, symbols or pictures, or reorganise and illustrate them.

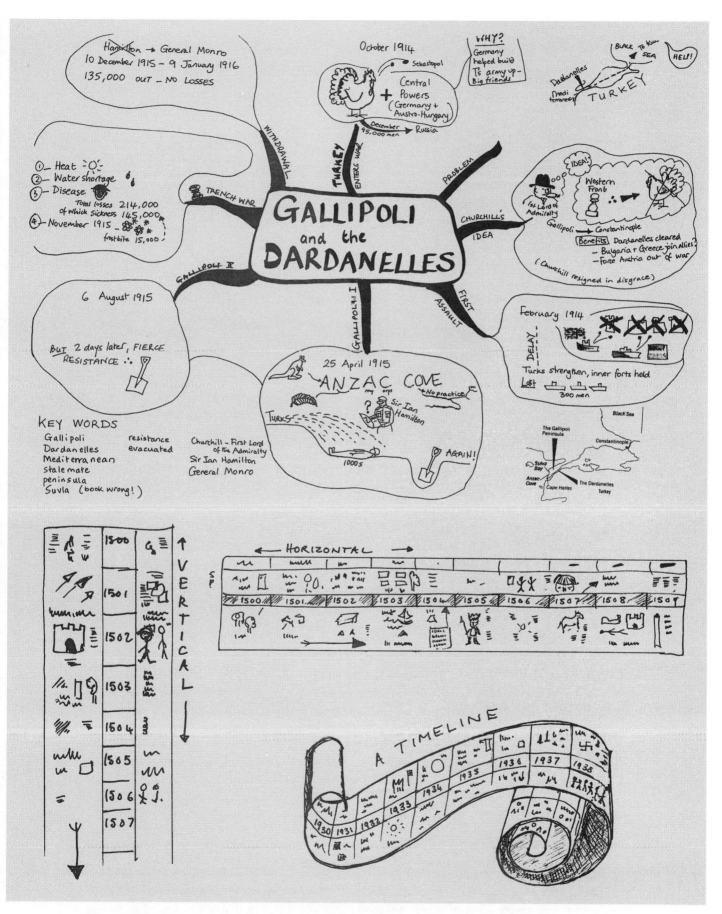

Figure 7.23 These timelines can be put on the wall, filed with revision notes or rolled up in an elastic band and kept in a pocket for revision.

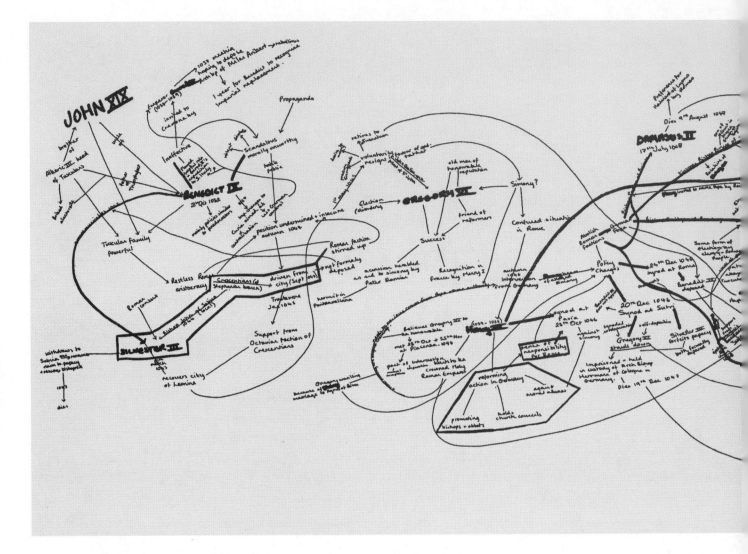

Figure 7.24 This version of Susie's mind-map is part of a roll of paper measuring 1 × 4 metres. It has been greatly reduced to the point where the writing is almost illegible. But the idea of linkages is clear – though clearer on the original, which is large and in colour.

- A skeleton timeline with dates and main events, which has been put together by either the teacher or the pupil himself, can be enlarged and added to at a later date and made more visually memorable by adding pictures, symbols and colour (Figures 7.25 and 7.26 over page).

One student (Susie) found making a chronological timeline unsatisfactory for her revision – as were her linear notes. She wanted to create something that showed both the chronology and the links. She found mind-map timelines (Figure 7.24) answered her needs:

I first experimented with mind-maps after obtaining a poor mark in my mock history GCSE, despite thorough revision. The new revision method I developed was really helpful as it condensed large volumes of information into just a few points, themes and events that were linked by colour-coded lines. As many of the individual points reappeared in different situations, the fact that I could link every event with lines prevented me from learning the same facts twice. Afterwards, when I was given essay titles, I could just

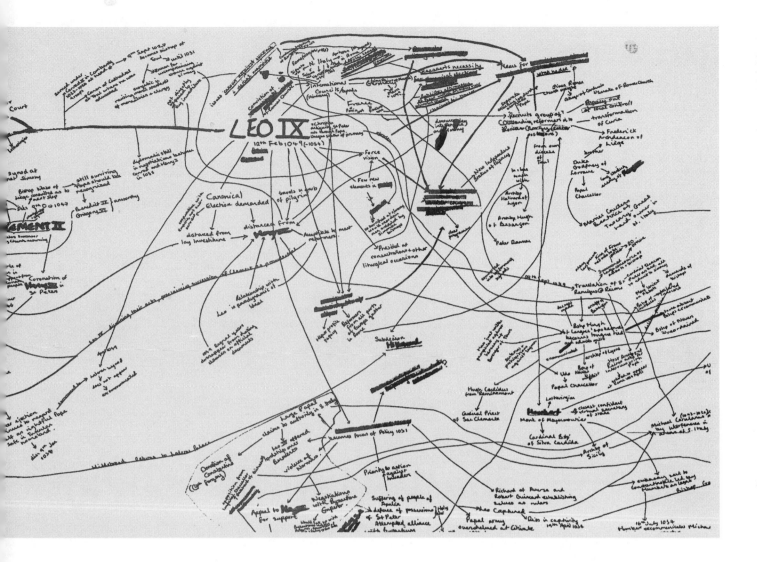

find them on my map and the plan would be there, surrounded by all the information I would need and including the colour-coded cross links that then allowed me to see how the essay could be structured.

In the exam I felt really prepared because I had a thorough plan for any essay title they could give me. I knew all of the points because of having thought so carefully about how to phrase them, colour them, and where to place them on the map. My grade definitely reflected this improved revision technique.

Now that I am doing A-levels, I am creating the map you can see in the picture, as the course progresses. It takes about ten minutes each night to add any new links, events or themes that I have come across onto the map, and this has helped me to remember all of the new information. I have even seen links, contradictions and patterns between topics and events that were not originally pointed out during class. This has increased my understanding in lessons and is very satisfying. All of the information is really coming together, and I am having to add fewer and fewer new points as the same points tend to reappear in different focuses within the subject.

<u>The League of Nations: Successes and Failures</u>
N.B. You need to look particularly carefully at the dates referred to in any questions on the League of Nations.

Successes:

Social and Humanitarian Work

The post-WWI refugee problem was solved, famine was alleviated, World Health Organization did good work in combatting disease, drug trafficking was clamped down on, the slave trade in Asia was lessened, and general promotion of the rights of women and developing nations took place. The Mandates Commission did some good work - the very idea of independence for colonies was then new - and the ILO is widely seen as the League's greatest success.

Administration of Plebiscites

A new idea based on principle of self-determination; was especially successful in Upper Silesia and the Ruhr Coalfield.

| 1919 | 1920 | 1921 | 1922 | 1923 | 1924 | 1925 | 1926 | 1927 | 1928 | 1929 | 1930 | 1931 | 1932 | 1933 | 1934 | 1935 | 1936 |

Failures:

Disarmament Conferences, 1920s and 1930s

In 1919 Germany's disarmament was held to be the first step in a more general process, as suggested in Wilson's fourteen points. However, apart from the Washington Conferences of 1921-2 which had some success with naval disarmament [see later], the general process never took place, and this only served to embitter many Germans further. In 1933 Hitler came to power in Germany and began to rearm; nothing was done and by the late thirties all major world powers were rearming.

Figure 7.25 Skeleton timeline waiting for details of the successes and failures of the League of Nations to be filled in. (See Sheet X in the Worksheet section.)

Cards to sort and pair

Sets of revision cards, in all subjects, can just as well be used for sorting and pairing as for network circles. Activities with these cards may appear childish in the context of secondary school, but so much of what is to be revised needs palatable and varied repetition to strengthen the memory trace. Valuable learning results from gathering the information and making the cards. Short, repeated games with the cards, either alone or with friends who are revising the same syllabus, will build confidence. Fear of the possibility of not being able to remember something in an exam increases the likelihood of not remembering, so confidence is crucially important, especially for candidates with any kind of learning difficulty.

Packs of revision cards invite repetitive use, partly because they highlight crucial material to be learned for exams and partly because they are a simple and playful device. Here are three examples of revision cards and activities to go with them.

1. Question and answer on separate cards

Two or three students might play pelmanism or 'pairs' with a set (10/15 pairs) of cards like the ones shown in the top box on page 266, but much of the multisensory learning will be missed if players ignore the italicised points in the following instructions:

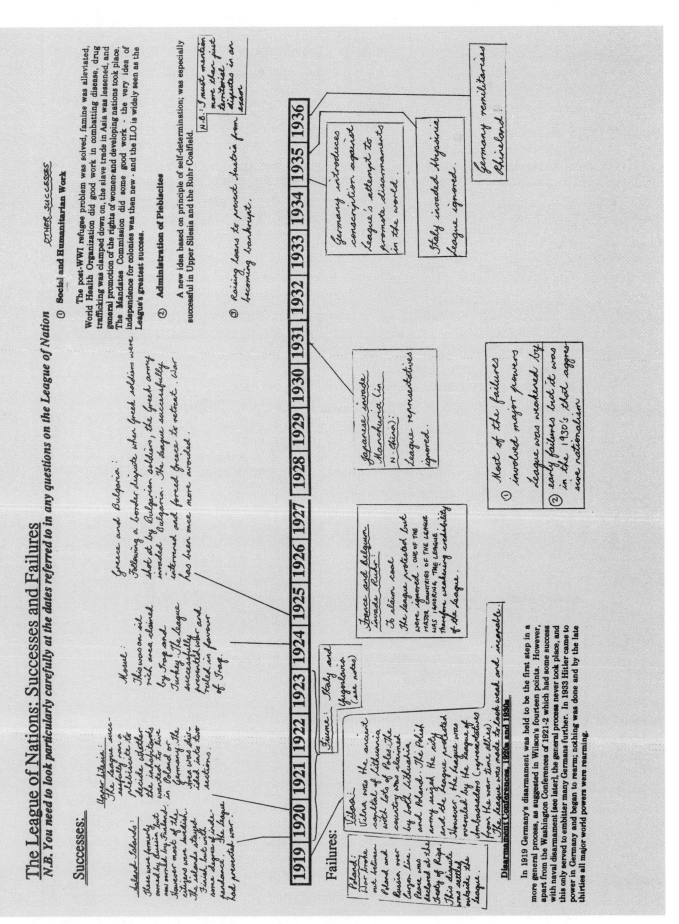

Figure 7.26 Completed timeline charting successes and failures of the League of Nations.

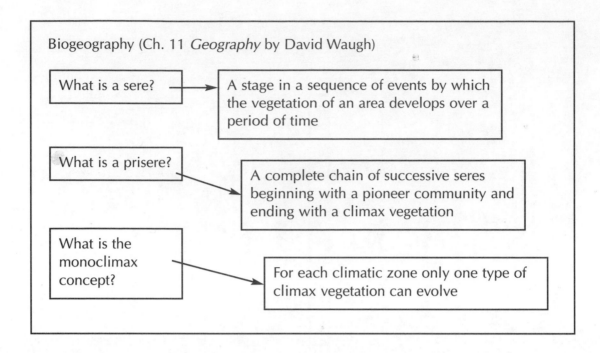

Biogeography (Ch. 11 *Geography* by David Waugh)

What is a sere? → A stage in a sequence of events by which the vegetation of an area develops over a period of time

What is a prisere? → A complete chain of successive seres beginning with a pioneer community and ending with a climax vegetation

What is the monoclimax concept? → For each climatic zone only one type of climax vegetation can evolve

- Mark question cards with a question mark on the back.
- Scatter cards, face down, and take turns to turn over a question card.
- *Read this aloud and say what you expect to find on the matching card.*
- Turn a card hoping to find the pair, *read it aloud.*
- *If the second card does not match the first, say what you would expect to find on its pair.*
- Turn both cards face down again in the same spot.
- Next person's turn.
- If the pair matches, take it and have another go.
- The winner has the most pairs.

2. Question and answer, on front and back of single card

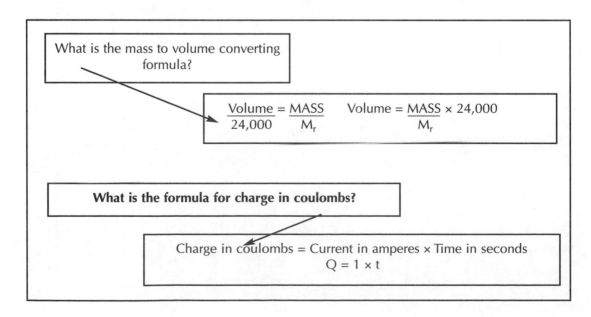

What is the mass to volume converting formula?

$$\text{Volume} = \frac{\text{MASS}}{24{,}000} \cdot \frac{}{M_r} \qquad \text{Volume} = \frac{\text{MASS} \times 24{,}000}{M_r}$$

What is the formula for charge in coulombs?

Charge in coulombs = Current in amperes × Time in seconds
$$Q = 1 \times t$$

This is an effective way to learn formulae, using these cards alone or by turns with a class-mate (which is worth doing because it encourages both to say the formulae aloud):

- Work through the full pack as fast as possible, reading one side of each card aloud.

- Then, from memory, say/write what should be on the other side, before turning it over to check.

- It is worth repeating the pack against the clock, with the aim of responding faster each time.

- Keep extracting cards until only the really problematic ones remain: this is the pack to repeat.

An activity with cards might form half the process for learning formulae; the other half would be in using them to work practice questions.

Don't waste cards on formulae that will be given on the exam paper, but be certain to know which they are.

Information not fully understood is hard to remember. If understanding is the problem, students must seek an explanation; they will not remember, in the stress of an exam, if they don't understand.

3. Cards to lay out in patterns or sequences

It is important to say the cards aloud and to set them out in the same way each time. Saying and hearing the language and forming the pattern by hand will reinforce memory in, for example, foreign language learning, so that, when it comes to an exam there will be spatial and auditory traces to support recall (see Chapter 6 for more suggestions):

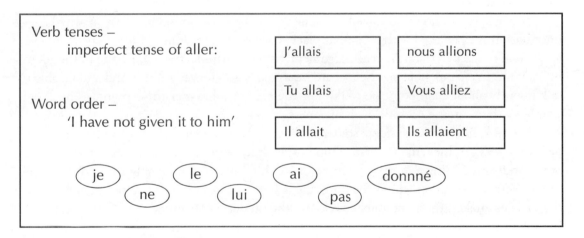

Verb tenses –
    imperfect tense of aller:

J'allais	nous allions
Tu allais	Vous alliez
Il allait	Ils allaient

Word order –
    'I have not given it to him'

je   ne   le   lui   ai   pas   donnné

Colour and shape reinforce memory traces for some learners (not all) and are sometimes extremely helpful to recall. This is an area worth experimenting with, e.g. students might colour code parts of speech in the French sentence above, or categorise them by the shape of a frame as below:

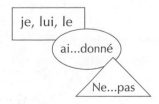

je, lui, le

ai...donné

Ne...pas

Wall posters – biology

Brontë, a dyslexic student, transformed her A-level biology notes into a series of large coloured posters, which she stuck on her bedroom wall. The creative work that went into planning and making the posters, especially with their colour, size and spatial layout, and the fact that she was constantly looking at them, made them easy for her to re-visualise in her exams (Figure 7.27).

Mind-maps on the wall – history

Eleanor, an A level student who had no learning difficulties, put the whole of her English history syllabus and the whole of her American history syllabus (see Figure 2.20 on pages 66–7) in two giant mind-maps on her bedroom wall. She made them out of a series of A4 maps created from class notes written through the year. She had drawn a few of the mind-maps in lessons and homework; the others she made during revision. The mind-maps were colourful and very detailed, and she used them, often when going to bed, either to work through the ideas on one sheet or to get a sense of the whole period and the way events were linked and developed. Figure 7.28 shows one of the A4 sheets drawn from class notes

Memory pegs

Understanding and remembering develop from connections a learner makes between what he already knows and what he is trying to learn. Sometimes artificial links made between an aspect of his personal life and the information he is trying to remember will act as pegs on which to hang new knowledge. Almost anything really familiar to the individual will work.

A peg system known to have been effective since Cicero used it is one in which new information is associated with a familiar place. Cicero increased his ability to speak fluently for several hours by visualising each argument, as he prepared a speech, in one of the rooms in his house. When delivering the speech, he would 'visit' a room in his mind and be able to talk fluently about each point he could 'see' there. He could order these points as he chose, simply by the route he took through his house.

Figure 7.29 shows a dyslexic student following this system and transforming a page in her textbook, 'Achievements of common agricultural policy' (CAP), into images of her home and surrounding countryside. In an exam this student will be able to re-visualise the images acting as pegs on which she hung the achievements of CAP. The personal nature of the images makes them uniquely vivid to the student concerned and correspondingly bewildering to anyone else – the message of this revision method is that pegs must be personal.

There are variations on this theme, which all work by personal associations. Susan, an A-level chemistry student and subsequently an educational psychologist, revised groups of chemicals by imagining them at focal points on a familiar walk: at a gate, one group, at an oak tree, another. Visualising one location recalled the chemistry attached to it, and Susan was able to recall the rest of the information by 'walking' in either direction from any point along the route.

Greg, an undergraduate, revising for his finals in geology and bored by the mass of detail, learned each day's topics in association with the meal his mother cooked for supper. Imagining the smell, taste, appearance and texture of curried chicken or mushroom omelettes served to peg and recall a day's revision.

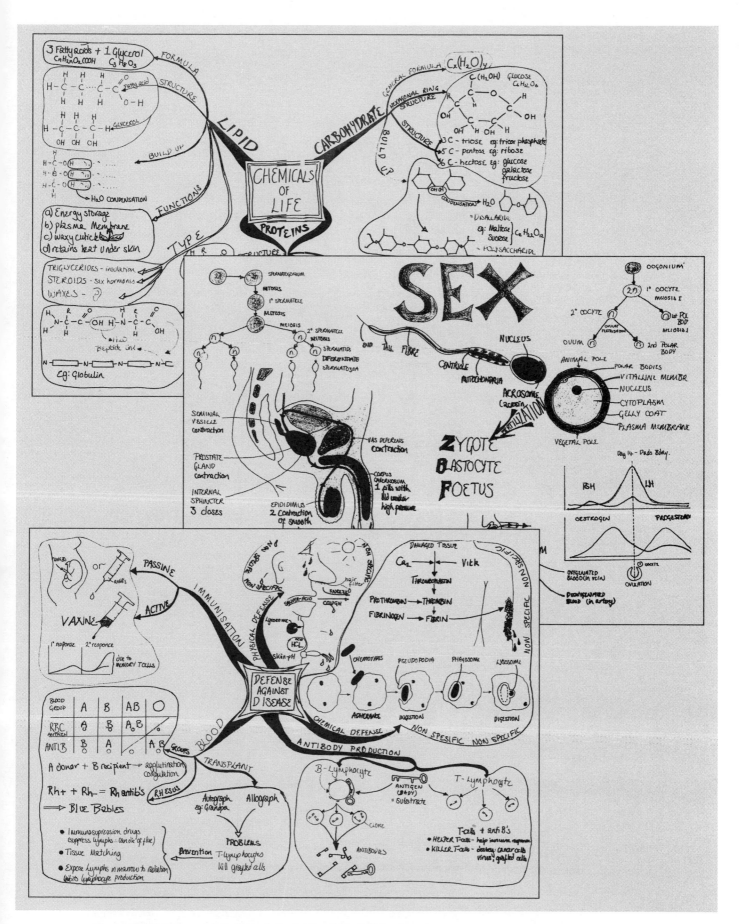

Figure 7.27 'Defense against disease', 'Sex', 'Chemicals of life': coloured
A3 posters pinned up on bedroom walls – a constant reminder.

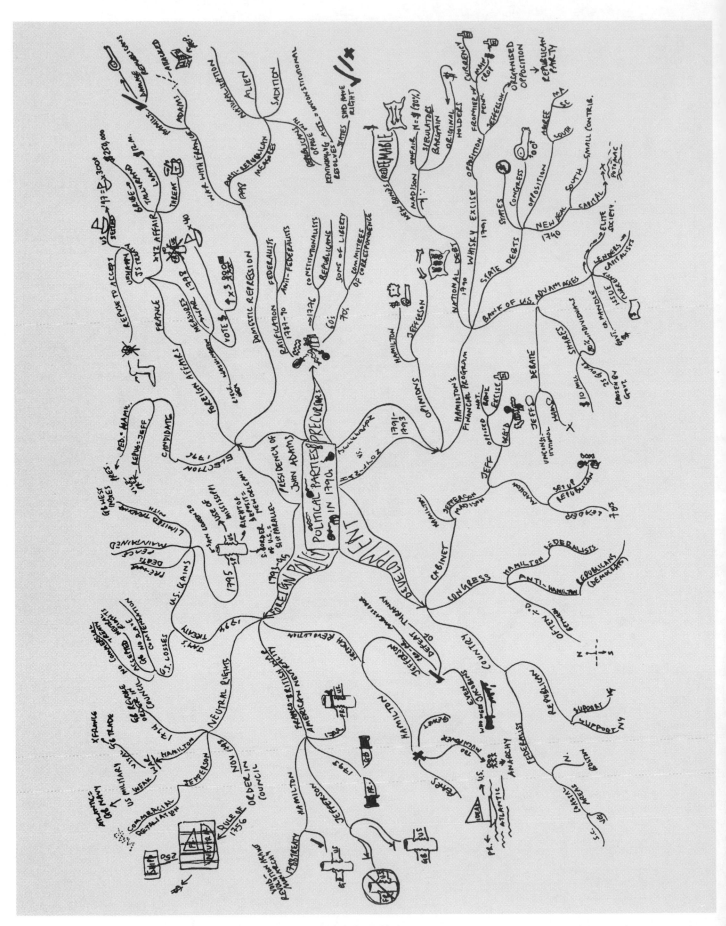

Figure 7.28 'Political parties in the 1790s', one of several A4 mind-maps covering an A-level history syllabus. These were fastened together and put up as a revision overview on bedroom walls.

Some achievements of CAP

Achieved a larger measure of self sufficiency. This reduces the costs and dependence on unreliable imports

Created higher yields due to input of capital for machinery and fertiliser

In NW Europe the average farm size has increased almost to the recommended level

Amalgamation of fields – in parts of France the number of fields has been reduced to one-eighth of the 1950 total

Production has changed according to demands, e.g., less wheat and potatoes and more sugar beet and animal products

Subsidies to hill farmers have reduced rural depopulation

Poorer farmers gain an opportunity to receive a second income by working in nearby factories ('five o'clock farmers') or from tourism

Higher income for farmers

Subsidies have reduced the risk of even higher unemployment in such rural areas as the Mezzogiorno

Reduced reliance on crops imported from developing countries who themselves have a food shortage

A surplus one year can offset a possible crop failure in another year

Some problems still facing CAP

An increase in food prices, especially in the net importing EEC countries of West Germany and the UK

Creation of food surpluses – the so called 'mountains and lakes'

Selling of surplus products at reduced prices to Eastern European countries (causes both political and economic opposition)

Increased gap between the favoured 'core' agriculture regions and the periphery

Peripheral farm units still very small and often uneconomic

High costs of subsidies. 'Industrial' countries such as the UK object to 70% of the EEC budget being spent on agriculture

'Five o'clock farmers' spend insufficient time on their farms. In France 15%, and in West Germany 30%, of farmers have a second income

Destruction of hedges to create larger fields destroys wild life and increases the risk of soil erosion

By reducing imports from developing countries the latter's main source of income is lost thus increasing the trade gap between the two areas

Figure 7.29 'Cicero's house': a peg system used here to transform textbook information about common agricultural policy (CAP) into personal imagery – home, garage and surroundings. When re-visualised in an exam, the images act as pegs on which to hang the information they represent.

One bun, two shoe . . .

One	bun		Six	sticks
Two	shoe		Seven	heaven
Three	tree		Eight	gate
Four	door		Nine	wine
Five	hive		Ten	hen

Notice that the images are easy to imagine and their names rhyme
with the numbers they represent.

This pegging system has been used successfully for years by students wanting to remember all sorts of lists of facts: case studies, legal documents, body parts, procedures, treaties. Dyslexic students, many of whom have difficulties learning inert data, can find it very useful as a revision tool, particularly as it can hold information in a sequence and depends on visualisation rather than rote learning.

Say you are revising some geography and want to remember the eight characteristics of a Central Business District (CBD), visualising is the key strategy (Figure 7.30). First, you have to think of some sort of link between a bun and the first item on your list:

- You want to remember 'vertical zoning with land use changes within multi-storey blocks' so you think of a tall pile of buns leaning up against an office block, each bun with a different type of filling.

- Take this one step further – don't just think of it, close your eyes and *picture* it. That's the way to store it in your memory, and that's the way to retrieve it too. Close your eyes again and you will be able to see the eight pictures you created, and these will give you the information you need to write about a CBD in the exam.

Revising set texts: English and foreign literature

Dyslexic students may have many strengths in their responses to literature, but their short-term memory difficulties and slow reading can make revision of a whole novel or play an uphill struggle. When the exams are approaching and time is short, the size of the task is daunting because it seems, against other smaller, more compartmentalised chunks of revision, to be too time-consuming.

It is crucial, therefore, that any revision is effective and done before the pressure is on. Gaining a thorough knowledge of the text will be achieved by strenuous processing: focusing on themes, recording ideas and selecting quotations.

When one considers the multi-tasking that is going on when a student is revising literature – decoding the words, visualising the setting and characters, considering the language, remembering the plot, identifying the themes, selecting the pivotal moments and telling quotations, noting ideas – it is obvious why the dyslexic student is daunted. But remove

The Characteristics of a Central Business District

1. BUN   **Vertical zoning** Land use changes within multi-storey blocks *(picture buns stacked vertically with different fillings)*

2. SHOE   **Office concentration** Central location needed for clients and workforce. *(Visualise a large shoe in centre of town with people streaming towards it)*

3. TREE   **Concentration of retailing** High threshold shops and department stores with wide ranges. Specialist shops further out *(Visualise trees with big shops and stores amongst the branches)*

4. DOOR   **Absence of manufacturing** Only a few specialised activities such as newspapers *(Picture yourself in a CBD, opening a factory door and finding nothing there)*

5. HIVE   **Low residential population** High rents, so only a few luxury flats, especially in large cities *(You are a bee, flying above the city, there are one or two luxury hives in the centre, but masses of hives in the outskirts)*

6. STICKS **Pedestrianisation** Since 1960s traffic movement limited within the CBD. Safer shopping *(Imagine pedestrians with sticks walking about the CBD)*

7. HEAVEN **Multi-storey development** High land values encourage buildings to grow upwards for floor space *(See buildings with their tops in heaven, angels measuring floor space)*

8. GATE   **Comprehensive redevelopment** Clearance of sites for complete redevelopment, sometimes to inner city *(Imagine a heap of rubble, a building site, a gate)*

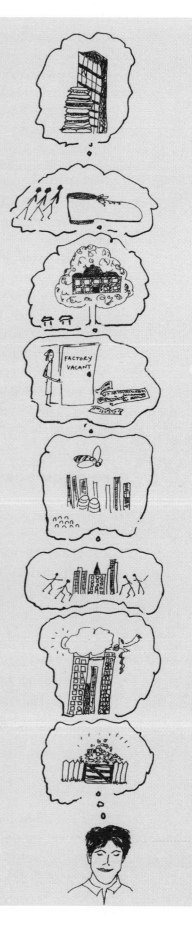

Figure 7.30 'One bun, two shoe' – this pegging system relies on visualising to help the student remember a list of points.

'decoding the words' from the equation and the task immediately becomes more manageable, and our student is on a level playing field with his peers: listening to the tape of the text will leave his mind free both to visualise and to think about the themes of the text. Being able to visualise and play with the ideas are the keys to enjoyment, understanding and memory of literature.

Some pupils have difficulty remembering the sequence of a novel or play – which scene or event came first – and it may be important to have this chronology in place when they have to answer a context question or provide evidence for an argument. A mind-map summary, with quotations and symbols, can be invaluable in providing that whole picture.

Novels and plays on tape are becoming increasingly available from school, university and public libraries. They are usually read by professional actors, whose variety of accents, expression and timing not only adds greatly to an appreciation of the text but also helps with understanding it.

A good range of foreign texts on tape is harder to get hold of – but it's worth trying. Grant & Cutler (www.grantandcutler.com) is a good source for these. Listening while following the text not only helps with comprehension through the reader's tone of voice but also presents a wonderful opportunity for reinforcing sound/symbol correlation for the dyslexic student whose word recognition, pronunciation or spelling may need this multisensory reinforcement.

For a good overall understanding of a foreign classical text it is well worth reading a translation of it aloud, with as much expression as possible, onto tape. The desperate student may want to memorise a literal translation to help him through the difficult bits of the text – listening to the tape again and again will probably work.

A revision session

Preparation

- Find a good, unabridged tape of the text – order from the public or school library, or from Listening Books. Enlist the help of a parent, or the special needs or literature teacher, if the tape is difficult to obtain.
- Collect a list of essay titles from a teacher or from old exam papers or revision guides.
- Buy some highlighters.
- Collect and sort your class notes.
- Choose about four exam questions or themes and write each one on a separate piece of paper. Have an additional sheet for 'random thoughts'.
- Prepare an A3 sheet on which to make a mind-map summary of the book or play.

Revision

Making a mind-map summary of the text while you listen provides a picture of the whole play or novel on one sheet – ideal for later revision (Figure 7.31). Selecting a pictorial symbol and quotation to mark each scene or chapter will focus your attention while you read and listen. It will also provide the stimulus for memory when you re-visualise the map during the exam.

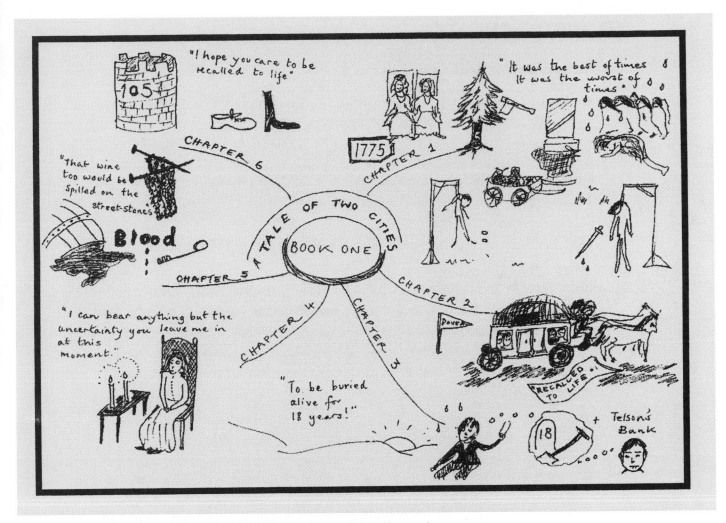

Figure 7.31 Including the most memorable quotes and images from each
chapter of *A Tale of Two Cities* provided the student with excellent revision:
revisiting the novel, visualising, selecting and rejecting, sequencing – and
having a visual record of the book.

- With the text open, your blank question sheets in front of you, and your pen and
  highlighters at the ready, switch on the tape. If you are listening to a play (one by
  Shakespeare, for example), it is rewarding to follow the text while listening to the
  tape (see page 39). This can also work for a novel, but sometimes the speed of reading
  on the tape is either too fast or too slow.

- Stop the tape when you want to write a point down on one of the question sheets,
  draw a symbol on your mind-map, or highlight a quotation or passage on the text.

- When you have an idea, *always* write it down on your spare sheet for 'random thoughts'.
  However memorable it is, you will probably forget it unless you write it down!

- File your sheets and mind-maps after every session – they will provide excellent last-
  minute revision by triggering your memory of the scenes, characters and ideas from
  the text.

Revising poetry

Learning poetry and quotations

There need be no particular problems here for the dyslexic student, so long as he starts early enough so that he has time to counteract the 'forgetting curve' – and uses multisensory techniques:

- *Speaking the verse aloud with expression and gesture* will help with memory. Actors learn their lines more easily when they move about and link their lines to tones of voice and body language.
- *Selecting an image* for each line, each verse or each quotation – either by drawing it, visualising it, or both.
- *Mind-mapping* so that the whole poem can be seen on one page – each line or verse with a picture symbol. When the map is finished, the pupil should turn over the page, re-visualise the map and say the poem aloud, using the symbols as landmarks.
- *Putting the verse onto tape* (rehearsing first and being very careful to read it accurately):
  - saying the title of the poem or category of quotations to follow (e.g. *Anthem to Doomed Youth*)
  - *pause*
  - first line or verse: 'What passing bells for these who die as cattle?'
  - *pause*
  - second line: 'Only the monstrous anger of the guns' . . . and so on. This works well because it is using both oral and aural skills. When the student plays the tape again, his ear will anticipate the line, he will speak it himself and then be able to check his version against the original. When the tapes are played again and again, the poems and quotations can be learnt almost subliminally.

Some pupils may prefer simply to record the poem onto tape without pauses and then, when playing it back, try to say the poem along with the tape.

In the case of quotations, a student can make his own brief introduction: 'There is church imagery throughout the poem' and then list examples of it. He will not only need to be able to recognise the quote once the voice on tape has begun the line but also need to be able to generate the list himself: 'Which quotes do I know to support this idea?' and say them or write them down.

Poetry criticism

Writing essays in any subject presents overload for a dyslexic person – having ideas, planning, remembering, writing, spelling, punctuating. The secret is always to break the process into stages so that the thinking is done before the more problematical writing stage. Unlike other subjects, where good revision of the facts at least prepares the student for most essay questions, the unseen poem or the comparison of a known with an unknown poem, adds a new element to the equation.

Preparation will be most effective if the student concentrates on the elements of criticism that can be applied to most good poems and practises answering the sort of questions he will address whichever poem or poems he may be presented with.

Although the mind-map of questions in Figures 7.32 and 7.33 provide a formal structure for the way the student thinks about the poem, the ideas and responses that it should generate will be personal and can be used flexibly, whatever the question posed. Laying the questions out spatially will help some dyslexic students with to remember them by their place on the page – a template for criticism with the poem in the middle. The spatial arrangement will also encourage the student to keep adding ideas and, because all the evidence is on the same page, he will be able to see the links between them more easily.

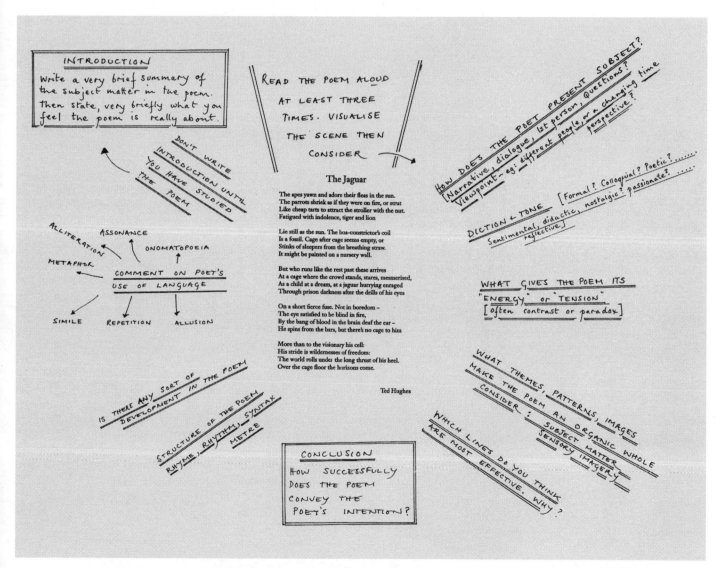

Figure 7.32 The questions around 'The Jaguar' can be applied to any poem and will encourage the pupil to do his thinking and noting before he starts writing (for a blank mind-map, with questions and a space for a poem, see Sheets Y and Z in the Worksheet section).

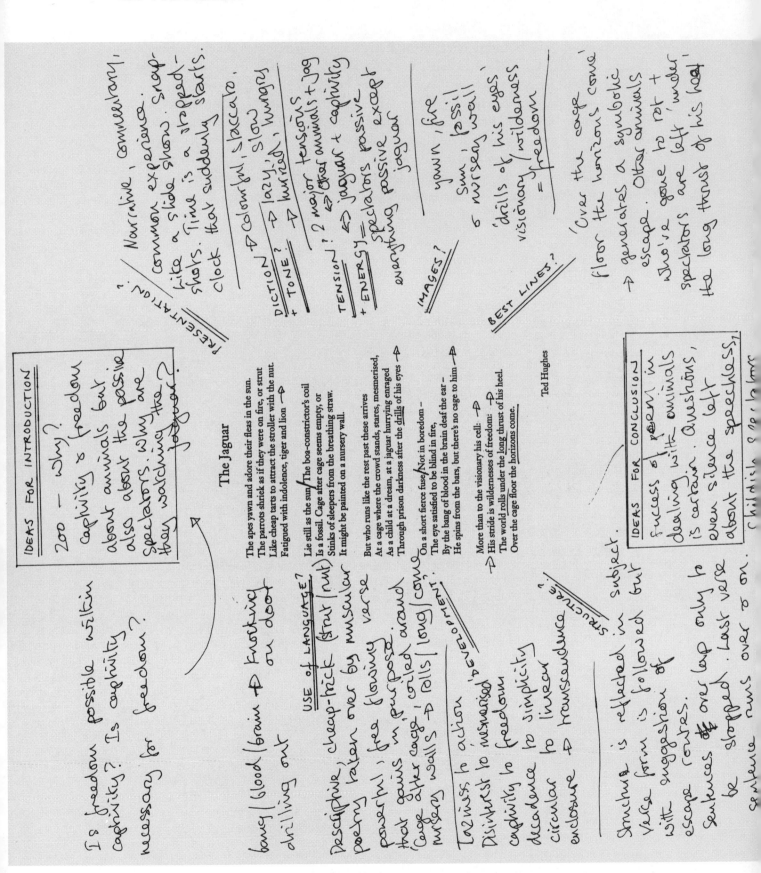

IDEAS FOR INTRODUCTION

Zoo – why?
captivity & freedom
about animals but
also about the passive
spectators. Why are
they watching the jaguar?

Is freedom possible within
captivity? Is captivity
necessary for freedom?

PRESENTATION? Narrative, commentary,
common experience. Snap-
shots. Time is a stopped-
clock that suddenly starts.

DICTION → colourful, staccato.
+ TONE? → lazy, slow
→ hurried, hungry

TENSION? 2 major tensions
→ other animals + jaguar
→ jaguar + captivity

+ ENERGY? → spectators passive
spectators passive except
everything passive jaguar

IMAGES? yawn, fire
sun, (oasis!)
6 nursery wall
'drills of his eyes'
visionary/wilderness
= freedom

BEST LINES? 'Over the cage
floor the horizons come'
→ generates a symbolic
escape. Other animals
who've gone to pot +
spectators are left 'under
the long thrust of his heel'

The Jaguar

The apes yawn and adore their fleas in the sun.
The parrots shriek as if they were on fire, or strut
Like cheap tarts to attract the stroller with the nut.
Fatigued with indolence, tiger and lion →

Lie still as the sun. The boa-constrictor's coil
Is a fossil. Cage after cage seems empty, or
Stinks of sleepers from the breathing straw.
It might be painted on a nursery wall.

But who runs like the rest past these arrives
At a cage where the crowd stands, stares, mesmerised,
As a child at a dream, at a jaguar hurrying enraged
Through prison darkness after the drills of his eyes →

On a short fierce fuse. Not in boredom –
The eye satisfied to be blind in fire,
By the bang of blood in the brain deaf the ear –
He spins from the bars, but there's no cage to him →

More than to the visionary his cell:
His stride is wildernesses of freedom:
The world rolls under the long thrust of his heel.
Over the cage floor the horizons come.

Ted Hughes

USE of LANGUAGE?
bang/blood/brain → frantic
drilling out

Descriptive, cheap-trick (strut/nut)
poem taken over by muscular
powerful, free flowing verse
that gains in purpose.
'cage after cage, coiled around'
→ rolls/long/coiled?
nursery walls → transcendence?

STRUCTURE?
Laziness to action
Disinterest to mesmerised DEVELOPMENT
captivity to freedom
decadence to simplicity
circular to linear
enclosure → transcendence

Structure is reflected in subject.
Verse form is followed but
with suggestion of
escape routes.
Sentences overlap only to
be stopped. Last verse
runs over & on.
Childish & regular

IDEAS FOR CONCLUSION
Success of poem in
dealing with animals
is certain. Questions,
even silence left
about the speechless?

Figure 7.33 This mind-map has been worked on by a student in preparation for an exam – and an unknown essay question.

Summaries

Contents

Summaries and Worksheets may be copied for teaching purposes.

1 How teachers can help dyslexic students

There will be a minority of students in every class who underachieve because they have underlying difficulties in some of the basic subskills of learning – visual and auditory memory and perception, sequencing skills, speed of processing, or hand–eye co-ordination. These students can achieve their potential if they and their teachers recognise their difficulties and work around them. Letting them off work is not helpful. They will need extra guidance and a reassurance from you that they too are capable of producing excellent work. Praise is a great motivator.

Dyslexics often have great strengths. They frequently are amongst the most interesting pupils in the school. The crucial skills of abstract reasoning, imagination and intelligence are unaffected by dyslexia.

You will have noticed that dyslexic students often have problems in these areas:

Organisation

The dyslexic person's poor organisation is due to short-term memory and sequencing difficulties. These have a knock-on effect on all his academic work. As a tutor, form teacher or other helper you can give practical help. Time-consuming to begin with, it should save time in the long run, both for the child, and for his frustrated teachers.

Suggestions:

- Give help rather than criticism – suggest systems and provide support.
- Show him how to file his papers and computer notes.
- Encourage him to have copies of lesson and homework timetables for school, home, schoolbag.
- Train him always to write his homework down in a particular place.
- Make periodic checks on his notes.
- Remind him to put his name on his books, his garments, his equipment.

Reading

Dyslexic students are often slow, inaccurate and therefore, reluctant, readers – they may have to read material twice to take in and remember it. They frequently misread exam questions.

Suggestions:

- Promote the use of books on tape (unabridged versions) for set texts and also general reading, especially Shakespeare and the meatier novels. Pupils will need warning so they have time to get or order them from the library.
- Recommend alternative textbooks to make the curriculum accessible for weaker readers.
- Teach reading skills. See *The Art of Efficient Reading* by Spache and Berg (Macmillan).
- Ensure photocopied handouts are clear and the print not too small. Enlarged text can be a help for a dyslexic person who wants to highlight, make notes or colour code.
- Give practice in reading and analysing exam questions.

Reading unseen material aloud in class

There is no point in asking dyslexic pupils to read aloud without warning – it will put them off your subject and make them dread lessons. Moreover, when they are stressed, they can't internalise what they are reading.

Suggestions:

- Discover which pupils hate reading aloud. Give one-to-one practice to increase confidence.
- Talk to them about the problem – and reassure them that you won't call on them to read. This will reduce their anxiety and enable them to concentrate during your lesson.

Note-taking

Note-taking can be a giveaway. A dyslexic student's notes may be incomplete, inaccurate, illegible and, therefore, of little use for revision. The worst scenario is of the student who gets his notes or diagrams down reasonably well but does not 'hear' or internalise what is being said because he has had to concentrate hard on the mechanical aspects of the task.

When copying from the board, the dyslexic student with poor visual perception or memory is likely to be slow and inaccurate, especially if the words are foreign or technical, or the teacher's writing is not clear. Diagrams will take him longer. Spatial difficulties may make it hard for him to copy geometry, charts, maps and diagrams.

The process of writing notes and using pauses and class discussion time to catch up may prevent him from participating orally in the lesson – which is probably his best way of learning and remembering. As students go up the school and more sophisticated skills are required, the problem tends to get more acute.

Suggestions:

You can:
- Check which pupils are having difficulties (before too much ground has been lost) – by asking them whether they feel they are coping, by looking at their notes and by testing their understanding.
- Give a lesson on note-taking: how to organise the page, how to indicate different hierarchies, how to recognise main points.
- Suggest a consistent system of abbreviations.
- Teach subject-specific vocabulary, so that words are better understood and spellings practised.
- Give, at the beginning of the lesson, a clear outline of what you hope to cover and, while teaching, emphasise which are the important points.
- Make a point of not giving explanations while students are writing or copying
- Suggest typing rather than hand-writing.
- Encourage the laptop user to learn to touch-type so that he can concentrate better on the meaning rather than on the typing. He will also be able to keep his eyes on the board while copying. This will improve accuracy.
- Encourage laptop users to use the computer's full resources: e.g. drawing software etc.

Essay writing

Dyslexic pupils can get a block about writing essays. When making curriculum choices, they may avoid essay-writing subjects. The most common and serious problem is the lack of structuring and sequencing in their essays. As dyslexic people are often lateral thinkers, the problems of organisation are compounded. In addition their writing may be much slower than their thinking, so good ideas and connections get forgotten as they struggle with the writing and spelling.

Suggestions:

- Train dyslexic students to tackle essay writing in five stages: analysing the question, brainstorming, planning, writing and then checking.
- Encourage idea generation through brainstorming before they start writing.
- Teach mind-mapping for those who can 'see' and organise an essay's structure, hierarchies and balance better when ideas and evidence are arranged spatially.
- If there is a marked discrepancy in the quality of a pupil's spoken and written expression, or if his handwriting does not stand up to the pressure of writing under timed conditions (he writes too slowly or writes illegibly), recommend that he learns to touch-type and use a word processor as soon as possible.

Learning work

Memorising will take longer and need more reinforcement, particularly rote learning. Conventional methods may not work effectively.

Suggestions:

- Teach these pupils to think much more about *how* they are learning something. If their methods are inefficient, they should try other, more active, methods. The more active, or interactive, the methods are, the more likely they are to be successful, for example: drawing, speaking aloud, discussing, summarising, explaining, testing, mind-mapping or using tape.
- Show dyslexic students the 'forgetting curve' and demonstrate to them how timed reviews can enable them to transfer their learning from short- to long-term memory.

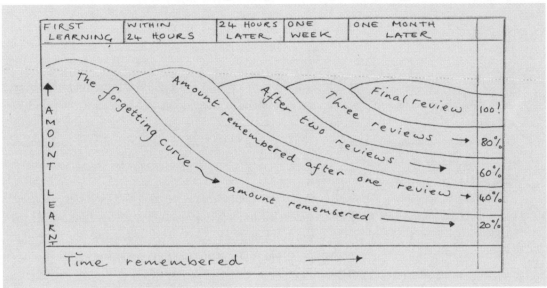

Language learning

There are many good reasons why dyslexics are particularly weak in language learning:

- **visual perception and memory difficulties** – so they do not notice spellings, accents, gender; they copy inaccurately and are poor at checking and learning
- **auditory perception and memory difficulties** – so they do not hear slight differences in sound or stress, or hear where one word ends and another begins. Rote learning takes longer
- **sequencing difficulties** – which affect spelling, word order (for both reading and writing), learning of declensions and conjugations

Suggestions:

- Teach them to integrate saying, hearing, seeing and writing as much as possible for learning tasks. In this way a weak channel (perhaps the eye) is supported by a stronger one; having to say the word makes the student focus better with his eye on the letters and uses the memory in his ear, lips and tongue – which are the major senses for language learning.
- Reading aloud to check work makes a tremendous difference – the ear picks up errors that the eye does not notice, accents can be 'heard', sequences of words that look right may sound wrong (the latter being the more reliable test).
- Memorising work should be 'out loud' and 'a little and often' (see the 'forgetting curve').
- These students should not rely on their own vocabulary books for learning – inaccurate copying makes this hazardous (wrong genders, wrong spellings, misplaced accents etc.).

Maths

For many dyslexic students the organisation of calculators, geometrical instruments, sharp pencils, rulers – as well as the organisation of work on the page – are major areas of weakness. Reading or copying fast and accurately from the board or a textbook, hitting the right buttons on the calculator and extracting the relevant information from exam questions are also problem areas. Dyslexic students make silly mistakes as they work – misreading signs, misplacing decimal points. Others work intuitively, missing out the working altogether. Some dyslexics may not process fast enough to understand properly in the lesson or to get enough practice to reinforce the memory trace.

Suggestions:

- Train them in organisation – tutors and parents could help here.
- Saying numbers and symbols aloud when copying or using the calculator – then the mismatch between eye and ear alerts the student to any inaccuracy.
- Always ask, 'Does this answer seem reasonable?' – especially where decimal place value is involved.
- For multi-stage problems, encourage them to write on every other line. This will help the teacher, the examiner and the student to follow the workings, and is of particular value for expressions containing indices as a way of keeping the index well and truly raised and separate from the rest of the expression.
- Paper with wide lines is better for these students than plain paper.
- Dyslexic and dyspraxic students will find larger diagrams better to work with because they are easier to label and less cluttered visually.
- Encourage pupils to show working – as the intuitive approach runs out sooner or later for even the very brightest. For the less mathematically gifted, method marks will prove an essential part of their final GCSE percentage.
- Teachers should take particular care to keep their blackboard workings and explanations clear and concise so that dyslexic students can follow the sequence easily.
- Teach students to make mental pictures of an operation (e.g. transformations) by getting them to first draw them and then visualise the images on their mental screen. This will strengthen understanding and memory and provide a link for more advanced work. The use of colour coding on the blackboard can clarify explanations. It can be used to separate questions or notes and examples and is particularly effective when cancelling algebraic expressions, because pupils can see at a glance where each part has 'gone'.

Dr Harry Chasty, one-time Head of the Dyslexia Institute wrote:

'If children can't learn in the way we teach, we must teach them in the way they can learn.'

2 Dyslexic difficulties – a page for students

Use a highlighter to mark any difficulties that you feel apply to you.

Notes

Are your notes incomplete, inaccurate, illegible – and therefore of little use for future revision? Can you get your notes or diagrams down reasonably well, but in doing so miss the explanations because you have to concentrate hard on the process of drawing, or writing and remembering the words? Where there is copying words or diagrams from the board, are you slower than the rest, and inaccurate too? Do you have to use class discussion time to catch up with notes and does this prevent you from participating in the lesson or asking questions? The problem doesn't go away with time, so some alternative must be decided on: someone else's notes? An outline from the teacher? A good/different textbook? A laptop? At least make the teacher aware of your difficulty.

Reading

Reading needs to be an automatic skill for learning from books to be enjoyable. Do you have to reread material in order to understand and remember what you have read? Under pressure, do you read exam questions inaccurately? Are you a slow, reluctant or inaccurate reader? Use books on tape so that you don't miss out on books, set texts or plays that others are reading. Do you hate reading aloud? If so, you must tell your teachers you would rather not read aloud in class.

Essays

Your written work is probably scruffy, but the most common and important problem is the structuring and sequencing in essays. Is your thinking much faster than your writing? Do good ideas get lost when you try to write and think at the same time? Are you beginning to get a block about writing essays at all? Do you try to avoid essay-writing subjects when making curriculum choices? Learning to touch-type and using a word processor will make a great difference to your fluency. You should brainstorm and then plan your essays so that you do the thinking and organising *before* you start writing.

Languages

Any spelling, writing, and reading difficulties that you may have with your own language will make foreign language learning hard for you. You might find you have difficulty relating sounds to symbols, being able to break down words into syllables, seeing stems and endings, recognising stress, hearing slight differences in sound, being able to sequence letters in a word and words in a sentence, and being able to copy accurately from a book or from the board. Are the words you have copied into your vocab book correct? Do these difficulties make vocabulary learning, remembering grammar, learning verb conjugations and tenses, speaking the foreign language, copying and checking hard for you? If so, you should explain your difficulties to your teacher and ask for special help in learning multisensorily – speaking aloud as you learn, using pictures, using mnemonics and repetition.

Organisation

Sequencing and short-term memory problems have an effect on organisation. Do you have problems with filing, remembering and finding books and files, writing down what your homework is and then remembering to give it in, planning the day and managing time? If so, you should ask one of your teachers to help you to get a system organised.

Learning work

Do learning tasks take you longer, and is work learnt one day and forgotten the next? You must think much more about *how* you are learning something, then how and when to revise it, if you are to transfer the material from short- to long-term memory.

3 Homework from a parent's point of view

What is it?

- Discuss with the student a reliable system for getting homework down in each subject.
- Comply meticulously with any school systems, e.g. checking and signing a homework book.
- Keep telephone numbers/e-mail addresses of reliable classmates.
- Take a copy of the homework timetable and know when homework has to be handed in.
- Find out the timescale for course work; there is often an opportunity for further supervised drafts if the student meets deadlines.
- Help the student to know what he is supposed to be doing, but try not to nag.
- Can you access homework assignments via the school network?

When should homework be done and where?

- Topics for negotiation: fix homework time for each day of the week. If a child agrees that the timing is reasonable (neither interfering with a favourite TV programme nor inconveniencing a family meal) he should expect to stick to it without fuss.
- Is his work-space warm, light and quiet? Listening to music may be helpful (blocks out other distractions in the house), but watching television won't be.
- Does he have a generous table surface and shelves to keep books and files in good order?
- Keep up a supply of kit, items that encourage multisensory work and organised filing (see page 122): hole punch and protectors, scissors, glue, A3 paper, highlighters, replace dried up felt tips, plastic wallets, index cards and box, dividers, tape-recorder and blank tapes, printer ink, files in various styles, a bag big enough to carry school gear, etc.

How can you help?

- If a teenager doesn't feel in control, he may not let parents help, so limit your area of interest to something acceptable to him and try to get a copy of the textbook if at all possible.
- Agree a topic with him and get him to decide what he would like you to do.
- If the work is learning, concentrate on finding a multisensory method and avoid testing until the learning is largely secure.

Examples of useful activities:

- Test him on his foreign vocabulary after he has learnt it.
- Look at his history mind-map while he describes it from memory.
- Ask him geography questions he has written out while reading.
- Agree key science questions to read on to tape; leave pauses for replies.
- Listen with him to the tape of his Shakespeare play while he follows the text.
- Get him to check a piece of writing by reading it aloud.

General support:

- Remind him to download or file his day's work, or negotiate a weekly 'housekeeping' session. Take an interest in content and presentation as well as organisation.
- It may be possible to e-mail work from home to be printed and handed in at school.
- Keep computers and printers in working order; success at school may depend on them.
- Remind or help him to repack his bag for school next day, checking by timetable, not memory.

4 Homework from a school's point of view

The value of homework

Dyslexic students need homework, probably more than others, for the following reasons:

- Specific difficulties may have prevented them from getting a firm grasp of lessons during the day. They need to review topics while there is still a memory trace.
- Poor memory skills need the support of 'another go' at new ideas, information and vocabulary. Without a review, too little will be secured in long-term memory.
- Slightly slower processing may result in less practice during the day than for others (e.g. fewer maths examples worked). A chance of further practice is crucial, especially for confidence.
- Teaching styles may, inadvertently, play on learning weaknesses. In this case, dyslexic students need an opportunity to digest new material in a way that suits them better (e.g. rote learning vocabulary by speaking aloud, note-taking by mind-mapping).

Helping with homework

Dyslexic students would benefit from the following in relation to homework:

Skills training:

- They do not 'pick' up how to read from memory, take notes, plan essays, organise papers or learn by heart. These types of skill need teaching in class if they are to be used in homework.

Structure in school:

- Homework needs to be set regularly.
- There needs to be enough time for dyslexic students to understand and write it down fully and in the right place (homework diary or laptop, rather than the back of an exercise book or a scrap of paper). It may need to be set earlier in the lesson than is convenient to the teacher.
- Homework regularly available on a school's network – accessible, in an ideal world, from home – is an excellent fail-safe system. Equally motivating to disorganised and forgetful students is the opportunity to type homework and give it in electronically, especially if teachers then comment and return it by the same method.
- A reward system for homework consistently handed in.
- Unwavering pursuit of homework not handed in – a clear line of retribution. Close monitoring is surprisingly often welcomed by children whose organisation is out of control.
- Always marked, commented on or tested.
- Always preserved in whatever way (exercise book, file, on computer etc.).

Feedback:

- Students need a constructive 'teaching' comment – and an insistence that they read it.
- Easily legible comments: 'But I can't read his writing' is often a student's excuse for skipping straight to the grade at the end of his work.
- Any progress (forwards or backwards) from one effort to the next needs to be noted – dyslexic pupils, whose output is often so erratic, really need to know where they are.

Alternative ways of working with the same material:

- The more variety in channels and methods of processing new information, the more likely dyslexic students are to enjoy/understand/remember it.
- Engaging visual and spatial skills to present verbal information helps memory and results in useful items for revision. For many, reproducing the day's work in a computerised format – graph, chart, diagram, timeline, model, mind-map, notes, colour etc. – can lessen the boredom of homework (may even give pleasure) and be doubly valuable if the task extends some computer skills.

The chance of help with homework at school:

- A homework club after school – not as a punishment.
- Subject clinics, perhaps during lunch breaks. These could be run by staff, but be manned by students. Such an arrangement could provide a creative area of development for older students (excellent material for a curriculum vitae) and there is nothing like teaching for learning.

Parents of dyslexic students:

They are a vital resource, but their ignorance of what is going on in class and consequent anxiety can be counterproductive. In addition, parents may feel managing homework is a matter between school and child, and they may wish to avoid interfering. However, responding to the following difficulties will make it easier for them to be more effective:

- Parents need to be able to rely on what a homework diary says.
- They may need to know the timetable, the syllabus and the timing of tests, coursework and exams.
- They may need some textbooks at home.
- They may need to feel able to consult teachers – electronic communication is efficient and quick.
- They may need guidance in their role, e.g. taking part responsibility for homework being done to a good standard, negotiating a routine with their child, checking homework diaries and communicating with tutors.

General comments:

- Some schools, while having an excellent homework policy, may not realise just how important the detailed execution of it is to dyslexic students.
- Parents may be grateful for occasional 'training sessions' to involve them in the school's system and because their role changes subtly as their children grow up.

5 Some thoughts on exam concessions

It is important that exam concessions to students with dyslexia are understood, fair and seen to be fair. The last thing a dyslexic examinee needs is to have other students, or even teachers, making comments about the unfairness of this extra time or permission to have a word processor or amanuensis.

Extra time

The student needs to understand that extra time is awarded to him, not just to enable him to have more time for writing down what he knows, but to enable him to:

- Read and analyse exam questions, documents or extracts slowly and carefully – using a highlighter to mark keywords. He may need to read written material more than once to be sure of getting at the meaning.
- Subvocalise while he is reading maths or science questions so that he has both a visual and an auditory check on numbers, symbols and instructions.
- Plan his essays and written answers. A common difficulty for a dyslexic student is his short-term memory capacity; he cannot do several language-processing activities simultaneously, particularly if one involves writing at speed. He needs to break down the tasks into stages. For essays, he should first analyse the question carefully, brainstorm, plan – and then write.
- Check his work when he has finished. As a result of his problems with spelling and punctuation, missing out words and accuracy with numbers, accents and foreign spellings, he is likely to have made many more mistakes than other students.
- Practise reading back his work under his breath, especially foreign language work or work that needs punctuating or clarifying.

Word processing

A dyslexic student who cannot synchronise his thinking with his handwriting or cannot write comfortably or legibly at speed is handicapped compared to his peers. He will benefit enormously from using a word processor. Again, there are certain provisos. The student should be advised:

- To learn to touch-type – otherwise he is simply exchanging one non-automatic skill (handwriting) for another (typing).
- Not to imagine that, because he has a word processor and can therefore switch paragraphs about, he does not need to plan his work. Certainly, corrections will be easier, but it is very difficult in the exam room to alter the fundamental structure of an essay when you are well into it. The temptation to start typing straight away has to be resisted.
- Using a word processor in exams can transform the experience of writing for a student who, in the past, has often not had time to check his work, been unable to read his own handwriting when done at speed and been exhausted by the ordeal.

Amanuensis

- Using an amanuensis is not as easy as it sounds. Both pupil and helper need to practise the technique on old exam papers so that problems can be identified and dealt with in advance.

6 Recognising the child in an educational psychologist's report

Look for answers to these three questions:

1. **Is there a spiky profile?** – a disparity between scores across the range of intelligence test sub-skills – (see Figure 8.1)

    *   Two frequently used intelligence tests are the Weschler Intelligence Scale for Children (WISC III) and the British Abilities Scale (BAS II).
    *   These give two IQ scales: Verbal and Performance.
    *   Subtest scores are graded 1–19; the average score is 10.
    *   The results of both scales are combined to give a full-scale IQ. Treat this with caution because it may disguise the extent of both weaknesses and strengths. Study the full range of subscores.
    *   General effect in the classroom – puzzling discrepancies in achievement, resulting in disappointment, frustration and, possibly, bad behaviour.

2. **Is there a big discrepancy between Verbal and Performance Scale scores?** This can be a useful guide to secondary schoolteachers:

    *   As well as considerable variation between scores across all the intelligence test subskills, there may also be a marked difference between Verbal and Performance IQ scores.
    *   A big discrepancy either way will result in mismatches between ability and performance in the classroom.
    *   One criterion for concessions in public exams is: 'Is there a significant discrepancy between his ability to express himself orally and in writing?'
    *   Verbal scores in particular may indicate academic potential.

3. **What is the whole picture – not just the cognitive profile?**

    *   Relate cognitive profile to the wider picture of the child's home, temperament, educational history and current school setting.
    *   Self-esteem and motivation in the face of dyslexia are strong factors for success, as is firm daily support from well-informed parents and teachers.

Some facts common to most educational psychologists' reports

Background information

*   This gives a history of the problem and relevant information about the child's family and schooling.

General intellectual ability testing

*   This is an assessment of cognitive strengths and weaknesses.
*   The commonly used intelligence test, WISC, is a 'closed' test, i.e. one to be used by educational psychologists only.
*   WISC does not require children to read or write.

Literacy attainments

This group of tests aims to establish the child's current level of literacy skills. It usually breaks down into the following:

Reading	Accurate decoding of single unrelated words. Speed of reading, aloud/silently. Comprehension of sentences/continuous prose.
Spelling	Single-word spelling accuracy.
Handwriting	Manual speed and legibility – often a copying task.
Free writing	Quality of content, fluency, sentence structure, spelling, handwriting, punctuation and speed of production when these are all performed simultaneously.

Conclusions

- These relate the pattern of strengths and weaknesses described in the foregoing tests to the child's practical experience in school and at home.
- They try to suggest a picture of the child's future academic development in the light of these findings.

Recommendations

These give advice on:

- The nature of specialist support deemed appropriate.
- Suggestions for how parents and teachers can help at home and in school.
- Recommendations for concessions in GCSE and A-level exams.

Subtests scores in WISC are sometimes regrouped to give information in three specific areas:

Verbal Comprehension (calculated from Information, Similarities, Vocabulary and Comprehension) shows the use of language in thinking across a variety of question and answer tests.

Perceptual Organisation (calculated from Picture Completion, Picture Arrangement, Block Design ad Object Assembly) shows the ability to use non-verbal material in logical ways.

Freedom from Distractability (calculated from Arithmetic and Digit Span) measures the use of auditory memory and sequencing in verbal problem-solving without losing concentration.

Profiles

Students with 'spiky' profiles like those in Figure 8.1 are likely to have difficulties in the classroom. It is unreasonable to expect these children to achieve in school consistently near the level of their highest subscores or even at a level that is average in their personal range. They are far more likely to seesaw between raising expectations and failing to reach them, depending on the type of task they are performing and their state of mind at the time.

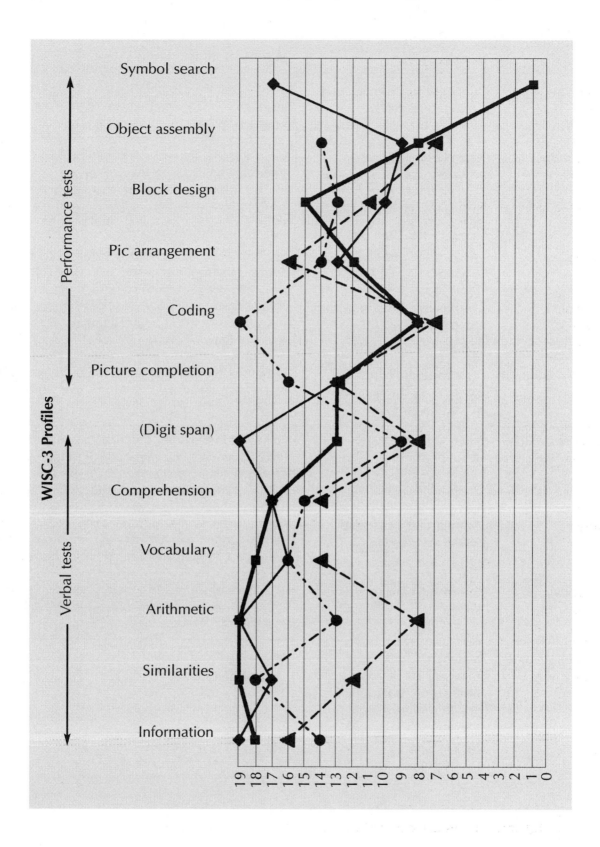

Figure 8.1 The 'spiky' profiles of four students with specific learning difficulties.

Skill	Means	May cause difficulties in
Short-term auditory memory	Cannot hold information while processing it	Mental arithmetic, multiplication tables, learning by heart, following instructions, spelling, remembering what he has heard, attentive listening
Visual memory	Remembering shapes or patterns	Checking spelling, accurate reading, copying shapes, language learning, diagrams
Auditory sequencing	Managing sequential order in material heard	Oral spelling or tables, dictionary and reference skills, following instructions, note-taking
Visual sequencing	Organising symbols or shapes in order	Spelling (especially irregular words), copying, arithmetical routines, some aspects of DT
Visuomotor skill (or hand–eye co-ordination)	Co-ordination of vision with movement	Handwriting, ball skills, PE, clumsiness, using instruments in maths, conducting experiments in science, drawing
Visuospatial ability	Perception of objects in space, position, distance, speed, abstract form	Page layout, aspects of handwriting, relative size, map work, shape work in maths, team sports
Listening or auditory comprehension	Processing the spoken word	Following instructions, attending to any verbal material, distractible, low attention span, easily confused, literacy learning. May depend on following others, looking at gesture, pointing
Auditory discrimination	Hearing fine differences between sounds	Even when this is said to be satisfactory there may still be hidden difficulties with phonology, which will affect literacy and foreign language learning
Phonological awareness	Perception of sounds within words	Sequence of sounds in words, segmentation of syllables, rhyme, alliteration, automatic sound/symbol recognition
Speed of information processing	Inefficiency with the management of streams of information, especially written symbols, as in copying	Most classroom activities

Table 8.1 Understanding the psychologist's report: explanations of some common terms

IQ scale scores are categorised as:			
60–79	exceptionally low	110–119	above average
80–89	below average	120–129	high
90–109	average	130+	exceptionally high

7 Special Educational Needs Code of Practice

Some implications for teachers, students and parents

Boxed quotations are taken from the Code of Practice.

Definition of special educational needs

> 'Children have special educational needs if they have a learning difficulty which calls for special educational provision to be made for them.'

Definition of a learning difficulty in the context of dyslexia

> 'Children have a learning difficulty if they have a significantly greater difficulty in learning than the majority of children of the same age.'

The principles highlighted in the *Code of Practice Identification, Assessment and Provision in the Secondary Sector* are:

> - 'Provision for pupils with special educational needs should match the nature of their needs'
>
> - 'There should be regular recording of a pupil's special educational needs, the action taken and the outcomes.'

There has recently been a fundamental shift of emphasis towards:

1. 'Teacher competency' rather than 'pupil deficit'.
2. Assessment as a continuing process that arises from the learning context.
3. Fine-tuning the understanding of individual need as the result of continuous assessment.
4. A greater practical partnership between school, parent and student.
5. Action.

Following on from these five principles, teachers, parents and children will need to think about:

1. **Identifying children with learning difficulties**. Anyone, including the child himself, can and should sound the alert. Emphasis here is laid on early identification.
2. **Taking steps to define what problems are caused from within the child**. Where dyslexia is a possibility, Martin Turner, Head of psychology at the Dyslexia Institute, takes the view that 'Psychological tests are indicated to help diagnose this disability'. He views dyslexia as 'a cognitive deficit, that is a specific difficulty with the management of certain kinds of (mainly verbal) information.' He states that 'dyslexia comes from within and is not simply the result of external factors such as poor teaching or a lack of opportunity. The dyslexic child is likely to have weaknesses in one or more of the following areas:

   - short-term memory
   - phonological awareness
   - speed of information processing.'

These, in his view, create obstacles to teaching as well as learning, and an educational psychologist's assessment can play a valuable part in overcoming them. 'An objective psychometric assessment aims to secure information that reflects an individual's development at the biological or cognitive–developmental level. The objectivity as well as the information itself is of obvious value in helping to establish a clear pattern of individual strengths as well as weaknesses' (Turner, 1999).

3. **Taking steps to define what external factors are aggravating those problems.** The Code of Practice lays increased emphasis on the responsibility of teachers and the context in which learning takes place. Assessment should now be a continuous process related to progress in the classroom, and adjustments to teaching methods should be made in the light of the learner's progress.

4. **Thinking out and applying methods that manage the child's difficulties in such a way as to improve his learning**. The Code of Practice defines this step to be beyond the level of normal classroom differentiation, on the assumption that this differentiation, as already applied, has not been enough to close the gap in performance between the child with special educational needs and his peers.

5. **Evaluating, fine-tuning and recording action in the light of the child's progress.** For this to be a success there needs to be sensitive communication among teachers, parents and child, and a flexible, sustained approach from all concerned.

Much of this may prove difficult, time-consuming or expensive to carry out. It is, however, right at the heart of successful learning for the child in secondary school who has special educational needs. Teachers can overcome many of the apparent difficulties, and methods devised to help individual children often benefit the whole class.

Various pitfalls

The teenager with special educational needs

- probably doesn't want to know
- rarely wants to be treated differently from his peers
- is afraid of being/appearing stupid
- dreads failure in his attempts to overcome his problems, on top of his failure to keep up in school
- would probably prefer to denigrate his self-image than be seen to take risks
- his morale and energy for change are likely to be at their lowest ebb

Suggestions:

- A skilful educational psychologist can do much to make a student feel good about himself.
- Discovering or confirming cognitive strengths often does more than compensate for a clear delineation of weaknesses.
- Informed attention from experienced adults – particularly from his teachers – may free a child from anxiety and a feeling of isolation, particularly if this attention takes the form of constructive action.
- Adults (teachers, parents, educational psychologists, doctors, counsellors), being able to take a long view, can encourage/insist on necessary action. For example, they may recognise the ultimate value of a literacy course, even at secondary level, where a teenager might not.
- Experienced adults will know how to break complex provision into manageable steps. To use a computer instead of a pen, for instance the steps might be:
  1. take touch-typing lessons
  2. use a computer and touch-typing skills at home for some homework

3. use a laptop to word process class work in a few subjects where teachers see clearly the improvement this brings

4. use a laptop for all written work

5. word process school exams

6. word process public exams.

- Engaging a teenager in tackling his own problems is also likely to increase the maturity of his outlook (often lagging behind that of his peers) and greatly improve his sense of self-worth.

> 'Young people with special educational needs have a unique knowledge of their own needs and circumstances and their own views about what sort of help they would like to help them make the most of their education. They should feel confident that they will be listened to and that their views are valued.'

- Genuine success in the classroom, apparent and publicly acknowledged, is likely to result from appropriate help – this kind of success is the key to long-term progress both in morale and in quality of learning.

Parents

- Parents may initially know very little about their child's condition.
- They often feel disproportionate anxiety.
- This combination of ignorance and fear can lead to overbearing control and confrontational relations with school, both of which teenagers resent.

Suggestions:

- Accept and learn about dyslexia.
- Take a long view – what position does the teenager wish to be in in a few years from now? What steps would be necessary to reach that goal?
- To help in the short term, open and maintain good communication with all relevant adults, particularly teachers. Keep your side of any bargain made with the school or your child.
- Support your child's current curriculum with time planning, alternative textbooks, help with reading, essay planning, revision – any area that is acceptable to a particular teenager and for which you have time and expertise or access to other helpers.
- Try to put your child in charge as much as possible. Contrive compromises. Keep cool!

Teachers

> 'All teachers are teachers of pupils with special educational needs.'

The guiding principle of the Code of Practice for teachers is:

However:

- It is extremely difficult to pay constant attention to particular individuals while teaching a whole class.
- The curriculum does not allow time to dawdle.
- The rest of the class is probably impatient to get on.

- Teachers may not always recognise or understand the nature of difficulties that individuals experience in their subject.
- They may have little experience in how to help.
- They may not wish to change their ways.

Suggestions:

- Use every available source of information about any child who is underachieving in your subject: your experience of the child in class, his own view of the situation, other teachers' views, assessment reports, the home scene etc.
- Keep your eye on the demands of your particular subject – reading, note-taking, essay writing, diagram drawing, mastering technical vocabulary, rote learning, sequencing, calculating, revising etc.
- How does the individual child respond to them?
- How can you help an individual meet those demands?
- Many of your suggestions will benefit others in the class.
- Make ongoing use of the school SENCO. That expertise is intended to help teachers adapt their teaching.
- Seek and take into account the pupil's view. An individual's explanation of his difficulty often contains the seeds of a solution and, especially at secondary school level, his active commitment will be a *sine qua non* for his progress.
- Engage parents in specific practical action – e-mail can be very useful as it is instant and informal.
- Keep expectations high and be quick to praise.
- Don't give up! If teachers do, the child probably will too. The message of the Code is: if a teacher's methods aren't working, change them.

> 'A child with special educational needs should have their needs met.'

The spirit of the recent Code of Practice is to ensure that:
The education of children with special educational needs at all ages should therefore be regarded as a matter of policy that engages governors, head teacher, subject teachers, pastoral staff, special needs staff, child and parents in responsibility for a sustained effort to that end.

8 Emotional intelligence – the 'ping' factor

Educational Emotional Awareness

Theory: We all have 'emotional intelligence' and can use emotion to help us to learn.
Principle: Knowing what you know the better to access it – metacognition.
Transfer: Once analysed and understood, the process can be taught to others.

'The Ping Factor': a small but momentarily perfect instance of realisation – Ping!
1. A dramatic moment,   –   it involves the emotions
2. A moment of insight   –   an affective impact analysed
3. A moment of learning   –   the significance of the cameo is captured
4. Weighing the significance   –   seeing what the benefit might be
5. Leads to shift/change   –   understanding of the learning situation shifts

The Cyclical Nature of Problem-solving

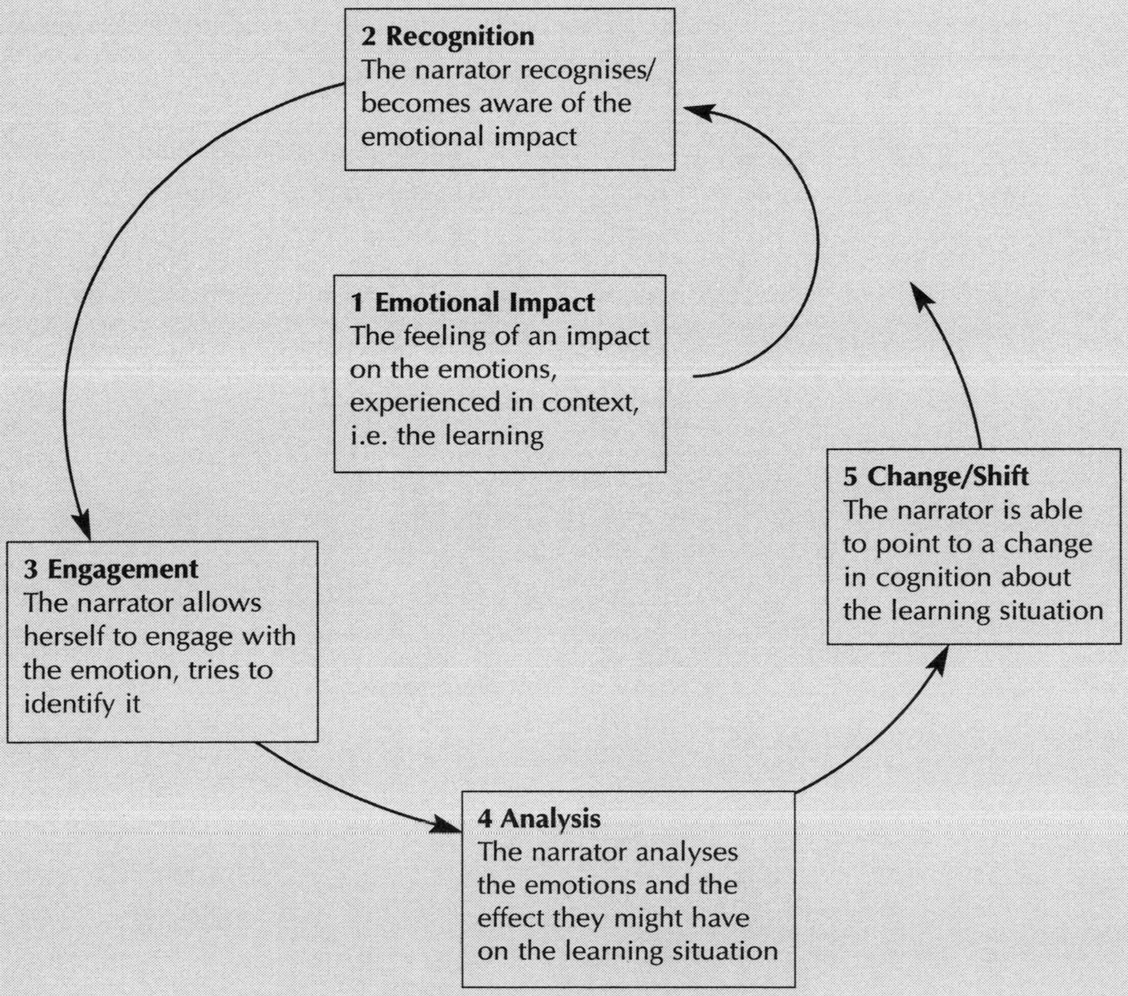

2 Recognition
The narrator recognises/
becomes aware of the
emotional impact

1 Emotional Impact
The feeling of an impact
on the emotions,
experienced in context,
i.e. the learning

5 Change/Shift
The narrator is able
to point to a change
in cognition about
the learning situation

3 Engagement
The narrator allows
herself to engage with
the emotion, tries to
identify it

4 Analysis
The narrator analyses
the emotions and the
effect they might have
on the learning situation

Figure 8.2 Educational emotional awareness. Based on a teacher's
experience, which she narrated and formalized in the diagram.

Making use of emotional intelligence

Emotions have a part to play in the process of learning. Feelings often run high, but it is not so often that the sources of these feeling are articulated and used to adapt or enhance classroom experience. If they are, it is usually the sources of negative feeling – exasperation, discouragement and boredom – that teachers and learners dwell on. There is much to gain from exploring *positive* emotions.

Most learners and teachers will recognise the experience of a small but momentarily perfect instance of realisation – a student may suddenly get a sense of wholeness in the topic he is studying; a teacher may realise that he has taught something in such a way that one student at least has truly understood. These small but perfect cameo moments are dramatic – ping! They are expressed, not in words, but in a surge of good feeling – delight, excitement, euphoria – although they may then be swept aside as bells ring and the day strides on. A problem has been solved, the emotions have registered the solution, but nothing has been made of that affective impact. Yet, a little time spent analysing this emotional impact would afford the best chance of radical improvement to teaching and learning.

The purpose of such an analysis would be to cause a shift or a change in understanding about the learning situation. Figure 8.2 illustrates the cyclical nature of problem-solving and traces steps to analyse and capture the significance of these small flashes of insight. The analysis starts with a moment of emotional impact in the classroom and works through its recognition and acceptance to a rationalisation of its professional significance.

The understanding generated by emotional intelligence is every bit as useful to teachers and learners as the understanding generated by intelligence in the more academic sense of the word. Emotional understanding applied to the process of learning leads not merely to the implication of change but to a greater self-confidence and, hence, to a greater capacity for change.

Worksheets

Contents

These worksheets may be copied for teaching purposes. Many are best enlarged onto A3

(See Chapter 5 page 158.)

(See Chapter 5 page 159.)

(See Chapter 5 page 176.)

This can be used most effectively if it is enlarged, photocopied onto card and cut up into segments. Students are then asked to reassemble the circle, justifying the placing of each segment (see Chapter 5 page 179).

This type of sheet is particularly useful for learners who have difficulty matching sound to symbol, or recognising the difference between sounds that are nearly the same. They will need help as they track along the line, circling the sound they are looking for, and saying it aloud – or differentiating between, say, 'le' and 'les', 'eu' and 'au' or 'é' and 'è'. It is a good idea to start with one sound and work on that – seeing and saying at once will help with reading, speaking and spelling. Other sheets can easily be made to cope with other sound patterns or other languages (see Chapter 6 page 190).

(See Chapter 6 page 209.)

This should be used in conjunction with Worksheet N. A student should think of a keyword and draw a picture symbol that will remind him of the ending he wants to remember. This exercise is effective in focusing attention on which endings are masculine and which are the exceptions to the rule, but to remember the information the student must re-visualise the map and draw it from memory three or four times (see Chapter 6 page 209).

(See Chapter 6 page 209.)

(See Chapter 6 page 217.)

Photocopied onto card and cut out, these labels, and the English and French verb tense examples that go with them, provide a useful sorting exercise for students who are unsure of their tenses. The exercise sparks useful discussion and provides a quick diagnosis of weaknesses. It is best to work in English first and use only two or three tenses. When these are certain the student will be confident enough to tackle the others (see Chapter 6 page 217).

Sheet S   Five-finger checklist 321

(See Chapter 6 page 220.)

Sheet T   Latin mind-map (Active Voice) 322

Students who find it difficult to remember a linear sequence often find a spatial arrangement far easier to memorise. This mind-map will be even more memorable if the student draws his own symbols and reminders on it to help him remember the different endings. Speaking the conjugations aloud, with rhythm and emphasis, will further help the learning process (see Chapter 6 page 219).

Sheet U   Latin mind-map (Passive Voice) 323

The position of the tenses on this passive voice map match those on the previous map. The learner can easily visualise *where*, for example, the future tense is. He can remember the endings by his pictures of, for example, a boar, berries etc. – whichever mnemonic links do the trick for him (see Chapter 6 page 219).

Sheet V   What happened in the exams? 324

(See Chapter 7 page 234.)

Sheet W   Daily revision timetables 325

Colour blocking (e.g. blue for work, yellow for leisure, crimson for sleep) the cells in these tables will help students form a realistic preview of their revision time-patterns (see Chapter 7 page 235).

Sheet X   League of Nations skeleton timeline 326

The history teacher who laid out this format completed it for himself (see page 265) while setting it as preparation for a class essay (see Chapter 7 page 264).

Sheet Y   Mind-mapping poetry 327

The rationale for sheet Z (see Chapter 7 page 277).

Sheet Z   Blank poetry mind-map 328

(See Chapter 7 page 277.)

**Visual imagery for
comprehension and memory**

• Draw three to four representational pictures in sequence like a cartoon.

• Draw one picture to represent the main idea of the passage.

Great Expectations Chapter Fourteen

Once, it had seemed to me that when I should at last roll up my shirt-sleeves and go into the forge, Joe's 'prentice, I should be distinguished and happy. Now the reality was in my hold, I only felt that I was dusty with the dust of the small coal, and that I had a weight upon my daily remembrance to which the anvil was a feather. There have been occasions in my later life (I suppose as in most lives) when I have felt for a time as if a thick curtain had fallen on all its interest and romance, to shut me out from anything save dull endurance any more. Never has that curtain dropped so heavy and blank, as when my way in life lay stretched out straight before me through the newly entered road of apprenticeship to Joe.

I remember that at a later period of my 'time', I used to stand about the churchyard on Sunday evenings, when night was falling, comparing my own perspective with the windy marsh view, and making out some likeness between them by thinking how flat and low both were, and how on both there came an unknown way and dark mist and then the sea. I was quite as dejected on the first working-day of my apprenticeship as in that after-time; but I am glad to know that I never breathed a murmur to Joe while my indentures lasted. It is about the only thing I am glad to know of myself in that connection.

Visualising helps understanding and remembering

- Read the poem at least three times.

- Translate the words into pictures in your mind.

Now draw four representational pictures in sequence like a cartoon.

'Child on Top of a Greenhouse' Theodore Roethke

The wind billowing out the seat of my britches,
My feet crackling splinters of glass and dried putty,
The half-grown chrysanthemums staring up like accusers,
Up through the streaked glass, flashing with sunlight,
A few white clouds all rushing eastward,
A line of elms plunging and tossing like horses
And everyone, everyone pointing up and shouting!

Formulate one picture to represent the idea of the poem

Make images to improve comprehension and memory

1

2

3

Image to peg the main idea

4

Make abbreviations:

1. Which words in this passage would it help to abbreviate and why?
2. What symbols could be used for them?
3. Where else could they be used?

Text:

Words	Why?	Abbreviations	Use again?

Recognising signal words:

❖ Which words give structure to the information?

❖ How would they affect note-taking?

Text:

Words	Effect on note-taking

Thinking about Writing

Requirements for Writing
at Keystage 3 Attainment Target 3 Level 7

When I am writing:

1. Am I confident that I can find the words to say what I mean?

   - Can I make characters live and grow in my stories?

   - Can I make the reader feel he is 'there'?

   - Do I know what it means to 'vary my style'?

   - Do I organise my ideas clearly enough for a reader to follow them?

   - Do I understand about grammar, and do I recognise when mine is not correct? Do I know how to put it right?

   - Can I call up just the right word when I need it?

   - Can I spell reliably – both regular and irregular words?

   - Is my handwriting easy to read? Is it attractive?

   - Do I organise my paragraphs so that the order of my ideas is clear to the reader?

   - Does my punctuation help a reader to follow my meaning?

Question the Question

1.	Topic Area	Underline the words that indicate the subject matter.
2.	Limiting Words	Highlight the words that control the slant required on the topic area.
3.	Directive	Circle the words that suggest the structure into which your answer should fit, *the use you are to make of what you know.*

Illustration Question
Taken from English GCSE OCR 1999
Non-Fiction and Media Texts

'"Following Fashion is a Waste of Money."
Argue your own point of view on this subject.'

Question the Question

1.	Topic Area	<u>Following Fashion</u>
2.	Limiting Words	**Waste of Money, own view**
3.	Directives	Argue

Analysing an Essay Question

Examiners' most common criticism of the essays they mark at GCSE and A Level is that candidates have not answered the question.

There are basically two kinds of essay question: one asks you to give information and the other asks you to use it. Most exam questions combine the two. You should ask yourself:

'Am I being asked for a straightforward presentation of facts (describe, outline, trace) or am I being asked to process information in some way (assess, discuss, evaluate)? Am I being asked to do a bit of both?'

Examples of common directives and their meanings:

Describe: Offer a detailed account

Trace: Note turning points and stages

Contrast: Show differences between

Compare: Explore both similarities and differences

Summarise: Identify key ideas, present concisely

Discuss: Consider all sides of the argument

The point of this work on question analysis is to save you from writing everything you know about a topic, regardless of the question, or from reproducing a good essay you have previously written that is not strictly the answer to your current question.

Question the Question – trials

History Advanced Level
(OCR Paper 16 The Normans in England)

'How accurate is the judgement that throughout his reign
Edward the Confessor was a puppet of the House of Godwin?'

Topic area:

Limiting words:

Directive:

Religious Studies GCSE
(MEG Paper 6 Judaism)

'Describe two ways in which Jews may celebrate the Sabbath in the home
and explain the importance of these celebrations.'

Topic area:

Limiting words:

Directive:

Geography Year 8
(ISEB Geomorphological Processes)

'With reference to examples you have studied, show how man can reduce
either coastal erosion and its effects or coastal flooding and its effects.'

Topic area:

Limiting words:

Directive:

Question the Question – analysis of trials

'How accurate is the judgement that throughout his reign
Edward the Confessor was a puppet of the House of Godwin?'

Topic area:	Edward the Confessor, the House of Godwin
Limiting words:	Judgement, throughout reign, puppet
Directive:	How accurate?

'Describe two ways in which Jews may celebrate the Sabbath in the home
and explain the importance of these celebrations.'

Topic area:	Jews, the Sabbath
Limiting words:	Two ways, celebrate, in the home, importance
Directive:	Describe, explain

'With reference to examples you have studied, show how man can reduce
either coastal erosion and its effects or coastal flooding and its effects.'

Topic area:	Coastal erosion, coastal flooding, effects
Limiting words:	Either/or, examples studied, man, reduce
Directive:	With reference to, show how

Mistiming Essays

Understanding:
- Am I slow to assess what I know in answer to exam questions – and to make a choice?

- Do I waste time panicking or daydreaming?

- Does stress block my thinking?

Remembering:
- Does worry about time make me forget?

- Do my ideas wander from the main point?

- Does writing one idea make me forget the others?

- Do I forget what I am saying in the middle?

Organising:
- Does a muddle of ideas prevent me from writing?

- Do I have so much to say I cannot select ideas and put them in order?

- Do I rush in and then run out of things to write?

- Do I have good ideas out of place and struggle to fit them into my essay?

Writing:
- Is my handwriting hard work, slow, messy?

- Is it fast, needing many corrections, illegible?

- Does worry about spelling restrict my vocabulary?

- Do I hate checking?

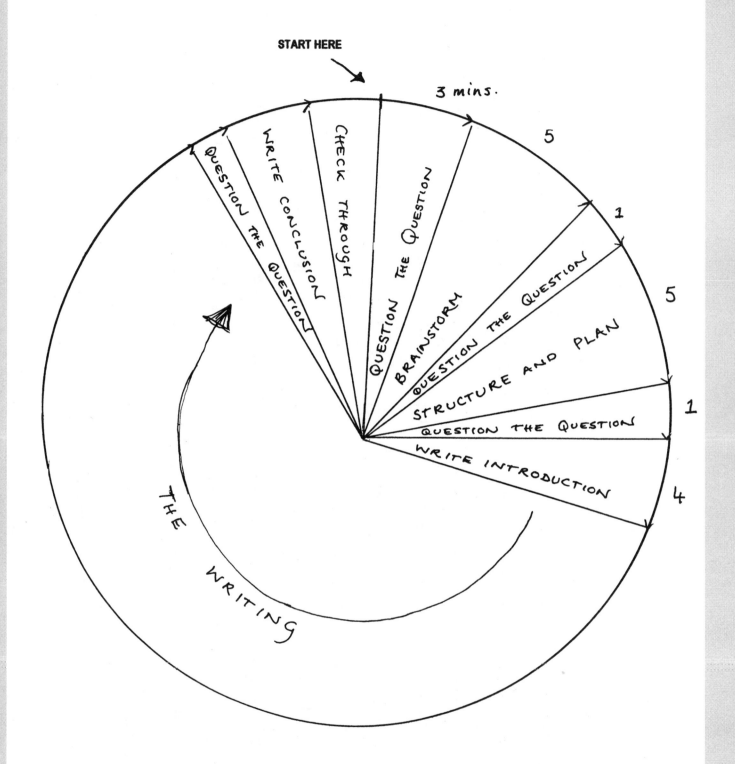

Eu une le de une des eau un ce une eu une eu ces les eau un eu des ce de un ces de

une le ce des le ces dans eau un en les eau de eu un des une de eau une

dans eu le ce en des ces un eu ce peu ces de une dans eu un eu ces le des

eau les en de une eu un ces en une de le eau le des eu ce un ce Eu une le

de une des eau un ce une eu ces les eau un eu des ce de un ces de une le ce des

des le ces dans eau un les eau de eu un des une de eau une dans eu le ce des

en ces un eu ce peu ces de une dans eu un eu ces le des eau les de une eu

un ces une de le eau le des en eu ce un ce des eau les de une eu un ces

une de des eau les les de une eu un en ces une de la de eau une dans eu le ce

des ces eu une le de une des eau un ce une eu ces les en eau un eu des ce

en de un ces de une eau un ce des le ces en dans eau un les eau de eu un des

une de eau une dans eu le ce des ces un eu ce peu ces de une dans eu un eu

Making a mind-map to help remember masculine endings

To learn the rules of gender a student can turn a rather forbidding list of rules into a mind-map.

To help him to learn which endings were usually masculine, this student wrote an 'ending' on each branch of a mind-map and then chose words with those endings, and drew a picture to remind himself of each example. The exceptions to the rules are made very clear in an extra box. Having done this, he then turned the page over and visualised the mind map, describing it aloud as he did so. He was able to remember the rules without any difficulty. Doing your own map is the key to remembering it – someone else's won't do!

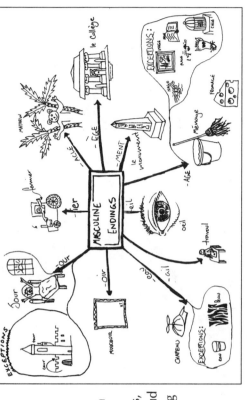

Nouns with these endings are usually masculine

-acle	-ège	-ment	-age	-ail/eil	-eau	-oir	-ier	-our
Le spectacle	Le collège	Le document	Le chauffage	Le travail	Le chapeau	Le miroir	Le fermier	Le four
Un obstacle	Le privilège	Un appartement	Le chomage	Le vitrail	Le chateau	Le tiroir	Le quartier	Le tour (turn)
Le miracle	Le sortilège	Un argument	Le fromage	Un oeil	Le bateau	Le bougeoir	Le palier	Le secours
	Le piège	Un environnement	Le mènage		L'oiseau	Le mouchoir	Le métier	Le jour
			Exceptions		**Exceptions**			**Exceptions**
			La page		L'eau			La tour (tower)
			La plage		La peau			La cour
			La nage					
			La rage					
			La cage					
			une image					

Masculine groups of words

Trees	Compass points	English words	Colours	Days of the week months and seasons	Metals and chemicals	Most nouns ending in –a-i-o-u **Exceptions:** loi, foi, radio	Most plants

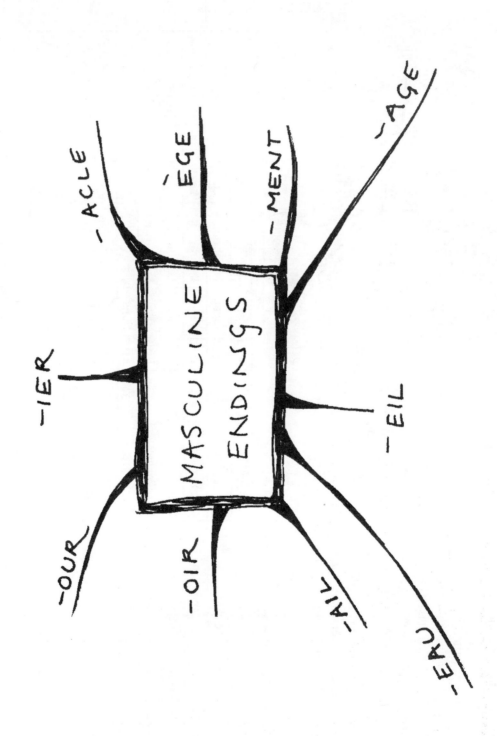

GUESS MASCULINE!

LEARN EXCEPTIONS
une éponge
la poudre

aire - la locataire
ure - la signature
oire - une armoire
ère - la croisière

LONGER
=re
ENDINGS

60% NOUNS - MASC

MASCULINE
=ge
un orage - storm
un mélange
un dérapage - skid

FEMININE

FEMININE

-re MASCULINE IF
le fiacre - cab
le nombre =number

=e
la poule - hen
la chemise - shirt
la poste - post office

An exercise for gender rules:
Strictly following the mind map above, fill in the gender box for each word.

la	température		le	livre
☐	lumière		☐	métier
☐	tonnerre		☐	ruban
☐	symbole		☐	saucisse
☐	maquillage		☐	siège
☐	quiétude		☐	incendiaire
☐	sang		☐	temoignage
☐	éponge		☐	poubelle

Exceptions to the guide lines on the mind-map:

le symbole
une éponge
le tonnerre

The gender of only these three out of sixteen words needs to be learned.

Present

Infinitive

Future

Imperfect

Pluperfect

Perfect

Conditional

I give	you are giving	he carries
they eat	they are skiing	I run
I was sleeping	you used to sleep	he was shouting
they were skiing	I used to paint	we were coming
you were walking	she was drinking	I used to live
I have slept	you drank	he has swum
he skated	they have eaten	you jumped
I will read	you are going to ski	she will run
we will give	we are going to give	they will sing
I had slept	you had walked	she had eaten
we had skated	you had sung	they had come
I would like	you would enjoy	he would laugh
you would cook	you would want	you would cry
to cry	to laugh	to run
to write	to wear	to like

je donne	tu donnes	il porte
elles aiment	ils font	je cours
je dormais	tu venais	il portait
ils aimaient	vous écriviez	nous venions
vous aviez	elle buvait	je donnais
j'ai porté	vous allez venir	Il a bu
nous avons mangé	ils ont vendu	vous êtes venus
tu aimeras	tu as donné	je vais voir
nous donnerons	je porterai	elles chanteront
vous marcherez	il donnera	elle avait mangé
nous avions dormi	j'avais chanté	Elles donneraient
nous mangerions	je voudrais	Il aimerait

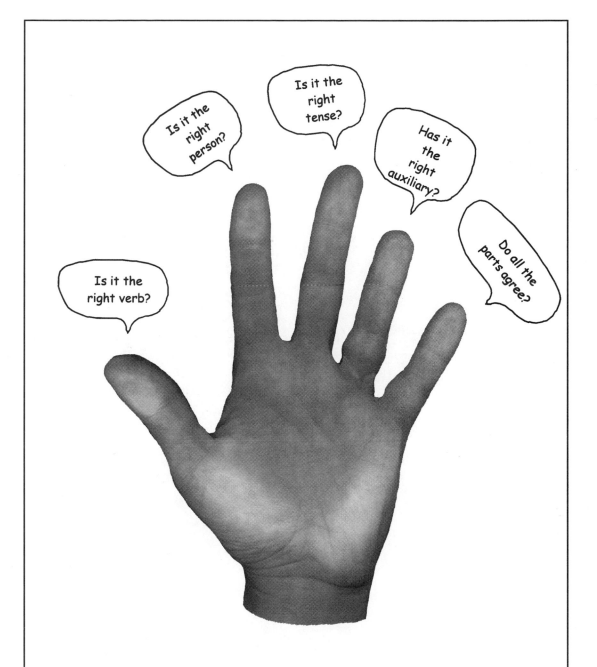

Always check your translations – you can pick up a lot of
mistakes if you do the following:

- Learn the five-finger checklist and count each one off as you
  check each verb.
- Check the gender of your nouns – do the article and adjective
  agree?
- Read your work aloud (under your breath if you are in an
  exam!) and ask yourself: 'Does this sound right?'

Active Voice

Present tense

amo	moneo
amas	mones
amat	monet
amamus	monemus
amatis	monetis
amant	monent
rego	audio
regis	audis
regit	audit
regimus	audimus
regitis	auditis
regunt	audiunt

Future tense

amabo	monebo
amabis	monebis
amabit	monebit
amabimus	monebimus
amabitis	monebitis
amabunt	monebunt
regam	audiam
reges	audies
reget	audiet
regemus	audiemus
regetis	audietis
regent	audient

Pluperfect tense

amaveram	monueram
amaveras	monueras
amaverat	monuerat
amaveramus	monueramus
amaveratis	monueratis
amaverant	monuerant
rexeram	audiveram
rexeras	audiveras
rexerat	audiverat
rexeramus	audiveramus
rexeratis	audiveratis
rexerant	audiverant

Future perfect tense

amavero	monuero
amaveris	monueris
amaverit	monuerit
amaverimus	monuerimus
amaveritis	monueritis
amaverint	monuerint
rexero	audivero
rexeris	audiveris
rexerit	audiverit
rexerimus	audiverimus
rexeritis	audiveritis
rexerint	audiverint

Perfect tense

amavi	monui
amavisti	monuisti
amavit	monuit
amavimus	monuimus
amavistis	monuistis
amaverunt	monuerunt
rexi	audivi
rexisti	audivisti
rexit	audivit
reximus	audivimus
rexistis	audivistis
rexerunt	audiverunt

Imperfect tense

amabam	monebam
amabas	monebas
amabat	monebat
amabamus	monebamus
amabatis	monebatis
amabant	monebant
regebam	audiebam
regebas	audiebas
regebat	audiebat
regebamus	audiebamus
regebatis	audiebatis
regebant	audiebant

Passive Voice

Present tense

amor	moneor
amaris	moneris
amatur	monetur
amamur	monemur
amamini	monemini
amantur	monentur
regor	audior
regeris	audiris
regitur	auditur
regimur	audimur
regimini	audimini
reguntur	audiuntur

Future tense

amabor	monebor
amaberis	moneberis
amabitur	monebitur
amabimur	monebimur
amabimini	monebimini
amabuntur	monebuntur
regar	audiar
regeris	audieris
regetur	audietur
regemur	audiemur
regemini	audiemini
regentur	audientur

Perfect tense

amatus sum	monitus sum
amatus es	monitus es
amatus est	monitus est
amati sumus	moniti sumus
amati estis	moniti estis
amati sunt	moniti sunt
rectus sum	auditus sum
rectus es	auditus es
rectus est	auditus est
recti sumus	auditi sumus
recti estis	auditi estis
recti sunt	auditi sunt

Pluperfect tense

amatus eram	monitus eram
amatus eras	monitus eras
amatus erat	monitus erat
amati eramus	moniti eramus
amati eratis	moniti eratis
amati erant	moniti erant
rectus eram	auditus eram
rectus eras	auditus eras
rectus erat	auditus erat
recti eramus	auditi eramus
recti eratis	auditi eratis
recti erant	auditi erant

Future perfect tense

amatus ero	monitus ero
amatus eris	monitus eris
amatus erit	monitus erit
amati erimus	moniti erimus
amati eritis	moniti eritis
amati erunt	moniti erunt
rectus ero	auditus ero
rectus eris	auditus eris
rectus erit	auditus erit
recti erimus	auditi erimus
recti eritis	auditi eritis
recti erunt	auditi erunt

Imperfect tense

amabar	monebar
amabaris	monebaris
amabatur	monebatur
amabamur	monebamur
amabamini	monebamini
amabantur	monebantur
regebar	audiebar
regebaris	audiebaris
regebatur	audiebatur
regebamur	audiebamur
regebamini	audiebamini
regebantur	audiebantur

What happened in the exams?

The best moment to do an exam debriefing is as soon as possible after the event, when the memory (and perhaps the pain) is still fresh. There is a lot to learn from previous experiences. It is useful for pupils to fill in and then file a debriefing sheet so that it can be produced before the next exam preparation. Detailed and focused questions – and answers – are most helpful.

	Did you plan your answers?	Did you finish?	Best revision method?	Were your notes good enough?	Did you make any silly mistakes?	Did you use a word processor?	Resolutions for next time?	Marks?
English								
History								
Maths								
French								
Biology								
Geography								
Chemistry								
Physics								

Revision timetables – fill these in with your own preferred times; be prepared to change times if they don't suit you after all.

Best times to revise	Times	Number of hours
Before breakfast		
Breakfast		
Morning		
Lunch		
Afternoon		
Tea		
Early evening		
Supper		
Late evening		

	Mon	Tues	Wed	Thurs	Fri	Sat	Sun
Before breakfast							
Breakfast							
Morning							
Lunch							
Afternoon							
Tea							
Early evening							
Supper							
Late evening							

The League of Nations: Successes and Failures
N.B. You need to look particularly carefully at the dates referred to in any questions on the League of Nations.

Successes:

Social and Humanitarian Work

The post-WWI refugee problem was solved, famine was alleviated, World Health Organization did good work in combating disease, drug trafficking was clamped down on, the slave trade in Asia was lessened, and general promotion of the rights of women and developing nations took place. The Mandates Commission did some good work - the very idea of independence for colonies was then new - and the ILO is widely seen as the League's greatest success.

Administration of Plebiscites

A new idea based on principle of self-determination; was especially successful in Upper Silesia and the Ruhr Coalfield.

1919	1920	1921	1922	1923	1924	1925	1926	1927	1928	1929	1930	1931	1932	1933	1934	1935	1936

Failures:

Disarmament Conferences, 1920s and 1930s

In 1919 Germany's disarmament was held to be the first step in a more general process, as suggested in Wilson's fourteen points. However, apart from the Washington Conferences of 1921-2 which had some success with naval disarmament (see later), the general process never took place, and this only served to embitter many Germans further. In 1933 Hitler came to power in Germany and began to rearm; nothing was done and by the late thirties all major world powers were rearming.

Mind-mapping Poetry

This mind-map can be used as a tool for writing about poetry or as a way of approaching a new poem or as a revision exercise.

The topics: these are the important elements to consider when studying a poem.

The format: psychologists tell us that the brain takes greater pleasure in circles than in linear sequences. In the case of this map the links between topics are clearer; the separate elements are more easily recalled from their position on the page; there is a sense of building to complete a whole picture of the poem; the whole is instantly visible in a way that a page of sequential writing is not; the poem is always in the centre.

Revision: 'Recognising' a poem you have studied by looking over the notes you have written will not work as effective revision. The mental processing involved in 'looking over' will not be vigorous enough to give you a coherent or lasting impression of each poem.

Use this exercise to give yourself a fresh approach to poems you have studied. You will find that if you respond to each suggestion, at the end you will have processed your understanding of the poem into words.

- The instruction to read the poem *aloud* is crucial – much of the feeling and meaning of poetry is conveyed by sound. You have probably never read it yourself aloud.

- Initially you may have little to say in response to some of these prompts, but take the one you find easiest first and that will lead you into the poem.

- The one about 'energy' or 'tension' and the one about 'an organic whole' are the ones to pay most attention to. You will enjoy finding the 'most effective' lines – they will be your favourites.

- Take the trouble to write out your 'conclusion' and 'introduction', even if you do some or all of the others orally.

- You might link your conclusion to the title of the group of poems to which this particular poem belongs.

- Try to memorise the general headings (not your answers) on the map by looking away from it and visualising it on your mental screen – you will probably remember the topics by their position in the circle. They may all have a part to play in your exam answer.

- Remember the 'forgetting curve' and re-visualise the map again.

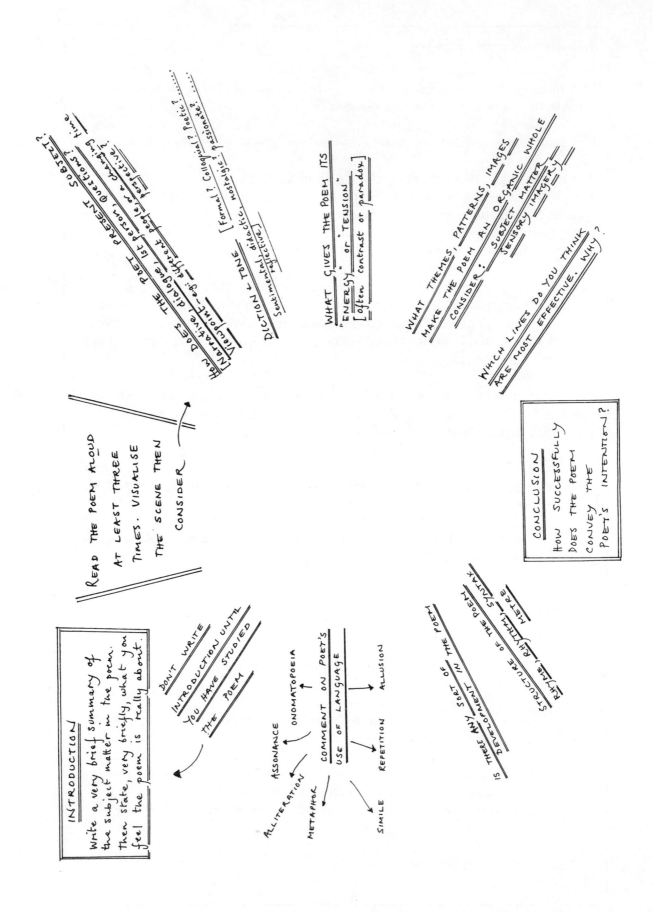

READ THE POEM ALOUD AT LEAST THREE TIMES. VISUALISE THE SCENE THEN CONSIDER

[NARRATIVE] Viewpoint — e.g: dramatic/dialogue/literary

The POET 1st person / 3rd person perspective
How DOES the PRESENT question/dramatise?
Subject?
dramatic / narrative / reflective time

DICTION + TONE [Formal? Colloquial? Poetic? Sentimental, didactic, nostalgic? passionate? reflective]

WHAT GIVES THE POEM ITS "ENERGY" or "TENSION" [often contrast or paradox]

WHAT THEMES, PATTERNS, IMAGES MAKE THE POEM AN ORGANIC WHOLE
CONSIDER: SUBJECT MATTER — SENSORY IMAGERY

WHICH LINES DO YOU THINK ARE MOST EFFECTIVE. WHY?

CONCLUSION
How SUCCESSFULLY DOES THE POEM CONVEY THE POET'S INTENTION?

METRE
RHYME / RHYTHM
STRUCTURE / SYNTAX
DEVELOPMENT of THE POEM
IS THERE ANY SORT OF THE POEM

COMMENT ON POET'S USE OF LANGUAGE
ONOMATOPOEIA
ALLUSION
ASSONANCE
REPETITION
ALLITERATION
METAPHOR
SIMILE

DON'T WRITE INTRODUCTION UNTIL YOU HAVE STUDIED THE POEM

INTRODUCTION
Write a very brief summary of the subject matter in the poem. Then state, very briefly, what you feel the poem is really about.

References and Resources

Adams K (1995) Straight A's in GCSE. London: HarperCollins.

Baddeley A (1982) Your Memory: A Users' Guide. London: Penguin Books Ltd.

Baum H (1982) Biochemist's Songbook. London: Taylor & Francis.

Breznitz Z (1991) The beneficial effect of accelerating reading rate on dyslexic readers' reading comprehension. In: Snowling M, Thomson M (eds) Dyslexia: Integrating Theory and Practice. London: Whurr.

Buzan T with Israel L. Get Ahead: A Short Cut to Straight A's. Video: 1WCV 1008.

Buzan T (1993) The Mind Map Book. London: BBC Books.

Buzan T (1990) Use Your Head. London: BBC Publications.

Collins (1999) Easy Learning Dictionary. London: Harper Collins.

Cover to Cover Cassettes Ltd., PO Box 112, Marlborough, Wiltshire SN8 3UG. Telephone: 01264 731 227. Website: covertocover.co.uk.

De Leeuw M, De Leeuw E (1987) Read Better, Read Faster. London: Penguin Books Ltd.

Galaburda A, Director of the Dyslexia Neuro-anatomical Laboratory at Beth Israel Hospital in Boston, as reported in the New York Times 15 September, 1991.

Grant & Cutler, 55–57 Great Marlborough Street, London W1B 2AY. Email: grantandcutler.com

Kelly V (1991) Curriculum-based study skills. In: Snowling M, Thomson M (eds) Dyslexia: Integrating Theory and Practice. London: Whurr Publishers.

Letts Literature Guides. London: BPP Ltd.

Listening Books, 12 Lant Street, London SE1 1QH. Telephone: 0207 407 9417. Website: www.listening-books.org.uk.

Multimedia Textbooks, Glaston Hall, Spring Lane, Glaston, Oakham, Rutland LE15 9BZ.

Nicholson R, Fawcett A (2001) Automaticity Deficit and Puplis with Dyslexia. BDA Website: www.bdainternationalconference.org/presentations

Oakhill J, Garnham A (1988) Becoming a Skilled Reader. Oxford: Blackwell.

Oakhill J, Yuill N (1991) Remediating comprehension difficulties. In: Snowling M, Thomson M (eds) Dyslexia: Integrating Theory and Practice. London: Whurr.

Oxford Hachette French Dictionary (1994–97) CD Rom, Oxford University Press.

Rack J (2001) Biological Bases of Developmental Dyslexia. Dyslexia Review.

Ramsden E (1994) Key Science Chemistry. Cheltenham: Stanley Thornes Ltd.

Sharma M (1992) Maths and Dyslexia Conference, Cheltenham.

Spache GD, Berg P (1978) The Art of Efficient Reading. New York: Macmillan Publishing Co, Inc.

Tallal P (1991) Rutgers Center for Molecular and Behavioral Neurosciences, as reported in the New York Times 15 September 1991.

The Talking Bookshop, 11 Wigmore Street, London W1U 1PE. Telephone: 0207 491 4117. Website: talking-books.co.uk.

Waugh D (1998) The Wider World. Windsor: Nelson.

Index